J. P. TARCHER, INC.
Los Angeles
Distributed by St. Martin's Press
New York

THE AQUARIAN CONSPIRACY

PERSONAL AND SOCIAL TRANSFORMATION IN THE 1980s

BY MARILYN FERGUSON

Foreword by John Naisbitt

Lines from the poem "Olbers' Paradox" from Lawrence Ferlinghetti, *Who Are We Now?*, copyright © 1976 by Lawrence Ferlinghetti, reprinted by permission of New Directions. Lines from the poem "A Ritual to Read to Each Other," copyright © 1961 by William Stafford, from his volume *Stories That Could Be True*, reprinted by permission of Harper & Row Publishers, Inc. Lines from the poem "God Is a Verb," from Buckminster Fuller, *No More Second-Hand God*, reprinted by permission of the author. Lines from the poem "The Thought of Something Else," copyright © 1965 by Wendell Berry, from his volume *Openings*, reprinted by permission of Harcourt Brace Jovanovich, Inc., New York. The passage from *Gandhi the Man* by Eknath Easwaran reprinted by permission of Nilgiri Press, Box 477, Petaluma, California 94952.

Library of Congress Cataloging in Publication Data

Ferguson, Marilyn
  The aquarian conspiracy.

  Bibliography pp. 442–450
  Includes indexes.
  1. Change (Psychology) 2. Social change. I Title
BF637.C4F47 1980   303.4   79–91722

ISBN 0-87477-458-6 (paper)

Design by John Brogna

Manufactured in the United States of America

10 9 8 7 6 5 4

For
Eric, Kris, and Lynn

Time, events, or the unaided individual action of the mind will sometimes undermine or destroy an opinion without any outward sign of change. . . . No conspiracy has been formed to make war on it, but its followers one by one noiselessly secede. As its opponents remain mute or only interchange their thoughts by stealth, they are themselves unaware for a long period that a great revolution has actually been effected.

–ALEXIS DE TOCQUEVILLE

And I strive to discover how to signal my companions . . . to say in time a simple word, a password, like conspirators: Let us unite, let us hold each other tightly, let us merge our hearts, let us create for Earth a brain and a heart, let us give a human meaning to the superhuman struggle.

–NIKOS KAZANTZAKIS

This soul can only be a conspiracy of individuals.

–PIERRE TEILHARD DE CHARDIN

Contents

Foreword by John Naisbitt   13

Acknowledgments   15

Introduction   17

CHAPTER 1   The Conspiracy   23

CHAPTER 2   Premonitions of Transformation
and Conspiracy   45

CHAPTER 3   Transformation: Brains Changing,
Minds Changing   65

CHAPTER 4   Crossover: People Changing   85

CHAPTER 5   The American Matrix for
Transformation   119

CHAPTER 6   Liberating Knowledge:
News from the Frontiers
of Science   145

CHAPTER 7   Right Power   189

CHAPTER 8   Healing Ourselves   241

CHAPTER *9*   Flying and Seeing:
              New Ways to Learn   279

CHAPTER *10*   The Transformation of Values
              and Vocation   323

CHAPTER *11*   Spiritual Adventure:
              Connection to the Source   361

CHAPTER *12*   Human Connections:
              Relationships Changing   387

CHAPTER *13*   The Whole-Earth Conspiracy   405

Afterword   418

Guidelines for Successful Projects   430

APPENDIX *A*   *Summary of Questionnaire
              Responses*   432

APPENDIX *B*   *Resources for Change*   435

Readings and References   441

Index   450

Foreword

For some months in 1981, people from many different backgrounds were telling me about an amazing new book. *The Aquarian Conspiracy* (a title that struck me as oxymoronic) was clearly becoming the rage among the "new age" constituency. But what got me to read it was the enthusiasm of business people.

Rarely has a book articulated and documented what so many of us were secretly thinking. It brought to mind Ralph Waldo Emerson's essay, "Self Reliance," which makes the point that true genius is saying what is in your heart, because it is in everyone's heart. That is the genius of *The Aquarian Conspiracy*.

After reading the book, I reached Marilyn through her office in Los Angeles; we have been friends ever since. When introducing her at a conference in Florida, I said that my book, *Megatrends*, was the soft-core document on change; *The Aquarian Conspiracy* was "the hard-core stuff." *Megatrends* spoke of changes in our society; *The Aquarian Conspiracy* dealt with the change in ourselves, in our souls.

During times of great change, people seek some kind of structure. Such a search for parameters accounts in part for the current religious revival. Hundreds of new churches have been established during the last two decades, helped in part by electronic media; many of these churches have highly structured fundamentalist beliefs. A similar proliferation of new religious groups occurred 150 years ago, when we were in the midst of another basic shift, from an agricultural to an industrial economic base.

There is, however, a rapidly growing population to whom such external structures are not appealing; these are the ''inner-directed,'' people inclined to reach down inside to their own spiritual resources. So we are experiencing a simultaneous revival in *personal spirituality*. The individualism of the new spirituality is fed by the individualistic nature of an information society, and also by the trend I have called the ''high-touch response'' to all of the high-tech in today's society.

It is to this spirit that *The Aquarian Conspiracy* speaks. The book was ahead of its time. Because the spirituality phenomenon has gathered momentum, the book's insights and precepts are truer today than when it was published seven years ago.

Some have criticized Marilyn Ferguson as too optimistic. In this I look to Albert Camus for counsel. Camus said that there is only one philosophical question: suicide. And if you decide not to take that course, optimism is the necessary condition to get through life. Pessimists are of no help at all. The optimism of *The Aquarian Conspiracy* is an affirmation of life's possibilities.

I envy those of you who are about to read *The Aquarian Conspiracy* for the first time. It is one of the most extraordinary books of our age.

JOHN NAISBITT
Washington, D.C.
June 1987

Acknowledgments

There can be no full accounting of my debt to the hundreds of persons who contributed to this project in various ways since its inception in 1976, but they know who they are and will recognize their input here and there. To them, and to the busy people who took the time to respond to the Aquarian Conspiracy survey, my thanks.

A special thank-you to Anita Storey, longtime friend and co-worker, for her unflagging support, insights, and humor... and to Sandra Harper, an extraordinary research assistant, agent of serendipity ... and to my children, Eric, Kris, and Lynn Ferguson for demonstrating understanding beyond their years during an often trying period.

Many who helped are quoted in the book in the context of their specific expertise. For dialogue, feedback, and encouragement, I'm grateful to Marthe Bowling, David Bresler, Harris Brotman, Nancie Brown, Meg Bundick, Jo Capehart, Dorothy Fadiman, James Fadiman, Elaine Flint, Jerry Harper, Marjorie King, Jytte Lokvig, Jack McAllister, M. S. McDonald, Brendan O'Regan, Karen Rose, Bob Samples, Judith Skutch, Robert A. Smith, III, Dick Traynham, and Brian van der Horst.

Thanks to Janice Gallagher and Victoria Pasternack for their dedicated editorial efforts; to Mary Lou Brady, publisher's assistant, for her friendship and liaison.

Most of all, my profound thanks to Jeremy Tarcher, whose sustained editorial creativity and commitment to this project made him the kind of publisher writers dream about but never expect to find.

Introduction*

In the early 1970s, while researching a book about the brain and consciousness, I was deeply impressed by scientific findings demonstrating human capacities well beyond our idea of "the norm." At that time the social implications of this research were essentially unexamined in science and unknown to the public. The research was specialized, scattered through many disciplines, technically written, and published two or three years after the fact in journals that circulate primarily to specialty libraries.

While science, in its objective fashion, was generating surprising data about human nature and the nature of reality, I saw that hundreds of thousands of individuals were coming upon subjective surprises of their own. Through systematic explorations of conscious experience, using a variety of methods, they were discovering such phenomena of mind as accelerated learning, expanded awareness, the power of internal imagery for healing and problem solving, and the capacity to recover buried memories; insights from these explorations changed their values and relationships. They were reaching out now for any information that would help them make sense of their experiences.

Perhaps because it was one of the first attempts at synthesis, my book, *The Brain Revolution: The Frontiers of Mind Research*, made me an unofficial clearinghouse for researchers who saw the implications of their findings, individuals wanting to compare notes, and media people looking for background on the

*An Afterword for the 1987 edition of *The Aquarian Conspiracy*, which might also be read along with this introduction, appears at the end of this book.

17

burgeoning interest in consciousness. To meet this apparent need for connection and communication, in late 1975 I began publishing a twice-monthly newsletter, *Brain/Mind Bulletin*, encompassing research, theory, and innovation relating to learning, health, psychiatry, psychology, states of consciousness, dreams, meditation, and related subjects.

The newsletter was a lightning rod for energy I had greatly underestimated. The immediate response—an avalanche of articles, correspondence, and calls—confirmed that rapidly growing numbers of people were exploring new territory, both in radical science and radical experience. As I traveled around the country, lecturing and covering conferences, I found these pioneers everywhere. And the new perspectives were being put to work. The social activism of the 1960s and the "consciousness revolution" of the early 1970s seemed to be moving toward a historic synthesis: social transformation resulting from personal transformation—change from the inside out.

In January, 1976, I published an editorial, "The Movement That Has No Name." It said, in part:

Something remarkable is underway. It is moving with almost dizzying speed, but it has no name and eludes description.

As *Brain/Mind Bulletin* reports on new organizations—groups focusing on new approaches to health, humanistic education, new politics, and management—we have been struck by the indefinable quality of the *Zeitgeist*.

The spirit of our age is fraught with paradox. It is at the same time pragmatic and transcendental. It values both enlightenment and mystery . . . power and humility . . . interdependence and individuality. It is simultaneously political and apolitical. Its movers and shakers include individuals who are impeccably Establishment allied with one-time sign-carrying radicals.

Within recent history "it" has infected medicine, education, social science, hard science, even government with its implications. It is characterized by fluid organizations reluctant to create hierarchical structures, averse to dogma. It operates on the principle that change can only be facilitated, not decreed. It is short on manifestos. It seems to speak to something very old. And perhaps, by integrating magic and science, art and technology, it will succeed where all the king's horses and all the king's men failed.

Perhaps, I wrote, the indefinable force is an idea whose time has come, and it is robust enough now to be named. Yet how could one characterize this groundswell?

The reader response to the editorial and the requests from other journals for permission to reprint it confirmed that many were sensing and seeing the same forces.

Months later, while outlining a not-yet-titled book about the emerging social alternatives, I thought again about the peculiar form of this movement: its atypical leadership, the patient intensity of its adherents, their unlikely successes. It suddenly struck me that in their sharing of strategies, their linkage, and their recognition of each other by subtle signals, the participants were not merely cooperating with one another. They were in collusion. "It"—this movement—was a conspiracy!

At first I was reluctant to use the term. I didn't want to sensationalize what was happening, and the word *conspiracy* usually has negative associations. Then I came across a book of spiritual exercises in which the Greek novelist, Nikos Kazantzakis, said he wished to signal his comrades, "like conspirators," that they might unite for the sake of the earth. The next day the *Los Angeles Times* carried an account of Canadian Prime Minister Pierre Trudeau's speech to the United Nations Habitat Conference in Vancouver; Trudeau quoted from a passage in which the French scientist-priest Pierre Teilhard de Chardin urged a "conspiracy of love."

Conspire, in its literal sense, means "to breathe together." It is an intimate joining. To make clear the benevolent nature of this joining, I chose the word *Aquarian*. Although I am unacquainted with astrological lore, I was drawn to the symbolic power of the pervasive dream in our popular culture: that after a dark, violent age, the Piscean, we are entering a millennium of love and light—in the words of the popular song, "The Age of Aquarius," the time of "the mind's true liberation."

Whether or not it was written in the stars, a different age seems to be upon us; and Aquarius, the waterbearer in the ancient zodiac, symbolizing flow and the quenching of an ancient thirst, is an appropriate symbol.

Over the next three years, a period of endless research, rethinking, and revision of this book, the title got around. It invariably provoked a startled, amused reaction as the conspirators recognized themselves and their collusion to change social institutions, modes of problem solving, and distribution of power. Some signed their letters as "co-conspirators" or addressed correspondence to me "c/o The Aquarian Conspiracy." The label seemed fitting for the solidarity and intrigue of the movement.

As its networks grew, the conspiracy became truer with every passing week. Groups seemed to be organizing spontaneously all over the country and abroad. In their announcements and internal communications, they expressed the same conviction: "We are in the midst of a great transformation. . . ." "In this period of cultural awakening . . ." Conspirators connected me with other conspirators: politicians, stewards of corporate or private wealth, celebrities, professionals trying to change their professions, and "ordinary" people accomplishing miracles of social change. These, in turn, put me in touch with still others and *their* networks.

Help came in many forms: research assistance, leads, privately circulated papers, books and articles, expertise, critiques of the manuscript in its various drafts, encouragement, assistance in uncovering the rich history of the transformative vision. Those who helped wanted nothing in the way of recognition; they only wanted others to feel what they have felt, to glimpse our collective potential.

In late 1977, to check out my own assessment of the conspiracy and the views of its adherents, I sent questionnaires to two hundred and ten persons engaged in social transformation in many different areas.* One hundred and eighty-five responded. They represented many different fields and walks of life. Although many are well known and a few even famous, most are people whose names are not widely recognizable. Only three asked for anonymity; this is indeed an "open conspiracy."

Participants are not identified in connection with their questionnaire statements, although the names of many appear in the text because they have also expressed their views publicly. The conspiracy should not become associated with personalities. Once identified, individuals who have worked quietly for change might find it hard to function under scrutiny. More important, artificial distinctions might be drawn as to who is or is not a conspirator. Names would focus attention on the wrong thing; a conspirator can be anyone.

Much as I was hesitant at first to use the word *conspiracy*, when I began writing the first draft of this book I shied away

---

*The questionnaire is summarized in Appendix A.

from the word *transformation*. It connoted great, perhaps impossible, change. Yet we seem to know now that our society must be remade, not just mended, and the concept has come into common usage. People speak freely of transforming this or that institution or procedure, and individuals are less self-conscious about discussing their own transformation—an ongoing process that has changed the tenor of their lives.

There are risks, of course, in drawing attention to the once-anonymous movement that has operated so effectively without publicity. There is always the possibility that this great cultural realignment will be co-opted, trivialized, exploited; indeed, that has already happened to some extent. And there is a danger that the trappings and symbols of transformation will be mistaken for the difficult path.

But whatever the risks of disclosure, this conspiracy, whose roots are old and deep in human history, belongs to all of us. This book charts its dimensions—for those who belong to it in spirit but have not known how many others share their sense of possibility, and for those who despair but are willing to consider the evidence for hope.

Like the charting of a new star, naming and mapping the conspiracy only makes visible a light that has been present all along but unseen because we didn't know where to look.

> *Marilyn Ferguson*
> *Los Angeles, California*
> *January 1980*

CHAPTER 1

The Conspiracy

After the final no there comes a yes
And on that yes the future of the world depends.

—*WALLACE STEVENS*

A leaderless but powerful network is working to bring about radical change in the United States. Its members have broken with certain key elements of Western thought, and they may even have broken continuity with history.

This network is the Aquarian Conspiracy. It is a conspiracy without a political doctrine. Without a manifesto. With conspirators who seek power only to disperse it, and whose strategies are pragmatic, even scientific, but whose perspective sounds so mystical that they hesitate to discuss it. Activists asking different kinds of questions, challenging the establishment from within.

Broader than reform, deeper than revolution, this benign conspiracy for a new human agenda has triggered the most rapid cultural realignment in history. The great shuddering, irrevocable shift overtaking us is not a new political, religious, or philosophical system. It is a new mind—the ascendance of a startling worldview that gathers into its framework breakthrough science and insights from earliest recorded thought.

The Aquarian Conspirators range across all levels of income and education, from the humblest to the highest. There are schoolteachers and office workers, famous scientists, government officials and lawmakers, artists and millionaires, taxi drivers and celebrities, leaders in medicine, education, law, psychology. Some are open in their advocacy, and their names may be familiar. Others are quiet about their involvement, believing they can be more effective if they are not identified with ideas that have all too often been misunderstood.

There are legions of conspirators. They are in corporations, universities and hospitals, on the faculties of public schools, in factories and doctors' offices, in state and federal agencies, on city councils and the White House staff, in state legislatures, in volunteer organizations, in virtually all arenas of policy-making in the country.

Whatever their station or sophistication, the conspirators are linked, made kindred by their inner discoveries and earthquakes. You can break through old limits, past inertia and fear, to levels of fulfillment that once seemed impossible . . . to richness of choice, freedom, human closeness. You can be more productive, confident, comfortable with insecurity. Problems can be experienced as challenges, a chance for renewal, rather than stress. Habitual defensiveness and worry can fall away. *It can all be otherwise.*

In the beginning, certainly, most did not set out to change society. In that sense, it is an unlikely kind of conspiracy. But they found that their *lives* had become revolutions. Once a personal change began in earnest, they found themselves rethinking everything, examining old assumptions, looking anew at their work and relationships, health, political power and "experts," goals and values.

They have coalesced into small groups in every town and institution. They have formed what one called "national non-organizations." Some conspirators are keenly aware of the national, even international, scope of the movement and are active in linking others. They are at once antennae and transmitters, both listening and communicating. They amplify the activities of the conspiracy by networking and pamphleteering, articulating the new options through books, lectures, school curricula, even Congressional hearings and the national media.

Others have centered their activity within their specialty, forming groups within existing organizations and institutions, exposing their co-workers to new ideas, often calling on the larger network for support, feedback, back-up information.

And there are millions of others who have never thought of themselves as part of a conspiracy but sense that their experiences and their struggle are part of something bigger, a larger social transformation that is increasingly visible if you know where to look. They are typically unaware of the national networks and their influence in high places; they may have found only one or two kindred spirits in their workplace, neighborhood, or circle of friends. Yet even in small groups—twos and threes, eights and tens—they are having their impact.

You will look in vain for affiliations in traditional forms: political parties, ideological groups, clubs, or fraternal organizations. You find instead little clusters and loose networks. There are tens of thousands of entry points to this conspiracy. Wherever people share experiences, they connect sooner or later with each other and eventually with larger circles. Each day their number grows.

However bold and romantic this movement may seem, we shall see that it has evolved from a sequence of historical events that could hardly have led elsewhere ... and it expresses deep principles of nature that are only now being described and confirmed by science. In its assessment of what is possible, it is rigorously rational.

"We are at a very exciting moment in history, perhaps a turning point," said Ilya Prigogine, who won the 1977 Nobel prize for a theory that describes transformations, not only in the physical sciences but also in society—the role of stress and "perturbations" that can thrust us into a new, higher order.

Science, he said, is proving the reality of a "deep cultural vision." The poets and philosophers were right in their intimations of an open, creative universe. Transformation, innovation, evolution—these are the natural responses to crisis.

The crises of our time, it becomes increasingly clear, are the necessary impetus for the revolution now under way. And once we understand nature's transformative powers, we see that it is our powerful ally, not a force to be feared or subdued. *Our pathology is our opportunity.*

In every age, said scientist-philosopher Pierre Teilhard de Chardin, man has proclaimed himself at a turning point in history. "And to a certain extent, as he is advancing on a rising spiral, he has not been wrong. But there are moments when this impression of transformation becomes accentuated and is thus particularly justified."

Teilhard prophesied the phenomenon central to this book: a conspiracy of men and women whose new perspective would trigger a critical contagion of change.

Throughout history virtually all efforts to remake society began by altering its outward form and organization. It was assumed that a rational social structure could produce harmony by a system of rewards, punishments, manipulations of power. But the periodic attempts to achieve a just society by political experiments seem to have been thwarted by human contrariness . . . and now what?

The Aquarian Conspiracy represents the Now What. We have to move into the unknown: The known has failed us too completely.

Taking a broader view of history and a deeper measure of nature, the Aquarian Conspiracy is a different kind of revolution, with different revolutionaries. It looks to the turnabout in consciousness of a critical number of individuals, enough to bring about a renewal of society.

"We cannot wait for the world to turn," said philosopher Beatrice Bruteau, "for times to change that we might change with them, for the revolution to come and carry us around in its new course. We ourselves *are* the future. We *are* the revolution."

THE PARADIGM SHIFT

New perspectives give birth to new historic ages. Humankind has had many dramatic revolutions of understanding—great leaps, sudden liberation from old limits. We discovered the uses of fire and the wheel, language and writing. We found that the earth only *seems* flat, the sun only *seems* to circle the earth, matter only *seems* solid. We learned to communicate, fly, explore.

Each of these discoveries is properly described as a "paradigm shift," a term introduced by Thomas Kuhn, a science historian and philosopher, in his landmark 1962 book, *The Structure of Scientific Revolutions*. Kuhn's ideas are enormously helpful, not only because they help us understand how a new perspective emerges but also how and why such new views are invariably resisted for a time.

A paradigm is a framework of thought (from the Greek *paradigma*, "pattern"). A paradigm is a scheme for understanding and explaining certain aspects of reality. Although Kuhn was writing about science, the term has been widely adopted. People speak of educational paradigms, paradigms for city planning, the paradigm shift in medicine, and so on.

A paradigm shift is a distinctly new way of thinking about old problems. For example, for more than two centuries, leading thinkers assumed that Isaac Newton's paradigm, his description of predictable mechanical forces, would finally explain everything in terms of trajectories, gravity, force. It would close in on the final secrets of a "clockwork universe."

But as scientists worked toward the elusive ultimate answers, bits of data here and there refused to fit into Newton's scheme. This is typical of any paradigm. Eventually, too many puzzling observations pile up outside the old framework of explanation and strain it. Usually at the point of crisis, someone has a great heretical idea. A powerful new insight explains the apparent contradictions. It introduces a new principle . . . a new perspective. By forcing a more comprehensive theory, the crisis is not *destructive* but *instructive*.

Einstein's Special Theory of Relativity formed the new paradigm that superseded Newton's physics. It resolved much unfinished business, anomalies and riddles that would not fit into the old physics. And it was a stunning alternative: The old mechanical rules were not universal; they did not hold at the level of galaxies and electrons. Our understanding of nature shifted from a clockwork paradigm to an uncertainty paradigm, from the absolute to the relative.

A new paradigm involves a principle that was present all along but unknown to us. It includes the old as a partial truth, one aspect of How Things Work, while allowing for things to work in other ways as well. By its larger perspective, it transforms traditional knowledge and the stubborn new observations, reconciling their apparent contradictions.

The new framework does more than the old. It predicts more accurately. And it throws open doors and windows for new exploration.

Given the superior power and scope of the new idea, we might expect it to prevail rather quickly, but that almost never happens. The problem is that you can't embrace the new paradigm unless you let go of the old. You can't be half-hearted, making the change bit by bit. "Like the gestalt switch," Kuhn said, "it must occur all at once." The new paradigm is not "figured out" but suddenly seen.

New paradigms are nearly always received with coolness, even mockery and hostility. Their discoveries are attacked for their heresy. (For historic examples, consider Copernicus, Galileo, Pasteur, Mesmer.) The idea may appear bizarre, even fuzzy, at first because the discoverer made an intuitive leap and does not have all the data in place yet.

The new perspective demands such a switch that established scientists are rarely converted. As Kuhn pointed out, those who worked fruitfully in the old view are emotionally and habitually attached to it. They usually go to their graves with their faith unshaken. Even when confronted with overwhelming evidence, they stubbornly stick with the wrong but familiar.

But the new paradigm gains ascendance. A new generation recognizes its power. When a critical number of thinkers has accepted the new idea, a collective paradigm shift has occurred. Enough people have caught onto the new perspective, or have grown up with it, to form a consensus. After a time that paradigm, too, is troubled by contradictions; another breakthrough occurs, and the process repeats itself. Thus science is continually breaking and enlarging its ideas.

Real progress in understanding nature is rarely incremental. All important advances are sudden intuitions, new principles, new ways of seeing. We have not fully recognized this process of leaping ahead, however, in part because textbooks tend to tame revolutions, whether cultural or scientific. They describe the advances as if they had been logical in their day, not at all shocking.

In retrospect, because the bridge of explanation was laid out painstakingly in the years after the intuitive leap, the big ideas seem reasonable, even inevitable. We take them for granted—but at first they sounded crazy.

By naming a sharply recognizable phenomenon, Kuhn made us conscious of the ways of revolution and resistance. Now that we are beginning to understand the dynamics of revolutionary insights, we can learn to foster our own healthy change and we can cooperate to ease the collective change of mind without waiting for the fever of a crisis. We can do this by asking questions in a new way—by challenging our old assumptions. These assumptions are the air we breathe, our familiar furniture. They are part of the culture. We are all but blind to them, yet they must give way to more fundamental perspectives if we are to discover what doesn't work—and why. Like the *koans* Zen masters give their novices, most problems cannot be solved at the level at which they are asked. They must be reframed, put into a larger context. And unwarranted assumptions must be dropped.

The King in a *New Yorker* cartoon announces that he can *so* repair Humpty Dumpty—but he needs *more* horses and *more* men. In just that irrational mode we try to solve problems with our existing tools, in their old context, instead of seeing that the escalating crisis is a symptom of our essential wrongheadedness.

For example, we ask how we are going to provide adequate national health insurance, given the increasingly high cost of medical treatment. The question automatically equates health with hospitals, doctors, prescription drugs, technology. Instead we should be asking how people get sick in the first place. What is the nature of wellness? Or we argue about the best methods for teaching the curriculum of public schools, yet rarely question whether the curriculum itself is appropriate. Even more rarely have we asked, What is the nature of learning?

Our crises show us the ways in which our institutions have betrayed nature. We have equated the good life with material consumption, we have dehumanized work and made it needlessly competitive, we are uneasy about our capacities for learning and teaching. Wildly expensive medical care has made little advance against chronic and catastrophic illness while becoming steadily more impersonal, more intrusive. Our government is complex and unresponsive, our social support system is breaking at every stress point.

The potential for rescue at this time of crisis is neither luck, coincidence, nor wishful thinking. Armed with a more sophisticated understanding of how change occurs, we know that the very forces that have brought us to planetary brinksmanship carry in them the seeds of renewal. The current disequilibrium — personal and social — foreshadows a new kind of society. Roles, relationships, institutions, and old ideas are being reexamined, reformulated, redesigned.

For the first time in history, humankind has come upon the control panel of change—an understanding of how transformation occurs. We are living in *the change of change*, the time in which we can intentionally align ourselves with nature for rapid remaking of ourselves and our collapsing institutions.

The paradigm of the Aquarian Conspiracy sees humankind embedded in nature. It promotes the autonomous individual in a decentralized society. It sees us as stewards of all our resources, inner and outer. It says that we are *not* victims, not pawns, not limited by conditions or conditioning. Heirs to evolutionary riches, we are capable of imagination, invention, and experiences we have only glimpsed.

Human nature is neither good nor bad but open to continuous transformation and transcendence. It has only to discover itself. The new perspective respects the ecology of everything: birth, death, learning, health, family, work, science, spirituality, the arts, the community, relationships, politics.

The Aquarian Conspirators are drawn together by their parallel discoveries, by paradigm shifts that convinced them they had been leading needlessly circumscribed lives.

PERSONAL PARADIGM SHIFTS: SEEING THE HIDDEN PICTURES

As experienced by an individual, the paradigm shift might be compared to the discovery of the "hidden pictures" in children's magazines. You look at a sketch that appears to be a tree and a pond. Then someone asks you to look more closely—to look for something you had no reason to believe was there. Suddenly you see camouflaged objects in the scene: The branches become a fish or a pitchfork, the lines around the pond hide a toothbrush.

Nobody can talk you into seeing the hidden pictures. You are not *persuaded* that the objects are there. Either you see them or you don't. But once you have seen them, they are plainly there whenever you look at the drawing. You wonder how you missed them before.

Growing up, we experienced minor paradigm shifts — insights into the principles of geometry, for instance, or a game, or a sudden broadening of our political or religious beliefs. Each insight enlarged the context, brought a fresh way of perceiving connections.

The opening up of a new paradigm is humbling and exhilarating; we were not so much wrong as partial, as if we had been seeing with a single eye. It is not more knowledge, but a *new knowing*.

Edward Carpenter, a remarkably visionary social scientist and poet of the late nineteenth century, described such a shift:

If you inhibit thought (and persevere) you come at length to a region of consciousness below or behind thought ... and a realization of an altogether vaster self than that to which we are accustomed. And since the ordinary consciousness, with which we are concerned in ordinary life, is before all things founded on the little local self ... it follows that to pass out of that is to die to the ordinary self and the ordinary world.

It is to die in the ordinary sense, but in another, it is to wake up and find that the "I," one's real, most intimate self, pervades the universe and all other beings.

So great, so splendid, is this experience, that it may be said that all minor questions and doubts fall away in the face of it; and certain it is that in thousands and thousands of cases, the fact of its having come even once to an individual has completely revolutionized his subsequent life and outlook on the world.

Carpenter captured the essense of the transformative experience: enlargement, connection, the power to permanently transform a life. And, as he said, this "region of consciousness" opens to us when we are quietly vigilant rather than busily thinking and planning.

Both accidentally and deliberately, people have had such experiences throughout history. Deep inner shifts may occur in response to disciplined contemplation, grave illness, wilderness treks, peak emotions, creative effort, spiritual exercises, controlled breathing, techniques for "inhibiting thought," psychedelics, movement, isolation, music, hypnosis, meditation, reverie, and in the wake of intense intellectual struggle.

Over the centuries, in various parts of the world, technologies for inducing such experiences were shared among a few initiates in each generation. Scattered brotherhoods, religious orders, and small groups explored what seemed to be extraordinary reaches of conscious experience. In their esoteric doctrines, they sometimes wrote of the liberating quality of their insights. But they were too few, they had no way to disseminate their discoveries widely, and most of earth's inhabitants were preoccupied with survival, not transcendence.

Quite suddenly, in *this* decade, these deceptively simple systems and their literature, the riches of many cultures, are available to whole populations, both in their original form and in contemporary adaptations. Drugstore racks and airport newsstands offer the wisdom of the ages in paperback. University extension classes and weekend seminars, adult education courses, and commercial centers are offering techniques that help people connect to new sources of personal energy, integration, harmony.

These systems aim to fine-tune the mind and body, to expand the brain's sensing, to bring the participants to a new awareness of vast untapped potential. When they work, it's like adding sonar, radar, and powerful lenses to the mind.

The widespread adaptation of such techniques and the spread of their use throughout society were predicted in the 1950s by P. W. Martin, when "consciousness" research was first under way. "For the first time in history, the scientific spirit of inquiry is being turned upon the other side of consciousness. There is a good prospect that the discoveries can be held this time and so become no longer the lost secret but the living heritage of man."

As we will see in Chapter 2, the idea of a rapid transformation of the human species, beginning with a vanguard, has been articulated by many of history's most gifted thinkers, artists, and visionaries.

All of the systems for widening and deepening consciousness employ similar strategies and lead to strikingly similar personal discoveries. And now, for the first time, we know that these subjective experiences have their objective counterparts. Laboratory investigation, as we shall see, shows that these methods integrate the brain's activity, making it less random, provoking it into higher organization. *Brains undergo a quite literal accelerated transformation*.

The transformative technologies offer us passage to creativity, healing, choices. The gift of insight—of making imaginative new connections—once the specialty of a lucky few, is there for anyone willing to persist, experiment, explore.

In most lives insight has been accidental. We wait for it as primitive man awaited lightning for a fire. But making mental connections is our most crucial learning tool, the essence of human intelligence: to forge links; to go beyond the given; to see patterns, relationships, context.

The natural consequence of these subtle sciences of the mind is insight. The process can be so accelerated that we are dizzied, even a little frightened, by the unfolding of new possibilities. Each empowers us to understand better and predict more precisely what will work in our lives.

Little wonder that these shifts in awareness are experienced as awakening, liberating, unifying—transforming. Given the reward, it makes sense that millions have taken up such practices within a scant few years. They discover that they don't have to wait for the world "out there" to change. Their lives and environments begin to transform as their minds are transformed. They find that they have a sane, healthy center, the wherewithal to deal with stress and to innovate, and that there are friends out there.

They struggle to convey what has happened to them. They have no tidy rationale, and they may feel somewhat foolish or pretentious in talking about their experiences. They try to describe a sense of awakening after years of being asleep, the coming together of broken parts of themselves, a healing and homecoming.

For many, the reaction of friends and relatives is painfully patronizing, not unlike that of the elders who warn an adolescent against being too naive and idealistic. Explaining oneself is difficult indeed.

TRUST, FEAR, AND TRANSFORMATION

Having found a core of strength and sanity within, those who have learned that they can trust themselves are more comfortable about trusting others. Those who are cynical about change are usually cynical about themselves and their own ability to change for the better. Transformation, as we shall see, requires a certain minimum of trust.

We may fear loss of control. We may suspect that we will find in ourselves the dark unconscious forces portrayed by religious teachings and Freud. We may worry that we will stray too far from family and friends and find ourselves alone.

And we are sensibly afraid of getting our hopes up. We walk around this possibility as if it were a magician's trick. We check its pockets, we look for mirrors and trick panels. The more sophisticated we are, the more suspicious we are. After all, we are familiar with many brands of deception and self-deception—game playing, political propaganda, "putting up a good front," the fancy footwork of advertising.

We have been disappointed before, swindled by promises that seemed—and were—too good to be true. And it is plain that the gold of transformation has inspired a whole generation of counterfeiters.

The new array of choices seems too rich and varied; the promise too open-ended. Our worries are our safe boundaries; over time we have learned to identify with our limits. Now, leery of trusting the promise of an oasis, we defend the merits of the desert.

"The truth is," said *New York Times* columnist Russell Baker, "I don't feel good most of the time and don't want to. Moreover, I do not comprehend why anyone else should want to." It's perfectly normal not to feel good, he said. In our drawerful of cultural biases is the conviction that unhappiness is the mark of sensitivity and intelligence.

"We can learn to savor the scars of our remorse," said Theodore Roszak, "until finally we take our whole identity from them. That is what seems rock-solid and ultimately 'serious' to many of us—that harshly jaundiced candor and grim resignation.... We finish by believing that sin is the reality of the self. . . . Even more efficiently than a police force, it is distrust of self that makes people vulnerable and obedient."

Those who worry that the new ideas will shake the culture to its roots are right, he said. Our conformity has been due in part to our fear of ourselves, our doubts about the rightness of our own decisions.

The transformative process, however alien it may seem at first, soon feels irrevocably right. Whatever the initial misgivings, there is no question of commitment once we have touched something we thought forever lost—our way home. Once this journey has begun in earnest, there is nothing that can dissuade. No political movement, no organized religion commands a greater loyalty. This is an engagement with life itself, a second chance at meaning.

COMMUNICATING AND LINKING

If these discoveries of transformation are to become our common heritage for the first time in history, they must be widely communicated. They must become our new consensus, what "everybody knows."

In the early nineteenth century, Alexis de Tocqueville observed that cultural behavior and unspoken beliefs typically change long before people openly concede to each other that times have changed. Lip service is given for years — generations — to ideas long since privately abandoned. No one conspires against these old shells of belief, Tocqueville said, so they continue to have power and discourage innovators.

Long after an old paradigm has lost its value, it commands a kind of hypocritical allegiance. But if we have the courage to communicate our doubts and defection, to expose the incompleteness, the rickety structure, and the failures of the old paradigm, we can dismantle it. We don't have to wait for it to collapse on us.

The Aquarian Conspiracy is using its widespread outposts of influence to focus on the dangerous myths and mystiques of the old paradigm, to attack obsolete ideas and practices. The conspirators urge us to reclaim the power we long ago surrendered to custom and authority, to discover, under the clutter of all our conditioning, the core of integrity that transcends conventions and codes.

We are benefiting from the phenomenon predicted in 1964 by Marshall McLuhan: the *implosion* of information. The planet is indeed a global village. No one anticipated how quickly technology would be put to work in the service of the individual, how quickly we would be able to communicate and agree. The conformity that grieved Tocqueville is giving way to a rising authenticity, an epidemic unparalleled in history.

Now we can indeed find each other. We can tell each other what we have abandoned, what we now believe. We can conspire against the old, deadly assumptions. We can *live* against them.

Global communications have encircled our world beyond any possibility of retreat. Now the whole planet is alive with instantaneous links, networks of people poised for communication and cooperation.

Those of like mind can join forces as quickly as you can photocopy a letter, quick-print a flyer, dial a telephone, design a bumper sticker, drive across town, form a coalition, paint a poster, fly to a meeting... or simply live openly in accordance with your change of heart.

"Perhaps for the first time in the history of the world," said psychologist Carl Rogers in 1978, "people are being really open, expressing their feelings without fear of being judged. Communication is qualitatively different from our historical past—richer, more complex."

Human catalysts like the Aquarian Conspirators describe the new options—in classrooms, on TV, in print, in film, in art, in song, in scientific journals, on the lecture circuit, during coffee breaks, in government documents, at parties, and in new organizational policies and legislation. Those who themselves might have been timid about questioning the prevailing opinion take heart.

Transformative ideas also appear in the guise of health books and sports manuals, in advice on diet, business management, self-assertion, stress, relationships, and self-improvement. Unlike "how-to" books of the past, these emphasize attitude, not behavior. Exercises and experiments are designed for direct experience from a new perspective.

For only that which is deeply felt can change us. Rational arguments alone cannot penetrate the layers of fear and conditioning that comprise our crippling belief systems. The Aquarian Conspiracy creates opportunities wherever possible for people to experience shifts of consciousness. Hearts as well as minds must change. Communication must be not only wide but deep.

Agreement can be communicated in many ways, sometimes even in silence, as Roszak pointed out to a large gathering in Vancouver in 1976 at the World Symposium on Humanity:

> In our time a secret manifesto is being written. Its language is a longing we read in one another's eyes. It is the longing to know our authentic vocation in the world, to find the work and the way of being that belong to each of us ... I speak of the Manifesto of the Person, the declaration of our sovereign right to self-discovery. I cannot say if those who have answered its summons are indeed millions, but I know that its influence moves significantly among us, a subterranean current of our history, that awakens in all those it touches an intoxicating sense of how deep the roots of the self reach, and what strange sources of energy they embrace. . . .

Penetrating to the roots of fears and doubts, we can change radically. Individuals are beginning to sustain social concern and action in ways never accomplished by outer influences: persuasion, propaganda, patriotism, religious injunctions, threats, preachments of brotherhood. A new world, as the mystics have always said, is a new mind.

FROM DESPAIR TO HOPE

Contemporary social critics too often speak from their own despair or a kind of cynical chic that belies their own sense of impotence. "Optimism is considered to be in poor taste," as philosopher Robert Solomon noted in *Newsweek*. "What seems to be concern betrays itself as self-indulgent, a self-righteous bitterness that declares society 'depraved' in order that one may pity oneself for being 'caught' in it. One blames the world for one's own unhappiness—or political failures."

If we are to find our way across troubled waters, we are better served by the company of those who have built bridges, who have moved beyond despair and inertia. The Aquarian Conspirators do not hope because they know less than the cynics but because they know *more*: from personal experience, from leading-edge science, and from grapevine news of successful social experiments occurring all over the world.

They have seen change in themselves, their friends, their work. They are patient and pragmatic, treasuring small victories that add up to a large cultural awakening; they know that opportunity appears in many guises, that dissolution and pain are necessary stages in renewal, and that "failures" can be powerfully instructive. Aware that deep change in a person or an institution can only come from within, they are gentle in their confrontation.

They are doers and workers who face the bad news every day and keep working. They have chosen life, whatever the cost. And most of all, they now know the power they have together.

SEEING THE EMERGENT CULTURE

Western society is at a pivotal point. Many key thinkers have had the paradigm shift about how paradigm shifts happen, a revolution in understanding how revolutions begin: in the ferment of questions, in the quiet recognition that the old won't do.

As a serious student of the conditions necessary for revolution, Tocqueville tried in the late 1840s to warn the governing powers in France about the possibility of overthrow. He was convinced that the government and the Court had so offended the people that democratic passions would soon overturn the government. On January 27, 1848, Tocqueville, a deputy, rose in the Chamber of Deputies. "They tell me that there is no danger because there are no disturbances," he said. "They say that as there is no visible perturbation on the surface of society, there are no revolutions beneath it. Gentlemen, allow me to say that I think you are wrong. Disturbance is not abroad but it has laid hold of men's minds."

Within four weeks the people revolted, the king fled, and the Second Republic was proclaimed.

Cultural transformation announces itself in sputtering fits and starts, sparked here and there by minor incidents, warmed by new ideas that may smoulder for decades. In many different places, at different times, the kindling is laid for the real conflagration—the one that will consume the old landmarks and alter the landscape forever.

In *Democracy in America* Tocqueville wrote that the hallmark of impending revolution is a critical period of agitation, in which there is enough communication for a few key reformers to stimulate each other, for "new opinions to suddenly change the face of the world."

A revolution, as we shall see, is first visible in tendencies—altered behavior and trends that are easily misunderstood, explained within the context of the old paradigm as something they aren't. And to confuse matters further, these new behaviors may be mimicked and exaggerated by those who do not understand their basis in inner turnabout. All revolutions attract mercenaries, thrill seekers, and the unstable, as well as the truly committed.

A revolution that is just getting under way, like a scientific revolution, is initially dismissed as crazy or unlikely. While it is clearly in progress, it seems alarming and threatening: In retrospect, when power has changed hands, it appears to have been foreordained.

Unaware of how values and frameworks have shifted historically, unaware of the continuous yet radical nature of change, we tend to drift into and out of cultural revolutions without knowing who fired the first shot and why. We are untrained in expectancy, in feeling the tremors of coming cultural upheaval, in seeing subtle darkening or brightening on the horizon.

Social, scientific, and political revolutions all take their contemporaries by surprise—except for the "visionaries" who seem to have detected the coming change from early, sketchy information. Logic alone, as we shall see, is a poor prophet. Intuition is necessary to complete the picture.

By definition, revolutions are not linear, one step at a time, event A leading to event B, and so on. Many causes operate on each other at once. Revolutions shift into place suddenly, like the pattern in a kaleidoscope. They do not so much proceed as crystallize.

"To the blind," warns an old saying, "all things are sudden." The revolution described in *The Aquarian Conspiracy* is not in the distant future. It is our imminent future and, in many ways, our dynamic present. For those who see it, the new society within the old is not a counterculture, not a reaction, but an *emergent* culture—the coalescence of a new social order. It has been characterized as a collection of "Parallel Cultures" by a group in England:

> We are people who agree on the need to overcome alienation and mutual hostility in society through the strategy of

building new values-based cultures amid the existing ones. These new cultures will co-exist with the old and perhaps eventually replace them.

We believe that organized confrontation, knocking the system or piecemeal reform serve only to preserve the basic alienation of society.... Most of our energies are going into the positive strategy of culture-building.

We find the single dimension of Left-Centre-Right power struggles to be almost entirely within the old, alienated way of life. Far from being radical, the extremes are as much a part of the old culture as the status quo they oppose.

The Third Way is not a group or a strategy, just a context.... Make no mistake, it is radical. The struggle for social values is a *new dimension* in radical social action, a way which is neither Right nor Left.

The Whole Earth Papers, a series of monographs, described the new movement as "provolutionary... an ascent of consciousness and paradigm shifts.... Our crises do not represent breakdown but break*through* in advancing the human community."

Michael Lerner, co-founder of a California health network, Commonweal, reporting on efforts to call attention to environmental stress, said, "We could not sustain this dark excavation if we did not sense that our work is another tiny part of a global movement.... Perhaps others will recognize the two polarities in the collective experience of our time: the stress caused by what we have created and called down on life, and the true grace of our spirit and courage as we seek a new way."

Stress and transformation ... these paired ideas are a theme, a litany, in the literature of the Aquarian Conspiracy.

Announcing its 1978 convention in Toronto, the Association for Humanistic Psychology referred to "this period of extraordinary evolutionary significance.... The very chaos of contemporary existence provides the material for transformation. We will search new myths and world visions."

The energy of this movement represents a kind of "field of force," said Arianna Stassinopoulos, a British social critic. It is gathering those who, "stirred by aspirations born of the new ideas, begin to manifest a new force, a new consciousness, a new power." The ideas that begin with the few radiate to the many.

The *Times* of London columnist Bernard Levin, remarking on

the nearly ninety thousand who attended a 1978 "Festival for Mind and Body" just outside London, foresaw a rapid spread of popular interest in transformation:

> What the world lives by at the moment just will not do. Nor will it; nor do very many people suppose any longer that it will. Countries like ours are full of people who have all the material comforts they desire, yet lead lives of quiet (and at times noisy) desperation, understanding nothing but the fact that there is a hole inside them and that however much food and drink they pour into it, however many motorcars and television sets they stuff it with, however many well-balanced children and loyal friends they parade around the edges of it . . . it *aches*.
>
> Those who attended the festival were seeking something—not certainty, but understanding: understanding of themselves. Almost every path on view began in the same place, inside the seeker.
>
> The question is being asked more insistently today than ever before in all history. . . . The crowds pouring through the turnstiles at Olympia are only the first drop in the wave that must soon crash over the politicians and ideologues and drown their empty claims fathoms deep in a self-confidence born of a true understanding of their own nature.

A 1979 symposium on the future of humanity said in its announcement: "Our first great challenge is to create a consensus that fundamental change is possible—to create a climate, a framework, which can integrally organize and coordinate the forces which are today striving for growth along seemingly separate paths. We will create an irresistibly vibrant vision, a new paradigm for constructive humanistic action. . . . Until we have created that master context, all talk of strategy is meaningless."

This book is about that master context. It is a book of evidence (circumstantial in some cases, overwhelming in others), pointing unmistakably to deep personal and cultural change. It is a guide to seeing paradigms, asking new questions, understanding the shifts, great and small, behind this immense transformation.

It is about the technologies, conspirators, networks—the perils, ambitions, promises—of change. It is also an attempt to show that what has been considered an elitist movement by some is profoundly inclusive, open to anyone who wants to be part of it.

We will explore the historic roots of the idea that a conspiracy can generate a new society, the premonitions of transformation over the years. We will review the evidence that the human brain has awesome capacities to transform and innovate, the variety of methods used to foster such transformation, and individual accounts of experiences that have changed people's lives.

We will see how cultural and historic circumstances led to the current readiness of this society for change and how America had long prefigured in visions of the turning point. We will see the pattern of the new world through our new models of nature, stunning new insights evident in the convergence of many branches of science, breakthroughs that promise a new age of discovery.

We will look at the undercurrents of change in politics and the emergence of networks as a new social form—the institution of our age, an unprecedented source of power for individuals. We will explore the profound paradigm shifts under way in health, learning, the workplace, and values. In each of these areas we will see evidence of the withdrawal of popular support from established institutions.

We will take up the "spiritual adventure" behind the Aquarian Conspiracy, the search for meaning that becomes an end in itself. We will trace the powerful, often disruptive, effect of the transformative process on personal relationships. And, finally, we will consider the evidence for potential worldwide change.

Throughout, specific projects and people will serve as illustrations, although none is cited as proof or authority. Rather, these are bits of a great mosaic, an overwhelming new direction of human effort and the human spirit at this point in history. For many, they will serve as creative inspiration, models of change, options to be adapted by the individual.

These new paradigms will raise some questions many may have preferred to leave unasked. Readers may confront certain crucial issues in their own lives. New perspectives have a way of altering old beliefs and values; they may penetrate denials and defenses of long standing. The ramifications of even a small personal revolution can seem more alarming to us than great impending cultural change.

In the course of this journey we will come to understand

certain powerful key ideas that can enrich and expand our lives, ideas that until now were mostly the province of specialists and policymakers.

We will construct bridges between the old and new worlds. When you understand the basic change taking place in any one major area, it is easier to make sense of the others. This discovery of a new pattern transcends explanation. The shift is qualitative, sudden, the result of neurological processes too rapid and complex to be tracked by the conscious mind. Although logical explanations can be laid out up to a point, the seeing of a pattern is not sequential but all-at-once. If a new concept does not click into place for you on first encounter, read on. As you move through the book you will come upon many related ideas, connections, examples, metaphors, analogies, and illustrative stories. In time, patterns will emerge, the shifts will occur. From the new perspective, old questions may seem suddenly irrelevant.

Once you have grasped the essence of this transformation, many otherwise inexplicable events and trends in the immediate environment or in the news may fall into place. It is easier to understand changes in one's family, one's community, the society. In the end we will see many of the darkest events in the context of a brightening historic picture, much as one stands back from a pointillist painting to get its meaning.

In literature there is a trusted device known as the Black Moment, the point where all seems lost just before the final rescue. Its counterpart in tragedy is the White Moment—a sudden rush of hope, a saving chance, just before the inevitable disaster.

Some might speculate that the Aquarian Conspiracy, with its promise of last-minute turnabout, is only a White Moment in Earth's story; a brave, desperate try that will be eclipsed by tragedy—ecological, totalitarian, nuclear. *Exeunt* humankind. Curtain.

And yet . . . is there another future worth trying for?

We stand on the brink of a new age, Lewis Mumford said, the age of an open world, a time of renewal when a fresh release of spiritual energy in the world culture may unleash new possibilities. "The sum of all our days is just our beginning."

Seen with new eyes, our lives can be transformed from accidents into adventures. We can transcend the old conditioning, the dirt-poor expectations. We have new ways to be born, humane and symbolic ways to die, different ways to be rich, communities to support us in our myriad journeys, new ways to be human and to discover what we are to each other. After our tragic wars, alienation, and the bruising of the planet, perhaps this is the answer Wallace Stevens meant—after the final No, the Yes on which the future of the world depends.

The future, Teilhard said, is in the hands of those who can give tomorrow's generations valid reasons to live and hope. The message of the Aquarian Conspiracy is that there is ripeness for a Yes.

2

Premonitions of Transformation and Conspiracy

It started in the morning as I woke. In a dream before waking I heard a beat, a drum, a march from the first Neanderthal shamans through the Vedic seers and all the patriarchs. There was a sense that no one could stop it.

—MICHAEL MURPHY, Jacob Atabet

The emergence of the Aquarian Conspiracy in the late twentieth century is rooted in the myths and metaphors, the prophecy and poetry, of the past. Throughout history there were lone individuals here and there, or small bands at the fringes of science or religion, who, based on their own experiences, believed that people might someday transcend narrow "normal" consciousness and reverse the brutality and alienation of the human condition.

The premonition was recorded, from time to time, that a minority of individuals would someday be yeast enough to leaven a whole society. Serving as a magnet culture, they would attract order around them, transforming the whole.

The central idea was always the same: Only through a new mind can humanity remake itself, and the potential for such a new mind is natural.

These courageous few have been history's radar, a Distant Early Warning System for the planet. As we will see, some of

45

them expressed their insights in a romantic vein, others as intellectual concepts, but all were pointing to a larger view. "Open your eyes," they were saying, "there is more." More depth, height, dimension, perspectives, choices than we had imagined. They celebrated the freedom found in the larger context and warned of the dangerous blindness of the prevailing view. Long before global war, ecological stress, and nuclear crisis struck, they feared for the future of a people without a context.

Although they themselves moved beyond the dominant ideas of their day, they carried few of their contemporaries with them. Most often they were misunderstood, lonely, even ostracized. Until this century, with its rapid communication, there was little chance for linkage among these scattered individuals. Their ideas, however, served as fuel for future generations.

Those who had premonitions of transformation believed that future generations might detect the invisible laws and forces around us: the vital networks of relationship, the ties among all aspects of life and knowledge, the interweaving of people, the rhythms and harmonies of the universe, the connectedness that captures parts and makes them wholes, the patterns that draw meaning from the web of the world. Humankind, they said, might recognize the subtle veils imposed on seeing; might awaken to the screen of custom, the prison of language and culture, the bonds of circumstance.

The themes of transformation have emerged with increasing strength and clarity over time, gathering impetus as communication expanded. At first the traditions were transmitted intimately, by alchemists, Gnostics, cabalists, and hermetics. With the invention of moveable type in the mid-fifteenth century, they became a kind of open secret but were available only to the literate few and were often suppressed by church or state.

Among the bold and isolated voices were Meister Eckhart, the German churchman and mystic of the fourteenth century; Giovanni Pico della Mirandola in the fifteenth; Jacob Boehme, a German, in the sixteenth and seventeenth; Emanuel Swedenborg in the seventeenth and eighteenth.

We are spiritually free, they said, the stewards of our own evolution. Humankind has a choice. We can awaken to our true nature. Drawing fully from our inner resources we can achieve a new dimension of mind; we can see more.

"I see through the eye, not with it," said poet-engraver William Blake, who lived in the late eighteenth and early nineteenth centuries. The enemy of whole vision, he said, was our reasoning power's divorce from imagination, "closing itself in, as steel." This half-mind was forever making laws and moral judgments and smothering spontaneity, feeling, art. To Blake, his age itself stood as the accuser, characterized by fear, conformity, jealousy, cynicism, the spirit of the machine. Yet this dark force was only a "Spectre," a ghost that could be exorcised from the minds it haunted.

"I will not cease from Mental Fight," he vowed, "Till we have built Jerusalem/In England's green and pleasant land." Blake, like later mystics, saw the American and French revolutions as only initial steps toward worldwide liberation, spiritual as well as political.

In 1836, nine years after Blake's death, a handful of American intellectuals fell into conversation at Harvard's bicentennial celebration, discovered their mutual interest in and excitement about new philosophical trends, and formed the nucleus of what is historically known as the American Transcendentalist movement.

The Transcendentalists—Ralph Waldo Emerson, Henry Thoreau, Bronson Alcott, and Margaret Fuller, along with several dozen others — rebelled against what seemed the dead, dry intellectualism of the day. Something was missing—an invisible dimension of reality they sometimes called the Oversoul. They sought understanding from many sources: experience, intuition, the Quaker idea of the Inner Light, the *Bhagavad Gita*, the German Romantic philosophers, historian Thomas Carlyle, poet Samuel Coleridge, Swedenborg, the English metaphysical writers of the seventeenth century.

Their term for intuition was "transcendental reason." They anticipated the consciousness research of our time in their belief that the brain's other mode of knowing is not an alternative to normal reasoning but a kind of transcendent logic—too fast and complex for us to follow with the step-by-step reasoning powers of our everyday consciousness.

Just as Boehme influenced Swedenborg who influenced Blake, so all three influenced the Transcendentalists; the Transcendentalists, in turn, affected literature, education, politics, and economics for generations, influencing Nathaniel Hawthorne, Emily Dickinson, Herman Melville, Walt Whitman, John Dewey, the founders of the British Labor party, Gandhi, Martin Luther King.

In the late nineteenth and early twentieth centuries, industrialism flourished. Widespread social transformation based on a change of heart still seemed a distant dream, but in England Edward Carpenter predicted that one day the tradition of the centuries would lose its form and outline, like melting ice in water. Networks of individuals would slowly form; widening circles would meet, overlap, and finally close around a new center for humankind. "Or, rather, the world-old center once more revealed."

This ultimate connection would be like the linked fibers and nerves of a body, lying within the outer body of society. The networks would move toward that elusive dream, "the finished, free society."

Carpenter also said that the insights of the Eastern religions might be the seed for this great change, enlarging the Western view of reality.

In *Cosmic Consciousness*, written in 1901, Richard Bucke, a Canadian physician, described the experience of an electrifying awareness of oneness with all life. Persons who experienced such states of consciousness were becoming more numerous, he said, walking the earth and breathing the air with us, but at the same time walking another earth and breathing another air of which we know little. "This new race is in the act of being born from us, and in the near future it will occupy and possess the earth."

In 1902 William James, the great American psychologist, redefined religion not as dogma but as experience—the discovery of a new context, an unseen order with which the individual might achieve harmony. Our ordinary consciousness filters out awareness of this mysterious, enlarged dimension, yet until we have come to terms with its existence we must beware lest we make a "premature foreclosure on reality."

Of all the creatures of earth, James said, only human beings can change their pattern. "Man alone is the architect of his destiny. The greatest revolution in our generation is that human beings, by changing the inner attitudes of their minds, can change the outer aspects of their lives."

Gradually Western thinkers were beginning to attack the very foundations of Western thought. We were naive in our expectation that mechanistic science would explain the mysteries of life. These spokesmen for a larger worldview pointed out how our institutions were violating nature: Our education and philosophy failed to value art, feelings, intuition.

In the 1920s Jan Christian Smuts, the Boer general who was twice prime minister of South Africa, formulated a brilliant concept that anticipated many scientific breakthroughs of the late twentieth century. In *Holism and Evolution*, Smuts called attention to an invisible but powerful organizing principle inherent in nature. If we did not look at wholes, if we failed to see nature's drive toward ever higher organization, we would not be able to make sense of our accelerating scientific discoveries.

There is a whole-making principle in mind itself, Smuts said. Just as living matter evolves to higher and higher levels, so does mind. Mind, he said, is inherent in matter. Smuts was describing a universe becoming ever more conscious.

The idea of expanding powers of mind unfolded in literature, too. "New" human beings of deeper sensibility appeared often in the fiction of Hermann Hesse. In his enormously popular novel *Demian* (1925), Hesse depicted a fraternity of men and women who had discovered paranormal abilities and an invisible bond with one another. "We were not separated from the majority of men by a boundary," the narrator said, "but simply by another mode of vision." They were a prototype of a different way of life.

In 1927 Nikos Kazantzakis, the great Greek novelist, envisioned a union of such individuals—those who might create for earth a brain and a heart, might "give a human meaning to the superhuman struggle," comrades he might signal "with a password, like conspirators." What we have called God is the evolutionary drive of consciousness in the universe, he believed. "The new earth exists only in the heart of man."

In *The Open Conspiracy: Blueprints for a World Revolution* (1928), novelist-historian H. G. Wells proposed that the time was nearly ripe for the coalescence of small groups into a flexible network that could spawn global change. "All this world is heavy with the promise of greater things," Wells once said, "and a day will come, one day in the unending succession of days, when beings who are now latent in our loins shall stand upon this earth as one stands upon a footstool and shall touch the stars."

Carl Jung, the Swiss psychoanalyst, was drawing attention to a transcendent dimension of consciousness usually ignored in the West, the union of the intellect with the intuitive, pattern-seeing mind. Jung introduced an even larger context, the idea of the collective unconscious: a dimension of shared symbols, racial memory, pooled knowledge of the species. He wrote of the "daimon" that drives the seeker to search for wholeness.

In 1929 Alfred North Whitehead, a philosopher-mathematician, published *Process and Reality*, a book that described reality as a flux whose context is the mind, rather than something tangible "out there." He tried to articulate remarkable principles in nature which were formally discovered by research generations later.

After a visit to the United States in 1931, Pierre Teilhard de Chardin sailed back to China from the San Francisco Bay.[1] En route the Jesuit paleontologist framed an essay, "The Spirit of the Earth," inspired by his growing conviction that a conspiracy of individuals from every layer of American society was engaged in an effort "to raise to a new stage the edifice of life."

Back in Peking he set forth his major thesis: Mind has been undergoing successive reorganizations throughout the history of evolution until it has reached a crucial point—the discovery of its own evolution.

This new awareness—evolving mind recognizing the evolutionary process—"is the future natural history of the world." It will eventually become collective. It will envelop the planet and will crystallize as a species-wide enlightenment he called "Omega Point." Certain individuals, attracted to a transcendent vision of the future and to each other, seemed to be forming a spearhead in the "family task" of bringing humanity into this larger awareness. "The only way forward is in the direction of a common passion, a conspiracy."

And, as he told a friend, nothing in the universe could resist "the cumulative ardor of the collective soul," a large enough number of transformed persons working together.

Although many resist the idea that mind evolves, he said, it will gain eventual acceptance. "A truth once seen, even by a single mind, always ends by imposing itself on the totality of human consciousness." Evidence for this evolutionary thrust was issuing from all the sciences, he said, and those who refused to see it were blind. "Evolution is a condition to which all theories must bow, a curve all lines must follow."

No one can call himself modern who disregards this evolutionary thrust, he said. To our descendants it will be as familiar and instinctive an idea as the third dimension of space is to a baby.

The Phenomenon of Man was limited to private circulation during Teilhard's lifetime because the church forbade him to pub-

---

[1]Teilhard was the individual most often named as a profound influence by the Aquarian Conspirators who responded to a survey (see Introduction and Appendix). His books, once repressed, have now sold many millions and have been translated into virtually every language. The next most frequently mentioned influences are Aldous Huxley, Carl Jung, and Abraham Maslow.

lish it. In it, he warned that a mind awakened to this evolutionary concept may experience fear and disorientation. It must create a new equilibrium for everything that had once been tidy in its inner world. "It is dazzled when it emerges from its dark prison."

There is now incontrovertible evidence that we have entered upon the greatest period of change the world has ever known, he said. "The ills from which we are suffering have had their seat in the very foundation of human thought. But today something is happening to the whole structure of human consciousness. A fresh kind of life is starting."

We are the children of transition, not yet fully conscious of the new powers that have been unleashed: "There is for us in the future not only survival but superlife."

Historian Arnold Toynbee said in 1935 that a creative minority, "turning to the inner world of the psyche," could summon the vision of a new way of life for our troubled civilization. He also predicted that the most significant development of the age would be the influence of the Eastern spiritual perspective on the West.

In the late 1930s a Polish count, Alfred Korzybski, pointed out yet another aspect of consciousness—language. Language molds thought, he said, laying out the principles of General Semantics. We confuse it with reality; it creates false certainties. With words we try to isolate things that can only exist in continuity. We fail to see process, change, movement. If we are to experience reality, Korzybski and his followers said, we must acknowledge the limits of language.

In *The Wisdom of the Heart*, essays published on the eve of World War II, Henry Miller warned of the difficulty of expressing new realities within the limits of language:

> There exist today all over the world a number of modern spirits who are anything but modern. They are thoroughly out of joint with the times, and yet they reflect the age more truly, more authentically than those who are swimming with the current. In the very heart of the modern spirit there is a schism. The egg is breaking, the chromosomes are splitting to go forward with a new pattern of life. Those of us who seem most alien . . . are the ones who are going forward to create the life as yet inchoate.
>   We who are affected cannot make ourselves clear. . . .
> This is the era when apocalyptic visions are to be fulfilled. We are on the brink of a new life, entering a new domain.

In what language can we describe things for which there are as yet no new names? And how describe relations? We can only divine the nature of those to whom we are attracted, the forces to which we willingly yield obedience. . . .

Even in the early days of the war, philosopher Martin Buber said he sensed a rising hunger for relatedness. "On the horizon I see moving up, with the slowness of all events of true human history, a great dissatisfaction unlike all previous dissatisfactions." Men would no longer rise in rebellion merely against one oppressor or another but against the distortion of a great yearning, "the effort toward community."

In a 1940 letter Aldous Huxley said that although he was profoundly pessimistic about collective humanity at the moment, he was "profoundly optimistic about individuals and groups of individuals existing on the margins of society." The British author, living in Los Angeles, was the hub of a kind of pre-Aquarian conspiracy, an international network of intellectuals, artists, and scientists interested in the notion of transcendence and transformation. They disseminated new ideas, supported each other's efforts, and wondered whether anything would ever come of it. Many of Huxley's interests were so advanced that they did not come into their own until the decade after his death. When such ideas were heresies, he was a proponent of consciousness research, decentralization in government and the economy, paranormal healing, the uses of altered awareness, visual retraining, and acupuncture.

He was also an early supporter of Ludwig von Bertalanffy, a German biologist who framed a science of context he first called perspectivism, later General Systems Theory. This theory, which has grown steadily in its influence in many different disciplines, sees all of nature—including human behavior—as interconnected. According to General Systems Theory, nothing can be understood in isolation but must be seen as part of a system.

In the business-as-usual postwar era, there were those who sensed approaching upheaval, an awakening to our cultural conditioning. Even as he was describing the alienation and conformity of *The Lonely Crowd*, sociologist David Riesman speculated that the trance might be broken. "Many currents of change in America escape the notice of the reporters of this best-reported nation on earth. . . . America is not only big and rich, it is mysterious, and its capacity for the humorous or

ironical concealment of its interests matches that of the legendary inscrutable Chinese."

Reisman's book and others fostered new awareness of the
prison of conformity. They questioned hidden assumptions
and called attention to contradictions—the first step in breaking
an old paradigm.

In the mid-1950s psychoanalyst Robert Lindner touched off
controversy by his prophetic warning that there was an impending "mutiny of the young":

> Into them we have bred our fears and insecurities, upon
> them we have foisted our mistakes and misconceptions. In
> our stead they are expressing the unrelieved rage, the ten-
> sion, and the terrible frustration of the world they were
> born into.... They are imprisoned by the blunders and
> delusions of their predecessors, and like all prisoners, they
> are mutineers in their hearts.

Must We Conform? asked the title of a book he wrote in 1956.
"The answer is a resounding No! *No*—not only because in the
end we are creatures who cannot... but *no* because there is an
alternate way of life available to us here and now. It is the way
of positive rebellion, the path of creative protest."

The key was enlarged awareness, Lindner said—recognition
of how we are crippled by unconscious fears and motives. "I
believe profoundly that the tide can be turned."

The eminent psychologist Gardner Murphy was predicting
in the 1950s that the growing scientific curiosity about consciousness would lead to "new realms of experience." The
more we played on "the other side of the mind," the more we
exploited these gifts no culture had ever fully exploited, the less
likely our old assumptions would hold—not even the ideas of
Darwin and Freud. Radically different ideas would emerge,
Murphy said, "and we shall fight frantically against them, of
course."

New ideas... new people. C. S. Lewis, novelist and essayist,
described what seemed to him a kind of secret society of new
men and women, "dotted here and there all over the earth."
One could learn to recognize them, he said, and clearly they
recognized each other.

In a 1960 French best-seller, *The Morning of the Magicians*,
Louis Pauwels and Jacques Bergier described an "open conspiracy" of intelligent individuals transformed by their inner
discoveries. The members of this network might be contempo-

rary stewards of a long line of esoteric wisdom, Pauwels and Bergier said. Had they surfaced only now from the secret traditions of the alchemists and Rosicrucians?

Perhaps a few were finding what many had yearned for. Concluding his monumental *Literature and Western Man* (1960), J. B. Priestley assessed the widespread hunger for completion. Schizophrenic Western culture was desperately searching for its center, for some balance between inner and outer life. "The inner world of the whole age...is trying to compensate for some failure in consciousness, to restore a balance destroyed by one-sidedness, to reconcile the glaring opposites."

Only religion can carry the load of the future, he said, not the religion of churches, but the spiritual dimension that transcends custom and politics.

> Even if we believe that the time of our civilization is running out fast, like sugar spilled from a torn bag, we must wait. But while we are waiting, we can try to feel and think and behave *as if* our society were already beginning to be contained by religion ... *as if* we were finding our way home again in the universe. We can stop disinheriting ourselves. . . . We can challenge the whole de-humanizing, depersonalizing process that is taking the symbolic richness, the dimension of depth out of men's lives, inducing the anesthesia that demands violence, crudely horrible effects, to feel anything at all.
>
> Instead of wanting to look at the back of the moon, remote from our lives, we can try to look at the back of our own minds.

Just behaving "as if" might show us the way home—might prove the step toward healing, justice, order, real community. "And if we only declare what is wrong with us, what is our deepest need, then perhaps the despair and death will, by degrees, disappear. . . ."

In his final novel, *Island* (1963), Huxley portrayed such a society, in which healing relied on powers of mind, extended "families" provided comfort and counsel, learning was rooted in doing and imagining, commerce bowed to ecology. To emphasize the urgent need for awareness, trained mynah birds flew about crying "Attention! Attention!"

Most critics reviewed *Island* as a spoof, less successful than Huxley's darker vision, *Brave New World*. But Huxley had not only described a world he believed possible but had created it as a composite of practices known to exist in contemporary cultures. In the words of Dr. MacPhail in *Island*:

> To make the best of both worlds, Oriental and European, the ancient and modern—what am I saying? To make the best of *all* the worlds—the worlds already realized within the various cultures and, beyond them, the worlds of still unrealized potentialities.

Indeed, diverse cultures were impinging on each other more by the day. In his enormously influential *Understanding Media* (1964), Marshall McLuhan described the coming world as a "global village," unified by communications technology and rapid dissemination of information. This electrified world, with its instant linkage, would bear no resemblance to the preceding thousands of years of history.

In this age we have become conscious of the unconscious, McLuhan pointed out. Although most of us still continue to think in the old fragmented patterns of the slow days, our electronic linkage brings us together "mythically and integrally." McLuhan saw coming change: Increasing numbers were aspiring to wholeness, empathy, deeper awareness, revolting against imposed patterns, wanting people to be open.

And we would be remade, he said, by the flood of new knowledge.

> The immediate prospect for fragmented Western man encountering the electric implosion within his own culture is his steady and rapid transformation into a complex person... emotionally aware of his total interdependence with the rest of human society....
>
> Might not the current translation of our entire lives into the spiritual form of information make of the entire globe, and of the human family, a single consciousness?

Introducing "World Perspectives," a series of books published by Harper & Row beginning in the 1960s, Ruth Ananda Ashen wrote of a "new consciousness" that might lift humankind beyond fear and isolation.[2] We are now contending with

---

[2]The "World Perspectives" series included many authors whose thinking was influential in the Aquarian Conspiracy, among them Lancelot Law Whyte, Lewis Mumford, Erich Fromm, Werner Heisenberg, René Dubos, Gardner Murphy, Mircea Eliade, Kenneth Boulding, Marshall McLuhan, Milton Mayerhoff, Ivan Illich and Jonas Salk.

fundamental change since we now understand evolution itself. There is now abroad "a counterforce to the sterility of mass culture . . . a new, if sometimes imperceptible, spiritual sense of convergence toward human and world unity."

The new series of books was planned to encourage "a renaissance of hope," to help the mind grasp what had eluded it in the past. Having discovered his own nature, man now has new choices "for he is the only creature who is able to say not only 'no' to life but 'yes.'"

Steadily, as increasing numbers of influential thinkers speculated on the possibilities, the transformative vision became more credible.

Psychologist Abraham Maslow described an innate human drive beyond basic survival and emotional needs — a hunger for meaning and transcendence. This concept of "self-actualization" rapidly gained adherents.

"It is increasingly clear," Maslow wrote, "that a philosophical revolution is under way. A comprehensive system is swiftly developing, like a tree beginning to bear fruit on every branch at the same time." He described a group he thought of as Transcenders, "advance scouts for the race," individuals who far exceeded the traditional criteria for psychological health. He compiled a list of around three hundred creative, intelligent individuals and groups of individuals whose lives were marked by frequent "peak experiences" (a term he coined). This was his Eupsychean Network—literally, "of good soul." Transcenders were irresistibly drawn to each other, he said; two or three such people would find each other in a roomful of a hundred, and they were as likely to be businessmen, engineers, and politicians as poets and priests.

In England Colin Wilson, in a 1967 postscript to his famous study of alienation, *The Outsider*, called attention to a critical issue being addressed quietly in the United States by Maslow and others: the possibility of human metamorphosis—the vision of a world hospitable to creativity and mystical experience.

No analogy, even that of metamorphosis, could quite capture the suddenness or radicalness of the transformation ahead, according to John Platt, a physicist at the University of Michigan. Only dreamers like Wells and Teilhard had seen "the enormous sweep and restructuring and unity and future of it. It is a quantam jump, a new state of matter."

And this transformation would come within a generation or two, Platt said. "We may now be in the time of the most rapid change in the whole evolution of the human race . . . a kind of cultural shock front."

In 1967 Barbara Marx Hubbard, a futurist moved by Teilhard's vision of evolving human consciousness, invited a thousand people around the world, including Maslow's network, to form a "human front" of those who shared a belief in the possibility of transcendent consciousness. Hundreds responded, including Lewis Mumford and Thomas Merton. Out of this grew a newsletter and later a loose-knit organization, the Committee for the Future.

Erich Fromm, in *Revolution of Hope* (1968), foresaw a "new front," a movement that would combine the wish for profound social change with a new spiritual perspective; its aim would be the humanization of a technological world.

Such a movement, which could happen within twenty years, would be nonviolent. Its constituency would be Americans already eager for new direction, including old and young, conservatives and radicals, all social classes. "The middle class has begun to listen and to be moved," Fromm said. Neither state nor political parties nor organized religion could provide either an intellectual or spiritual home for this thrust. Institutions were too bureaucratic, too impersonal.

The key to the success of the movement would be its embodiment in the lives of its most committed members, who would work in small groups toward personal transformation, nourishing each other, "showing the world the strength and joy of people who have deep convictions without being fanatical, who are loving without being sentimental . . . imaginative without being unrealistic . . . disciplined without submission."

They would build their own world amid the alienation of the contemporary social milieu. They would probably engage in meditation and other reflective states of consciousness to become more open, less egocentric, more responsible. And they would replace narrow loyalties with a wide, loving, critical concern. Their style of consumption would "serve the needs of life, not the needs of producers."

The flags were going up.

Carl Rogers described the Emerging Man; Lewis Mumford, the New Person, the age that would "make the Renaissance look like a still-birth." Jonas Salk said that humankind was moving into a new epoch. Evolution, he said, favors "the survival of the wisest. . . . Who are they? What must they do? How can they discover themselves and others with whom to work?"

Educator John Holt called for "a radically new kind of human being." Philosopher Lancelot Law Whyte stressed the urgency of a network: "We who already share intimations of this emergent attitude must become aware of one another . . . collect allies by timely signals."

The only possibility for our time, said Joseph Campbell, the mythologist, in 1968, is "the free association of men and women of like spirit . . . not a handful but a thousand heroes, ten thousand heroes, who will create a future image of what humankind can be."

In 1969 the noted French political writer Jean-François Revel predicted that the United States was about to experience "the second great world revolution"—an upheaval that would complete the first revolution, the rise of democracy in the West. In *Without Marx or Jesus* he predicted the emergence of *homo novus*, a new human being. Revel believed that the undercurrent of spiritual concern in the United States, evident in the burgeoning interest in Eastern religions, presaged profound change in the only country on the planet free enough for bloodless revolution.

Revel saw the coming second revolution as an emergent pattern amid the chaos of the 1960s; the social movements, the new mores and fashions, protests and violence. Indeed, many of the activists were turning inward, a direction that seemed heretical to their comrades in the conventional Left. They were saying that they could not change society until they changed themselves. Irvin Thomas, a social activist of the 1960s, recalled later:

> A funny thing happened on the way to Revolution. There we were, beating our breasts for social change, when it slowly began to dawn on us that our big-deal social-political struggle was only one parochial engagement of a revolution in consciousness so large that it has been hard to bring it into focus within our reality.

And Michael Rossman, one of the leaders of the Berkeley Free Speech Movement, and other leaders of the supposedly alienated campus rebels spoke in low tones of a curious development. In their thrust for change they had begun to experience "the scariness of real choice and possibility. . . . There was a sense that the surface of reality had somehow fallen away altogether. Nothing was any longer what it seemed."

Was this what it meant to make the world strange and new

again? Creating and naming the movement had "alleviated the responsibility for facing an unsought and terrifyingly wild field of choice in a universe in which somehow anything had become possible." Like the sorcerers in the popular books of Carlos Castaneda, Rossman and his friends had succeeded, however briefly, in "stopping the world." Confrontation was a less and less attractive strategy as it became more and more evident that, as Walt Kelly's cartoon character Pogo once observed, "We have met the enemy and they are us."

When the revolution went inside, television cameras and newspaper reporters could not cover it. It had become, in many ways, invisible.

To many of the activists idealism seemed the only pragmatic alternative. Cynicism had proved a self-fulfilling prophecy. Economist-educator Robert Theobald urged the creation of a new coalition, a linkage of all those committed to social change in an age of rapid communication.

> We live at a peculiar moment in history. If we look at the reality of the world from the viewpoint of the industrial era, it is clear that there is no hope. . . . But there is another way to look at our situation. We can discover the large number of people who have decided to change. . . . If we do this, it seems equally impossible that we shall fail to solve our problems.

We had not fallen into crisis after crisis because our ideals had failed but because we had never applied them, Theobald said. A return to the highest hopes and dreams of the Founding Fathers might rescue us. We determine which future we create by the views we hold.

In *The Transformation* (1972), George Leonard described the current period as "unique in history," the beginning of the most thoroughgoing change in the quality of human existence since the birth of civilized states. "It does not entail throwing over our civilized values and practices but subsuming them under a higher order."

And also in 1972 anthropologist Gregory Bateson predicted that the next five to ten years would be comparable to the Federalist period in United States history. Public, press, and politicians would soon be debating the new ideas, much as the creators of the American democracy searched for consensus in the eighteenth century. The efforts of the young and their interest in Oriental philosophy represented more sanity than the conventions of the establishment, Bateson said. In his 1970 best-seller, *The Greening of America*, Charles Reich had focused on the outward symbols of change, especially the change in dress and lifestyle among the young; but Bateson pointed out that it was "not only long-haired professors and long-haired youth" who were thinking differently. Thousands of business-men and even legislators had begun *wishing* for such change.

In her book, *The Crossing Point* (1973), M. C. Richards, artisan and poet, said:

> One of the truths of our time is this hunger deep in people all over the planet for coming into relationship with each other.
>
> Human consciousness is crossing a threshold as mighty as the one from the Middle Ages to the Renaissance. People are hungering and thirsting after experience that feels true to them on the inside, after so much hard work mapping the outer spaces of the physical world. They are gaining courage to ask for what they need: living intercon-nections, a sense of individual worth, shared oppor-tunities. . . .
>
> Our relationship to past symbols of authority is chang-ing because we are awakening to ourselves as individual beings with an inner rulership. Property and credentials and status are not as intimidating any more. . . . New sym-bols are rising: pictures of wholeness. Freedom sings within us as well as outside us. . . . Sages and seers have foretold this second coming. People don't want to feel stuck, they want to be able to change.

Change came most easily in geographical regions with a well-known tolerance for experiment. California had generated the first waves of campus unrest in the 1960s. In the 1970s the state began acquiring an international reputation as centerstage for the new, unnamed drama. Increasing numbers of re-searchers and innovators, interested in the expansion of awareness and its implications for society, relocated on the West Coast.

Jacob Needleman, professor of philosophy at San Francisco State University and a transplanted Easterner, warned in *The New Religions* (1973) that the nation must come to terms with the new spiritual-intellectual alliances in California. "Sooner or later we are going to have to understand California—and not simply from the motive of predicting the future for the rest of the country.... Something is struggling to be born here." The West Coast, he said, was not paralyzed by the European bias that dominated the cynical East Coast intellectual establishment: the divorce of the human mind from the rest of the cosmos. "Without wishing to sound darkly mysterious, I would have to say that there broods over this state a strong sense of greater universal forces."

Distinguished thinkers from many disciplines were describing an imminent transformation. The director of policy research at Stanford Research Institute, Willis Harman, said that if materialism had been the philosophical base for the Old Left, spirituality seemed likely to play that role for the New Left, a matrix of linked beliefs—that we are invisibly joined to one another, that there are dimensions transcending time and space, that individual lives are meaningful, that grace and illumination are real, that it is possible to evolve to ever higher levels of understanding.

Should these new coalitions prevail, Harman said, and some sort of transcendental premise dominate the culture, the result would be a social and historical phenomenon as great and pervasive as the Protestant Reformation.

Harman was one of the group of scholars and policy analysts who helped write *The Changing Image of Man*, a landmark study prepared for the Charles Kettering Foundation by the Stanford Research Institute in 1974. This remarkable document laid the groundwork for a paradigm shift in understanding how individual and social transformation might be accomplished. "The emergence of a new image and/or a new paradigm can be hastened or slowed by deliberate choice," the study noted, adding that crisis can be stimulated.

Despite growing scientific evidence for vast human potential, the study said, communicating the new image is difficult. Reality is richer and more multidimensional than any metaphor. But perhaps it is possible to lead people toward "the direct experiencing of what language can only incompletely and inadequately express.... There does indeed appear to be a path, through a profound transformation of society ... to a situation where our dilemmas are resolvable."

George Cabot Lodge, statesman and Harvard business professor, said, "The United States is in the midst of a great transformation, comparable to the one that ended medievalism and shook its institutions to the ground.... The old ideas and assumptions that once made our institutions legitimate are being eroded. They are slipping away in the face of a changing real-

ity, being replaced by different ideas as yet ill-formed, contradictory, unsettling."

A Stanford physicist, William Tiller, said that the nameless
movement had achieved a state of "critical mass" and could not
be stopped. The metaphor of a critical mass was also used by
Lewis Thomas, president of the Sloan-Kettering Institute, in
The Lives of a Cell (1974). Only in this century were we close
enough and numerous enough to begin the fusion around the
earth, a process that might now move very rapidly. Human
thought might be at an evolutionary threshold.

Art historian Jose Arguelles described "a strange disquietude
that permeates the psychic atmosphere, an unstable Pax
Americana." The revolution of the 1960s had planted the seeds
of apocalypse; the psychedelic drugs, however abused, had
given a visionary experience of self-transcendence to a sufficient number of individuals, so that they might well determine
the future of human development—"not a Utopia, but a collectively altered state of consciousness."

"We are living at a time when history is holding its breath,"
said Arthur Clarke, author of *Childhood's End* and *2001*, "and
the present is detaching itself from the past like an iceberg that
has broken away from its moorings to sail across the boundless
ocean."

Carl Rogers, who in privately circulated papers predicted the
emergence of a new kind of autonomous human being,
acclaimed the 1976 launching by California citizens and legislators of a network called Self Determination. Even if it didn't
spread to other states, he said, "it's a strong indication that the
emerging individuals do, in fact, exist and are becoming aware
of like-minded others."

But it wasn't just California. Human Systems Management,
an international coalition of management scientists, launched a
network from Columbia University in New York City: "A
search is on for special people, and they are not on any list
which can be bought. We must seek each other out, find each
other, link up with each other. It's not known how many we
are, where we are...."

And by 1976 Theodore Roszak was saying that soon no politics could survive unless it did justice to the spiritual subver-
sives, "the new society within the shell of the old." The grass-
roots, do-it-yourself revolution of Erich Fromm's prediction
was happening ten years early.

Networking was now a verb, and it was done by conferences, phone calls, air travel, books, phantom organizations,

papers, pamphleteering, photocopying, lectures, workshops, parties, grapevines, mutual friends, summit meetings, coalitions, tapes, newsletters. Funds came from grants, petty cash, and wealthy supporters, all with a peculiarly American pragmatism. Experiences and insights were shared, argued, tested, adapted, and shaken down into their usable elements very quickly.

There were now networks of academics, including college presidents and regents, lending their clout to the idea of evolving consciousness, and loose-knit groups of bureaucrats looking for ways to put government muscle behind the new ideas. A humanistic law network talked about ways to transform the bitter, adversarial nature of the justice system, and a low-profile international network of physicists engaged in studying consciousness.

The transformative vision was shared by individuals in many social movements—networks about madness, death and dying, alternative birth, ecology, nutrition. A web of "holistic" doctors, another of medical students and faculty on various campuses, formulated radical ways of thinking about health and disease. Maverick theologians and members of the clergy pondered "the new spirituality" that rose as churches declined. There were networks of innovative, "transpersonal" educators, caucuses of legislators, and a melding of economists-futurists-managers-engineers-systems theorists, all seeking creative, humanistic alternatives. A few captains of industry and finance. Foundation officials and university programmers, artists and musicians, publishers and television producers. A surprising clutch of celebrities. Scions of Old American Wealth. Ex-political radicals, minus their rhetoric, now in positions of influence.

In the late 1970s the circles began closing rapidly. The networks overlapped, linked. There was an alarming, exhilarating conviction that something significant was coming together.

Who dream the dream which all men always declare futile, Edward Carpenter had said, *Who dream the hour which is not yet on earth—and lo! it strikes.*

A series of resounding clicks, and the networks became the long-prophesied conspiracy.

3

Transformation: Brains Changing, Minds Changing

It is necessary; therefore, it is possible.
—G.A. BORGHESE

In the durable Victorian fantasy, *Flatland*, the characters are assorted geometric shapes living in an exclusively two-dimensional world. As the story opens, the narrator, a middle-aged Square, has a disturbing dream in which he visits a one-dimensional realm, Lineland, whose inhabitants can move only from point to point. With mounting frustration he attempts to explain himself—that he is a Line of Lines, from a domain where you can move not only from point to point but also from side to side. The angry Linelanders are about to attack him when he awakens.

Later that same day he attempts to help his grandson, a Little Hexagon, with his studies. The grandson suggests the possibility of a Third Dimension—a realm with up and down as well as side to side. The Square proclaims this notion foolish and unimaginable.

That very night the Square has an extraordinary, life-changing encounter: a visit from an inhabitant of Spaceland, the realm of Three Dimensions.

At first the Square is merely puzzled by his visitor, a peculiar circle who seems to change in size, even disappear. The visitor explains that he is a Sphere. He only seemed to change size and disappear because he was moving toward the Square in Space and descending at the same time.

Realizing that argument alone will not convince the Square of the Third Dimension, the exasperated Sphere creates for him an experience of depth. The Square is badly shaken:

> There was a dizzy, sickening sensation of sight that was not like seeing; I saw a Line that was no Line; Space that was not Space. I was myself and not myself. When I could find voice, I shrieked aloud in agony, "Either this is madness or it is Hell."
>
> "It is neither," calmly replied the voice of the Sphere. "It is Knowledge; it is Three Dimensions. Open your eyes once again and try to look steadily."

Having had an insight into another dimension, the Square becomes an evangelist, attempting to convince his fellow Flatlanders that Space is more than just a wild notion of mathematicians. Because of his insistence he is finally imprisoned, for the public good. Every year thereafter the high priest of Flatland, the Chief Circle, checks with him to see if he has regained his senses, but the stubborn Square continues to insist that there is a third dimension. He cannot forget it, he cannot explain it.

The common wisdom about transcendent moments is that they can never be properly communicated, only experienced. "The Tao that can be described is not the Tao...." Communication, after all, builds upon common ground. You might describe purple to someone who knows red and blue, but you cannot describe red to someone who has never seen it. Red is elemental and irreducible. Neither could you describe saltiness, sandiness, light.

There is an irreducible sensory aspect to those experiences sometimes vaguely described as transcendent, transpersonal, spiritual, altered, nonordinary, or peak. These sensations—light, connection, love, timelessness, loss of boundaries—are further complicated by paradoxes that confound logical description. As the hapless Square said, in trying to describe the Third Dimension, "I saw a Line that was no Line."

However futile their efforts, those who have been moved by such extradimensional experiences are forced to try to describe them in the language of space and time. They say they felt something that was high or deep, an edge or an abyss, a far country, a frontier, No Man's Land. Time seemed fast or slow; the discoveries were old and new, prophetic and remembered, strange yet familiar. Perspective shifted sharply, if just for a moment, transcending the old contradictions and confusion.

As we saw in Chapter 2, some eminently sane and distinguished people believe that the human mind may have reached a new state in its evolution, an unlocking of potential comparable to the emergence of language. Is this awesome possibility a utopian dream... or a fragile reality?

Until a few years ago, claims that consciousness can be expanded and transformed rested on subjective evidence. Suddenly, first in the handful of laboratories of a few pioneer scientists, then in thousands of experiments around the world, the undeniable evidence began coming forth.

Awakening, flow, freedom, unity, and synthesis are not "all in the mind," after all. They are in the brain as well. Something in conscious functioning is capable of profound change. The subjective accounts have been correlated with concrete evidence of physical change: higher levels of integration in the brain itself, more efficient processing, different "harmonics" of the brain's electrical rhythms, shifts in perceptual ability.

Many researchers say they have been shaken by their own findings about changes in conscious functioning because of the implications for widespread social change. There are hard facts to face, not just soft speculation.

It would take an additional book—a library, rather—to fully survey the subject of this chapter and the next: the evidence of change; the triggers, tools, and discoveries of personal transformation; and the experiences of people undergoing the process here and now. In any event, transformations of consciousness are more to be experienced than studied.

Bear in mind that these two chapters are panoramic, a synopsis of a vast, deep realm. They will serve their purpose if they convey a sense of the feelings and insights involved in the transformative process, if here and there they connect with something in the reader's life. We will look at changes of mind, of brain and body, of life direction.

We need, first of all, a working definition of transformation if we are to grasp its power over the lives of individuals and the way it generates deep social change. The Aquarian Conspiracy is both cause and effect of such transformation.

TRANSFORMATION: A DEFINITION

The term *transformation* has interestingly parallel meanings in mathematics, in the physical sciences, and in human change. A transformation is, literally, a forming over, a restructuring. Mathematical transforms, for example, convert a problem into new terms so that it can be solved. As we shall see later, the brain itself functions by complex mathematical transforms. In the physical sciences, a transformed substance has taken on a different nature or character, as when water becomes ice or steam.

And of course, we speak of the transformation of people—specifically the transformation of consciousness. In this context consciousness does not mean simple waking awareness. Here it refers to the state of being *conscious of one's consciousness.* You are keenly aware that you have awareness. In effect, this is a new perspective that sees other perspectives—a paradigm shift. The poet e.e. cummings once rejoiced that he had found "the eye of my eye ... the ear of my ear." *Seeing Yourself See,* one book title put it. This awareness of awareness is another dimension.

Significantly, ancient traditions describe transformation as new *seeing*. Their metaphors are of light and clarity. They speak of insight, vision. Teilhard said that the aim of evolution is "ever more perfect eyes in a world in which there is always more to see."

Most of us go through our waking hours taking little notice of our thought processes: how the mind moves, what it fears, what it heeds, how it talks to itself, what it brushes aside; the nature of our hunches; the feel of our highs and lows; our misperceptions. For the most part we eat, work, converse, worry, hope, plan, make love, shop—all with minimal thought about how we *think*.

The beginning of personal transformation is absurdly easy. *We only have to pay attention to the flow of attention itself.* Immediately we have added a new perspective. Mind can then observe its many moods, its body tensions, the flux of attention, its choices and impasses, hurting and wishing, tasting and touching.

In mystical tradition, the mind-behind-the-scenes, the part that watches the watcher is called the Witness. Identifying with a wider dimension than our usual fragmented consciousness, this center is freer and better informed. As we'll see, this wider perspective has access to universes of information processed by the brain at an unconscious level, realms we usually can't penetrate because of static or control from the surface mind—what Edward Carpenter called "the little, local self."

A mind not aware of itself—*ordinary* consciousness—is like a passenger strapped into an airplane seat, wearing blinders, ignorant of the nature of transportation, the dimension of the craft, its range, the flight plan, and the proximity of other passengers.

The mind aware of itself is a pilot. True, it is sensitive to flight rules, affected by weather, and dependent on navigation aids, but still vastly freer than the "passenger" mind.

Anything that draws us into a mindful, watchful state has the power to transform, and anyone of normal intelligence can undertake such a process. Mind, in fact, is its own transformative vehicle, inherently prepared to shift into new dimensions if only we let it. Conflict, contradiction, mixed feelings, all the elusive material that usually swirls around the edges of awareness, can be reordered at higher and higher levels. Each new integration makes the next easier.

This consciousness of consciousness, this witness level, is sometimes referred to as a "higher dimension," an expression that has often been misunderstood. Psychiatrist Viktor Frankl pointed out that no moral judgment is implied:

> *A higher dimension is simply a more inclusive dimension.* If, for example, you take a two-dimensional square and extend it vertically so that it becomes a three-dimensional cube, then you may say that the square is included in the cube.... Between the various levels of truth there can be no mutual exclusiveness, no real contradiction, for the higher includes the lower.

The Square in *Flatland* tried to explain himself to the Linelanders as a "Line of Lines." Later the Sphere described himself as a "Circle of Circles." As we'll see, the human transformative process, once it begins, is geometric. In a sense, the fourth dimension is just this: *to see the other three with new eyes.*

CONSCIOUS EVOLUTION

The idea that we have wide options of consciousness is hardly new. At the dawn of the Renaissance, Pico della Mirandola wrote:

> With freedom of choice and with honor, as though the maker and molder of thyself, thou mayest fashion thyself in whatever shape thou shalt prefer. Thou shalt have the power to generate into the lower forms of life which are brutish. Thou shalt have the power, out of thy soul's judgment, to be reborn into the higher forms. . . .

Then, as now, philosophers argued whether human nature is good or evil. Today science, of all disciplines, offers us another option: The human brain and behavior are almost unbelievably plastic. True, we are conditioned to be afraid, defensive, and hostile, yet we also have the capacity for extraordinary transcendence.

Those who believe in the possibility of impending social transformation are not optimistic about human nature; rather, they trust the transformative process itself. Having experienced positive change in their own lives—more freedom, feelings of kinship and unity, more creativity, more ability to handle stress, a sense of meaning—they concede that others may change, too. And they believe that if enough individuals discover new capacities in themselves they will naturally conspire to create a world hospitable to human imagination, growth, and cooperation.

The proven plasticity of the human brain and human awareness offers the possibility that *individual evolution* may lead to *collective evolution*. When one person has unlocked a new capacity its existence is suddenly evident to others, who may then develop the same capacity. Certain skills, arts, and sports, for example, are developed consummately in particular cultures. Even our "natural" abilities must be encouraged. Human beings do not even walk or talk spontaneously. If babies are kept in cribs in institutions with nothing to do but stare at the ceiling, they will walk and talk very late, if ever. These capacities must be released; they evolve in interaction with other human beings and the environment.

We only know what the brain can do by calling on it. The genetic repertoire of any species includes an almost infinite number of potentialities, more than can be tapped by any one environment or during a single lifetime. As one geneticist put it, it's as if we all have grand pianos inside us, but only a few learn to play them. Just as human beings learn to defy gravity in gymnastic feats or discriminate between hundreds of varieties of coffee, so we can perform gymnastics of attention and subtleties of interior sensing.

Millennia ago humankind discovered that the brain can be teased into profound shifts of awareness. The mind can learn to view itself and its own realities in ways that seldom occur spontaneously. These systems, tools for serious inner exploration, made possible the conscious evolution of consciousness. The growing worldwide recognition of this capacity and how it can be accomplished is the major technological achievement of our time.

In a famous passage, William James urged his contemporaries to heed such shifts:

Our normal waking consciousness, rational consciousness as we call it, is but one special type of consciousness, while all about it, parted from it by the filmiest of screens, there lie potential forms of consciousness entirely different.

We may go through life without suspecting their existence, but apply the requisite stimulus, and at a touch they are there in all their completeness....

No account of the universe in its totality can be final which leaves these other forms of consciousness quite disregarded.

THE WAYS WE CHANGE

There are four basic ways in which we change our minds when we get new and conflicting information. The easiest and most limited of these we might call *change by exception*. Our old belief system remains intact but allows for a handful of anomalies, the way an old paradigm tolerates a certain number of odd phenomena that hang around its edges before the breakthrough to a larger, more satisfying paradigm. An individual who engages in change by exception may dislike all members of a particular group, except one or two. He may consider psychic phenomena nonsense yet still believe that his great-aunt's dreams came true. These are dismissed as "the exceptions that prove the rule" instead of the exceptions that *disprove* the rule.

Incremental change occurs bit by bit, and the individual is not aware of having changed.

Then there is *pendulum change*, the abandonment of one

closed and certain system for another. The hawk becomes a dove, the disenchanted religious zealot becomes an atheist, the promiscuous person turns into a prude—and vice versa, all the way around.

Pendulum change fails to integrate what was right with the old and fails to discriminate the value of the new from its over-statements. Pendulum change rejects its own prior experience, going from one kind of half-knowing to another.

Change by exception, incremental change, and pendulum change stop short of transformation. The brain cannot deal with conflicting information unless it can integrate it. One simple example: If the brain is unable to fuse double vision into a single image, it will eventually repress the signals from one eye. The visual cells in the brain for that eye then atrophy, causing blindness. In the same way, the brain chooses between conflicting views. It represses information that does not fit with its dominant beliefs.

Unless, of course, it can harmonize the ideas into a powerful synthesis. That is *paradigm change*—transformation. It is the fourth dimension of change: the new perspective, the insight that allows the information to come together in a new form or structure. Paradigm change refines and integrates. Paradigm change attempts to heal the delusion of either-or, of this-or-that.

In many ways, it is the most challenging kind of change because it relinquishes certainty. It allows for different interpretations from different perspectives at different times.

Change by exception says, "I'm right, except for _____." *Incremental change* says, "I was almost right, but now I'm right." *Pendulum change* says, "I was wrong before, but now I'm right." *Paradigm change* says, "I was partially right before, and now I'm a bit more partially right." In paradigm change we realize that our previous views were only part of the picture—and that what we know now is only part of what we'll know later. Change is no longer threatening. It absorbs, enlarges, enriches. The unknown is friendly, interesting territory. Each insight widens the road, making the next stage of travel, the next opening, easier.

Change itself changes, just as in nature, evolution evolves from a simple to a complex process. Every new occurrence alters the nature of those to follow, like compound interest. Paradigm change is not a simple linear effect, like the ten little Indians in the nursery rhyme who vanish one by one. It is a sudden shift of pattern, a spiral, and sometimes a cataclysm.

When we wake up to the flux and alteration of our own awareness we augment change. Synthesis builds on synthesis.

STRESS AND TRANSFORMATION

Given the proper circumstances, the human brain has boundless capabilities for paradigm shifts. It can order and reorder itself, integrate, transcend old conflicts. Anything that disrupts the old order of our lives has the potential for triggering a transformation, a movement toward greater maturity, openness, strength.

Sometimes the perturbing element is obvious stress: a job loss, a divorce, serious illness, financial troubles, a death in the family, imprisonment, even sudden success or a promotion. Or it may be subtle intellectual stress: a close relationship with someone whose views differ markedly from those we have always held; a book that shakes our beliefs; or a new environment, a foreign country.

Personal stress as well as the collective stress of our age, the much-discussed future shock, can be agents of transformation, once we know how to integrate them. Ironically, for all our nostalgia for simpler times, the turbulent twentieth century may be driving us into the change and creativity dreamt of through the ages.

The entire culture is undergoing trauma and tensions that beg for new order. Psychiatrist Frederic Flach, remarking on this historic development, quoted the English novelist Samuel Butler, who said in *The Way of All Flesh:* "In quiet uneventful lives, the changes internal and external are so small that there is little or no strain in the process of fusion and accommodation. In other lives there is great strain, but there is also great fusion and accommodating power." Flach adds:

This power to fuse and accommodate which Butler described is indeed creativity. That was in 1885. Today fewer and fewer people find their lives quiet and uneventful. Changes take place at an accelerated pace and touch everyone in some way. In a world of increasingly complex stresses, personal and cultural, we can no longer afford to use our creative abilities only to solve specific problems here and there. Our health and our sanity require that we learn how to live lives that are genuinely creative.

We are troubled by many things we can't fit together, the paradoxes of everyday life. Work should be primarily meaningful, work should pay well. Children should have freedom, children should be controlled. We are torn between what others want of us and what we want for ourselves. We want to be compassionate, we want to be honest. We want security, we want spontaneity.

Warring priorities, stress, pain, paradoxes, conflicts—these prescribe their own remedies if we attend to them fully. When we deal indirectly with our tensions, when we stifle them or vacillate, we *live* indirectly. We cheat ourselves of transformation.

THE WAY OF AVOIDANCE

At the level of ordinary consciousness, we deny pain and paradox. We doctor them with Valium, dull them with alcohol, or distract them with television.

Denial is a way of life. More accurately, it is a way of diminishing life, of making it seem more manageable. Denial is the alternative to transformation.

Personal denial, mutual denial, collective denial. Denial of facts and feelings. Denial of experience, a deliberate forgetting what we see and hear. Denial of our capacities. Politicians deny problems, parents deny their vulnerability, teachers deny their biases, children deny their intentions. Most of all, we deny what we know in our bones.

We are caught between two different evolutionary mechanisms: denial and transformation. We evolved with the ability to repress pain and to filter out peripheral information. These are useful short-term strategies that allowed our ancestors to shunt aside stimuli that would be too much to bear in an emergency, just as the fight-or-flight syndrome aroused them to cope with physical danger.

The capacity for denial is an example of the body's sometimes short-sighted vision. Some of the body's automatic responses hurt over the long run more than they help. The formation of scar tissue, for example, prevents the nerves in the spine from reconnecting after an accident. In many injuries, swelling causes more damage than the original trauma. And it is the body's hysterical overreaction to a virus, rather than the virus itself, that makes us ill.

Our ability to block our experience is an evolutionary dead end. Rather than experiencing and *transforming* pain, conflict, and fear, we often divert or dampen them with a kind of unwitting hypnosis.

Over a lifetime, more and more stress accumulates. There is no release, and our consciousness narrows. The floodlight shrinks into the slender beam of a flashlight. We lose the vividness of colors, sensitivity to sounds, peripheral vision, sensitivity to others, emotional intensity. The spectrum of awareness becomes ever narrower.

The real alienation in our time is not from society but from self.

Who knows where it starts? Perhaps in our earliest years, when we skin a knee and some kindly adult distracts us with a joke or a cookie. Certainly the culture does not foster the habit of really experiencing our experiences. But denial would probably happen anyway because of our knack for masking whatever hurts, even at the cost of consciousness.

Avoidance is a short-term answer, like aspirin. Avoidance settles for chronic dull pain rather than brief acute confrontation. The cost is flexibility; just as an arm or leg contracts in chronic pain, so the full range of movement of consciousness goes into spasm.

Denial, however human and natural a response, exacts a terrible price. It is as if we settled for living in the anterooms of our lives. And, ultimately, it doesn't work. A part of the self keenly feels all the denied pain.

For most of a century, psychologists used a bureaucratic model of the mind: Conscious mind on top, commanding officer; Subconscious, like an unreliable first-lieutenant; and the Unconscious, far below, an unruly platoon of erotic energies, archetypes, curiosities. It comes as a shock, then, to learn that a Co-conscious has been operating alongside us—a dimension of awareness that Stanford psychologist Ernest Hilgard has called the Hidden Observer.

Laboratory experiments at Stanford have shown that another part of the self can acknowledge pain and other stimuli to which hypnotized subjects are oblivious. This aspect of consciousness is always present, always fully experiencing. And it can be quite readily called upon, as Hilgard's experiments demonstrated.

For example, with her hand immersed in ice water, one hypnotized woman steadily reported that she felt zero pain on a scale of zero to ten. But her other hand, with access to pencil and paper, reported an increase in pain: "0...2...4...7..." Other subjects gave contradictory verbal reports, depending on which "self" the hypnotist summoned.

Like stuck records, all our denied experiences and emotions reverberate endlessly in the other half of the self. Awesome energy goes into keeping this information cycling out of the range of ordinary awareness. Little wonder if we are fatigued, dis-eased, alienated.

We have two essential strategies for coping: the way of avoidance or the way of attention.

In his 1918 diary, Hermann Hesse recalled a dream in which he heard two distinct voices. The first told him to seek out forces to overcome suffering, to calm himself. It sounded like parents, school, Kant, the church fathers. But the second voice—which sounded farther off, like "primal cause"—said that suffering only hurts because you fear it, complain about it, flee it.

> You know quite well, deep within you, that there is only a single magic, a single power, a single salvation...and that is called loving. Well, then, love your suffering. Do not resist it, do not flee from it. Give yourself to it. It is only your aversion that hurts, nothing else.

The pain is the aversion; the healing magic is attention.

Properly attended to, pain can answer our most crucial questions, even those we did not consciously frame. The only way out of our suffering is through it. From an ancient Sanskrit writing: "Do not try to drive pain away by pretending that it is not real. If you seek serenity in oneness, pain will vanish of its own accord."

Conflict, pain, tension, fear, paradox...these are transformations trying to happen. Once we confront them, the transformative process begins. Those who discover this phenomenon, whether by search or accident, gradually realize that the reward is worth the scariness of unanesthetized life. The release of pain, the sense of liberation, and the resolution of conflict make the next crisis or stubborn paradox easier to confront.

THE WAY OF ATTENTION

We have the biological capacity to deny our stress—or trans-form it by paying attention to it. Recent discoveries about the brain help us understand both the psychological and physio-logical aspects of these two choices, and why the way of atten-tion is a deliberate choice.

The brain's right and left hemispheres interact all the time, but each also has certain functions of its own. These specialized functions of the hemispheres were first observed in the effects of injuries confined to one side of the brain or the other. Later, there were more sophisticated techniques to detect differences. Different pictures would be flashed simultaneously to the left and right visual fields, for example, or the left and right ears would hear different tones at the same time. Postmortem examination of brains showed subtle structural differences be-tween the sides. Eventually research found that brain cells pro-ducing certain chemicals were more concentrated on one side than the other.

The hemispheres can operate independently, as two separate centers of consciousness. This was dramatically demonstrated in the 1960s and 1970s when twenty-five patients around the world underwent "split-brain" surgery for the treatment of se-vere epilepsy. The connections between hemispheres were severed in the hope of confining seizures to one side.

After their recovery from the operation, the split-brain sub-jects, who appeared normal enough, were tested to determine whether there was a duality of conscious experience and to observe the separate functions of the two hemispheres. What tasks would each half-self be able to perform? What would it be able to describe?

The split-brain patient indeed proved to have two minds, capable of independent functioning. Sometimes the left hand literally did not know what the right hand was doing.

For example, the split-brain patient cannot tell the experi-menter the name of an object known only to the mute right hemisphere.[1] The subject claims not to know what the object is, although the left hand (controlled by the right brain) can re-trieve it from a pile of objects out of visual range. If the split-brain patient tries to copy simple shapes with the right hand

---

[1]These functions are reversed in some people, particularly in many left-handers. That is, language is in the right hemisphere rather than the left, spatial competence in the left rather than the right, etc.

(whose controlling left brain cannot comprehend spatial relationships), the left hand may attempt to finish the task.

We tend to identify the "I" with the verbal left brain and its operations, the part of us that can talk about and analyze experiences. The left hemisphere essentially controls speech. It adds, subtracts, hyphenates, measures, compartmentalizes, organizes, names, pigeonholes, and watches clocks.

Although the right hemisphere has little control over the speech mechanism, it understands language in some way and gives our speech its emotional inflection. If a certain region of the right brain is damaged, speech becomes monotonous and colorless. The right hemisphere is more musical and sexual than the left. It thinks in images, sees in wholes, detects patterns. It seems to mediate pain more intensely than the left.

In Marshall McLuhan's expression, the right brain "tunes" information, the left brain "fits" it. The left deals with the past, matching the experience of this moment to earlier experience, trying to categorize it; the right hemisphere responds to novelty, the unknown. The left takes snapshots, the right watches movies.

The right brain makes visual closure—that is, it can identify a shape suggested by only a few lines. It mentally connects the points into a pattern. As psychologists would put it, the right brain completes the gestalt. It is whole-making—holistic.

Detecting tendencies and patterns is a crucial skill. The more accurately we can get the picture from minimal information, the better equipped we are to survive.

We use pattern-seeing in mundane ways, as when we read a handwritten message with partially closed letters. The ability to close a pattern with limited information enables the successful retailer or politician to detect early trends, the diagnostician to name an illness, the therapist to see an unhealthy pattern in a person or family.

The right hemisphere is richly connected to the ancient limbic brain, the so-called emotional brain. The mysterious limbic structures are involved in memory processing and, when electronically stimulated, produce many of the phenomena of altered states of consciousness.

In the classic sense of "heart and mind," we can think of this right hemisphere-limbic circuit as the heart-brain. If we say, for example, "The heart has its reasons," we are referring to the deeply felt response processed by the "other side of the brain."

For both cultural and biological reasons, the left brain seems to dominate awareness in most of us. In some instances, researchers have reported, the left brain even takes over those tasks at which the right brain is superior.

We confine much of our conscious awareness to the very aspect of brain function that reduces things to their parts. And we sabotage our only strategy for finding meaning because the left brain, in habitually cutting off conflict from the right, also cuts off its ability to see patterns and to see the whole.

Without the benefit of a scalpel, we perform split-brain surgery on ourselves. We isolate heart and mind. Cut off from the fantasy, dreams, intuitions, and holistic processes of the right brain, the left is sterile. And the right brain, cut off from integration with its organizing partner, keeps recycling its emotional charge. Feelings are dammed, perhaps to work private mischief in fatigue, illness, neurosis, a pervasive sense of something wrong, something missing—a kind of cosmic homesickness. This fragmentation costs us our health and our capacity for intimacy. As we'll see in Chapter 9, it also costs us our ability to learn, create, innovate.

KNOWING AND NAMING

The raw stuff of human transformation is around and within us, omnipresent and invisible as oxygen. We are swimming in knowledge we have not claimed, all mediated by the realm of the brain that cannot name what it knows.

There are techniques that can help us name our dreams and dragons. They are designed to reopen the bridge between right and left to through traffic, to increase the left brain's awareness of its counterpart.

Meditation, chanting, and similar techniques increase the coherence and harmony in the brainwave patterns; they bring about greater synchrony between the hemispheres, which suggests that higher order is achieved. On occasion it appears that increasing populations of nerve cells are recruited into the rhythm, until all regions of the brain seem to be throbbing, as if choreographed and orchestrated. The usually dissynchronous patterns in the two sides seem to become entrained to each other. Brainwave activity in older, deeper brain structures may also show an unexpected synchrony with the neocortex.

One example of such a technique is focusing, a method developed by psychologist Eugene Gendlin of the University of Chicago. People using this technique learn to sit quietly and allow the feeling, or "aura," of a particular concern to well up.

In effect, they ask it to identify itself. Typically, after half a minute or so, a word or phrase pops into mind. If it is appropriate, the body responds unmistakably. As Gendlin described it:

> As these rare words come, one senses a sharpened feeling, or a felt relief, a felt shift, usually before one can say what this shift is. Sometimes such words are not in themselves very impressive or novel, but just these words have an experiential effect, and no others do.[2]

Research shows that these "felt shifts" are accompanied by a pronounced change in brainwave harmonics. A distinct, complex pattern seems to correlate with this experience of insight. The brain's activity is integrated at a higher level. And when a person reports feeling "stuck" there is a detectable collapse of those same EEG harmonics.

Whatever lowers the barrier and lets the unclaimed material emerge is transformative. Recognition—literally, "knowing again"—occurs when the analytical brain, with its power to name and classify, admits the wisdom of its other half into full awareness.

The organizing part of the brain can only understand that which it can fit into prior knowledge. Language draws the strange, the unknown, into full consciousness, and we say, "Of *course*..."

In Greek philosophy, *logos* ("word") was the divine ordering principle, fitting the new or strange into the scheme of things. Whenever we name things, we structure consciousness. As we look at the great social transformation under way, we will see again and again that naming awakens new perspectives: birth without violence, voluntary simplicity, appropriate technology, paradigm shift.

Language releases the unknown from limbo, expressing it in a way that the whole brain can know it. Incantations, mantras, poetry, and secret sacred words are all bridges that join the two brains. The artist faces a form, Martin Buber once said. "If he speaks the primary word out of his being to the form which appears, then the effective power streams out and the work arises."

---

[2]His example of felt shift: You take off on a journey with that familiar, uneasy feeling that you have forgotten something. As you sit on the airplane you rummage through the possibilities. You may recall an item you did indeed forget, but there is no sense of relief; you know that isn't *it*. When the "real" item comes to mind, there is a sharp recognition, a tangible shift, certainty that this was what was troubling you.

Given the complexity of the brain, it may be generations before science understands the processes that enable us to know without knowing that we know. But no matter; what counts is that *something* in us is wiser and better informed than our ordinary consciousness. With such an ally within our selves, why should we go it alone?

FINDING THE CENTER

The joining of the two minds creates something new. Whole-brain knowing is far more than the sum of its parts, and *different* from either.

John Middleton Murry, the British literary critic, said that the reconciling of mind and heart is "the central mystery of all high religion." In the 1940s Murry wrote that a growing number of men and women were becoming "a new kind of human being," fusing emotion and intellect. Most people, he said, turn away from inner conflict. They find comfort in faith, busyness, denial.

> But there were always a few on whom these opiates failed to work. . . . Heart and mind in them each insisted upon its rights, and the claims could not be reconciled. There was a deadlock in the center of their being, and they passed steadily into a condition of isolation, abandonment and despair. Their inward division was complete.
>
> Then came, out of that extreme and absolute division, a sudden unity. A new kind of consciousness was created in them. Mind and Heart, which had been irreconcilable enemies, became united in the Soul, which loved what it knew. The inward division was healed.

Murry called this new knowing the soul.[3] Over the centuries, accounts of transcendental experience often described it as a mysterious "center," the penetration of some unknown but central realm.[4] This transcendent center is in the lore of all cultures, represented in mandalas, in alchemy, in the king's

[3]Nikos Kazantzakis talked about harmonizing and modulating "both opposing forces" in the brain. From a transcendent peak you can see the brain's battle, he said; we must besiege every cell of the brain because that is where God is jailed, "seeking, trying, hammering to open a gate in the fortress of matter."

[4]Charles Lindbergh, describing an extraordinary mystical experience on his famous flight, said he felt "caught in the gravitational field between two planets."

chamber in pyramids ("fire in the middle"), the sanctum sanctorum, the holy of holies. "We sit around in a ring and suppose," wrote Robert Frost, "But the Secret sits in the middle and knows."

The escape from the prison of the two minds—the task of transformation—is the great theme pervading Hesse's novels: *Steppenwolf, Narcissus and Goldmund, The Glass Bead Game, Demian,* and *Siddhartha*. In 1921 he said that he hoped the spiritual wave from India would offer his culture "a corrective, refreshment from the opposite pole." Europeans unhappy with their overspecialized intellectual climate were not turning so much toward Buddha or Lao-tse, he said, as toward meditation, "a technique whose highest result is pure harmony, a simultaneous and equal cooperation of logical and intuitive thinking." The East contemplated the forest; the West counted the trees. Yet the need for completion emerges as a theme in the myths of all cultures. They wanted it all—and many transcended the split. The mind that knows the trees *and* the forest is a new mind.

The power of true center must be the most frequently mislaid artifact of human wisdom. It is as if the same message keeps washing ashore, and no one breaks the bottles, much less the code. True, Hesse said, many German professors were nervous that the intellectual West would drown in a Buddhist deluge. "The West, however," he observed dryly, "will not drown." Indeed, for all practical purposes, the West has only recently noticed the bottles that keep washing ashore and felt the tide that carries them.

Enumerating the variety of spiritual paths, Aldous Huxley urged "the central door" rather than purely intellectual or purely practical ways. "The best of both worlds . . . the best of *all* worlds." There is more to balance, as one Eastern thinker recently remarked, than not falling over.

The thrill of the new perspective cannot be sustained for an indefinite period. Inevitably and often, the individual lapses into old positions, old polarities, old ways. In *Mount Analog,* René Daumal described the slipping back:

> You cannot stay on the summit forever; you have to come down again. So why bother in the first place? Just this: What is above knows what is below, but what is below does not know what is above.

One climbs, one sees, one descends; one sees no longer, but one has seen.

There is an art of conducting oneself in the lower regions by the memory of what one saw higher up: "When one can no longer see, one can at least still know."

We live—as we shall see in the next chapter—by what we have seen.

4

Crossover: People Changing

*There is only one history of importance
and it is the history of what you once believed in and the history
of what you came to believe in.*
— *KAY BOYLE*

Toto, I've a feeling we're not in Kansas anymore.
— *DOROTHY*

 The difference between transformation by accident and transformation by a system is like the difference between lightning and a lamp. Both give illumination, but one is dangerous and unreliable, while the other is relatively safe, directed, available.

The intentional triggers of transformative experiences are numberless, yet they have a common quality. They focus awareness on awareness—a critical shift. For all their surface variation, most focus on something too strange, complex, diffuse, or monotonous to be handled by the brain's analytical, intellectual half: on breathing, repetitive physical movement, music, water, a flame, a meaningless sound, a blank wall, a koan, a paradox. The intellectual brain can only dominate awareness by affixing itself to something definite and bounded. If it is captured by a diffuse, monotonous focus, the signals from the other side of the mind can be heard.

Among the triggers of such experiences reported by the individuals who responded to the Aquarian Conspiracy questionnaire:

- Sensory isolation and sensory overload, because sharply altered input causes a shift in consciousness.
- Biofeedback—the use of machines that feed back tones or visual readouts of body processes like brainwave activity, muscle activity, skin temperature—because learning to control these processes requires an unusually relaxed and alert state.
- Autogenic training, an approach that originated in Europe more than fifty years ago—self-suggestions that the body is becoming relaxed, "breathing itself."
- Music (sometimes in combination with imagery or meditation), because of the brain's sensitivity to tone and tempo and because music engages the right hemisphere. Chanting. Painting, sculpting, pottery, and similar activities that give a creator a chance to become lost in the creation.
- Improvisational theatre, with its requirement of both total attention and spontaneity. Psychodrama, because it forces an awareness of roles and role playing. Contemplation of nature and other aesthetically overwhelming experiences.
- The "consciousness-raising" strategies of various social movements that call attention to old assumptions.
- Self-help and mutual-help networks—for example, Alcoholics Anonymous, Overeaters Anonymous, and their counterparts, whose twelve rules include paying attention to one's conscious processes and to change, acknowledging that one can choose behavior, and cooperating with "higher forces" by looking inward.
- Hypnosis and self-hypnosis.
- Meditation of every description: Zen, Tibetan Buddhist, chaotic, Transcendental, Christian, Kabbalist, kundalini, raja yoga, tantric yoga, etc. Psychosynthesis, a system that combines imagery and a meditative state.
- Sufi stories, koans, and dervish dancing. Various shamanic and magical techniques, which focus attention.
- Seminars like est, Silva Mind Control, Actualizations, and Lifespring, which attempt to break the cultural trance and open the individual to new choices.
- Dream journals, because dreams are the most available medium for information from beyond the range of ordinary consciousness.
- Arica, Theosophy, and Gurdjieffian systems, which syn-

thesize many different mystical traditions and teach techniques for altering awareness.

- Contemporary psychotherapies, like Viktor Frankl's Logotherapy, which involves a search for meaning and the use of "paradoxical intention," the direct confrontation of the source of fear. Primal Therapy and its spin-offs, which summon up experiences of early childhood pain. The Fischer-Hoffman process, a similar reentry into childhood anxieties, followed by an intense use of imagery for reconciliation with and forgiveness of one's parents for any negative early experiences. Gestalt therapy, the gentle forcing through of patterns of recognition, or paradigm shifts.
- Science of Mind, an approach to healing and self healing.
- A Course in Miracles, an unorthodox contemporary approach to Christianity based on a profound shift in perception.
- Countless body disciplines and therapies: hatha yoga, Reichian, the Bates system for vision improvement, T'ai Chi Ch'uan, aikido, karate, running, dance, Rolfing, bioenergetics, Feldenkrais, Alexander, Applied Kinesiology.
- Intense experiences of personal and collective change at Esalen in Big Sur, sensitivity groups at Washington's National Training Laboratories, encounter groups, informal groups of supportive friends.
- Sport, mountain-climbing, river-running, and similar physically exhilarating activities, which cause a qualitative shift in the sense of being alive. Wilderness retreats or solitary flying or sailing, which foster self-discovery and a sense of timelessness.

All of these approaches might be called *psychotechnologies*—systems for a deliberate change in consciousness. Individuals may independently discover a new way of paying attention and may learn to induce such states by methods of their own devising. Anything can work.[1]

As William James noted three-quarters of a century ago, the

[1]Much of the criticism of the psychotechnologies is based on the apparent contradictions between the behavior of individuals and their claims of personal change. Many people discuss their purported new awareness as if it were the latest film or diet; yet even this phase may precede real change. Some people feel as if they are changing in ways not evident to others. Still others go through apparent negative change, periods of withdrawal or emotionality, before achieving a new equilibrium. We can only guess about the changes in

key to expanded awareness is surrender. As the struggle is abandoned, it is won. "To go faster, you must slow down," said the hero of *Shockwave Rider*, John Brunner's novel of the future. A biofeedback researcher, chief of psychiatry at a famous medical center, told his colleagues, "You can only win these races by taking your foot off the accelerator."

The complexity of a method should not be confused with its effectiveness. Highly structured disciplines and intricate symbolism may benefit some, while others go through rapid change with simple technology. An approach that works for a while may suddenly seem inappropriate, or a method may seem to be making no significant difference, but in retrospect, one realizes that something important has happened.

Our nervous systems are organized in different ways, we are in varying states of health, and we have different histories of introspection, dreaminess, rigidity, anxiety. Just as there are natural athletes, so there are individuals to whom shifts of consciousness come easily. A diffuse, relaxed state of attention, the key to all these approaches, need not be coerced, only permitted. Effort interferes with the process, and some people have difficulty just letting go.

Many people seem to be neurologically resistant to the psychotechnologies, perhaps because they were more sensitive to pain as children or experienced more noxious input. They are likelier to have cut off the more emotionally responsive, pain-sensitive right hemisphere. Others are more resilient—perhaps because they were born innovators and explorers, have more flexible temperaments, or learned to cope with fear and pain early in life.

Because of the initial advantage or disadvantage in differing nervous systems, it seems at first that the rich get richer and the poor get discouraged. But improvement comes for everyone, just as practice makes us more adept skiers or swimmers, whatever our inherent talent.

Like physical exercise, the technologies are progressive in their effect, but you don't lose brain changes the way you lose muscle development if you don't persist. "No mirror becomes iron again," said Sufi poet Rumi, "no ripe grape becomes sour again."

---

another person; transformation is not a spectator sport. And we may even misread what has happened in ourselves, realizing only in retrospect that an important shift has occurred; or we may think we have changed forever in some way only to find ourselves lapsing on occasion into old thought patterns and behaviors.

STAGES OF TRANSFORMATION

No system promises a shift from ordinary human fragmentation to twenty-four-hour-a-day clarity. Transformation is a journey without a final destination. But there are stages in the journey, and they are surprisingly mappable, based on thousands of historical accounts and the proliferating reports of contemporary seekers. Some traps, caves, quicksand, and dangerous crossings are unique to the individual journey, but there are deserts, peaks, and certain strange buttes observed by nearly everyone who persists. Recognizing, then, that the map is not the transformational territory, we will describe the process in terms of four major stages.

The first stage is preliminary, almost happenstance: an *entry point*. In most cases, the entry point can only be identified in retrospect. Entry can be triggered by anything that shakes up the old understanding of the world, the old priorities. Sometimes it is a token investment, made out of boredom, curiosity, or desperation—a ten-dollar book, a hundred-dollar mantra, a university extension course.

For a great many, the trigger has been a spontaneous mystical or psychic experience, as hard to explain as it is to deny. Or the intense alternative reality generated by a psychedelic drug.

It is impossible to overestimate the historic role of psychedelics as an entry point drawing people into other transformative technologies. For tens of thousands of "left-brained" engineers, chemists, psychologists, and medical students who never before understood their more spontaneous, imaginative right-brained brethren, the drugs were a pass to Xanadu, especially in the 1960s.

The changes in brain chemistry triggered by psychedelics cause the familiar world to metamorphose. It gives way to rapid imagery, unaccustomed depths of visual perception and hearing, a flood of "new" knowledge that seems at once very old, a poignant primal memory. Unlike the mental states produced by dreaming or drinking, psychedelic awareness is not fuzzy but many times more intense than normal waking consciousness. Only through this intensely altered state did some become fully aware of the role of consciousness in creating their everyday reality.

Those who ingested psychedelics soon found that the historic accounts closest to their own experiences derived either from mystical literature or from the wonderland of theoretical physics—complementary views of "the all and the void," the very real dimension that cannot be measured in miles or minutes.

As one chronicler of the sixties remarked, "LSD gave a whole generation a religious experience." But chemical *satori* is perishable, its effects too overwhelming to integrate into everyday life. Non-drug psychotechnologies offer a *controlled*, sustained movement toward that spacious reality. The annals of the Aquarian Conspiracy are full of accounts of passages: LSD to Zen, LSD to India, psilocybin to Psychosynthesis.

For whatever glories the mushrooms and saturated sugar cubes contained, they were only a glimpse—coming attractions, but not the main feature.

The entry-point experience hints that there is a brighter, richer, more meaningful dimension to life. Some are haunted by that glimpse and drawn to see more. Others, less serious, stay near the entry point, playing with the occult, drugs, consciousness-altering games. Some are afraid to go on at all. Confronting the nonrational is unnerving. Here the unfettered mind suffers a kind of agoraphobia, a fear of its own awesome spaces. Those with a strong need to control may be frightened by touching a realm of multiple realities, multiple ways of seeing. They would rather keep to their right/wrong, black/white version of the world. They repress insights that contradict the old belief system.

Some hesitate because they don't know where to turn next. Fear of criticism stops others. They might look foolish, pretentious, even crazy, to family, friends, co-workers. They worry that the journey inward will seem narcissistic or escapist. Indeed those who persist past the entry point have to overcome a pervasive culture bias against introspection. The search for self-knowledge is often equated with self-importance, with a concern for one's own psyche at the expense of social responsibility. The popular criticism of psychotechnologies is typified by the term "the new narcissism," from a *Harper's* article by Peter Marin, and the "Me Decade," a pejorative introduced by Tom Wolfe in *New York* magazine.[2]

---

[2]Philosopher William Bartley remarked that it is odd that the charge of social and political irresponsibility should ever have been leveled at the consciousness movement, especially since so many of the social movements have borrowed its techniques. "There is nothing narcissistic," he said, "about attempting to transcend those things in life that lead people to narcissism."

The excesses of some of those involved in the psychotechnologies—the extravagant claims of hucksters and true believers, the tyranny of some purported teachers and gurus—antagonize public opinion. A wide and deep social

The isolation of those new to the transformative process is deepened by their inability to explain how they feel and why they are going on. If they try to describe the discovery of a kind of inner "all-rightness"—a potentially whole and healthy self waiting to be liberated—they are afraid of sounding egotistical.

There is a fear of being jilted. The knowledge from these experiences is often elusive, hard to reconstruct. What if these insights were only phantoms... illusions? In the past we have believed promises that were broken. We have seen mirages of fresh hope dissolve as we reach for them. The memory of these betrayals, large and small, says, "Don't trust...."

Even more common, as Abraham Maslow noted, is the fear of our own higher potentialities. "We enjoy and even thrill to the godlike possibilities we see in ourselves in peak moments. And yet we simultaneously shiver with weakness, awe, and fear before these same possibilities." An apparent lack of curiosity is often a defense. "Fear of knowing is very deeply a fear of doing," Maslow said. Knowledge carries responsibility.

There is a fear of the self, an unwillingness to trust our deeper needs. We worry that an impulsive aspect might take over. Suppose we find that what we really want of life is dangerously different from what we have. And there is a related fear that we will be sucked into a maelstrom of unusual experiences and, worse yet, that we might like them. Or we might become committed to some demanding discipline; if we were to take up meditation, we might start getting up at five in the morning or become vegetarian.

Man is afraid of things that cannot harm him, says a Hasidic scripture, and craves things that cannot help him. "But actually it is something within him that he is afraid of, and it is something within him that he craves." We fear and crave becoming truly ourselves.

Somewhere at the entry point we know that if we pursue this Holy Grail, nothing will ever be quite the same. We can always turn back from the entry point. The opportunity for retreat is at hand, like the emergency door atop the Space Mountain ride in Disneyland, an exit for those with second thoughts.

---

phenomenon is misunderstood by the magnifying of the sensational, the trivial, the least representative. Similarly, the psychotechnologies are sometimes criticized because of individual casualties, people who have psychotic breaks. Too much sun is sunburn, but we don't blame the sun. These systems tap into a power source that can be abused.

Mutual criticism and self-criticism within the consciousness movement address these problems with more rigor and concern than do the outside critics.

The second stage, for those who go on, is *exploration*—the Yes after the final No. Warily or enthusiastically, having sensed that there is something worth finding, the individual sets out to look for it. The first serious step, however small, is empowering and significant. The quest, as one spiritual teacher put it, *is* the transformation.

This exploration is the "deliberate letting" psychologist Eugene Gendlin describes. This letting permits the inner knowledge to come forward. It is an intentional release, as when we deliberately relax our grip on something. The grip is the contraction of our consciousness, our psychic spasm, which must be loosened before anything can change.

The psychotechnologies are designed to free that tight hold so that we might become buoyant, the way a lifeguard detaches the panicky grip of a drowning person so that he might be rescued.

Ironically, we go after transformative experiences in the only way we know how: as consumers, competitors, still operating from the values of the old paradigm. We may compare our experiences to others, wonder if we're "doing it right," getting there fast enough, making progress. We may be trying to replicate one particularly rewarding or moving experience. During this phase some individuals try many techniques and teachers, like comparison shoppers. In an age of supersonic travel and satellite communication, we tend to expect instant gratification, instant feedback, instant news. The process of transformation may be simmering underground like a geyser, but we cannot see it and are impatient for action.

Some fall at first into pendulum change. The initial method, e.g., Transcendental Meditation, running, est, Rolfing, is seen as the panacea for the world's ills. All other systems are dismissed.

In this false dawn of certainty, there is often eager proselytizing. The would-be evangelists quickly learn that no single system works for everyone. And the methods themselves — by repeated focusing of awareness—eventually lead to the realization that there will be no ultimate answers.

As science fiction writer Ray Bradbury said, "We all go on the same Search, looking to solve the old Mystery. We will not, of course, ever solve it. We will climb all over it. We will, finally, inhabit the Mystery...."

In the third stage, *integration*, the mystery is inhabited. Although there may be favorite methods or teachers, the individual trusts an inner "guru."

During the earlier stages there was probably some dissonance, sharp conflict between new beliefs and old patterns. Like the troubled society struggling to remake itself with old tools and structures, the individual tries at first to improve the situation rather than change it, to reform rather than transform.

Now there may be oscillation between exhilaration and loneliness because fear centers on the disruptive effect the transformative process may be having on the old itinerary: career direction, relationships, goals, and values. . . . There is a new self in an old culture. But there are new friends, new rewards, new possibilities.

A different kind of work is undertaken in this period—more reflective than the busy seeking of the exploration stage. Just as a paradigm shift in science is followed by a mopping-up operation, a pulling together of loose strands into the new framework, so those who undergo personal transformation have a left-brain need to know. Intuition has leaped ahead of understanding. What really happened? The individual experiments, refines, tests ideas, shakes them down, sharpens, expands.

Many explore subjects they had no former interest in or aptitude for in an attempt to learn something about shifts in conscious experience. They may look into philosophy, quantum physics, music, semantics, brain research, psychology. From time to time, the neophyte "scientist" draws back for a period of assimilation. The opening has been immense. Everything matters.

Ironically, while there is less need now for external validation or justification, *self*-questioning may reach the level of inquisition. Usually the individual emerges from such reevaluation with a new strength and sureness, grounded in purpose.

At entry point the individual discovered that there are other ways of knowing. In exploration he found that there are systems to bring about that other knowing. In integration, having seen that many of his old habits, ambitions, and strategies are not appropriate to his new beliefs, he learned that there are other ways of being.

Now in the fourth stage, *conspiracy*, he discovers other sources of power, and ways to use it for fulfillment and in service to others. Not only does the new paradigm work in his own life, but it seems to work for others. *If the mind can heal and transform, why can't minds join to heal and transform society?*

Earlier, when he was attempting to communicate the ideas of transformation, it was mostly to explain himself or to draw

friends and family into the process. Now the great social implications become apparent.

This is a conspiracy to enable transformation—not to impose
it on those who are neither ripe nor interested, but to make it
possible for those who are hungry for it. Michael Murphy,
co-founder of Esalen, suggested that the disciplines themselves
conspire for renewal. "Let's make that conspiracy apparent!
We can turn our daily common life into the dance the world is
meant for."

Paradoxically, there may be a hiatus in social activism during
this period while the individual assesses responsibilities, roles,
direction. After all, if he has the power to change society, even
in some small way, he had better pay attention. The whole idea
of leadership, power, and hierarchy is rethought. There is the
fear of destroying the great chance for social transformation by
falling into old behavior—defensiveness, egotism, or timidity.

No narrative of a transformative process can be fairly described as typical, since each is as unique as a fingerprint. But
the movement from stage to stage is a story frequently recounted.

A young clinical psychologist at a state hospital appended to
his Aquarian Conspiracy questionnaire a four-page letter that
classically described the process we have been discussing.
First, the *entry point*:

In the spring of 1974 I was just finishing my master's thesis
from a behavioral perspective in psychology. . . . One evening another graduate student and I decided to experiment
with LSD. During the evening I had an experience that I
was hard-pressed to explain or describe—the sudden feeling of a vortex opening in my head and ending somewhere
above me. I began to follow this with my awareness. As I
got further up I began losing control and felt much pressure and noise as well as bodily feelings of floating, zoom-
ing, etc. All of a sudden I popped out of the vortex.
Whereas before I had been looking around at a not-very
attractive married-housing campus complex, there now
stood before me the same buildings, incredibly beautiful in
ways I still can't describe. There was an order, complexity,
and simplicity, as if everything made sense in and of itself
with the other elements of the environment. In the core of
this experience I had the strong sensation that it was not
just the result of taking the drug.

During the days that followed, he asked fellow students and professors about the experience and was "immediately labeled a freak." As he continued questioning, one graduate student urged him several times to read the Don Juan books by Carlos Castaneda. At first he was skeptical. "I considered myself to be very scientific, and this stuff about an Indian sorcerer was too way-out for me." But he was desperate for an answer. He gave up his intellectual protests and entered the next stage, *exploration*:

I picked up the first book and within pages found that someone knew of the same experiences. I began to read all the books and decided to specialize in this area for my doctoral exams and dissertation. At this point I was not sure what I was going to specialize in as I did not know the name of what I was searching for.

After a summer of reading and furthering my experiential research, I had settled on my task: to utilize meditation as a standardized procedure for exploring human consciousness.

That summer he began to keep a journal of his thoughts and experiments and studied his own perceptual changes under the effects of LSD (ten sessions); he also used various strategies to achieve dramatic alterations of consciousness. Negative and sometimes frightening episodes led him to drop the drugs and curb the psychic games. "Meditation was a safer, surer way toward deep and stable exploration and change." A period of *integration* began in late 1974:

During the fall and spring I continued my personal search using meditation as the vehicle. I was writing a position paper for my doctoral exams on meditation and consciousness. I tried some of the things I was reading about, like out-of-body experiences, and decided there was a reality there—one I wasn't ready for. Besides, I knew from my reading that meditation was supposed to be practiced in a more productive manner.

Notice, he is more serious. He is no longer intrigued by paranormal abilities and tricks, wondering what he can learn to do, but now asks what he can *be*.

One night he had an extraordinary experience. He meditated before going to sleep and awoke to see a three-dimensional circular pattern pulsing in his visual field. The next day he drew pictures of the design, which he later identified as a *yantra*, a pattern used for contemplation in Eastern spiritual disciplines. When he learned that Carl Jung had written about the emergence of such patterns from the collective unconscious, he felt even more strongly that he could argue the psychological importance of meditation phenomena, even with the most skeptical professors in his graduate school.

In 1975 he did his dissertation on an experimental study of persons using meditation, relaxation training, and biofeedback. He was able to translate his findings to his dissertation committee, which included "a very structured behavioral psychologist" and a professor deeply involved in consciousness studies.

In 1976 he went to work at a state hospital. By 1977 he found himself in the fourth stage, *conspiracy*:

> I guess the rest of my account at this point is directed toward synthesis and entry into what you're calling the Aquarian Conspiracy. I want to continue my work in transpersonal psychology, meditation, biofeedback, and music meditation, while staying in mainstream clinical psychology.
>
> I have worked consistently toward raising the transpersonal banner at this hospital—slowly, because this state is not in the progressive swing the Bay Area and Los Angeles are in. However, the work with music meditation has progressed to the point where the hospital has given us a grant . . . I heard yesterday from interested people at an Ohio institution and today from Washington.
>
> I'm very pleased at the direction my meditation has taken me and try to remember to "hasten slowly" on this path. Little by little we are permeating the clinical fabric of treatment here. . . . We're using the experimental program in the Intensive Treatment Unit and find it works even with seriously ill schizophrenics.

Later he joined forces with a staff psychiatrist (an Oklahoman who had once spent time at a Zen center in California) and a psychology intern. The three had worked for more than a year on the need for reforming the overcrowded state hospital. Frustrated by the continuing resistance of the administration, they presented their ideas to a top state official in charge of institutions.

The official heard them out, then gave them a very straight look. "Maybe you can pull it off." And then he startled them by quoting from Carlos Castaneda, "Maybe this is your cubic centimeter of chance."[3]

The reorganization plan was adopted, virtually intact. The state mandated an application of the psychotechnologies in clinical care. An internal furor resulted, supervisors were shuffled around or removed, and the psychologist was asked to take a post as administrator of one of the units. He finally said no. "I realized that I didn't really want the money or status—that I really want to just work with patients."

He is now in private clinical practice and is a consultant to a state prison. He also serves on a state board charged with evaluating mental health facilities.

> It has been interesting to watch myself through this recent change in my life as I have really stepped off the cliff. . . . It's weird to watch my own risk-taking, not knowing where it will end up. The old negative feeling of potential failure is always around the corner, but my stronger feeling of centeredness always outshines these pesky creatures of the dark. I will look for my next cubic centimeter.

Neither typical nor unusual, the passage from casual experimentation to serious interest to commitment to conspiracy.

THE DISCOVERIES

The psychotechnologies — picks, pitons, compasses, binoculars — have aided in the rediscovery of inner landmarks variously named across cultures and across time. To understand more about the transformative process, we will look at these vistas. The discoveries, as we shall see, are mutually dependent and mutually reinforcing; they cannot be sharply isolated from each other. They are not sequential, either; some occur simultaneously. They deepen and change as well; none is finished once and for all.

Historically, transformation has been described as an *awakening*, a new quality of attention. And just as we marvel that we could have mistaken our dream world for reality once we have

[3]From *Journey to Ixtlan:* "All of us, whether or not we are warriors, have a cubic centimeter of chance that pops out in front of our eyes from time to time. The difference between an average man and a warrior is that the warrior is aware of this, and one of his tasks is to be alert, deliberately waiting, so that when his cubic centimeter pops out he has the necessary speed, the prowess, to pick it up."

come out of sleep, so those who experience an enlarged awareness are surprised that they had thought themselves awake
when they were only sleepwalking.

Each man, said Blake, is haunted until his humanity awakes.
"If the doors of perception were cleansed, we would see the
world as it is, infinite." And the Koran warns, "Men are asleep.
Must they die before they awake?"

The enlarged state of awareness reminds many of experiences in childhood when all the senses were sharp and open,
when the world seemed crystalline. Indeed, individuals who
preserve an urgent wakefulness into adulthood are rare. Sleep
researchers have discovered that most adults show physiological signs of sleepiness throughout their waking hours—and feel
that this state is perfectly normal.

In his famous "Ode on the Intimations of Immortality" William Wordsworth described the gradual shutdown of our
senses: The glory and the dream fade, the prison-house closes
in after childhood, and custom lies on us "heavy as frost."

The prison is our fragmenting, controlling, fretting attention — planning, remembering, but not *being*. In our need to
cope with everyday concerns, we forfeit our awareness of the
miracle of awareness. As the apostle Paul put it, we see through
a glass darkly, not face to face.

Again and again, the metaphor for new life is awakening. We
have been dead in the womb, not born.

One of the Aquarian Conspirators, a wealthy real-estate entrepreneur, reported in his questionnaire:

> It was at Esalen, my first trip there several years ago. I had
> just had a Rolfing session, and I walked outdoors.
>
> Suddenly I was overwhelmed by the beauty of every-
> thing I saw. This vivid, transcendent experience tore apart
> my limited outlook. I had never realized the emotional
> heights possible. In this half-hour solitary experience I felt
> unity with all, universal love, connectedness. This smash-
> ing time destroyed my old reality permanently.

He asked, as many have asked, "If this happened to me once,
why not again?"

A new understanding of *self* is discovered, one that has little
resemblance to ego, self-ishness, self-lessness. There are multiple dimensions of self; a newly integrated sense of oneself as
an individual . . . a linkage with others as if they are one-

self...and the merger with a Self yet more universal and primary.

On an individual level, we discover a self that does not compete. It is as curious as a child, delighted with testing its changing powers. And it is fiercely autonomous. It seeks self-knowledge, not gain, knowing it will never probe its own furthest reaches. As one recovered alcoholic put it, "The only person I need to be is myself. I can be really good at that. In fact, I can never fail if I am simply me and let you be you."

Redefining the self defuses competition. "The joy of this quest is not in triumph over others," Theodore Roszak said, "but in the search for the qualities we share with them and for our uniqueness, which raises us above all competition."

Self-knowledge is science; each of us is a laboratory, our *only* laboratory, our nearest view of nature itself. "If things go wrong in the world," Jung said, "something is wrong with me. Therefore, if I am sensible, I shall put myself right first."

The self released by the transformative process gathers in aspects that had been disenfranchised. Sometimes this is experienced by a woman as the capacity to act (the masculine principle), by a man as the emergence of nurturant feelings (the feminine principle). The reunion is picturesquely described in Buddhist literature as *sahaja*, "born together." As the innate nature reasserts itself, emotional turbulence diminishes. Spontaneity, freedom, poise, and harmony seem to increase. "It's like becoming real," said one respondent to the questionnaire.

We have been split at every level, unable to make peace with contradictory thoughts and feelings. Shortly before his suicide, poet John Berryman expressed the universal wish: "Unite my various soul...." When we respect and accept the fragmented identities, there is reunion and rebirth.

If there is rebirth, what dies? The actor, perhaps. And illusions—that one is a victim, or right, or independent, or capable of obtaining all the answers. Illusionectomy can be a painful operation, but there are profound rewards. "You shall know the truth," says a character in Brunner's *Shockwave Rider*, "and the truth shall make you you."

One Aquarian Conspirator spoke of experiencing "an internal momentum, a greater competence that seems to come from greater emotional openness, from being able to call on all aspects of oneself. When we say a person is powerful, we seem to be talking about an unapologetic self. It has nothing to do with position, either. Anyone can be powerful in this way."

An editor of a Boston-based magazine wrote that her most

vivid transformative experience was learning to see without the glasses she had worn for eighteen years. Using a method of mental stress-reduction designed by William Bates, she had a "flash" of clear vision.

> As I had that first flash, a strong force inside me seemed to be saying, "Now that you've let us see a little, we insist on seeing perfectly." I realized that we're all whole and perfect right now and we just don't experience that wholeness because we've covered it up. It takes less energy to be free and flowing than to be locked up in stress, and something inside us is dying to experience and express that flow. We learn by releasing and letting go, not by adding on.

This perfection, this wholeness, does not refer to superior achievement, moral rectitude, personality. It is not comparative and not even personal. Rather, it is an insight into nature—the integrity of form and function in life itself, connection with a perfect process. If only briefly, we recognize ourselves as children of nature, not as strangers in the world.

Beyond the personal reunification, the inner reconnection, the re-annexing of lost portions of oneself, there is the connection to an even larger Self—this invisible continent on which we all make our home. In his Aquarian Conspiracy questionnaire, a university professor told of being deeply affected by a long stay in remote areas of the Indonesian islands where he felt "a kind of magical circle, an unbroken unity with all life and cosmic processes, including my own life."

The separate self is an illusion. Several of the respondents to the questionnaire remarked on giving up the belief that they were encapsulated individuals. A psychologist said that she had to give up the idea of a striving self—"that 'I' existed in the way I had naively supposed, and that 'I' would be crowned finally with enlightenment."

The self is a field within larger fields. When the self joins the Self, there is power. Brotherhood overtakes the individual like an army . . . not the obligatory ties of family, nation, church, but a living, throbbing connection, the unifying I-Thou of Martin Buber, a spiritual fusion. This discovery transforms strangers into kindred, and we know a new, friendly universe.

There are new meanings to old words like "fellowship" and "community." "Love" may enter the vocabulary with increasing frequency; for all its ambiguity, its connotations of sentimentality, no word in English better approximates the new sense of caring and connectedness.

There emerges a new and different social consciousness, expressed by one man in terms of hunger and starvation:

> I can no longer protect myself from the reality of starvation by pretending that people who starve are nameless, faceless strangers. I know now who they are. They're just like me, only they're starving. I can no longer pretend that the collection of political agreements we call "countries" separates me from the child who cries out in hunger halfway around the world. We are one, and one of us is hungry. . . .

The group is the self of the altruist, someone once said. Sharpened empathy, a sense of participation in all of life, more sorrow, more joy, and an unsettling awareness of the multiplicity and complexity of causes make it hard to be self-righteous and judgmental.

Even beyond the collective Self, the awareness of one's linkage with others, there is a transcendent, universal Self. The passage from what Edward Carpenter called the "little, local self" to the Self that pervades the universe was also described by Teilhard as his first journey into "the abyss":

> I became aware that I was losing contact with myself. At each step of the descent a new person was disclosed within me of whose name I was no longer sure and who no longer obeyed me. And when I had to stop my exploration because the path faded beneath my steps, I found a bottomless abyss at my feet, and out of it comes—arising I know not from where—the current which I dare to call *my* life.

The fourth dimension is not another place; it is *this* place, and it is immanent in us, a process.

The *importance of process* is another discovery. Goals and endpoints matter less. Learning is more urgent than storing information. Caring is better than keeping. Means *are* ends. The journey is the destination.

We begin to see the ways in which we have postponed life, never paying attention to the moment.

When life becomes a process, the old distinctions between winning and losing, success and failure, fade away. Everything, even a negative outcome, has the potential to teach us and to further our quest. We are experimenting, exploring. In the wider paradigm there are no "enemies," only those useful, if irritating, people whose opposition calls attention to trouble spots, like a magnifying mirror.

Old sayings, once only poetry, now seem profoundly true. Like St. Catherine of Siena: "All the way to heaven is heaven." Cervantes: "The road is better than the inn." Garcia Lorca: "I will never arrive at Cordoba." C. P. Cavafy: "Ithaca has given you the beautiful voyage"...and Kazantzakis: "Ithaca is the voyage itself."

When you enjoy the trip, life is more fluid, less segmented; time is more circular and subtle. As process assumes importance, former values begin to shift, like wavy lines in a sheet-glass mirror. The focus changes: What was large may become small, distant, and what was trivial may loom like Gibraltar.

And we discover that *everything is process*. The solid world is a process, a dance of subatomic particles. A personality is a collection of processes. Fear is a process. A habit is a process. A tumor is a process. All of these apparently fixed phenomena are recreated every moment, and they can be changed, reordered, transformed in myriad ways.

The *bodymind connection* is a discovery that relates to process. Not only does the body reflect all the historical and present conflicts of the mind, but the reorganization of one helps reorganize the other. Psychotechnologies like Reichian therapy, bioenergetics, and Rolfing effect their transformations by restructuring and realigning the body. Intervention anywhere in the dynamic bodymind loop affects the whole.

A young trainee in a bodywork method called Neurokinesthetics described his own transformation:

> I'm amazed at how my life has changed and is still changing. The physical changes are numerous and I'm learning to pick up bodily cues from different systems, even those that are supposed to be autonomic. At the same time, my interaction with people is improving....
>
> In the early 1970s my friends and I were dissatisfied with the world. Our "solutions" were radical, rhetorical intellectualizations, basically studies in frustration. We knew the world had to change, but our answers weren't satisfactory because we weren't dealing with human suffering at the proper level.
>
> We cannot take charge of a situation if we can't control the environment—that is, our own bodies, physical, mental, and spiritual. That's true suffering.
>
> We don't need to be uptight. We can be in harmony with the environment, seeing the world from a clear perspec-

tive. As our bodies learn to flow, the more freely we can relate to other selves, to other people, to situations.

More consciousness means more awareness of the body. As we become more sensitive to the moment-to-moment, day-to-day effects of stressful emotions on the body, the subtle ways in which illness expresses conflict, we learn to deal with stress more directly. We discover our ability to handle stress, even when it escalates, by a different way of responding.

The body can also be a medium of transformation. In testing our limits in sport, dance, exercise we discover that the physical self is a changing, fluid, plastic bioelectrical system, not a thing. Like the mind, it harbors astonishing potentials.

One of the sweetest discoveries is *freedom* — passage to the place described in the *Upanishads* as "beyond grief and danger."

In our own biology is the key to the prison, the fear of fear, the illusion of isolation. Whole-brain knowing shows us the tyranny of culture and habit. It restores our autonomy, integrates our pain and anxiety. We are free to create, change, communicate. We are free to ask "Why?" and "Why not?"

"Just the fact of being slightly more aware changes the way in which you act," said Joseph Goldstein, a meditation teacher. "Once you've glimpsed what's going on, it's very difficult to get caught up in quite the same old way. . . . It's like some little voice in the background saying, 'What are you doing?'"

The psychotechnologies help break the "cultural trance"— the naive assumption that the trappings and truisms of our own culture represent universal truths or some culmination of civilization. The robot rebels, Galatea turns from statue to living flesh, Pinocchio pinches his arm and finds it isn't wooden.

A fifty-five-year-old sociologist described the onset of his freedom:

One Saturday morning in late September 1972 I was walking onto a tennis court to play for the n-to-the-nth-power time. I suddenly asked myself, "What am I doing this for?" . . . It was a sudden awareness that the world of conventional activities and socially accepted interpretations of reality was shallow and unrewarding.

I spent forty-eight years struggling unsuccessfully to find happiness and fulfillment in the social identities bestowed on me and in the pursuit of socially sanctioned goals.

I feel that I now have attained freedom just as fully and really as a runaway slave might have in the pre-Civil War period. At one point I became free of fears and guilt associated with my religious upbringing. At another there was a shift when I came to know myself not by my name, status, or role—but as a nameless free being.

Every society, by offering its automatic judgments, limits the vision of its members. From our earliest years we are seduced into a system of beliefs that becomes so inextricably braided into our experience that we cannot tell culture from nature.

Anthropologist Edward Hall has said that culture is a medium that touches every aspect of our lives: body language, personality, how we express ourselves, the way we design our communities. We are even captives of our idea of time. Our own culture, for example, is "monochronic," one thing at a time; whereas in many other world cultures time is "polychronic." In polychronic time, tasks and events begin and end according to their natural time for completion rather than rigid deadlines.

> For M-time people reared in the northern European tradition, time is linear and segmented like a road or a ribbon extending forward into the future and backward into the past. It is also tangible. They speak of it as being saved, spent, wasted, lost, made up, accelerated, slowed down, crawling, and running out.

Although monochronic time (M-time) is imposed, learned, and arbitrary, we tend to treat it as if it were built into the universe. The transformative process makes us more sensitive to the rhythms and creative drives of nature and to the oscillations of our own nervous systems.

Another liberation — freedom from "attachment" — is perhaps for most Westerners the least understood idea in Eastern philosophy. To us "nonattachment" sounds coldblooded, and "desirelessness" sounds undesirable.

We might more accurately think of nonattachment as nondependency. Much of our inner turbulence reflects the fear of loss: our dependence on people, circumstances, and things not really under our control. On some level we know that death, indifference, rejection, repossession, or high tide may leave us bereft in the morning. Still, we clutch desperately at things we cannot finally hold. Nonattachment is the most realistic of attitudes. It is freedom from wishful thinking, from always wanting things to be otherwise.

By making us aware of the futility of this wishful thinking, the psychotechnologies help free us from unhealthy dependencies. We increase our capacity to love without bargaining or expectations, to enjoy without emotional mortgages. At the same time, enhanced awareness adds luster to simple things and everyday events, so that what may seem a turn toward a more austere life is often the discovery of subtler, less perishable riches.

Another discovery: We are not liberated until we liberate others. So long as we need to control other people, however benign our motives, we are captive to that need. Giving them freedom, we free ourselves. And they are free to grow in their own way.

Andre Kostelanetz recalled how Leopold Stokowski radicalized orchestral form by freeing the musicians:

He dispensed with the uniform bowing of the strings, knowing that the strength of each player's wrist varies, and, to achieve the richest string tone, each player should have maximum elasticity. Leopold also encouraged the wind players to breathe as they wished. He didn't care, he said, how they made music as long as it was beautiful.

The bonds of culture are often invisible, and its walls are glass. We may think we are free. *We cannot leave the trap until we know we are in it*. None but ourselves, as Edward Carpenter observed long ago, are the "warders and jailers." Over and over, mystical literature depicts the human plight as needless imprisonment; it is as if the key were always within reach through the bars, but we never think to look for it.

Another discovery: *uncertainty*. Not just the uncertainty of the moment, which may pass, but oceanic uncertainty, mystery that washes across our beaches forever. Aldous Huxley said it in *The Doors of Perception*:

The man who comes back through the Door in the Wall will never be quite the same as the man who went out. He will be wiser but less cocksure, happier but less self-satisfied, humbler in acknowledging his ignorance yet better equipped to understand the relationship of words to things, of systematic reasoning to the unfathomable Mystery which it tries, forever vainly, to comprehend.

Or, as Kazantzakis expressed it, the real meaning of enlightenment is "to gaze with undimmed eyes on all darknesses."

The psychotechnologies do not "cause" uncertainty, any more than they manufacture freedom. They only open our eyes to both. The only loss is illusion. We only gain what was ours—unclaimed—all along. James Thurber knew: "There is no safety in numbers or anything else." Indeed, we never had security, only a caricature of it.

Many people have lived comfortably with a sense of mystery all their lives. Others, who have sought certainty as a hunter seeks his quarry, may be shaken to find that reason itself is a boomerang. Not only does everyday life produce unaccountable events, not only do people behave in ways we might term unreasonable, but even the outposts of rational thought—formal logic, formal philosophy, theoretical mathematics, physics—are mined with paradox. A great many of the Aquarian Conspirators said they discovered from their scientific training the limits of rational thought. Typical responses to the question, *What major ideas did you have to give up?*:

"Scientific proof as the only way to understand."
"That rationalism was it."
"Belief in the purely rational."
"That logic was all there really was."
"A linear view."
"The mechanistic worldview of science in which I had been trained."
"Material reality."
"Causality."
"I realized that science had limited its way of knowing nature."
"After many years of intellectual, left-brain pursuit of reality, an LSD experience taught me that there were alternate realities."

In effect, they gave up certainty.

In *Zen and the Art of Motorcycle Maintenance*, Robert Pirsig described the risk of pressing reason to its furthest reaches, where it turns back on itself. "In the high country of the mind," he observed, "one has to become adjusted to the thinner air of uncertainty, and to the enormous magnitude of the questions asked. . . ."

The more significant the question, the less likely there will be an unequivocal answer.

Acknowledging our uncertainty encourages us to experiment, and we are transformed by our experiments. We are free not to know the answer, we are free to change our position, we are free not to have a position. And we learn to reframe our problems. Asking the same question again and again without success is like continuing to search for a lost object in the places we have already looked. The answer, like the lost object, lies somewhere else altogether. Once we discover the power of challenging the assumptions in our old questions, we can foster our own paradigm shifts.

Here, as in many other instances, the discoveries are linked. An appreciation of process makes uncertainty bearable. A sense of freedom requires uncertainty, because we must be free to change, modify, assimilate new information as we go along. Uncertainty is the necessary companion of all explorers.

Paradoxically, if we give up the need for certainty in terms of control and fixed answers, we are compensated by a different kind of certainty—a direction, not a fact. We begin to trust *intuition*, whole-brain knowing, what scientist-philosopher Michael Polanyi called "tacit knowing." As we become attuned to the inner signals, they seem stronger.

One who becomes involved in the psychotechnologies realizes that those inner urgings and "hunches" do not contradict reason but represent transcendent reasoning, the brain's capacity for simultaneous analysis we cannot consciously track and comprehend. In *Mr. Sammler's Planet*, Saul Bellow wrote about the way we usually frustrate that knowing:

> Intellectual man had become an explaining creature. Fathers to children, wives to husbands, lecturers to listeners . . . the history, the structure, the reasons why. For the most part, in one ear and out the other. The soul wanted what it wanted. It had its own natural knowledge. It sat unhappily on the superstructures of explanation, poor bird, not knowing which way to fly.

The psychotechnologies lead one to trust the "poor bird" more, to let it fly. Intuition, that "natural knowledge," becomes a trusted partner in everyday life, available to guide even minor decisions, generating an ever more pervasive sense of flow and rightness.

Closely tied to intuition is *vocation*—literally, a "calling." As Antoine de Saint-Exupéry said of freedom, "There is no liberty except the liberty of someone making his way towards something."

Vocation is the process of making one's way toward something. It is a direction more than a goal. Following a peak experience, one of the conspirators, a housewife who later became a filmmaker, said, "I felt as if I'd been called to serve on somebody's plan for mankind." The conspirators typically say they feel as if they are cooperating with events rather than controlling them or suffering them, much as an aikido master augments his strength by aligning himself with existing forces, even those in opposition.

The individual discovers a new kind of flexible will that helps in the vocation. This will has sometimes been called "intention." It is the opposite of accident, it represents a certain deliberateness, but it doesn't have the iron quality we usually associate with the will.

To Buckminster Fuller, the commitment is "kind of mystical. The minute you begin to do what you want to do, it's really a different kind of life." Remarking on the same phenomenon, W. H. Murray said that commitment seems to enlist Providence. "All sorts of things occur to help one that would never otherwise have occurred. A whole stream of events issues from the decision, raising in one's favor all manner of unforeseen incidents and meetings and material assistance which no man could have dreamt would have come his way."

Vocation is a curious blend of the voluntary and the involuntary—choice and surrender. People remark that they feel strongly drawn in a particular direction or to certain tasks, and simultaneously convinced that they were somehow "supposed" to take just those steps. A poet and artist, M. C. Richards, said, "Life lies always at some frontier, making sorties into the unknown. Its path leads always further into truth. We cannot call it trackless waste, because as the path appears it seems to have lain there awaiting the steps ... thus the surprises, thus the continuity."

Former astronaut Edgar Mitchell became deeply interested in promoting the study of states of consciousness after his moon flight, and he launched an organization to raise funds for this purpose. At one point he remarked to a friend, "I feel almost as if I'm operating under orders. . . . Just when I think all is lost, I put my foot down over an abyss—and something comes up to hit it, just in time."

For some there is a conscious moment of choice. For others the commitment is recognized only in retrospect. Dag Hammarskjöld described the shift of his own life from the ordinary to the meaningful:

> I don't know who—or what—put the question, I don't know when it was put. I don't even remember answering. But at some moment I did answer to someone or something. And from that hour I was certain that existence is meaningful and that, therefore, my life in self-surrender had a goal.

Jonas Salk, discoverer of the first polio vaccine, also committed to an evolutionary model of social transformation, once said, "I have frequently felt that I have not so much chosen but that I have been chosen. And sometimes I wished to hell I could have disengaged!" He added that even so, those things he felt compelled to do despite his rationalizations proved immensely rewarding.

Speaking of his own experience, Jung said, "Vocation acts like a law of God from which there is no escape." The creative person is overpowered, captive of and driven by a demon. Unless one assents to the power of the inner voice, the personality cannot evolve. Although we often mistreat those who listen to that voice, he said, still "they become our legendary heroes."

By increasing our awareness of the inner signals, the psychotechnologies promote a sense of vocation, an inner direction awaiting discovery and release. Frederich Flach noted that when an individual has resolved his problems, when he is ready to meet the world with imagination and energy, things fall into place—a collaboration between person and events that seems to enlist the cooperation of fate:

> Carl Jung called this phenomenon "synchronicity." He defined it as "the simultaneous occurrence of two meaningfully but not causally connected events." ... At the very moment when we are struggling to sustain a sense of personal autonomy we are also caught up in vital forces that are much larger than ourselves so that while we may be the protagonists of our own lives, we are the extras or spear carriers in some larger drama. ...

This phenomenon sounds mystical only because we do

not understand it. But there are innumerable clues available given the right frame of mind—openness—the availability to synthesize the clues into a whole.

A number of conspirators describe a strong sense of mission. A typical account:

One day in spring 1977, while taking a walk after meditating, I had an electric feeling which lasted about five seconds in which I felt totally integrated with the creative force of the universe. I "saw" what spiritual transformation was trying to do, what my mission in life was, and several alternative ways I might accomplish it. I chose one and am making it happen. . . .

The dream of man's heart, Saul Bellow once said, is that life may complete itself in significant pattern. Vocation gives us such a pattern.

A sobering discovery — not guilt, not duty, but *responsibility* in the naked sense of its Latin roots — the act of giving back, responding. We can choose our mode of participation in the world, our response to life. We can be angry, gracious, humorous, empathetic, paranoid. Once we become aware of our habitual responses, we see the ways in which we have perpetuated many of our own tribulations.

By focusing on our thought processes, the psychotechnologies show us how much of our experience is generated by automatic responses and assumptions. A Los Angeles attorney recalled the blinding insight into responsibility that occurred in the 1960s when he was a first-year law student volunteering for a university experiment on the effects of LSD:

Suddenly I caught a glimpse, brief and shadowy at first, of my "real" self. I hadn't spoken to my parents in weeks; now I realized that, out of stupid pride, I'd needlessly hurt them by prolonging a feud that no longer held any emotional validity. Why hadn't I seen this before?

Moments later came another revelation, sharp and painful. I saw all the rich possibilities I'd recently squandered, breaking off with a young woman for what had seemed such good reasons at the time. Now I recognized all the jealousy I'd felt, my possessiveness, my suspicion. . . . My God, *I* was the one who had killed our romance, she hadn't.

Sitting there in the restaurant, I saw myself in a different, more "objective" light....I wasn't being tricked or manipulated. The troublemaker was *me*, only *me*, and always had been *me*. I began to sob without control. The weight of years of self-deception seemed to be lifting from me....

The experience certainly didn't "cure" me of my destructive personality traits, and yet on that single day I'd gained invaluable insights that would allow me, for the first time, to sustain a romantic relationship through all its peaks and valleys. Surely it was no coincidence that a few weeks later I met the woman who became—and remains—my wife.

Never again would he take LSD, he said, but the experience liberated him from slavery to his emotional makeup. "From then on I was free to struggle consciously and continually with it—a struggle that goes on to this day."

We often speak contemptuously of "the system," referring to an established power structure. Actually, if we realize that we are part of a dynamic system, one in which any action affects the whole, we are empowered to change it.

One est graduate said he reacted to this realization with mixed feelings:

Many mornings I wake up with a cold gray stone of fear in my solar plexus—fear that I really do matter...fear that being afraid won't stop me any more. If the discovery has frightened me, it has also awakened me. It explains me to myself in a way that says I have integrity and dignity. It says not only that I can make a difference, but *I am the difference in the world*.

Michael Rossman recalls the collective discovery by the organizers of the Free Speech Movement that they did have the power to *really* change things.

Nothing was any longer what it had seemed. Objects, encounters, events, all became mysterious....There was no avoiding that sense, I know it gave many people the creeps. We hardly ever mentioned it, and no one understood it, but we felt like audience and actors in the old Greek drama, playing our free parts in an inexorable script we already knew by heart. [There are] no words for that mind-wrenching simultaneity of free will and destiny.

...It may indeed be that we verge on breakthrough into

another plane of reality each time we act together to make the world strange and new, however modestly. Suppose the frameworks of individual perception can be broken so deeply by willfully and collectively changing social reality?

Each of us is—potentially—the difference in the world.

A belated discovery, one that causes considerable anguish, is that *no one can persuade another to change. Each of us guards a gate of change that can only be unlocked from the inside*. We cannot open the gate of another, either by argument or by emotional appeal.

To the individual whose gate of change is well defended, the transformative process, even in others, is threatening. The new beliefs and perceptions of others challenge the "right" reality of the unchanging person; something in himself may have to die. This prospect is frightening, for our identities are constituted more truly by our beliefs than by our bodies. The ego, that collection of qualms and convictions, dreads its own demise. Indeed, each transformation is a kind of suicide, the killing of aspects of the ego to save a more fundamental self.

At some point early in our lives, we decide just how conscious we wish to be. We establish a threshold of awareness. We choose how stark a truth we are willing to admit into consciousness, how readily we will examine contradictions in our lives and beliefs, how deeply we wish to penetrate. Our brains can censor what we see and hear, we can filter reality to suit our level of courage. At every crossroads we make the choice again for greater or lesser awareness.

Those who cannot communicate their own liberating discoveries may feel polarized at times from those closest to them. Eventually and reluctantly they accept the inviolate nature of individual choice. If, for whatever reasons, another person has chosen a life strategy of denial, which has its own heavy costs, we cannot reverse that decision; nor can we alleviate for another the chronic uneasiness that comes from a life of censored reality.

But there is a compensating discovery. Little by little, those who undertake the transformative process discern the existence of a vast *support network*.

"It's a lonely path," one of the conspirators said, "but you aren't alone on it." The network is more than a mere association of like-minded persons. It offers moral support, feedback, an opportunity for mutual discovery and reinforcement, ease, intimacy, celebration, a chance to share experiences and pieces of the puzzle.

Erich Fromm's blueprint for social transformation emphasized the need for mutual support, especially in small groups of friends: "Human solidarity is the necessary condition for the unfolding of any one individual." "No transformation, no Supermind, without such friends," said the narrator of Michael Murphy's novel, *Jacob Atabet*, based in part on the experiments and explorations of Murphy and his friends. "We are midwives to each other."

The immense fulfillment of the friendships between those engaged in furthering the evolution of consciousness has a quality impossible to describe, Teilhard once said. Barbara Marx Hubbard called the intense affinity "supra-sex" — an almost sensual longing for communion with others who have the larger vision. Psychologist Jean Houston wryly called it "swarming," and one conspirator spoke of "the network as fraternity."

There is a conspiracy to make it less risky for people to experience transformation, said a 1978 letter from John Denver, Werner Erhard, and Robert Fuller, past president of Oberlin College:

> Acknowledging to ourselves and to you that we are all members of this "conspiracy" to make the world a safer place for personal and social transformation brings us clarity of purpose and a sense of relatedness as we go about our business.
>
> In fact, the original meaning of conspiracy is to "breathe together," which expresses exactly what we have in mind. *We are together.*

In the novel *Shockwave Rider*, twenty-first-century society is a computer-monitored nightmare. The only sanctuary of privacy, individuality, and human nurturance is Precipice, a village that evolved from a shantytown of survivors of the Great Bay Quake. Its citizens protect it as an oasis and a prototype for deliverance from dehumanization. Around the country, an underground of sympathizers know of it.

Freeman, a fugitive from the authoritarian system, is helped by the underground. He later remarks, "Precipice is an awfully big place when you learn to recognize it."

So is the conspiracy. As its numbers increase, supportive

friendships become easier, even in stifling institutions and small towns.

The sense of community, the affirmation of mutual discoveries, gird the individual for an otherwise lonely enterprise. The network, as Roszak said, is a vehicle of self-discovery. "We turn to the company of those who share our most intimate and forbidden identity, and there we begin to find ourselves as persons."

Brief meetings are enough for recognition. Those who responded to the survey gave assorted accounts of how they found their allies:

- Through the grapevine, friends of friends: "When you're in such-and-such, look up so-and-so."
- Through synchronicity or "guidance": "They seemed to show up when I needed them."
- By making their interests known. Many are active in lecturing, writing, organizing, or running centers, but even those who are low-profile are usually not secretive.
- Most easily, at conferences, seminars, and other sites where those of similar interests are likely to congregate.
- "Everywhere!" In elevators and supermarkets, on airplanes, at parties, in offices. Some conspirators said they sometimes relate an anecdote among co-workers or strangers and watch for a reaction, for understanding. Like the primitive Christians, the Federalists, like a resistance movement, individuals band together, following the Buddhist dictum, "Seek out the brotherhood."

In her book, *On Waking Up*, Marian Coe Brezic described her new best friends as "a bunch of Practicing Grassroots Mystics":

They have mortgages to meet and bosses to please
and likely a mate who wonders what they're into . . .

Meanwhile and nevertheless
they're delving into the ancient wisdoms
rediscovered now and shared . . .
The kind of ideas you don't or can't explain
at the breakfast table
yet somehow putting a light on life.

Meet them at the produce bins
and these metaphysical friends
look like next-door neighbors who'll talk

about the price of one pear and what's happening to coffee unless you share their search. . . .

There is a strong sense of family—a family whose bond, as novelist Richard Bach expressed it, is not blood but respect and joy in each other's lives: "Rarely do members of one family grow up under the same roof." Community lends joy and sustenance to the adventure.

As the Parallel Cultures group says in its handbook, "We need support as our values change, and for that we have each other."

The most subtle discovery is *the transformation of fear.*

Fear has been our prison: fear of self, fear of loss, fear of fear. "What bars our way?" asked writer Gabriel Saul Heilig. "We still tremble before the Self like children before the falling dark. Yet once we have dared to make our passage inside the heart, we will find that we have entered into a world in which depth leads on to light, and there is no end to entrance."

The fear of failure is transformed by the realization that we are engaged in continuous experiments and lessons. The fear of isolation is transformed by discovery of the support network. The fear of not being efficient gradually falls away as we see past the culture's M-time and our priorities change.

The fear of being fooled or even looking foolish is transformed by the sudden recognition that *not* changing, not exploring, is a far more real and frightening possibility.[4]

Pain and paradox no longer intimidate us as we begin to reap the rewards of their resolution and see them as recurrent symptoms of the need for the transformation of disharmonies. Each survival and transcendence gives courage for the next encounter. The survivor knows the truth of Viktor Frankl's statement, "What is to give light must endure burning."

Fear of giving up any part of our current life inventory vanishes as we realize that all change is by choice. We only drop what we no longer want. Fear of self-inquiry is overcome because the self turns out to be not the dark, impulsive secret we had been warned about but a strong, sane center.

---

[4]There is no counterconspiracy except fear and inertia. Forty-four percent of the Aquarian Conspirators polled considered the greatest threat to widespread social transformation to be "popular fear of change." Other suggested factors were "conservative backlash" (20 percent), "excessive claims by advocates of change" (18 percent), and "divisiveness among advocates of change" (18 percent).

Sometimes a tiny child has mastered balance but is afraid to walk, and adults will try to tempt him by holding out a desirable toy. In a sense, transformative technologies are devices to get us to try our inner equilibrium. Eventually, trust in these systems becomes self-trust—or, more specifically, confidence in the process of change itself. We learn that fear, like pain, is just a symptom. Fear is a question: What are you afraid of, and why? Just as the seed of health is in illness, because illness contains information, our fears are a treasurehouse of self-knowledge if we explore them. Sometimes we call our fears by other names. We say we're sick and tired, angry, realistic; we say we "know our limits." Finding out what we are afraid of can break the code of many self-destructive behaviors and beliefs.

Once we experience the transformation of a fear we have trouble recapturing it, as if we have stepped far enough back from the fire to see that the burning buildings are only a part of a stage set or that the wizard is creating smoke from behind the curtain. Fear, it becomes evident, is a "special effect" of our consciousness. We will encounter fears and worries for the rest of our lives, but we now have a tool that makes all the difference.

THE TRANSFORMED LIFE

In the transformative process we become the artists and scientists of our own lives. Enhanced awareness promotes in all of us the traits that abound in the creative person: Whole-seeing. Fresh, childlike perceptions. Playfulness, a sense of flow. Risk-taking. The ability to focus attention in a relaxed way, to become lost in the object of contemplation. The ability to deal with many complex ideas at the same time. Willingness to diverge from the prevailing view. Access to preconscious material. Seeing what is there rather than what is expected or conditioned.

The transformed self has new tools, gifts, sensibilities. Like an artist, it spies pattern; it finds meaning and its own, inescapable originality. "Every life," said Hesse, "stands beneath its own star."

Like a good scientist, the transformed self experiments, speculates, invents, and relishes the unexpected.

Having done field work in the psychotechnologies, the self is a folk psychologist.

Awake now to the imprint of culture on itself, it attempts to

understand diversity with the curiosity and interest of an anthropologist. The practices of other cultures suggest endless
human possibilities.

The transformed self is a sociologist, too—a student of the
bonds of community and conspiracy. Like the physicist, it accepts ultimate uncertainty as a fact of life, it senses a realm
beyond linear time and blocked-out space. Like a molecular
biologist, it is awed by nature's capacity for renewal, change,
and ever-higher order.

The transformed self is an architect, designing its own environment. It is a visionary, imagining alternative futures.

Like a poet, it reaches for original metaphorical truths deep
in language. It is a sculptor, liberating its own form from the
rock of custom. With heightened attention and flexibility, it
becomes a playwright and is its own repertory company:
clown, monk, athlete, heroine, sage, child.

It is a diarist, an autobiographer. Sifting through the shards
of its past, it is an archaeologist. It is composer, instrument . . .
and music.

Many artists have said that when life itself becomes fully
conscious, art as we know it will vanish. Art is only a stopgap,
an imperfect effort to wrest meaning from an environment
where nearly everyone is sleepwalking.

The artist's material is always close at hand. "We live at the
edge of the miraculous," Henry Miller said, and T. S. Eliot
wrote that the end of all our exploring will be to arrive at our
starting point and know it for the first time. To Proust, discovery consisted not in seeking new landscapes but in having new
eyes. Whitman asked, "Will you seek afar off? You will come
back at last to things best known to you, finding happiness,
knowledge, not in another place but in this place . . . not in
another hour, but *this* hour."

For too long we have played games we did not care about by
rules we did not believe in. If there was art in our lives it was
paint-by-number. Life lived as art finds its own way, makes its
own friends and its own music, sees with its own eyes. "I go by
touching where I have to go," wrote poet Eric Barker, "obedient to my own illumined hand."

To the transformed self, as to the artist, success is never a
place to stay, only a momentary reward. Joy is in risking, in
making new. Eugene O'Neill scorned "mere" success:

Those who succeed and do not push on to greater failure
are the spiritual middle classers. Their stopping at success
is the proof of their compromising insignificance. How

pretty their dreams must have been!...Only through the unattainable does man achieve a hope worth living and dying for—and so attain *himself*.

A designer-engineer advised, "Do things in the spirit of design research. Be willing to accept a mistake and redesign. There is no failure."

If we take the artist-scientist's view toward life, *there is no failure*. An experiment has results: We learn from it. Since it adds to our understanding and expertise, however it comes out we have not lost. Finding out is an experiment.

As folk scientists we become sensitive to nature, relationships, hypotheses. For example, we can experimentally learn to tell our reckless impulses from genuine intuitions, getting a kind of long-range biofeedback for that inner sense of rightness.

The survey of Aquarian Conspirators asked for a choice of the four most important instruments for social change from a checklist of fifteen. More often than any other answer, "Personal Example" was checked.

More than a decade ago Erich Fromm was warning that no great radical idea can survive unless it is embodied in individuals whose lives are the message.

The transformed self is the medium. The transformed life is the message.

CHAPTER 5

The American Matrix for Transformation

We have it in our power to begin the world again.
—*THOMAS PAINE, Common Sense (1776)*

Tho' obscured, 'tis the form of the angelic land.
—*WILLIAM BLAKE, America (1817)*

Linked by television, millions of Americans had a collective peak experience on July 4, 1976, as they watched an armada of serene and beautiful sailing ships glide through New York harbor. Many were stirred by an unaccountable sense of hope and harmony, infused for a few hours with the nation's early vision and promise, remnants of the dream of unity, opportunity, and what Jefferson once called "the holy cause of freedom."

During that summer the European press noted the importance of the "American experiment," as the *London Sunday Telegraph* called it. Had it not been successful, "the idea of individual freedom would never have survived the Twentieth Century." *Neu Zurcher Zeitung* in Zurich said, "The American Bicentennial celebrates the greatest success story in modern history. The 1776 beacon, rekindled and invigorated in various ways — not least by puritan self-criticism — has endured." Stockholm's *Dagens Nyheter* observed that Americans are not bound together by social and cultural ties, family, or even language, so much as by the American dream itself.

But then we must ask, *whose* American dream? The dream is a chameleon; it has changed again and again. For the first immigrants, America was a continent to explore and exploit, a haven for the unwanted and the dissenters—a new beginning. Gradually the dream became an ascetic and idealized image of democracy, bespeaking the age-old hope for justice and self-governance. All too quickly, that dream metamorphosed into an expansionist, materialist, nationalist, and even imperialist vision of wealth and domination—paternalism, Manifest Destiny. Yet even then, there was a competing Transcendentalist vision: excellence, spiritual riches, the unfolding of the latent gifts of the individual.

There have been populist dreams in which a benevolent American government achieves lasting parity among people by redistributing wealth and opportunity. There are dreams of rugged individualism—and ideals of brotherhood, from sea to shining sea.

Like that of the founding fathers and of the American Transcendentalists of the mid-1800s, the dream of the Aquarian Conspiracy in America is a framework for nonmaterialist expansion: autonomy, awakening, creativity—and reconciliation.

As we shall see, there have always been two "bodies" of the American dream. One, the dream of tangibles, focuses on material well-being and practical, everyday freedoms. The other, like an etheric body extending from the material dream, seeks psychological liberation—a goal at once more essential and more elusive. The proponents of the latter dream have nearly always come from the comfortable social classes. Having achieved the first measure of freedom, they hunger for the second.

THE ORIGINAL DREAM

We have forgotten how radical that original dream was—how bold the founders of the democracy really were. They knew that they were framing a form of government that challenged all the aristocratic assumptions and top-heavy power structures of Western history.

The Revolutionaries exploited every available means of communication. They linked their networks by energetic letter writing. Jefferson designed an instrument with five yoked pens for writing multiple copies of his letters. The new ideas were spread through pamphlets, weekly newspapers, broadsides, almanacs, and sermons. As historian James MacGregor Burns noted, they also formulated their protests as official appeals to the king "shipped across the Atlantic after suitable hometown publicity."

Hardly anyone expected the American uprising to succeed. Thousands of colonists emigrated to Canada or hid in the woods, certain that the king's armies would tear the colonial regiments to shreds. Nor did a majority of the people support the struggle for independence, even in theory. Historians estimate that one-third favored independence, one-third favored retaining British ties, and one-third were indifferent.

"The American War is over," Benjamin Rush wrote in 1787, "but this is far from the case of the American Revolution. On the contrary, nothing but the first act of the great drama is over." Not only was the Revolution ongoing, as Rush said; it had preceded the military confrontation. "The war was no part of the revolution," John Adams reflected in 1815, "but only an effect and consequence of it." *The revolution was in the minds of the people*. This radical change in the principles, opinions, sentiments, and affections of the people was the real American Revolution. Long before the first shot is fired, the revolution begins. Long after truce is declared, it continues to overturn lives.

Although it is rarely noted in histories of the American Revolution, many of the arch-Revolutionaries came from a tradition of mystical fraternity. Except for such traces as the symbols on the reverse side of the Great Seal and the dollar bill, little evidence remains of this esoteric influence (Rosicrucian, Masonic, and Hermetic).[1] That sense of fraternity and spiritual enfran-

---

[1]The Adams family, which produced two American presidents, belonged to a Druidic sect that had been persecuted in England. In the American revolutionary period, Freemasonry was nearer its medieval beginnings and was more a mystical brotherhood than essentially the social lodge it became after widespread persecution of Masons in the nineteenth century.

Among the colonial Masons were George Washington, Benjamin Franklin, and Paul Revere. Fifty of the fifty-six signers of the Declaration of Independence are supposed to have been Masons. Historian Charles Ferguson described Washington's army as a "Masonic convention," noting that the revolutionaries relied on the brotherhood for most of their communications. Franklin obtained French aid by way of his Masonic connections in France, and Washington himself initiated Lafayette into the order.

Because the brotherhood was supposed to transcend national or political loyalties, revolutionary soldiers are said to have carefully returned the lost papers of a British field lodge; and the apparent laxness of some British generals was attributed to their hope for a quick and bloodless settlement so that Mason would not be set against Mason.

chisement played an important role in the intensity of the Revolutionaries and their commitment to the realization of a democracy.

"A New Order of the Ages Begins," says the reverse side of the Great Seal, and the Revolutionaries meant it. The American experiment was consciously conceived as a momentous step in the evolution of the species. "The cause of America is in great measure the cause of all mankind," Thomas Paine said in his inflammatory pamphlet *Common Sense*.

THE TRANSCENDENTALISTS— EXTENDING THE DREAM

In the early and middle nineteenth century, the American Transcendentalists restated and reinvigorated that second dream. As we will see in Chapter 7, they rejected traditional authority in favor of inner authority. Their term for autonomy was "self-reliance." Transcendentalism seemed to them a logical extension of the American Revolution—spiritual liberation as a counterpart to the freedoms guaranteed by the United States Constitution.

The autonomy of the individual was more important to them than allegiance to any government. If conscience did not concur with the law, Thoreau said, civil disobedience was called for.

The Transcendentalists supposedly threatened the older order with their "new ideas"; but the ideas were not new, only the prospect of applying them in a society. The eclectic Transcendentalists had drawn not only from Quaker and Puritan traditions but also from German and Greek philosophers and Eastern religions. Although they were charged with having contempt for history, they replied that humankind could be liberated from history.

They challenged the assumptions of the day in every realm: religion, philosophy, science, economy, the arts, education, and politics. They anticipated many of the movements of the twentieth century. Like the human-potential movement of the 1960s, the Transcendentalists maintained that most people had not begun to tap their own inherent powers, had not discovered their uniqueness or their mother lode of creativity. "But do your thing," Emerson said, "and I shall know you."

Among themselves they tolerated dissent and diversity, for they were sure that unanimity was neither possible nor desirable. They knew that each of us sees the world through our own eyes, our own perspective. Long before Einstein, they believed all observations to be relative. They sought companions, not disciples. Emerson's charge: Be an opener of doors to those who come after.

They believed that mind and matter are continuous. In contrast to the mechanistic Newtonian ideas prevalent in their day, they saw the universe as organic, open, evolutionary. Form and meaning can be discovered in the universal flux, they believed, if one appealed to intuition—"Transcendental Reason." More than a century before neuroscience confirmed that the brain has a holistic mode of processing, the Transcendentalists described flashes, intuitions, and a kind of simultaneous knowing. Generations before Freud, they acknowledged the existence of the unconscious. "We lie in the lap of immense intelligence," Emerson said.

But they did not reject intellectual knowledge; they believed reason and intuition to be complementary, mutually enriching. Functioning with both faculties one could be awake and live in "the enveloping now." (Emerson once said, "Every day is Doomsday.")

Inner reform must precede social reform, the Transcendentalists maintained; yet they found themselves campaigning on behalf of suffrage and pacifism and opposing slavery. And they were social innovators, establishing a cooperative community and an artists' collective.

To support themselves and bring their ideas to a larger public, they helped launch the Lyceum movement, traveling around the country in an early version of the lecture circuit, trying out their ideas in a variety of settings. Their journal, *The Dial*, edited by Margaret Fuller and later by Emerson (aided by Thoreau), had an impact far beyond its small circulation of one thousand, just as the Transcendentalists themselves had influence out of all proportion to their number.

Before the Civil War intervened, Transcendentalism had almost reached the proportions of a national grass-roots movement. Apparently many Americans of the day were attracted to a philosophy that stressed an inner search for meaning. Although the Transcendentalist movement was overwhelmed by the materialism of the late-nineteenth century, in various guises it entered the mainstream of world philosophy, to inspire literary giants like Whitman and Melville and to invigorate generations of social reformers.

TRANSFORMATION—AN AMERICAN DREAM

Historian Daniel Boorstin said of America, "We began as a Land of the Otherwise. Nothing is more distinctive, nor has made us more un-European than our disbelief in the ancient, well documented impossibilities."

There is a kind of dynamic innocence in the American notion that anyone who really wants to can beat the odds or the elements. Americans have little sense of keeping in their place. The myth of transcendence is perpetuated by a pantheon of wilderness explorers and moon explorers, record breakers in every field of endeavor, heroic figures like Helen Keller and "Lucky" Lindbergh.

Because the dream of renewal is built in, the American character is fertile ground for the notion of transformation. When a Stanford psychologist, Alex Inkeles, compared American character traits to those of Europeans, as evidenced in a 1971 poll, and then compared the most pronounced American traits to those observed in the culture two hundred years ago, he found a surprising continuity in ten traits.[2]

Americans take unusual pride in their freedoms and in their constitution, a pride that both impressed and irritated Tocqueville on his visit to the new republic.

Americans express greater self-reliance than Europeans. They are likelier to blame themselves for whatever has gone wrong, Inkeles said. They believe strongly in voluntarism, and they are "joiners." They are trusting, they think they can change the world, they believe that striving brings success, they are innovative and open.

The survey showed Americans to be more anti-authoritarian than Europeans and to have a stronger sense of the "quality" of the self, the importance of the individual.

These traits are clearly compatible with the process and discoveries of personal transformation discussed in Chapters 3 and 4: freedom, the self as powerful and responsible, connection to others, support network, autonomy, openness. *Personal transformation, in effect, is an enactment of the original American dream.*

---

[2]Over the same period there have been three major changes in the American character: an increasing tolerance of diversity, an erosion of the ethic of hard work and frugality, and a concern about the loss of control over the political system.

THE SECOND AMERICAN REVOLUTION

The Second American Revolution—the revolution to achieve freedom in a larger dimension—awaited critical numbers of agents of change and a means of easy communication among them. In 1969, in *Without Marx or Jesus*, Jean-François Revel described the United States as the most eligible prototype nation for world revolution. "Today in America—the child of European imperialism—a new revolution is rising. It is the revolution of our time . . . and offers the only possible escape for mankind today."

Real revolutionary activity, he noted, consists of *transforming reality*, that is, in making reality conform more closely to one's ideal. When we speak of "revolution" we must necessarily speak of something that cannot be conceived or understood within the context of old ideas. The stuff of revolution, and its first success, must be the ability to innovate. In that sense, there is more revolutionary spirit in the United States today, even on the Right, than elsewhere on the Left.

The relative freedom in the United States would make it possible for such a revolution to occur bloodlessly, Revel said. If that happened, and if one political civilization were exchanged for another, as seemed to be happening, the impact might be felt worldwide by osmosis. This radical transformation would need the simultaneous occurrence of smaller revolutions—in politics, society, international and interracial relations, cultural values, and technology and science. "The United States is the only country where these revolutions are simultaneously in progress and organically linked in such a way as to constitute a single revolution."

There also must be an internal critique of injustices, of the management of material and human resources, and of abuses of political power. Above all, there must be criticism of the culture itself: its morality, religion, customs, and arts. And there must be demand for respect of the individual's uniqueness, with the society regarded as the medium for individual development and for brotherhood.

Like Transcendentalism, Revel's revolution would encompass "the liberation of the creative personality and the awakening of personal initiative" as opposed to the closed horizons of more repressive societies. The perturbation would come from the privileged classes, he said, because that is the way of revolutions. They are launched by those disenchanted with the culture's ultimate reward system. If a new prototype of society is to emerge, rather than a coup d'état, dialogue and debate must occur at the highest levels.

Certainly the sixties saw great social turbulence; members of the middle and upper classes, especially, began to criticize existing institutions and speculate on a new society. Strong social and historical forces were converging to create the disequilibrium that precedes revolution. Americans were increasingly aware of the impotence of existing institutions—government, schools, medicine, church, business—to deal collectively with mounting problems.

The disenchantment with mores and institutions was most visible in the counterculture, but it spread quickly. The society's discontent and ripeness for new direction was evident in the rapid assimilation of counterculture concerns, values, behavior, fashion, and music.

Wave after wave of social protest reflected growing skepticism about authority,[3] more sensitivity to contradictions in the society—the juxtaposition of poverty and affluence, scarcity and consumerism. There were marches, lie-ins, sit-ins, be-ins, press conferences, riots. The civil rights movement, the antiwar movement, the Free Speech Movement, the ecology movement. Women's rights and gay rights. The Gray Panthers, antinuclear prayer vigils, taxpayers' revolts, demonstrations for and against abortion. All the groups cribbed strategies from their predecessors, including tactics for making the six o'clock news.

Meanwhile the rising interest in psychedelics dovetailed with media coverage of new discoveries about altered consciousness via meditation research and biofeedback training. The body-mind discoveries—the extraordinary connection between state of mind and state of health—buttressed the interest in human potential. Imported phenomena like acupuncture further challenged Western models of how things work.

One observer described the tumultuous events of the 1960s as the Great Refusal, when millions seemed to be saying no to

---

[3]The growing use of marijuana dealt a blow to authority: medical, legal, and parental. Hundreds of thousands of rural and small-town youths who might never have encountered marijuana in peacetime were introduced to the drug in Vietnam. Ironically, the introduction of major psychedelics, like LSD, in the 1960s was largely attributable to the Central Intelligence Agency's investigation into the substances for possible military use. Experiments on more than eighty college campuses, under various CIA code names, unintentionally popularized LSD. Thousands of graduate students served as guinea pigs. Soon they were synthesizing their own "acid." By 1973, according to the National Commission on Drug and Marijuana Abuse, nearly 5 percent of all American adults had tried LSD or a similar major psychedelic at least once.

conventions and concessions that had been taken for granted for generations. It was as if they were acting out Edward Carpenter's prophecy that the time would surely come when great numbers would rise up against mindless conformity, bureaucracies, warmaking, dehumanizing work, needless sickness. In discovering those regions of mind in which they transcend "the little, local self," human beings would create an agenda for the renewal of society.

To historian William McLoughlin, the sixties marked the beginning of America's fourth "great awakening," a cultural dislocation and revitalization that will extend into the 1990s.[4] These periodic awakenings, which take place over a generation or more, "are not periods of social neurosis but of revitalization. They are therapeutic and cathartic, not pathological." They result from a crisis in meaning: The ways of the culture no longer match the beliefs and behavior of the people. Although an awakening begins first with disturbance among individuals, it results in the shift of the whole worldview of a culture. "Awakenings begin in periods of cultural distortion and grave personal stress, when we lose faith in the legitimacy of our norms, the viability of our institutions, and the authority of our leaders."

American history, according to McLoughlin, is best understood as a millenarian movement, driven by a changing spiritual vision. Although it keeps redefining itself to meet contingencies and new experiences, there is one constant: "the fundamental belief that freedom and responsibility will perfect not only the individual but the world." This sense of a sacred collective purpose, which sometimes led to aggression in the past, has metamorphosed in this fourth awakening to a sense of the mystical unity of humankind and the vital power of harmony between human beings and nature.

McLoughlin calls attention to the model of social change formulated by anthropologist Anthony C.W. Wallace in a 1956 essay. Periodically, according to Wallace, the people in a given culture find that they can no longer travel its "mazeways," the orienting patterns and paths that have guided their predecessors. The "old lights" or customary beliefs do not fit current

[4]The Puritan Awakening (1610-1640) preceded the establishment of a constitutional monarchy in England. The first great awakening in America (1730-1760) led to the creation of the American republic; the second (1800-1830), to the solidification of the Union and the rise of Jacksonian participatory democracy; the third (1890-1920), to rejection of unregulated capitalistic exploitation and the beginning of the welfare state. Our fourth appears headed toward a rejection of unregulated exploitation of humankind and of nature and toward conservation and optimal use of the world's resources.

experience. Nothing is working because the solutions lie outside the accepted patterns of thought.

A few individuals, then great numbers, lose their bearings and begin to generate political unrest. As controversy grows, the traditionalists or "nativists," those who have most at stake in the old culture or who are most rigid in their beliefs, try to summon the people back to the "old lights." Mistaking symptoms for causes, they sanction or punish the new behaviors. Eventually, however, as McLoughlin described it, "accumulated pressures for change produce such acute personal and social stress that the whole culture must break the crust of custom, crash through the blocks in the mazeways, and find new socially structured avenues."

Then the "new light" is the consensus; it is first expressed in the more flexible members of the society who are willing to experiment with new mazeways or new lifestyles. Legal interpretation, family structure, sex roles, and school curricula change in response to the new vision, and gradually traditionalists drift into it as well.

Our present cultural transformation alarms conservatives and liberals alike with its radical new premises. Whereas conservatives have historically called for a return to civil law and order during periods of social turbulence, now "nativists" at both ends of the political spectrum are calling for a return to a lawful and orderly universe.

The fashionable label for psychological dissent, tantamount to the blanket charge of un-Americanism in the 1950s—is narcissism. Critics lump those seeking answers through inward search with hedonists and cultists, much as McCarthyites categorized political dissidents with criminals, drug addicts, and sexual deviants.

Someone is always trying to summon us back to a dead allegiance: Back to God, the simple-minded religion of an earlier day. "Back to the basics," simple-minded education. Back to simple-minded patriotism. And now we are being called back to a simple-minded "rationality" contradicted by personal experience and frontier science.

COMMUNICATIONS—OUR NERVOUS SYSTEM

In an unsettled period the questions and alternatives posed by a minority, the challenges to authority and established values, can spread rapidly throughout a culture. By amplifying both the unrest and the options, a society's communications network acts much like a collective nervous system. In this sense, the technology that seemed for a time to betray us into a dehumanized future is a powerful medium for human connection.

"At the present moment," Gertrude Stein said in 1945, "America is the oldest country in the world because she was the first country into the Twentieth Century." The United States, with its sophisticated communications technology and its history of exploiting news and promoting new images, was indeed the logical arena for the opening stages of the revolution Revel predicted.

Just as transformation builds on wider awareness and connection in the individual brain, so our social imagination has been painfully, exquisitely enlivened by a nerve network of electronic sensing. Our awareness is joined in high human drama: political scandals, war and peacemaking, riots, accidents, grief, humor. And just as modern physics and Eastern philosophies are introducing a more integrated worldview to the West, our fluent media nervous system is linking our social brain. "Electronic circuitry," Marshall McLuhan said not long ago, "is Orientalizing the West. The contained, the distinct, the separate, our Western legacy—are being replaced by the flowing, the unified, the fused."

These nerveways transmit our shocks and aches, our high moments and low, moon landings and murders, our collective frustrations, tragedies and trivia, institutional breakdowns in living color. They amplify the pain from alienated parts of our social body. They help break our cultural trance, crossing borders and time zones, giving us glimpses of universal human qualities that illuminate our narrow ways and show us our connectedness. They give us models of transcendence: virtuoso performers and athletes, brave survivors, floods and fires, everyday heroism.

Our collective nervous system mirrors our decadence. It arouses our right brains with music, archetypal dramas, startling visual sensations. It keeps our dream journal, taking notes on our fantasies and nightmares to tell us what we most want, what we most fear. If we let it, our technology can shock us out of the sleepwalking of the centuries.

Max Lerner compared the society to a great organism with its own nervous system. "In recent decades we have witnessed a neural overburdening of society, a strain not unlike that which an individual feels when he finds himself on the brink of fatigue or a breakdown." Yet technology might now be applied to move us further into the exploration of states of consciousness, he said. "The new awareness movements, the new search for self, may make for cohesion rather than disintegration."

The links in the expanding nervous system are not only the vast networks of commercial television and the daily newspapers and radio, but "other knowing"—innovative public television and small radio stations, small publishers, cooperatives of small magazines. There are newsletters, proliferating journals and magazines, self-published books. Every neighborhood has its quick-print shops, every supermarket and library its copying machines. Ordinary citizens have access to audio and video cassettes, computer time, home computers, cooperative use of national long-distance lines, inexpensive electronic typesetting equipment. Everybody can be a Gutenberg. We communicate by bumper stickers and T-shirts.

And our national penchant for self-questioning and search has turned increasingly inward, not only through the ever-present pop psychology and self-help books, but in original, radical sources: the literature of transformation. The books of Teilhard, forbidden publication in his lifetime, now sell in the millions. Abraham Maslow, Carl Jung, Aldous Huxley, Hermann Hesse, Carl Rogers, J. Krishnamurti, Theodore Roszak, and Carlos Castaneda are hot properties on drugstore paperback racks.

And there are "new-age" publications of all kinds: radio programs and newsletters, directories of organizations, lists of resources, Yellow Pages and handbooks, and new journals about consciousness, myth, transformation, the future. Thousands of spiritual titles roll off the presses in inexpensive editions.

The "statements of purpose" of some of the transformation-oriented publications are clear about their commitment. *East/West Journal*, based in the Boston area, expresses an intention to "explore the dynamic equilibrium that unifies apparently opposite values: Oriental and Occidental, traditional and modern. . . . We believe in people's freedom to chart the course of their lives as a boundless adventure. . . . We invite you to join us in this voyage of discovery, whose point of origin is everywhere and whose goal is endless."

New Dimensions Foundation in San Francisco, which produces a syndicated radio show featuring interviews with the leading spokespeople on the subject of transformation, launched an "audio journal"—tape cassettes edited from its tens of thousands of hours of interviews, dating back to 1973. New Dimension's purpose is "to communicate the vision and the infinite possibilities of human potential ... to use the media to present new ideas, new choices, new options, new solutions ... to promote more communication about the nature of personal and social change."

If we are to dream a larger American dream, we must go beyond our own experience, much as the authors of the Constitution immersed themselves in the political and philosophical ideas of many cultures and as the Transcendentalists synthesized insights from world literature and philosophy to frame their vision of inner freedom.

Most of all, we must let go of an inappropriate cynicism and dualism. Trust in the possibility of change and a sense of the connectedness of all of life are essential to social transformation.

Civilizations decline, Toynbee said, not so much because of invasions or other external forces but because of an internal hardening of ideas. The "elite creative minority" that once gave life to the civilization has been gradually replaced by another minority—still dominant, but no longer creative.

Creativity requires constant transformation, experimentation, flexibility. Cynicism, a chronic state of distrust, is antithetical to the openness necessary for a creative society. To the cynic, experiments are futile ... all conclusions are foregone. Cynics know the answers without having penetrated deeply enough to know the questions. When challenged by mysterious truths, they marshal "facts." Just as we must let go of dead philosophies, illusions, and old science to confront reality, so a country must keep challenging its traditions if it is to be transformed—if it wants renewal.

Through the heavy seas of crisis, through social movements and wars, depressions, scandals, betrayals, the United States has been consistently open to change. When a television interviewer asked Revel in 1978 for his current assessment of the potential for transformation in America, he said, "The United States is still the most revolutionary country in the world, the laboratory for society. All the experiments—social, scientific, racial, intergenerational—are taking place in the U.S."

The old hope of the Old World: a new world, a place for remaking oneself, a new start, a new life, freedom from tired identities and chafing limits. Historian C. Vann Woodward said, "The body of writings that make up Europe's America is enormous and still growing. Much of it has been speculative, uninformed, passionate, mythical,—about an America hoped for, dreamed of, despised, or instinctively feared."

Dreamed of . . . and feared. The very possibility that we can remake our destiny someplace is as threatening, in some ways, as the knowledge that there are systems for interior search.

"I say the sea is in," said poet Peter Levy. ". . . the new spirit is bluer than knowledge or history. In our lives, Europe is saying goodnight."

CALIFORNIA—LABORATORY FOR TRANSFORMATION

We protect ourselves from change, even from the hope of change, by our superstitious cynicism. Yet all exploration must be fueled by hope.

When the Wright brothers were attempting to fly the *Kitty Hawk*, an enterprising journalist interviewed people in their hometown, Dayton, Ohio. One elderly man said that if God had wanted man to fly, He would have given him wings, "and what's more, if anybody ever *does* fly, he won't be from Dayton!" Seventy years later the first human-powered machine, the *Gossamer Condor*, became airborne. It had been built and flown in California—and Californians were not surprised. *"If anybody ever does fly, he'll be from California."*

California, named for a mythical island, has been an island of myth in the United States, sanctuary of the endangered dream. "The flashing and golden pageant of California," Walt Whitman called it:

> I see in you, certain to come, the promise of thousands of years, till now deferred.
> . . . .
> The new society at last . . .
> clearing the ground for broad humanity, the true America.

If America is free, California is freer. If America is open to innovation, innovation is California's middle name. California is not so much different from the rest of the country as it is *more so*, a writer observed as early as 1883. California is a preview of our national paradigm shifts as well as our fads and fashions.

In 1963 social critic Remi Nadeau predicted that California would soon be not the outpost but the wellspring of American culture. If Californians are developing a new society, "the effect on the nation may be more than incidental." California seemed a kind of "forcing house" of national character. "Having left behind the social inhibitions of his old hometown, the

Californian is a sort of American in the making. What the American is becoming, the Californian is already."

California, Nadeau said, is a magically honest and sometimes frightening mirror in which every national evil—and national good—can best be studied. "California contains not only a great danger, but a great hope.... Nowhere does the conflict between individual freedom and social responsibility have a more open arena or show a more advanced stage of struggle."

The essence of the democratic experiment is tested in the laboratory of California. Having tended our national myth, California, purveyor of our electronic and celluloid myths, transmits it to those looking for hope. If it can work in California, maybe it can be adapted and put to work elsewhere.

The idea of America as the land of opportunity is more visible in California than anywhere, said James Houston, author of *Continental Drift*. "California is still the state where anything seems possible, where people bring dreams they aren't allowed to have anyplace else. So the rest of the country watches what goes on, because it's like a prophecy."

A political writer referred to California as "a high-pressure microcosm of America, a fertile testing ground for national prominence in any field, particularly politics." James Wilson, in *Challenge of California*, made the point that the lack of party organization makes it easy for new groups to gain ascendancy in California. "These forces endeavor not so much to wrest power from those who hold it as to create power where none has existed before."

David Broder, a national political columnist, said in 1978 that California's government is "more provocative in its program assumptions and more talented in its top-level administration than any other in America today, including the government in Washington. The competition in performance and reputation between Sacramento and Washington will continue in coming years.... California is big enough to provide a yardstick for measuring Washington's performance."

In 1949, Carey McWilliams said in *California: The Great Exception* that the main difference between California and the rest of the country was that "California has not grown or evolved so much as it has been hurtled forward, rocket-fashion. The lights went on all at once and have never dimmed."

Certainly California's wealth has been a major factor in the tilt of power and influence toward the West Coast. It is rich—the seventh richest "country" in the world—and it accounts for 12 percent of the Gross National Product of the United States. It is the most populous state in the country. Los Angeles

County alone exceeds the population of forty-one states. A phenomenon that exists "only in California" may be very large indeed.

Californians had an early opportunity to become disenchanted with the mirage of a consumer heaven. Michael Davy, associate editor of *The Observer* in London, and that paper's former Washington correspondent, said in 1972:

> Californians have the time, the money, and the assurance of future comfort that leaves them with no alternative but to confront their anxieties. Hitherto, only a tiny elite in any society has ever asked itself the question: What am I? The rest have either been too busy staying alive or have been ready to accept a system of belief handed down by the elite. In California, not only is there no general system of belief, but millions of people have the opportunity—and many of them the education—to worry about that dreadful void.

In an article titled "Anticipating America" in *Saturday Review* in late 1978, Roger Williams said that there is another California than the place America has come to imitate, mock, and envy. "One might call it California the future, the frontier—not frontier in the old Western sense but in the new national sense of innovativeness and openness."

California's continuing growth reinforces the openness, he said, forcing the state to face its larger problems head-on. "It is a sense of paradise possibly lost, as well as a pervasive feeling of community, that makes California the nation's most aggressive attacker of major social problems." Williams remarked on Californians' pervasive interest and involvement in public affairs, in commissions and agencies. California pioneered in major protective legislation for the environment, coastline conservation, energy research, and nuclear safeguards, he noted.

Boorstin once described the United States as a Nation of Nations, so shaped by the visions of its immigrants that it is international. Similarly, California is enriched by a diversity of cultures, influenced by an Asian and European influx, a junction of East and West, frontier for immigrants from the American East, South, and Midwest. More than half its inhabitants were born elsewhere.

California is also a synthesis of what C. P. Snow called the Two Cultures—Art and Science. Physicist Werner Heisenberg attributed the vitality and "human immediacy" of historic

Munich to its historic blend of art and science. California is that blend in the United States. An estimated 80 percent of the country's pure science is pursued in California; its residents include more Nobel laureates than any other state, and a majority of the members of the National Academy of Sciences are Californians. The arts, both as business and avant-garde experimentation, are a major enterprise in California. One public official estimated that nearly half a million people in greater Los Angeles "strive to make their living through the arts." The nation's entertainment is produced largely in California. Actors, writers, musicians, painters, architects, and designers comprise a major industry. For better or for worse, they are in large measure creating the nation's culture.

Historian William Irwin Thompson said that California is not so much a state of the Union as it is a state of mind, "an imagi-nation that seceded from our reality a long time ago." In leading the world in making a transition from industrial to postindustrial society, from hardware to software, from steel to plastic, from materialism to mysticism, "California became the first to discover that it is fantasy that leads reality, not the other way around." What we envision we can make real.

The California dream of sun and economic freedom, like the expansionist American dream, has always had a second body, a transcendental vision of another kind of light and another kind of freedom.

"The California Transcendentals" is the term given by critic Benjamin Mott to writers like Robinson Jeffers, John Muir, and Gary Snyder. "It's not just that, like Frost and Emerson, the California Transcendentals ask a certain height of us. They do. It's that at times they seem to be the only writers left in any region of this country with a clear idea of what elevation is. . . . Their true region is everywhere. In literary terms, they're indispensable."

If anything holds Californians together, Michael Davy suggested in 1972, it is "a search for a new religion," a vision that might emerge from "the mish-mash of Esalen-type thinking, revolutionary chatter, Huxleyan mysticism." Whatever the origin of these new stirrings, he said, they might well have import for the entire country.

"There is an orientalism in the most restless pioneer," Thoreau once said, "and the farthest west is but the farthest east." Gustave Flaubert also associated the farthest west with the farthest east: "I kept dreaming of Asiatic journeys, of going overland to China, of impossibilities, of the Indies or of

California." When Thoreau and Flaubert wrote those words in the nineteenth century, the West Coast was already dotted with centers and study groups revolving around Buddhism and "Hindoo" teachings. Today the influence of Eastern thought in California is pervasive.

California is "a different kind of consciousness and a different kind of culture," historian Page Smith said, possibly because of the large geographical transition made by its immigrants in the last century. "People leapt across whole barriers from Nebraska and Kansas, fifteen hundred miles to the Pacific Coast, and for a time there was a degree of isolation." The state was also influenced by the long Spanish period and proximity to Mexico, the mild climate, the sense of a fresh start common to immigrant populations, and the lack of tradition.

It makes sense that the Aquarian Conspiracy would be most evident in a pluralistic environment friendly to change and experimentation, among people whose relative wealth has given them the opportunity to become disenchanted with the materialist dream in its most hedonistic form, with few traditions to overturn, tolerance of dissent, an atmosphere of experimentation and innovation, and a long history of interest in Eastern philosophy and altered states of consciousness.

CALIFORNIA AND THE AQUARIAN CONSPIRACY

In 1962 *Look* magazine sent a team headed by Senior Editor George Leonard to prepare a special issue on California. The trends *Look* reported reveal the early roots of the Aquarian Conspiracy in California. They quote a San Francisco lay leader: "In California, the old social compartments are being broken down, and we are creating a new aristocracy—an aristocracy of those who care. Membership is restricted only by the capacity for concern."

The magazine reported that California seemed to be developing "a new kind of society and perhaps even a new kind of person able to cope with it." One of the phenomena the reporters mentioned was the apparent depth of relationships between friends, which they attributed to there being few relatives at hand.

Aldous Huxley, *Look* noted, was among the California residents calling for a new national constitutional convention. "Many Californians are holding, in a sense, constitutional conventions," the magazine reported, "at centers such as the one

in Santa Barbara [Center for the Study of Democratic In-
stitutions], the Center for Advanced Study in the Behavioral
Sciences in Palo Alto, and the Stanford Research Institute; at
board meetings of great corporations or planning groups; in
state and city governments, and sometimes even in the living
rooms of tract houses whose inhabitants came not so long ago
from Iowa, Maine, or Georgia."

Californians believe that anyone who cares to try can help
shape the future, *Look* said, and quoted Alan Watts: "Traditional patterns of relating, based on locality, are askew. Old
thought patterns are being broken down. What people in the
East can't see is that new patterns are being developed."

In the 1950s and 1960s, Aldous Huxley, then living in Los
Angeles, was among those who encouraged Michael Murphy
and Richard Price in their 1961 decision to open Esalen, the
residential center in California's Big Sur area that helped midwife much of what came to be known as the human-potential
movement. Seminar leaders in Esalen's first three years included Gerald Heard, Alan Watts, Arnold Toynbee, Linus
Pauling, Norman O. Brown, Carl Rogers, Paul Tillich, Rollo
May, and a young graduate student named Carlos Castaneda.

It was perhaps typical of the serendipity of those days that
one evening in 1962 heavy fog on the treacherous coastal high-
way through Big Sur forced a vacationing Abraham Maslow to
seek shelter at the nearest residence. Maslow drove down the
unmarked driveway through a tangle of shrubs to inquire
about accommodation for the night. He had arrived in time for
an Esalen study group that was unpacking a case of twenty
copies of his latest book.

Maslow's alliance with Esalen was an important linkage of
networks on the two coasts. And in 1965 George Leonard and
Michael Murphy joined forces. Leonard's account of their first
meeting and subsequent collaboration conveys the intellectual
excitement and visionary quality of the movement's earliest
days. It also reveals the genesis of popular misunderstandings
about what it meant.

In 1964 and 1965 Leonard traveled around the country, working on what he believed would be the most important story of
his career. It would run in two or three subsequent issues of
Look, he anticipated, and he intended to call it "The Human
Potential."[5]

---

[5]Leonard's article, which eventually ran to twenty thousand words, was never
published. *Look* decided it was "too long and too theoretical."

Several people had mentioned a rather mysterious young man named Michael Murphy, who ran a seemingly unclassifiable institute on the wild Big Sur coast of central California. I was told that Murphy, like the hero of Maugham's *The Razor's Edge*, had gone to India seeking enlightenment, had lived for eighteen months at the Aurobindo Ashram in Pondicherry. . . . The institute was supposedly a forum for new ideas, especially those that combined the wisdom of East and West. I heard that Esalen's first brochure flew under the title of a series of 1961 lectures by Aldous Huxley: "Human Potentialities."

As Leonard recalled their first meeting:

The dinner was magical. Murphy's knowledge of Eastern philosophy was encyclopedic, and he talked about it as if it were a delicious tale of suspense and adventure. He had a strong sense of history and a compelling vision of the future. Nor was Murphy the kind of guru-seeker you can sometimes spot by the vague look in their eyes. . . . This seeker was on a decidedly American *sadhana*. You could easily see him in a warm-up suit, never in a flowing white robe. . . .

After dinner we drove to my house and continued talking for hours. The meeting of minds, of visions, was extraordinary, with each of us bringing just what was needed in the way of background knowledge to dovetail with that of the other. While Murphy had been studying Eastern philosophy and humanistic psychology, I had been studying social and political movements in the United States.

They met at a vivid moment in the nation's history, Leonard recalls: Lyndon Johnson was pushing an idealist civil rights bill and his "war on poverty." There was a sense of changing consciousness in the country as social movements proliferated: sexual liberation, the Free Speech Movement, concern for the rights of Chicanos and American Indians, and, above all, the civil rights movement led by Martin Luther King.

In the spirit of those times, it was natural to think in terms of "movements." Just as the civil rights movement would break down the barriers between the races, and thus other barriers, a human potential movement would help break down the barriers between mind and body, between Eastern wisdom and Western action, between individual and society, and thus between the limited self and the potential self.

Soon Leonard, Murphy, and others were not only planning residential programs at Esalen but seeking ways the insights of this new human-potential movement could be applied to the larger society. They saw its relevance to education, politics, health care, race relations, and city planning. Such divergent notables as B. F. Skinner and S. I. Hayakawa led Esalen seminars in the fall of 1965, along with Watts, Carl Rogers, J. B. Rhine, and others. Leonard said:

> It was a heady time. Will Schutz and Fritz Perls came to live at Esalen. New methods proliferated. The Esalen lodge became a carnival of innovation. . . . In 1967 the institute opened a branch in San Francisco to take on urban problems. I joined forces with the distinguished black psychiatrist Price Cobbs to lead marathon interracial confrontations. Mike Murphy moved to the city. Best yet—oh, glorious, golden days of grace!—all this happened pretty much out of the public eye.
>
> Then came the media—the television and radio reports, the magazine articles, the books—and we were faced with the contradictions, the paradoxes, and the heartaches that inevitably accompany any serious challenge to cultural homeostasis.

Time's education section included what Leonard called a fairly objective article about Esalen in the fall of 1967, and United Press International covered Esalen's move to San Francisco.

> But it remained for a remarkable piece of writing in the December 31, 1967, issue of the *New York Times Sunday Magazine* to open the floodgates.
>
> I had learned by then that much of the publishing world used a very simple method of certification and reality testing: Until something appeared in the *New York Times*, you couldn't be sure it was real. When something appeared in a *favorable* light in the *Times*, you could bet it was not only real but worthy of further coverage. . . .
>
> So here we had "Joy is the Prize" by Leo Litwak, telling of the author's personal experience in a five-day Will Schutz encounter group and speculating on the Esalen vi-

sion. The article had the requisite air of initial skepticism
and closing irony but was generally positive.... Within
days of its publication, editors all over New York were
being bombarded with queries about doing a story, a
show, a book on this strange place on the California coast
and the "movement" it portended.

Esalen did not welcome the publicity. Its policy had been to
cooperate with reporters but to discourage coverage whenever
possible.

Although only 15 percent of Esalen's programs were encounter groups, Litwak had written about an encounter group,
which led other reporters and the public to associate Esalen
with them forever. Some reporters, bewildered by the wealth
of new ideas at Esalen, finding them hard to categorize, settled
for cynicism. Others became true believers, Leonard said,
and "helped create false expectations that led to eventual
disillusionment."

Inevitably, human-potential centers were springing up
around the country. At various times Murphy and Price were
approached by individuals wanting to affiliate with Esalen,
using the name for their own centers. They refused but actively
encouraged all competition.

The new society forming had spiritual underpinnings that
were hard to identify. Jacob Needleman, reflecting in 1973 on
his first years in California, said:

The person I was then could never have undertaken to
write this book [*The New Religions*].... Even apart from my
intellectual convictions, there was this whole matter of
California. As a transplanted Easterner, I felt duty-bound
not to take anything in California very seriously. I certainly
felt no need to *understand* California.... To me it was a
place desperately lacking in the experience of limitation....

I still do not claim to understand California, but I am
certain that it cannot be taken lightly from any point of
view.... Something is struggling to be born here.

...I wish I could state clearly what it is about California
that makes so many of its people—and not just the
young—so much more accessible to the cosmic dimension
of human life.... But the undeniable fact is that by and
large the West Coast does not exhibit the sort of intellectualism found in our eastern cities, an intellectualism

rooted in [the] European sense of the human mind as autonomous and outside nature.

In any case, it is not reality which Californians have left behind; it is Europe.... I began to see that my idea of intelligence was a modern European idea; the mind, unfettered by emotion, disembodied, aristocratically articulate.... I saw that I had judged California on its lack of the European element.

The Aquarian Conspiracy, needless to say, is nurtured in California.[6] Its "agents" from the Boston-Cambridge area, from New York and Washington, London, Denver, Minneapolis, Houston, Chicago, and hundreds of smaller cities rally in California from time to time for sustenance and courage.

The large "consciousness" conference, a California invention of the early 1970s, was a perfect device for this national crossfertilization. Beginning in 1975, California groups began organizing road shows—conferences and seminars all over the country.[7] In many cities strong local links were then established, and subsequent programs were staged by locals. Conference budgets tried to provide for continuous liaison. Small workshops proved even more flexible strategies for moving people about the country. Through such meetings the conspirators typically pooled the names of friends and contacts, quickly enlarging and linking the networks. Cassette tapes of conference lectures were disseminated by the thousand.

Ironically, while the eastern United States tends to patronize the West Coast as a bizarre relative, Radio Television Belgium sent a team to Los Angeles to film a documentary on how the 1960s counterculture had affected the 1970s, explaining that "what happens in California will eventually happen in Europe."

If California has once again anticipated the next step, the prospects for national change are strong indeed.

[6]Although nearly half of those responding to the Aquarian Conspiracy questionnaire now live in California, most were born in the East or Midwest. The role of California and its immigrants as catalysts for social transformation was proclaimed in the invitation to a 1979 conference in Sacramento, "California Renaissance," sponsored by the Association for Humanistic Psychology. Participants were to look at the "significance, promise, and dangers of the California experience" in terms of personal and planetary evolution.

[7]Two of the earliest such conferences were sponsored, interestingly, by the Lockheed Corporation. They were held in the San Jose area in 1971 and featured scientists and physicians.

DESPERATION AND RENEWAL

James Alan McPherson, a young Black who won the Pulitzer Prize for fiction, recently traced the advancement of freedoms from the Magna Carta to the Charter of the United Nations. "In the gradual elaboration of basic rights," he said, "an outline of something much more complex than 'black' and 'white' had begun." A new citizenship becomes possible in which "each United States citizen [could] attempt to approximate the ideals of the nation, be on at least conversant terms with all its diversity, and carry the mainstream of the culture inside himself."

Each American would be a synthesis of high and low, black and white, city and country, provincial and universal. "If he could live with these contradictions, he would be simply a representative American."

He quoted the Spanish philosopher, Miguel de Unamuno, who called attention to the adoption of the word *desperado* in English: "It is despair, and despair alone, that begets heroic hope, absurd hope, mad hope." McPherson added:

> I believe that the United States is complex enough to induce that sort of despair that begets heroic hope. I believe that if one can experience its diversity, touch a variety of its people, laugh at its craziness, distill wisdom from its tragedies, and attempt to synthesize all this inside oneself without going crazy, one will have earned the right to call oneself "citizen of the United States." . . . One will have begun on that necessary movement.

This movement from a hopeless person to a desperado, he said, is "the only new direction I know."

American society has at hand most of the factors that could bring about collective transformation: relative freedom, relative tolerance, affluence enough to be disillusioned with affluence, achievements enough to know that something different is needed. We have been temperamentally innovative, bold, and confident. Our national myth says that we can have the alternative if we have the imagination and the will.

"To be an American," said social and literary critic Leslie Fiedler, "is precisely to *imagine* a destiny rather than inherit one. We have always been inhabitants of myth rather than history."

To imagine a destiny, to transcend a past . . . We have little to lose by the remaking of our family institutions. We have begun to know our complex selves: our roots, our collective mid-life crisis, our sexuality and death and renewal, our paradoxical yearning for both freedom and order, our costly addictions. We sense the limits of our old science, the dangers of our top-heavy hierarchies, and we see the context of our planet.

We begin to feel our tangible and spiritual connection with other cultures. We have awakened our power to learn and to change.

And we have ideas.

Afraid or not, we seem to have made it past the entry point into real transformation: past the cultural shake-up, the violence, the fascination and excesses, the fear of the new and uncharted. We have begun to imagine the possible society.

CHAPTER **6**

Liberating Knowledge: News from the Frontiers of Science

Any truth creates a scandal.
—MARGUERITE YOURCENAR, *The Memoirs of Hadrian*

Our discoveries about the startling nature of reality are a major force for change, undermining common-sense ideas and old institutional philosophies. "The 1980s will be a revolutionary time," said physicist Fritjof Capra, "because the whole structure of our society does not correspond with the world-view of emerging scientific thought."

The agenda of the coming decade is to act on this new scientific knowledge—discoveries that revise the very data base on which we have built our assumptions, our institutions, our lives. It promises far more than the old reductionist view. It reveals a rich, creative, dynamic, interconnected reality. Nature, we are learning, is not a force over which we must triumph but the medium of our transformation.

The mysteries we will explore in this chapter are not remote from us, like black holes in outer space, but *ourselves*. Our brains and bodies. The genetic code. The nature of change. The widening and shrinking of conscious experience. The power of imagination and intention. The plastic nature of intelligence and perception.

We live what we know. If we believe the universe and ourselves to be mechanical, we will live mechanically. On the other hand, if we know that we are part of an open universe, and that our minds are a matrix of reality, we will live more creatively and powerfully.

If we imagine that we are isolated beings, so many inner tubes afloat on an ocean of indifference, we will lead different lives than if we know a universe of unbroken wholeness. Believing in a world of fixity, we will fight change; knowing a world of fluidity, we will cooperate with change.

As Abraham Maslow said, a fear of knowing is very deeply a fear of doing, because of the responsibility inherent in new knowledge. These new discoveries reveal aspects of nature too rich for analysis, yet we can understand them. On some level—call it heart, right brain, gut, collective unconscious—we recognize the rightness, even the simplicity of the principles involved. They fit with deeply buried knowledge within us.

Science is only confirming paradoxes and intuitions humankind has come across many times but stubbornly disregarded. It is telling us that our social institutions and our very ways of existence violate nature. We fragment and freeze that which should be moving and dynamic. We construct unnatural hierarchies of power. We compete when we might cooperate.

If we read the handwriting on the wall of science, we see the critical need to change—to live with nature, not against it.

Discoveries from many realms of science—brain research, physics, molecular biology, research on learning and consciousness, anthropology, psychophysiology—have come together in revolutionary ways, yet the emergent picture is by no means well known. Word from the scientific frontier usually leaks back only through highly specialized channels, sometimes garbled. But it concerns us all; it is news to be broken, not a diary to be classified.

Before we look at the discoveries, we'll consider briefly the reasons we have heard the news only in bits, if at all. Certainly no one censors it. Part of the communication problem, as we shall see, is the strangeness of what is being found; part results from the extreme specialization of the researchers and their own lack of an overview. Very few people are synthesizing the information being gathered in far-flung places. It is as if military scouts were continually returning from reconnaissance missions with observations and there were no generals to put it all together.

Once upon a time, everybody "did" science. Long before science was a career, people tried to understand nature for their own amusement and excitement. They collected specimens, experimented, built microscopes and telescopes. Although some of these hobby scientists became famous, it hardly occurs to us that they were untrained in the formal sense; they wrote no dissertations for graduate schools.

And we were all scientists, too—curious children, testing substances on our tongues, discovering gravity, peering under rocks, seeing patterns in the stars, wondering what makes the night scary and the sky blue.

Partly because the educational system has taught science only in a reductionist, left-brain style and partly because of the society's demands for practical applications of technology, the romance of science fades quickly for most youngsters. Those who love nature but dislike dissecting small animals soon learn to avoid high-school biology. Students who enroll in psychology courses, hoping to learn something about how people think and feel, find themselves learning more about rats and statistics than they ever wanted to know.

In higher education, science narrows further. The humanities-oriented sheep and the science-oriented goats are herded into their respective pens; at many universities, the science and humanities centers are blocks apart. Most students sidestep any science beyond the minimum required hours; the science majors are funnelled into their specialties, subspecialties, and microspecialties. By graduate school, they can scarcely communicate with each other.

Most of us end up feeling that science is something special, separate, outside our ken, like Greek or archeology. A minority pursue it narrowly, and we have C. P. Snow's Two Cultures, Science and Art, each a little superior, a little envious, and tragically incomplete.

Each scientific discipline is an island, as well. Specialization has kept most scientists from trespassing into "fields" other than their own, both from fear of looking foolish and from the difficulty of communication. Synthesis is left to the hardy few, the irrepressibly creative researchers whose breakthroughs make work for the whole industry.

At a recent annual meeting of the American Association for the Advancement of Science (founded to foster interdisciplinary exchange), anthropologists reportedly met in one

Philadelphia hotel to hear reports about the probable causes for the extinction of tribes. At the same hour, hundreds of biologists convened in a nearby hotel to discuss the reason for the extinction of species. The two groups—in their separate hotels—came up with the same answer: *over-specialization*.

Specialization has spawned another problem: technical and mathematical languages—a Tower of Babel.

In brain science alone, half a million papers are published annually. Neuroscience has become such an esoteric discipline, so narrowly subspecialized, that the researchers have extraordinary difficulty in communicating even among themselves. Only a handful of researchers are trying to make sense of the whole.

The second reason for the communications gap is the utter strangeness of the new worldview. We are required to make paradigm shift after paradigm shift, to drastically alter our old beliefs and to see from a new perspective.

It has been said that science replaces common sense with knowledge. Indeed, our most advanced intellectual adventures carry us into wonderlands beyond the boundaries of logical, linear understanding. There is a much-quoted observation of the great biologist, J. B. S. Haldane, that reality is not only stranger than we conceive but stranger than we *can* conceive.

There is no bottom line in nature. There is no deepest place where it all makes tidy sense. This can be frightening. It can make us feel as if we are regressing to childhood, when nature seemed immense, mysterious, potent. Later we learned to sort facts from fancy, and mystery was reduced to "explanations." "Facts" about lightning or magnetism or radio waves, for example, led us to think that nature was understood or about to be understood. This mistaken view, held by most scientists in the late-nineteenth century, carried over into popular misunderstanding of the powers of science.

Now, when our most advanced science begins to sound mythic and symbolic—when it relinquishes hope of achieving ultimate certainty—we are disbelieving. It is as if we are being asked to re-create the awe and credulity of early childhood, before we knew what a rainbow "really" was.

As we shall see, the new science goes beyond cool, clinical observations to a realm of shimmering paradox, where our very reason seems endangered. Yet, just as we can take advantage of great technological developments of our civilization, like the transistor, our lives can be liberated by the new worldview of radical science, whether we understand the technicalities or not.

Many of the vital insights of modern science are expressed in mathematics, a "language" most of us neither speak nor understand. Ordinary language is inadequate to deal with the nonordinary. Words and sentences have given us a false sense of understanding, blinding us to the complexity and dynamics of nature.

Life is not constructed like a sentence, subject acting on object. In reality many events affect each other simultaneously. Take, for example, the impossibility of sorting out who-did-what-first or who-caused-what-behavior in a family. We construct all of our explanations on a linear model that exists only as an ideal.

Semanticists like Alfred Korzybski and Benjamin Whorf warned that Indo-European languages trap us in a fragmented model of life. They disregard relationship. By their subject-predicate structure, they mold our thought, forcing us to think of everything in terms of simple cause and effect. For this reason it is hard for us to talk about—or even *think* about—quantum physics, a fourth dimension, or any other notion without clearcut beginnings and endings, up and down, then and now.

Events in nature have simultaneous multiple causes. Some languages, notably Hopi and Chinese, are structured differently and can express nonlinear ideas with less strain. They can, in effect, "speak physics." Like the ancient Greeks, whose philosophy strongly influenced the left-brained West, we say, "The light flashed." But the light and the flash were *one*. A Hopi would more accurately say, "Reh-pi!"—"Flash!"

Korzybski warned that we will not grasp the nature of reality until we realize the limitation of words. Language frames our thought, thereby setting up barriers. The map is *not* the territory. A rose is *not* a rose is a rose; the apple of August 1 is *not* the apple of September 10 or the wizened fruit of October 2. *Change and complexity always outrun our powers of description.*

Ironically, even most scientists do not relate scientific knowledge to everyday life. Peer pressure discourages them from searching for wider meaning or significance "outside their field." They keep what they know compartmentalized and irrelevant, like a religion practiced only on holy days. Only a few have the intellectual rigor and personal courage to try to integrate their science into their lives. Capra remarked that most physicists go home from the laboratory and live their lives as if Newton, not Einstein, were right—as if the world were fragmented and mechanical. "They don't seem to realize the philosophical, cultural, and spiritual implications of their theories."

Our quantifying instruments—electron microscopes, computers, telescopes, random-number generators, EEGs, statistics, test tubes, integral calculus, cyclotrons—have finally given us passage to a realm beyond numbers. What we find is not nonsense but a kind of meta-sense—not illogical, but transcending logic as we once defined it.

Creating a new theory, Einstein once said, is not like erecting a skyscraper in the place of an old barn. "It is rather like climbing a mountain, gaining new and wider views, discovering unexpected connections between our starting point and its rich environment. But the point from which we started out still exists and can be seen, although it appears smaller and forms a tiny part of our broad view...."

SEEING THE NEW WORLD

Like the Flatlanders, we have been at least one dimension short. This dimension, however strange it may seem at first, in a very real sense is the genesis of our world—our real home.

This chapter will take us through several scientific doorways into that other dimension. Technical terms have been kept to a minimum so that the "story line" can better be followed. Those who want to pursue the data will find technical references at the back of the book.

The left brain is a useful companion on a voyage of discovery—up to a point. Its measuring genius has brought us to our present respect for, and intellectual belief in, the larger dimension. But in many ways it is like Virgil in Dante's *Divine Comedy*. Virgil could escort the poet through Hell and Purgatory, where everything was reasonable, where, for example, the punishment fit the crime.

But when Dante came to the perimeters of Paradise, Virgil had to stay behind. He could confront the mystery but he could not penetrate it. Beatrice, the poet's muse, accompanied him into the place of transcendence.

Nonlinear understanding is more like "tuning in" than traveling from point to point. The scientific discoveries discussed in this chapter take us into a country whose cartography is felt rather than traced.

When the left brain confronts the nonlinear dimension, it keeps circling around, breaking wholes into parts, retracing its data, and asking inappropriate questions, like a reporter at a funeral. *Where, when, how, why?* We have to inhibit its questions for the moment, suspend its judgment, or we cannot "get" the other dimension, any more than you can see both perspectives of the optical-illusion staircase at the same time—or be swept away by a symphony while analyzing the composition.

A world without space and time is not completely foreign to our experience. It is a little like our dreams, where past and future seem to run together, where locations shift mysteriously.

Recall the model of the paradigm shift introduced by Thomas Kuhn: Every important new idea in science sounds strange at first. As the physicist Niels Bohr put it, great innovations inevitably appear muddled, confusing, and incomplete, only half-understood even by their discoverers, and a mystery to everyone else. There is no hope, Bohr said, for any speculation that does not look absurd at first glance. Bohr once remarked of an idea advanced by his famous colleague Werner Heisenberg, "It isn't crazy enough to be true." (As it turned out, it wasn't.[1])

If we stubbornly refuse to look at that which seems magical or incredible, we are in distinguished company. The French Academy announced at one point that it would not accept any further reports of meteorites, since it was clearly impossible for rocks to fall out of the sky. Shortly thereafter a rain of meteorites came close to breaking the windows of the Academy.

If scientists are slow to accept new information, the public is usually even slower. Erwin Schrödinger, the great physicist, once said that it takes at least *fifty years* before a major scientific discovery penetrates the public consciousness—half a century before people realize what truly surprising beliefs are held by leading scientists. The human species can no longer afford the luxury of such long double-takes or the leisurely changes of heart of entrenched scientists. The cost is too great: in our ecology, our relationships, our health, our conflict, our threatened collective future. We are duty-bound to search, question, open our minds.

A major task of the Aquarian Conspiracy is to foster paradigm shifts by pointing out the flaws in the old paradigm and showing how the new context explains more—makes more sense. As we will see, the most powerful transformative ideas

---

[1]Charles Richet, who won the Nobel prize for his discovery of allergic shock, was criticized when he undertook to study clairvoyance. "I didn't say it was possible," Richet responded. "I only said it was true."

from modern science connect like parts of a puzzle. They support each other; together they form the scaffolding for a wider worldview.

Each of these major ideas is a whole in itself, a system for understanding a spectrum of phenomena in our lives and in society. Each also has uncanny parallels to ancient poetic and mystical descriptions of nature. Science is only now verifying what humankind has known intuitively since the dawn of history.

In *The Morning of the Magicians* Pauwels and Bergier speculated that an open conspiracy exists among scientists who have discovered these metaphysical realities. Many of the Aquarian Conspirators are scientists, a fraternity of paradigm breakers who cross into each other's territory for new insights. Many more have an intense lay interest in the frontiers of research. They draw their models for social change from scientific insights about how nature really, radically works. Other conspirators have become interested in science because they want to understand the physical basis for experiences they have had through the psychotechnologies.[2]

By supporting programs where scientists from many disciplines can discuss the implications of their work for society and for personal change, the Aquarian Conspiracy plays an important educational role. For example, a fairly typical program staged in New York in late 1978 featured two physicists, Nobel laureate Eugene Wigner and Fritjof Capra; psychologist Jean Houston, a researcher in altered states of consciousness; brain scientist Karl Pribram; and Swami Rama, a yogi who became famous in the early 1970s when the Menninger Foundation and other laboratories verified his remarkable ability to control physiological processes (including virtually stopping his heart). Their topic: "New Dimensions of Consciousness."

The brochure for the conference, also typical, characterized the convergence of science and intuition:

> Today we are on the brink of a new synthesis. In the past four centuries western science has experienced a continous shattering and reforming of its basic concepts. Now the

[2]In a sense, the Aquarian Conspirators represent the Two Cultures: typically, they are involved in both science and the arts. A high percentage of those surveyed play a musical instrument; engage regularly in arts or crafts; and/or read fiction, poetry, and science fiction. From science they seek more than information; they seek meaning—the essential quest of the artist.

scientific community has begun to recognize striking correlations between their findings and those expressed
abstrusely by ancient mystics. This is a convocation of visionary men and women pioneering this new synthesis.

Similar programs have been presented all around the
country—at universities and science museums, in the inner
chambers of establishment science—with titles like *On the Ultimate Nature of Reality, The Physics of Consciousness, Consciousness
and Cosmos, Consciousness and Cultural Change.*

BRAIN AND CONSCIOUSNESS RESEARCH

Until the 1960s there were relatively few scientists studying the
brain and even fewer researching the interaction between the
brain and conscious experience. Since then brain and consciousness research has become a thriving industry. The more
we know in this field, the more radical our questions become.
"There will be no end to this enterprise," said John Eccles, a
Nobel-laureate neuroscientist, "not for centuries."

Beginning in the sixties biofeedback research demonstrated
that human subjects can control delicate, complex, internal
processes long believed to be involuntary. In the laboratory,
people were trained to speed up and slow down their heart
rate, alter the electrical activity on the surface of the skin, shift
from rapid beta-rhythm brainwaves to slower alpha-rhythm.
Human subjects learned to "fire" (cause a bioelectrical action
in) a single motor nerve cell. A pioneer researcher in biofeedback, Barbara Brown, has remarked that this deep biological
awareness reflects the mind's ability to alter every physiological
system, every cell in the body.

Although biofeedback subjects knew how these shifts felt,
they were helpless to explain how they were achieved. On one
level biofeedback seems like a straightforward phenomenon;
monitoring bodily information by machine readout, tone cues,
or lights one can identify the sensations associated with fluctuations in feedback. But there is a mysterious gap between *intention* and physiological action. How can one's will select a single
cell out of billions and cause it to discharge? Or release a specific chemical? Or limit the flow of gastric juices? Or alter the
rhythmic behavior of populations of brain cells? Or dilate capillaries to increase hand temperature?

Awareness is wider and deeper than anyone had guessed; intention, more powerful. Clearly, human beings have not begun to exploit their potential for change.

Biofeedback phenomena sent researchers scurrying back to the handful of scientific reports on yogis reported to have such control—without feedback. Until the phenomenon was verified in biofeedback laboratories, it had been widely assumed that the yogis had somehow tricked the few investigators willing to look at their feats.

Emerging at the same time were laboratory studies of meditation and other altered states of consciousness. Distinctive physiological changes in EEG, respiration, and electrical activity on the skin surface were found in meditators. The higher-amplitude, more rhythmic, slower brainwave patterns confirmed the claims of the psychotechnologies that practitioners achieve greater internal harmony.

During that same period, split-brain research (discussed in Chapter 3) demonstrated that human beings are indeed "of two minds" and that such centers of consciousness can function independently from each other in a single skull. The importance of this research, which opened a related field studying brain-hemisphere specialization, cannot be overstated. It helped us understand the distinctive nature of "holistic" processes; the mysterious knowing that had been insisted upon, disputed, and doubted over the centuries. The phenomenon of "intuition" was now vaguely situated on the neuroanatomical map.

The quantifying brain confirmed the reality of its qualitatively different "minor" hemisphere—an equal, if repressed, partner. Its powers were evident in the amazing performances of biofeedback subjects, the altered physiological processes measured in meditators, the strange double awareness in split-brain patients. More subtle techniques soon revealed the presence of the "other mind" in general perception. Researchers demonstrated that our attention is exquisitely selective, biased by belief and emotion; we can process information in parallel channels at the same time; we have extraordinary capacities for memory (if not always easy access to our data banks).

In the mid-seventies a series of breakthroughs opened an exciting new research field that is radicalizing what we know about how the brain works. Best known is the discovery of the class of brain substances known as endorphins or enkephalins, sometimes referred to as "the brain's own morphine" because they were first identified by their action at the brain sites where morphine has its effect. Like morphine, the endorphins are also analgesic.

The endorphins and the other brain substances of the class known as peptides added a new principle to brain function. The known chemical transmitters in the brain had been tracked; they work in a linear way, from cell to cell. But the new substances are more simultaneous in their action; they seem to modulate the activity of brain cells much as one tunes a radio and adjusts for volume. Some of them "broadcast" messages as well, which led Roger Guillemin, a Nobel-laureate researcher in the field, to suggest the existence of a "new" nervous system comprised of these substances.

Because the peptides are general and powerful in their action, their effects on the body and behavior are often dramatic. The endorphins, for example, have been shown to affect sexuality, appetite, social bonding, pain perception, alertness, learning, reward, seizures, and psychosis. Experiments have implicated the endorphins in the mysterious placebo effect, in which an inactive substance like a sugar pill produces relief because the patient expects it. Patients experiencing placebo relief from postoperative dental discomfort reported a recurrence of pain after they were given a chemical that interferes with the endorphins. Faith, inspired by the placebo, apparently releases endorphins. How it happens is as big a mystery as how intention works in biofeedback.

The endorphins may also be the system that enables us to push from our minds whatever we do not want to feel or think about—the chemistry of denial. Also, they are clearly involved in states of mental well-being. Infant animals distressed by separation from their mothers show a drop in endorphin levels. There is evidence that eating releases endorphins in the digestive system, which may explain the comfort some people obtain from food.

There are many different substances in the endorphin family and they produce different effects. Chemically, endorphins are molecules broken down from a very large molecule—itself recently found to be stored within an enormous molecule. The brain seems to take these chemicals out of "cold storage" as needed.

Mental states such as loneliness, compulsion, anguish, attachment, pain, and faith are not just "all in the head" but in the brain as well. Brain, mind, and body are a continuum.

Our thoughts — intention, fear, images, suggestion, expectation—alter the brain's chemistry. And it works both ways; thoughts can be altered by changing the brain's chemistry with drugs, nutrients, oxygen.

The brain is hopelessly complex. Biologist Lyall Watson spoke of the Catch-22 of brain research: "If the brain were so simple we could understand it, *we* would be so simple we couldn't!"

HOLISM AND SYSTEMS THEORY

Ironically, scientific insights into the brain's holistic talents—its right-hemisphere capacity to comprehend wholes—raise serious questions about the scientific method itself. Science has always tried to understand nature by breaking things into their parts. Now it is overwhelmingly clear that *wholes cannot be understood by analysis*. This is one of those logical boomerangs, like the mathematical proof that no mathematical system can be truly coherent in itself.

The Greek prefix *syn* ("together with"), as in *syn*thesis, *syn*ergy, *syn*tropy, becomes increasingly meaningful. When things come together something new happens. In relationship there is novelty, creativity, richer complexity. Whether we are talking about chemical reactions or human societies, molecules or international treaties, there are qualities that cannot be predicted by looking at the components.

Half a century ago in *Holism and Evolution* Jan Smuts tried to synthesize Darwin's evolutionary theory, Einstein's physics, and his own insights to account for the evolution of mind as well as matter.

Wholeness, Smuts said, is a fundamental characteristic of the universe—the product of nature's drive to synthesize. "Holism is self-creative, and its final structures are *more* holistic than its initial structures." These wholes — in effect, these unions — are dynamic, evolutionary, creative. They thrust toward ever-higher orders of complexity and integration. "Evolution," Smuts said, "has an ever deepening, inward spiritual character."

As we'll see shortly, modern science has verified the quality of whole-making, the characteristic of nature to put things together in an ever-more synergistic, meaningful pattern.

General Systems Theory, a related modern concept, says

that each variable in any system interacts with the other variables so thoroughly that cause and effect cannot be separated. A single variable can be both cause and effect. Reality will not be still. And it cannot be taken apart! You cannot understand a cell, a rat, a brain structure, a family, or a culture if you isolate it from its context. *Relationship is everything*.

Ludwig von Bertalanffy said that General Systems Theory aims to understand the principles of wholeness and self-organization at all levels:

> Its applications range from the biophysics of cellular processes to the dynamics of populations, from the problems of physics to those of psychiatry and those of political and cultural units. . . .
>
> General Systems Theory is symptomatic of a change in our worldview. No longer do we see the world in a blind play of atoms, but rather a great organization.

This theory says that history, while interesting and instructive, may not predict the future at all. Who can say what the dance of variables will produce tomorrow. . . next month . . . next year? Surprise is inherent in nature.

EVOLUTION: THE NEW PARADIGM

In Arthur Clarke's *Childhood's End*, the mysterious extraterrestrial Overlords, who have controlled Earth for a hundred years, explain that they are only interim protectors of humankind. Despite their greater intellectual powers, the Overlords are in an evolutionary cul-de-sac, whereas humanity has the capability of infinite evolution.

> Above us is the Overmind, using us as the potter uses his wheel. And your race is the clay that is being shaped on that wheel.
>
> We believe—it is only a theory—that the Overmind is trying to grow, to extend its powers and its awareness of the universe. By now, it must be the sum of many races, and long ago it left the tyranny of matter behind. . . . It sent us here to do its bidding, to prepare you for the transformation that is now at hand. . . .
>
> As to the nature of the change, we can tell you very

little . . . it spreads explosively, like the formation of crystals round the first nucleus in a saturated solution.

What Clarke described in literary metaphor, many serious scientists have expressed in academic terms. They suspect that we may be playing upon our own evolution, as on a musical instrument.

Darwin's theory of evolution by chance mutation and survival of the fittest has proven hopelessly inadequate to account for a great many observations in biology. Just as inadequacies in Newton's physics led Einstein to formulate a shocking new theory, so a larger paradigm is emerging to broaden our understanding of evolution.

Darwin insisted that evolution happened very gradually. Steven Jay Gould, a Harvard biologist and geologist, notes that on the eve of the publication of *The Origin of Species*, T. H. Huxley wrote Darwin, promising to battle on his behalf but warning that he had burdened his argument unnecessarily by this insistence. Darwin's portrayal of glacially slow evolution reflected in part his admiration of Charles Lyell, who promoted the idea of gradualism in geology. Evolution was a stately and orderly process in Darwin's view, Gould noted, "working at a speed so slow that no person could hope to observe it in his lifetime."

And just as Lyell rejected the evidence for cataclysm in geology, Darwin ignored problems in his own evidence. True, there seemed to be great gaps, missing rungs in the ladder of evolution, but he believed these were just imperfections in the geological record. Change only *seemed* abrupt.

But to this day fossil evidence has not turned up the necessary missing links. Gould called the extreme rarity in the fossil record of transitional forms of life "the trade secret of paleontology." Younger scientists, confronted by the continuing absence of such missing links, are increasingly skeptical of the old theory. "The old explanation that the fossil record was inadequate is in itself an inadequate explanation," said Niles Eldredge of the American Museum of Natural History.

Gould and Eldredge independently proposed a resolution of this problem, a theory that is consistent with the geological record. Soviet paleontologists have proposed a similar theory. *Punctuationalism* or *punctuated equilibrium* suggests that the equilibrium of life is "punctuated" from time to time by severe stress. If a small segment of the ancestral population is isolated at the periphery of its accustomed range, it may give way to a new species. Also, *the population is stressed intensely because it is living at the edge of its tolerance.* "Favorable variations spread quickly," Gould said. "Small peripheral isolates are the laboratory of evolutionary change."

Most species do not change direction during their tenure on earth. "They appear in the fossil record looking much the same as when they disappear," Gould said. A new species arises suddenly in the geological evidence. It does not evolve gradually by the steady change of its ancestors, but *all at once and fully formed.*

The old paradigm saw evolution as a steady climb up a ladder, whereas Gould and others liken it to a branching out of various limbs of a tree. For instance, anthropologists have discovered in recent years that at one time there were at least three coexisting hominids — creatures that had evolved beyond the ape. Earlier it was believed that these different specimens formed a sequence. Now it is known that one "descendant" was living at the same time as its presumed ancestors. Several different lineages split from the parent stock, the lower primates. Some survived and continued to evolve, while others disappeared. The large-brained Homo appeared quite suddenly.

The new paradigm attributes evolution to periodic leaps by small groups.[3] This changing view is significant for at least two reasons: (1) It requires a mechanism for biological change more powerful than chance mutation, and (2) it opens us up to the possibility of rapid evolution in our own time, when the equilibrium of the species is punctuated by stress. Stress in modern society is experienced at the frontiers of our psychological rather than our geographical limits. Pioneering becomes an increasingly psychospiritual venture since our physical frontiers are all but exhausted, short of space exploration.

Given what we are learning about the nature of profound change, transformation of the human species seems less and less improbable.

Gould pointed out that Europeans in the nineteenth century favored the idea of gradualism, both in geology and evolution; it fit more comfortably with the dominant philosophy, which abhorred revolutions, even in nature. Our philosophies limit

[3]Science writer George Alexander described the new theory: "Where gradualism would compare evolution to a slow stately parade in which great numbers drift in and out, rather like New York's St. Patrick's Day parade, punctuated equilibrium envisions a series of block parties or street fairs. These localized events ... stand basically alone."

what we let ourselves see, he said.[4] We need pluralistic philosophies that free us to see the evidence from many points of view.

> If gradualism is more a product of Western thought than a fact of nature, then we should consider alternative philosophies of change to enlarge our realm of constraining prejudices. In the Soviet Union, for example, scientists are trained with a very different philosophy of change.... They speak of the "transformation of quantity into quality." This may sound like mumbo jumbo, but it suggests that change occurs in large leaps following a slow accumulation of stresses that a system resists until it reaches the breaking point. Heat water and it eventually reaches a boiling point. Oppress the workers more and more and they suddenly break their chains.

Evolution may be speeded up by certain genetic mechanisms, according to new findings. Genes and segments of DNA have been shown to jump off and onto chromosomes in bacteria and certain other life forms, suggesting that the chromosomes may be modified continuously. Researchers have conjectured that such genetic rewriting may be expected in *all* forms of life.

Certain segments of the DNA don't appear to contribute to the gene's usual product at all. The discovery of these intervening sequences, which appear as nonsense in the context of the genetic code, was called "horrifying" by one of the researchers, Walter Gilbert of Harvard. As the British journal *New Scientist* observed, "Our very concept of a gene is now in doubt." DNA might not be the consistent archive biologists had supposed, but rather a flux—"a dynamic system in which clusters of genes expand and contract, roving elements hop in and out."[5]

[4]Art critic and historian Rudolf Arnheim pointed out that Europe seized upon the Second Law of Thermodynamics, when it was first formulated, to account for everything that seemed to be going wrong. "The sun was getting smaller, the earth colder," and the general decline into entropy was also evident in the lower standards of army discipline, social decadence, falling birth rate, more insanity and tuberculosis, poorer vision.

[5]The evolution that had been assumed to take thousands of years may well take only a generation, judging from the recent birth of a "siabon," the offspring of a male gibbon and a female siamang, two genetically dissimilar apes. Scientists now speculate that multiple rearrangements of genetic material rather than accumulated mutations may be the primary mechanisms by which species diverge.

Biochemist Albert Szent-Gyorgyi, discoverer of Vitamin C and a Nobel laureate, proposed that a drive toward greater order may be a fundamental principle of nature. He calls this characteristic *syntropy*—the opposite of entropy. Living matter has an inherent drive to perfect itself, he believes. Perhaps the cell periphery in a living organism actually feeds information back to the DNA at its core, changing the instructions. "After all," he said, "it was not known until a few years ago how the DNA issues its instructions to the cell in the first place. Some equally elegant process may alter those instructions."

He rejected the idea that random mutations account for the sophistication in living matter. Biological reactions are chain reactions, and the molecules fit together more precisely than the cogwheels of a Swiss watch. How, then, could they have developed by accident?

> For if any one of the very specific "cogwheels" in these chains is changed, then the whole system must simply become inoperative. Saying that it can be improved by random mutation of one link sounds to me like saying that you could improve a Swiss watch by dropping it and thus bending one of its wheels or axles. To get a better watch, you must change all the wheels simultaneously to make a good fit again.

Biologists have observed that there are many all-or-nothing "evolved" characteristics, such as the structure of birds for flight, that could not have occurred by random mutation and survival of the fittest. Half a wing would not have given any survival advantage. And wings would not have been of any use if the bone structure had not changed at the same time.

Evolution involves true transformation, re-forming of the basic structure, and not mere adding on.

Even in lower forms of life there are evolutionary achievements so stunning they humble our largest theories. In *African Genesis* Robert Ardrey recounted an incident in Kenya when Louis Leakey pointed out to him what appeared to be a coral-colored flower made up of many small blossoms, like a hyacinth. On close inspection, each oblong "blossom" turned out to be the wing of an insect. These, said Leakey, were flattid bugs.

Startled, Ardrey remarked that this was certainly a striking instance of protective imitation in nature. Leakey listened, looking amused, then explained that the coral flower "imitated" by the flattid bug does not exist in nature. Furthermore, each batch of eggs laid by the female includes at least one flattid bug with green wings, not coral, and several with wings of in-between shades.

> I looked closely. At the tip of the insect flower was a single green bud. Behind it were half a dozen partially matured blossoms showing only strains of coral. Behind these on the twig crouched the full strength of flattid bug society, all with wings of purest coral to complete the colony's creation and deceive the eyes of the hungriest of birds.
>
> There are moments when one's only response to evolutionary achievement can be a prickling sensation in the scalp. But still my speechlessness had not reached its most vacant, brain-numbed moment. Leakey shook the stick. The startled colony rose from its twig and filled the air with fluttering flattid bugs. . . . Then they returned to their twig. They alighted in no particular order and for an instant, the twig was alive with the little creatures climbing over each other's shoulders in what seemed to be random movement. But the movement was not random.
>
> Shortly the twig was still and one beheld again the flower.

How had the flattid bugs evolved so? How do they know their respective places, crawling over one another to get into position, like schoolchildren taking their places for a Christmas pageant?

Colin Wilson suggested that there is not only communal consciousness among the bugs but that their very existence is due to a telepathic genetic connection. The flattid-bug community is, in a sense, a single individual, a single mind, whose genes were influenced by its *collective* need.

Is it possible that we too are expressing a collective need, preparing for an evolutionary leap? Physicist John Platt has proposed that humankind is now experiencing an evolutionary shockfront and "may emerge very quickly into coordinated forms such as it has never known before . . . implicit in the biological material all along, as surely as the butterfly is implicit in the caterpillar."

THE SCIENCE OF TRANSFORMATION

When the puzzles and paradoxes cry out for resolution, a new paradigm is due. Fortunately, a deep and powerful new explanation for rapid evolution—biological, cultural, personal—is emerging.

The theory of dissipative structures won the 1977 Nobel prize in chemistry for a Belgian physical chemist, Ilya Prigogine. This theory may prove as important a breakthrough to science in general as the theories of Einstein were to physics. It bridges the critical gap between biology and physics—the missing link between living systems and the apparently lifeless universe in which they arose.

It explains "irreversible processes" in nature—the movement toward higher and higher orders of life. Prigogine, whose early interest was in history and the humanities, felt that science essentially ignored *time*. In Newton's universe time was considered only in regard to motion, the trajectory of a moving object. Yet, as Prigogine keeps saying, there are many aspects of time: decay, history, evolution, the creation of new forms, new ideas. Where in the old universe was there room for *becoming*?

Prigogine's theory resolves the fundamental riddle of how living things have been running uphill in a universe that is supposed to be running down.

And the theory is immediately relevant to everyday life—to *people*. It offers a scientific model of transformation at every level. It explains the critical role of stress in transformation—and the impetus toward transformation inherent in nature!

As we shall see, the principles revealed by the theory of dissipative structures are valuable in helping us understand profound change in psychology, learning, health, sociology, even politics and economics. The theory has been used by the United States Department of Transportation to predict traffic flow patterns. Scientists in many disciplines are employing it within their own specialties. The applications are infinite.

The essence of the theory is not difficult to understand once we get past some semantic confusion. In describing nature, physical scientists often use ordinary words in their most literal sense—words for which we also have abstract meanings and strongly loaded emotional values. To understand Prigogine's theory we need to withhold traditional value judgment about words like "complexity," "dissipation," "coherence," "instability," and "equilibrium."

First, let's look again for a moment at the way in which nature is saturated with order and alive with pattern: flowers and insect colonies, cellular interactions, pulsar and quasar

stars, the DNA code, biological clocks, the symmetrical ex-
changes of energy in the collision of subatomic particles, memory patterns in human minds.

Next, remember that at a deep level of nature, nothing is
fixed. These patterns are in constant motion. Even a rock is a
dance of electrons.

Some forms in nature are *open systems*, involved in a continuous exchange of energy with the environment. A seed, an
ovum, and a living creature are all open systems. There are also
human-made open systems. Prigogine gives the example of a
town: It takes in energy from the surrounding area (power, raw
materials), transforms it in factories, and returns energy to the
environment. In *closed systems*, on the other hand—examples
would be a rock, a cup of cold coffee, a log—there is no internal
transformation of energy.

Prigogine's term for open systems is *dissipative structures*.
That is, their form or structure is maintained by a continuous
dissipation (consumption) of energy. Much as water moves
through a whirlpool and creates it at the same time, energy
moves through and simultaneously forms the dissipative structure. All living things and some nonliving systems (for instance, certain chemical reactions) are dissipative structures. A
dissipative structure might well be described as a *flowing wholeness*. It is highly organized but always in process.

Now think about the meaning of the word *complex*: braided
together. A complex structure is connected at many points and
in many ways. The more complex a dissipative structure, the
more energy is needed to maintain all those connections.
Therefore it is more vulnerable to internal fluctuations. It is said
to be "far from equilibrium." (In the physical sciences, equilibrium does not mean healthy balance. It refers to ultimate random dispersal of energy. This equilibrium is a kind of death.)

Because these connections can only be sustained by a flow of
energy, the system is always in flux. Notice the paradox; the
more *coherent* or intricately connected the structure, the more
unstable it is. Increased coherence means increased instability!
This very instability is the key to transformation. The dissipation of
energy, as Prigogine demonstrated by his elegant mathematics,
creates the potential for sudden reordering.

The continuous movement of energy through the system results in fluctuations; if they are minor, the system damps them
and they do not alter its structural integrity. But if the fluctuations reach a critical size, they "perturb" the system. They increase the number of novel interactions within it. They shake it

up. The elements of the old pattern come into contact with each other in new ways and make new connections. *The parts reorganize into a new whole. The system escapes into a higher order.*

The more complex or coherent a structure, the greater the next level of complexity. Each transformation makes the next one likelier. Each new level is even more integrated and connected than the one before, requiring a greater flow of energy for maintenance, and is therefore still less stable. To put it another way, flexibility begets flexibility. As Prigogine said, at higher levels of complexity, "the nature of the laws of nature changes." Life "eats" entropy. It has the potential to create new forms by allowing a shake-up of old forms.

The elements of a dissipative structure cooperate to bring about this transformation of the whole. In such a shift, even molecules do not just interact with their immediate neighbors, Prigogine noted, "but also exhibit coherent behavior suited to the [needs of] the parent organism." At other levels, insects cooperate within their colonies, human beings within social forms.

One recently reported example of a new dissipative structure occurred when bacteria were placed experimentally in water, a medium in which this strain was unaccustomed to live. They began to interact in a highly organized way that enabled some of their number to survive.

The Zhabotinskii reaction, a dissipative structure in chemistry, caused something of a sensation among chemists in the 1960s. In this dramatic example of nature creating patterns in both space and time, beautiful scroll-like forms unfold in a solution in a laboratory dish while the colors of the solution oscillate, changing from red to blue at regular intervals. Similarly, when certain oils are heated, a complex pattern of hexagons appears on the surface. The higher the heat, the more complex the pattern. These shifts are sudden and nonlinear. Multiple factors act on each other at once.[6]

At first the idea of creating new order by perturbation seems outrageous, like shaking up a box of random words and pouring out a sentence. Yet our traditional wisdom contains parallel ideas. We know that stress often forces sudden new solutions;

[6]Nonlinearity is not mysterious. As an example in everyday life, Prigogine cites heavy freeway traffic. In light traffic you can drive in a linear way, moving more or less as you choose with minimum slowing or lane changing. But if traffic thickens, "there is a new regime—competition between events." You are not only driving but being *driven by* the system. All the cars are now affecting each other.

that crisis often alerts us to opportunity; that the creative process requires chaos before form emerges; that individuals are often strengthened by suffering and conflict; and that societies need a healthy airing of dissent.

Human society offers an example of spontaneous self-organization. In a fairly dense society, as individuals become acquainted with others, each soon has more points of contact throughout the system via friends and friends of friends. *The greater the instability and mobility of the society, the more interactions occur.* This means greater potential for new connections, new organizations, diversification. Much as certain cells or organs in a body specialize during the course of evolution, people with common interests find one another and refine their specialty by mutual stimulation and exchange of ideas.

The theory of dissipative structures offers a scientific model for the transformation of society by a dissident minority like the Aquarian Conspiracy. Prigogine has pointed out that the theory "violates the 'law of large numbers.'" And yet, historians have long noted that a creative minority can reorder a society. "The historical analogy is so obvious," Prigogine said. "Fluctuations, the behavior of a small group of people, can completely change the behavior of the group as a whole."

Critical perturbations—"a dialectic between mass and minority"—can drive the society to "a new average." Societies have a limited power of integration, he said. Any time a perturbation is greater than the society's ability to "damp" or repress it, the social organization will (a) be destroyed, or (b) give way to a new order.

Cultures are the most coherent and strangest of dissipative structures, Prigogine remarked. A critical number of advocates of change can create "a preferential direction" like the inner ordering of a crystal or magnet that organizes the whole.

Because of their size and density, modern societies are subject to large internal fluctuations. These can trigger shifts to a higher, richer order. In Prigogine's terms, they can become more pluralistic and diversified.

We are transformed through interaction with the environment. Science can now express as beautifully as the humanities the great and final paradox; our need to connect with the world (relationship) and to define our unique position in it (autonomy).

Prigogine acknowledged a strong resemblance between this "science of becoming" and the vision of Eastern philosophies, poets, mystics, and scientist-philosophers like Henri Bergson and Alfred North Whitehead. "A deep collective vision," he called it. He believes that the breakdown between the Two Cultures is *not* as Snow thought, that those in the humanities are not reading enough science and vice-versa.

"One of the basic aspects of the humanities is time—the way things change. The laws of change. As long as we had only these naive views of time in physics and chemistry, science had little to say to art." Now we move from a world of quantities in science to a world of qualities—a world in which we can recognize ourselves, "a human physics." This worldview goes beyond duality and traditional options into a rich, pluralistic cultural outlook, a recognition that higher-order life is not bound by "laws" but is capable of boundless innovation and alternate realities.

> And this point of view has been expressed by many poets and writers, Tagore, Pasternak.... The fact that we can quote the truth of the scientists and the truth of the poets is in a sense already proof that we can in some sense bridge the problem between the Two Cultures and have come to the possibility of a new dialogue.
>
> We are approaching a new unity—a non-totalitarian science, in which we don't try to reduce one level to another.

THE BRAIN AS A DISSIPATIVE STRUCTURE

Long before Prigogine's theory was experimentally confirmed, its significance stunned an Israeli researcher, Aharon Katchalsky. Katchalsky, also a physical chemist, had been studying dynamic patterns of brain function for many years. He was trying to understand how the brain integrates, what its rhythms and oscillations mean.

The brain seemed a perfect example of a dissipative structure. It is the ultimate in complexity. It is characterized by form and flow, interaction with the environment, abrupt shifts, sensitivity to being perturbed. It demands the lion's share of the body's energy—with only 2 percent of the body weight, it consumes 20 percent of the available oxygen. The ups and downs of its energy influx are characteristic of the unstable dissipative structure.

In 1972 Katchalsky organized a spring work session of top brain scientists at Massachusetts Institute of Technology to introduce Prigogine's recently advanced theory to neuroscience. Katchalsky also presented his own cumulative evidence of dynamic organizing properties in nature and how they are affected by sudden, sharp fluctuations.

The theory of dissipative structures might well tie dynamic brain patterns to transitions in the mind. Gestalt psychology, he commented, had long taken note of sudden transitions, jumps in perception. "The restructuring of an individual personality may take a sudden form, as in flashes of understanding, learning a new skill, falling in love, or the conversion experience of St. Paul."

At the same session, Vernon Rowland of Case Western Reserve University predicted that this approach to the brain would penetrate the old mystery: the difference that makes a whole more than the sum of its parts. Cooperation seemed to be a key; the more complex a system, the greater its potential for self-transcendence.

Although the theory was new to most participants, they quickly agreed that further study and synthesis should be undertaken. A whole new field seemed likely to emerge. Perhaps the idea of dissipative structures would be the key to further progress in brain research, which seemed urgently in need of something other than the current linear approach. It was decided that Katchalsky would chair future sessions, guide the work, and synthesize the results.

Two weeks later Katchalsky was slain by terrorists' bullets in the Lod Airport at Tel Aviv.

He had been hot on the trail of a truly promising connection. Consider the theory of dissipative structures as it may apply to the human brain and consciousness. It helps explain the transformative power of psychotechnologies—why they can break conditioning that is firmly resistant to change in ordinary states of consciousness.

Brainwaves reflect *fluctuations of energy*. Groups of neurons are experiencing enough electrical activity to show up on the EEG graph. In normal consciousness, small and rapid brainwaves (beta rhythm) dominate the EEG pattern in most people. We are more attentive to the external world than to inner experience in the beta state. Meditation, reverie, relaxation, and other assorted psychotechnologies tend to increase the slower, *larger* brainwaves known as alpha and theta. Inward attention, in other words, generates a larger fluctuation in the brain. *In altered states of consciousness, fluctuations may reach a critical level, large enough to provoke the shift into a higher level of organization.*

Memories, including deeply entrenched patterns of behavior and thought, are dissipative structures. They are patterns or forms stored in the brain. Remember that *small* fluctuations in a dissipative structure are suppressed by the existing form; they have no lasting effect. But larger fluctuations of energy cannot be contained in the old structure. They set off ripples throughout the system, creating sudden new connections. Thus, old patterns are likeliest to change when maximally perturbed or shaken—activated in states of consciousness in which there is significant energy flow.

Prigogine's theory helps to account for the dramatic effects sometimes seen in meditation, hypnosis, or guided imagery: the sudden relief of a lifelong phobia or ailment. An individual reliving a traumatic incident in a state of highly-focused inward attention perturbs the pattern of that specific old memory. This triggers a reorganization—a new dissipative structure.

The old pattern is broken.

The "felt shift" in Eugene Gendlin's focusing process, characterized by a sudden phase shift in the EEG's alpha harmonics, is probably the appearance of a new knowing—a new dissipative structure. Similar phase shifts in meditative states have been associated with subjective reports of insight.

A stuck thought pattern, an old paradigm, a compulsive behavior, a knee-jerk response . . . all of these are dissipative structures, capable of sudden enlargement. The new structure is like a larger paradigm. And the perturbation that provokes the new order in a dissipative structure is analogous to the crisis that helps force the shift to a new paradigm.

Again and again, the mandates of nature, repeated at all levels:

Molecules and stars, brainwaves and concepts, individuals and societies—all have the potential for transformation.

Transformation, like a vehicle on a downward incline, gathers momentum as it goes.

All wholes transcend their parts by virtue of internal coherence, cooperation, openness to input.

The higher on the evolutionary scale, the more freedom to reorganize. An ant lives out a destiny; a human being shapes one.

Evolution is a continuous breaking and forming to make new, richer wholes. Even our genetic material is in flux.

If we try to live as closed systems, we are doomed to regress.

If we enlarge our awareness, admit new information, and take advantage of the brain's brilliant capacity to integrate and reconcile, we can leap forward.

PSI: THE UNKNOWN IN PHYSICS AND PARAPSYCHOLOGY

To fully realize the extent to which nature's complexity transcends ordinary logic, one need only visit the never-never land of quantum physics or the parapsychology laboratories. In both theoretical physics and parapsychology, the Greek letter *psi* designates the unknown.

Jeremy Bernstein, a professor of physics at the Stevens Institute of Technology, said that he sometimes has the fantasy that it is 1905 and he is a professor of physics at the University of Berne.

> The phone rings and a person I have never heard of identifies himself as a patent examiner in the Swiss National Patent Office. He says that he has heard that I give lectures on electromagnetic theory and that he has developed some ideas which might interest me. "What sort of ideas?" I ask a bit superciliously.
>
> He begins discussing some crazy-sounding notions about space and time. Rulers contract when they are set in motion; a clock on the equator goes at a slower rate than the identical clock when it is placed at the North Pole; the mass of an electron increases with its velocity; whether or not two events are simultaneous depends on the frame of reference of the observer, and so on. How would I have reacted?
>
> Well, a great many of Albert Einstein's contemporaries would have hung up the phone. After all, in 1905 he didn't even have an academic job!

But a careful reading of his papers would have shown that they connected to what was known, Bernstein said. "A really novel genuine theory may appear at first sight to be quite crazy, but if it is any good it has this aspect of connectivity." It is not suspended in mid-air, and that distinguishes it from the purely crackpot.

Modern physics, letting itself out further and further into the unknown on that slender thread of connection, has revealed a reality that is very fluid, like the surrealistic melted clocks of Salvador Dali. Matter has only "a tendency to exist." There are no things, only connections. Only relationships. If matter collides, its energy is redistributed among other particles in a kaleidoscope of life and death, like Shiva's dance in Hindu mythology.

In place of a real and solid world, theoretical physics offers us a flickering web of events, relationships, potentialities. Particles make sudden transitions, "quantum leaps," behaving at times like units, yet mysteriously wavelike on other occasions. One current theory sees the universe as a "scattering matrix" in which there are no particles at all but only relationships between events.

At its primary level the universe seems to be paradoxically whole and undifferentiated, a seamlessness that *somehow* generates the intricate tapestry of our experience, a reality we cannot possibly visualize.

But mathematics can go where common sense cannot. Just as Prigogine formulated the mathematics to prove a strange, self-organizing, transcendent force in nature, so another mathematical proof threatens the underpinnings of post-Einsteinian physics, which was already beyond imagining for most of us.

This proof—Bell's theorem—was proposed in 1964 by J. S. Bell, a physicist working in Switzerland, and first confirmed experimentally in 1972. Physicist Henry Stapp, in a 1975 federal report, called it "the most profound discovery of science."

Bell's theorem was foreshadowed in 1935 when Einstein and two associates proposed an experiment they believed would demonstrate the fallacy of quantum logic, which Einstein found too uncertain for comfort. If the theory of quantum mechanics was correct, they said, then a change in the spin of one particle in a two-particle system would affect its twin simultaneously, even if the two had been widely separated in the meantime.

On the surface, the idea appeared absurd. How could two separated particles be thus connected? This challenge, later known as the Einstein-Podolsky-Rosen effect, did not refute quantum theory, as was intended. Instead it called attention to the bizarre nature of the subatomic world.

Which leads us to Bell's amazing theorem. Experiments show that if paired particles (which are identical twins in their polarity) fly apart and the polarity of one is changed by an experimenter, the other changes *instantaneously*. They remain mysteriously connected.

Bernard d'Espagnet, a physicist at the University of Paris, wrote in 1979, "The violation of Einstein's assumptions seems to imply that in some sense all these objects constitute an indivisible whole." This effect is probably not caused by a transfer of information, physicist Nick Herbert said, at least not in the usual sense. Rather it is "a simple consequence of the oneness of apparently separate objects . . . a quantum loophole through which physics admits not merely the possibility but the *necessity* of the mystic's unitary vision: 'We are all one.'"

Thoughtful physicists are struck by the curious parallels between their findings and ancient mystical descriptions of reality. These similarities were pointed out in *The Tao of Physics* by Fritjof Capra and *The Dancing Wu Li Masters* by Gary Zukav. Capra compared the organic, unified, and spiritual vision of reality in Eastern philosophy to the emerging paradigm of physics. Zukav's book takes its title from the Chinese expression for physics, *wu li*, which he translates as "patterns of organic energy."

"Bell's theorem not only suggests that the world is quite different than it seems," Zukav said, "it *demands* it. There is no question about it. Something very exciting is happening. Physicists have 'proved' rationally that our rational ideas about the world in which we live are profoundly deficient."

He notes the view of Geoffrey Chew, chairman of the physics department at the University of California at Berkeley: "Our current struggle [with advanced physics] may thus be only a foretaste of a completely new form of human intellectual endeavor, one that will not only lie outside physics but will not even be described as 'scientific.'"

In one sense, Zukav said, we may be approaching "the end of science." Even as we continue to seek understanding, we are learning to accept the limits of our reductionist methods. Only direct experience can give a sense of this nonlocal universe, this realm of connectedness. Enlarged awareness — as in meditation — may carry us past limits of our logic to more complete knowledge. The end of conventional science may mean "the coming of Western civilization, in its own time and in its own way, into the higher dimensions of human experience."

Many great physicists over the years have become deeply absorbed in the role of the mind in constructing reality. Schrödinger, for instance, remarked that exploring the relationship between brain and mind is the *only* important task of science. He once quoted the Persian mystic Aziz Nasafi:

The spiritual world is one single spirit who stands like unto
a light behind the bodily world and who, when any single
creature comes into being, shines through it as through a
window. According to the kind and size of the window,
less or more light enters the world.

Western thinking is still trying to objectify everything,
Schrödinger said. "It is in need of blood transfusion from Eastern thought." A Hindu sutra proclaims, "There is nothing in
the moving world but mind itself," a view echoed by physicist
John Wheeler: "May the universe in some strange sense be
'brought into being' by the vital act of participation?"

Niels Bohr, to symbolize his theory of complementarity, designed a coat of arms featuring the yin-yang symbol. The Taoist
saying, "The real is empty, and the empty is real," is not unlike
physicist Paul Dirac's statement, "All matter is created out of
some imperceptible substratum...nothingness, unimaginable
and undetectible. But it is a peculiar form of nothingness out of
which all matter is created."

The ultimate psi in physics remains unknowable. Reviewing
the big bang theory of the origins of the universe, Robert Jastrow, an astrophysicist who heads NASA's Goddard Institute
for Space Studies, pointed out that it is not exactly an explanation of cause. "If a scientist really examines the implications, he
would be traumatized. As usual, when the mind is faced with
trauma, it reacts by ignoring the implications—in science this is
called 'refusing to speculate'—or by trivializing the origin of the
world by calling it the Big Bang, as if the universe were merely
a firecracker."

Consider the enormousness of the problem: Science has
proved that the universe exploded into being at a certain
moment. It asks, what cause produced this effect? Who or
what put the matter and energy into the universe? Was the
universe created out of nothing or was it gathered together
out of pre-existing materials? And science cannot answer
these questions.

...It is not a matter of another year, another decade of
work, another measurement, or another theory. At this
moment it seems as though science will never be able to
raise the curtain on the mystery of creation.

Nature has no simple level, Prigogine pointed out. The

nearer we try to approach it, the greater the complexity we confront. In this rich, creative universe, the supposed laws of strict causality are almost caricatures of the true nature of change. There is "a more subtle form of reality, one that involves both laws and games, time and eternity.... Instead of the classical description of the world as an automaton, we return to the ancient Greek paradigm of the world as a work of art."

He and his associates in Brussels are now working on a concept he believes more important than the theory of dissipative structures—a new kind of uncertainty theory that applies to the everyday level of reality, not just in the realm of the very small and the very large. Predictable processes are altered by the unpredictable. Here, as in modern science in general, the key discoveries come as a surprise. "The impossible becomes possible."

Generating our world of apparent concreteness is a realm of unbroken wholeness; from that dimension where there is only potential we extract meaning—we sense, perceive, measure.

"Every phenomenon is unexpected," said Eugene Wigner, "and most unlikely until it has been discovered. And some of them remain unreasonable for a long time after they have been discovered."

Psychic phenomena—psi—are probably no less natural than the phenomena of subatomic physics but they are notoriously less predictable. And they are more threatening to many people. After all, we can disregard the eerie world of modern physics if we wish. It is one thing if an astrophysicist like Stephen Hawking of Cambridge University speaks of black holes "where space-time becomes so twisted up that it just comes to an end and all known laws of physics break down." We don't expect to encounter a black hole.

But it is quite another matter to acknowledge the unknown dimension in everyday life: the evidence for remote viewing (seeing at a distance, classically known as clairvoyance), telepathy (transfer of mental events), precognition (awareness of events in the future), psychokinesis (interaction of mind and matter), and synchronicity (meaningful coincidence, a composite of the other phenomena).

Except for synchronicity, these phenomena can be subjected to experimentation. Despite the unnaturalness of the laboratory setting, the importance of mental state, and the notorious elusiveness of psi, there is a mounting body of evidence that the phenomena irrefutably occur and that they can be facilitated by the psychotechnologies.

Human intention has been shown to interact with matter at a distance, affecting the particles in a cloud chamber, crystals, the rate of radioactive decay. An intention to "heal" has been demonstrated to alter enzymes, hemoglobin values, and the hydrogen-oxygen bond in water. The mode of transmission is unknown, just as there is a missing link between intention and biofeedback control and between suggestion and the brain chemistry involved in the placebo effect. Every human intention that results in physical action is, in effect, mind over matter. How consciousness and the physical world interact remains a mystery.

Once primarily the province of psychologists and psychiatrists, parapsychology has attracted a number of physicists in recent years.[7] Even so, theories on the mechanism of psi are sketchy, and most theories try instead to understand what helps or hinders the phenomena.

A recent survey of more than seven hundred parapsychological references reviewed a dizzying variety of approaches. Among the factors studied: effects of time and distance, forced choice, impulsivity, motivation, interpersonal factors, the experimenter effect, alterations of consciousness (dreams, hypnosis, biofeedback, drugs), brain correlates (density of alpha brainwaves, hemispheric specialization, brain injuries), personality profiles of low and high scorers (neuroticism, extraversion, creativity, psychosis), sex differences, age differences, birth order, belief, learning, decline effects, short-circuiting the ego, body language, responses in the autonomic nervous sys-

[7]Historically, many great scientists have been drawn to psi. Among the first officers of the Society for Psychical Research in Britain were three Nobel laureates: the discoverer of the electron, J.J. Thompson; the discoverer of argon, Lord Rayleigh (J.W. Strutt); and Charles Richet. William James, usually described as the father of American psychology, co-founded the American Society for Psychical Research. Among the Nobel laureates specifically interested in psi were Alexis Carrel, Max Planck, the Curies, Schrödinger, Charles Sherrington, and Einstein (who wrote the foreword for Upton Sinclair's book on telepathy, *Mental Radio*). Carl Jung and Wolfgang Pauli, a Nobel physicist, coauthored a theory about synchronicity. Pierre Janet, a great French scientist of the nineteenth century, actively investigated psi. Luther Burbank and Thomas Edison had a strong interest in the field.

Aquarian Conspirators surveyed (see Appendix) reported an extremely high level of belief in psi. Generally they had gone through a chronology of interest: first fascination, fear, or both; then avoidance of the phenomena as a distraction from the transformative process itself; and, finally, acceptance of them as natural, plausible, an extension of human creative powers and evidence of the essential unity of all life.

tem (changes in blood volume in capillaries, for example), and the effects of strobe lights.

Mind is invisible circuitry, tying us together. "So think as if your every thought were to be etched in fire upon the sky for all and everything to see," says the *Book of Mirdad*, "for so, in truth, it is." Psi is not a parlor game. The phenomena remind us that we have access to a source of transcendent knowing, a domain not limited by time and space.

FROM QUANTITY TO QUALITY: THE MISSING LINKS

In all of these scientific breakthroughs we discover qualitative shifts: transformations rather than gradual change. There are jumps—"missing links." For example:

The sudden shifts of brain activity observed in altered states of consciousness.

The gap between intention and physiological change in biofeedback . . . and between suggestion and analgesia in the placebo effect.

The suddenness of intuition—a jump to a solution with no clear logical steps in between. The right brain's gestalts, sudden wholes.

The "jumping genes" observed by molecular biologists. Mutations—transformations within the genetic code. The sudden appearances of new life forms in the course of evolution.

Quantum jumps in physics.

The transfer of information in psychic phenomena.

The shift of a dissipative structure to a higher order.

In our lives and in our cultural institutions we have been poking at qualities with tools designed to detect quantities. By what yardstick do you measure a shadow, a candle flame? What does an intelligence test measure? Where in the medical armamentarium is the will to live? How big is an intention? How heavy is grief, how deep is love?

We cannot quantify relationships, connectedness, transformation. Nothing in the scientific method can cope with the richness and complexity of qualitative shifts. In a transformative universe, history is instructive, but not necessarily predictive. As individuals, we are foolish if we set limits on our own or other people's potential based on past and present knowledge, including old science.

For those willing to listen, science itself is telling thrilling, open-ended mystery stories about a world rich beyond our imagining. Just as one who makes a clearing in the forest is increasing the periphery of contact with the unknown, we are only becoming wiser about the scope of the territory we have yet to explore.

A HOLOGRAPHIC WORLD

Some scientific discoveries are premature, molecular geneticist Gunther Stent observed in 1972. These intuitive or accidental discoveries are repressed or ignored until they can be connected to existing data. In effect, they await a context in which they make sense.

Gregor Mendel's discovery of the gene, Michael Polanyi's absorption theory in physics, and Oswald Avery's identification of DNA as the basic hereditary substance were ignored for years, even decades. Stent suggested that the existence of psychic phenomena was a similarly premature discovery, one that would not be appreciated by science, regardless of the data, until a conceptual framework had been established.

Recently a Stanford neuroscientist, Karl Pribram, proposed an all-encompassing paradigm that marries brain research to theoretical physics; it accounts for normal perception and simultaneously takes the "paranormal" and transcendental experiences out of the supernatural by demonstrating that they are part of nature.

The paradoxical sayings of mystics suddenly make sense in the radical reorientation of this "holographic theory." Not that Pribram was the least bit interested in giving credence to visionary insights. He was only trying to make sense of the data generated from his laboratory at Stanford, where brain processes in higher mammals, especially primates, have been rigorously studied.

Early in his career as a brain surgeon, Pribram worked under the famous Karl Lashley, who searched for thirty years for the elusive "engram"—the site and substance of memory. Lashley trained experimental animals, then selectively damaged portions of their brains, assuming that at some point he would scoop out the locus of what they had learned. Removing parts of the brain worsened their performance somewhat, but short of lethal brain damage, it was impossible to eradicate what they had been taught.

At one point Lashley said facetiously that his research proved that learning was not possible. Pribram participated in writing up Lashley's monumental research, and he was steeped in the mystery of the missing engram. How could memory be stored not in any one part of the brain but distributed throughout?

Later, when Pribram went to the Center for Studies in the Behavioral Sciences at Stanford,[8] he was still deeply troubled by the mystery that had drawn him into brain research: How do we remember? In the mid-sixties, he read a *Scientific American* article describing the first construction of a hologram, a kind of three-dimensional "picture" produced by lensless photography. Dennis Gabor invented holography in principle in 1947, a discovery that later earned him a Nobel prize, but the construction of a hologram had to await the invention of the laser.

The hologram is one of the truly remarkable inventions of modern physics—eerie, indeed, when seen for the first time. Its ghostlike image can be viewed from various angles, and it appears to be suspended in space. Its principle is well described by biologist Lyall Watson:

If you drop a pebble into a pond, it will produce a series of regular waves that travel outward in concentric circles. Drop two identical pebbles into the pond at different points and you will get two sets of similar waves that move towards each other. Where the waves meet, they will interfere. If the crest of one hits the crest of the other, they will work together and produce a reinforced wave of twice the normal height. If the crest of one coincides with the trough of another, they will cancel each other out and produce an isolated patch of calm water. In fact, all possible combinations of the two occur, and the final result is a complex arrangement of ripples known as an interference pattern.

Light waves behave in exactly the same way. The purest kind of light available to us is that produced by a laser, which sends out a beam in which all the waves are of one frequency, like those made by an ideal pebble in a perfect pond. When two laser beams touch, they produce an interference pattern of light and dark ripples that can be recorded on a photographic plate. And if one of the beams, instead of coming directly from the laser, is reflected first off an object such as a human face, the resulting pattern

[8]He worked on his landmark book, *Languages of the Brain*, in an office next door to Thomas Kuhn, who was writing *The Structure of Scientific Revolutions*.

will be very complex indeed, but it can still be recorded. The record will be a hologram of the face.

Light falls onto the photographic plate from two sources: from the object itself and from a reference beam, the light deflected by a mirror from the object onto the plate. The apparently meaningless swirls on the plate do not resemble the original object, but the image can be reconstituted by a coherent light source like a laser beam. The result is a 3-D likeness projected into space, at a distance from the plate.

If the hologram is broken, any piece of it will reconstruct the entire image.

Pribram saw the hologram as an exciting model for how the brain might store memory.[9] If memory is distributed rather than localized, perhaps it is holographic. Maybe the brain deals in interactions, interpreting bioelectric frequencies throughout the brain.

In 1966 he published his first paper proposing a connection. Over the next several years he and other researchers uncovered what appeared to be the brain's calculative strategies for knowing, for sensing. It appears that in order to see, hear, smell, taste, and so on, the brain performs complex calculations on the frequencies of the data it receives. Hardness or redness or the smell of ammonia are only frequencies when the brain encounters them. *These mathematical processes have little common-sense relationship to the real world as we perceive it.*

Neuroanatomist Paul Pietsch said, "The abstract principles of the hologram may explain the brain's most elusive properties." The diffuse hologram makes no more common sense than the brain. The whole code exists at every point in the medium. "Stored mind is not a *thing*. It is abstract relationships.... In the sense of ratios, angles, square roots, mind is a mathematic. No wonder it's hard to fathom."

Pribram suggested that the intricate mathematics might be performed via slow waves known to move along a network of fine fibers on the nerve cells. The brain may decode its stored memory traces the way a projected hologram decodes or deblurs its original image. The extraordinary efficiency of the holographic principle makes it attractive, too. Because the pat-

[9]Among those researchers who first suggested a tie between phenomena of consciousness and the holographic principle were Dennis Gabor, discoverer of holography; Ula Belas of Bell Telephone Laboratories; Dennis and Terence McKenna; physicists William Tiller and Evan Harris; biologist Lyall Watson; and inventors Itzhak Bentov and Eugene Dolgoff.

tern on a holographic plate has no space-time dimension, billions of bits of information can be stored in a tiny space—just as billions of bits are obviously stored in the brain.

But in 1970 or 1971, a distressing and ultimate question began troubling Pribram. If the brain indeed knows by putting together holograms—by mathematically transforming frequencies from "out there"—*who* in the brain is interpreting the holograms?

This is an old and nagging question. Philosophers since the Greeks have speculated about the "ghost in the machine," the "little man inside the little man" and so on. Where is the *I*—the entity that uses the brain?

Who does the actual knowing? Or, as Saint Francis of Assisi once put it, *"What we are looking for is what is looking."*

Lecturing one night at a symposium in Minnesota, Pribram mused that the answer might lie in the realm of gestalt psychology, a theory that maintains that what we perceive "out there" is the same as—*isomorphic* with—brain processes.

Suddenly he blurted out, "Maybe the *world* is a hologram!"

He stopped, a little taken aback by the implications of what he had said. Were the members of the audience holograms—representations of frequencies, interpreted by his brain and by one another's brains? If the nature of reality is *itself* holographic, and the brain operates holographically, then the world is indeed, as the Eastern religions have said, *maya:* a magic show. Its concreteness is an illusion.

Soon afterward he spent a week with his son, a physicist, discussing his ideas and searching for possible answers in physics. His son mentioned that David Bohm, a protégé of Einstein, had been thinking along similar lines. A few days later, Pribram read copies of Bohm's key papers urging a new order in physics. Pribram was electrified. *Bohm was describing a holographic universe.*

What appears to be a stable, tangible, visible, audible world, said Bohm, is an illusion. It is dynamic and kaleidoscopic—not really "there." What we normally see is the explicate, or *un*folded, order of things, rather like watching a movie. But there is an underlying order that is father to this second-generation reality. He called the other order implicate, or *en*folded. The enfolded order harbors our reality, much as the DNA in the nucleus of the cell harbors potential life and directs the nature of its unfolding.

Bohm describes an insoluble ink droplet in glycerine. If the fluid is stirred slowly by a mechanical device so that there is no diffusion, the droplet is eventually drawn into a fine thread that is distributed throughout the whole system in such a way that it is no longer even visible to the eye. If the mechanical device is then reversed, the thread will slowly gather together until it suddenly coalesces again into a visible droplet.

Before this coalescence takes place, the droplet can be said to be "folded into" the viscous fluid, while afterward it is unfolded again.

Next imagine that several droplets have been stirred into the fluid a different number of times and in different positions. If the ink drops are stirred continuously and fast enough, it will appear that a single permanently existing ink drop is continuously moving across the fluid. There is no such object. Other examples: a row of electric lights in a commercial sign that flashes off and on to give the impression of a sweeping arrow, or an animated cartoon, giving the illusion of continuous movement.

Just so, all apparent substance and movement are illusory. They emerge from another, more primary order of the universe. Bohm calls this phenomenon the *holomovement*.

Ever since Galileo, he says, we have been looking at nature through lenses; our very act of objectifying, as in an electron microscope, alters that which we hope to see. We want to find its edges, to make it sit still for a moment, when its true nature is in another order of reality, another dimension, where there are no *things*. It is as if we are bringing the "observed" into focus, as you would bring a picture into resolution, but the *blur* is a more accurate representation. The blur itself is the basic reality.

It occurred to Pribram that the brain may focus reality in a lenslike way, by its mathematical strategies. These mathematical transforms make objects out of frequencies. They make the blurred potential into sound and color and touch and smell and taste.

"Maybe reality isn't what we see with our eyes," Pribram says. "If we didn't have that lens—the mathematics performed by our brain—maybe we would know a world organized in the frequency domain. No space, no time—just events. Can reality be read out of that domain?"

He suggested that transcendental experiences—mystical states—may allow us occasional direct access to that realm. Certainly, subjective reports from such states often sound like descriptions of quantum reality, a coincidence that has led several physicists to speculate similarly. Bypassing our normal,

constricting perceptual mode—what Aldous Huxley called the
reducing valve—we may be attuned to the source or matrix of
reality.

And the brain's neural interference patterns, its mathematical processes, may be identical to the primary state of the universe. That is to say, our mental processes are, in effect, made
of the same stuff as the organizing principle. Physicists and
astronomers had remarked at times that the real nature of the
universe is immaterial but orderly. Einstein professed mystical
awe in the face of this harmony. Astronomer James Jeans said
that the universe is more like a great thought than a great
machine, and astronomer Arthur Eddington said, "The stuff of
the universe is mind-stuff." More recently, cyberneticist David
Foster described "an intelligent universe" whose apparent concreteness is generated by—in effect—cosmic data from an unknowable, organized source.

In a nutshell, the holographic supertheory says that *our brains
mathematically construct "hard" reality by interpreting frequencies
from a dimension transcending time and space. The brain is a hologram, interpreting a holographic universe.*

We are indeed participants in reality, observers who affect
what we observe.

In this framework, psychic phenomena are only by-products
of the simultaneous-everywhere matrix. Individual brains are
bits of the greater hologram. They have access under certain
circumstances to all the information in the total cybernetic system. Synchronicity—the web of coincidence that seems to have
some higher purpose or connectedness — also fits in with the
holographic model. Such meaningful coincidences derive from
the purposeful, patterned, organizing nature of the matrix.
Psychokinesis, mind affecting matter, may be a natural result
of interaction at the primary level. The holographic model
resolves one long-standing riddle of psi: the inability of instrumentation to track the apparent energy transfer in telepathy, healing, clairvoyance. If these events occur in a dimension transcending time and space, there is no need for energy
to travel from here to there. As one researcher put it, "There
isn't any *there*."

For years those interested in phenomena of the human mind
had predicted that a breakthrough theory would emerge; that it
would draw on mathematics to establish the supernatural as
part of nature.

The holographic model is such an integral theory catching all the wildlife of science and spirit. It may well be the paradoxical, borderless paradigm that our science had been crying for.

Its explanatory power enriches and enlarges many disciplines, making sense of old phenomena and raising urgent new questions. Implicit in the theory is the assumption that harmonious, coherent states of consciousness are more nearly attuned to the primary level of reality, a dimension of order and harmony. Such attunement would be hampered by anger, anxiety, and fear and eased by love and empathy. There are implications for learning, environments, families, the arts, religion and philosophy, healing and self-healing. What fragments us? What makes us whole?

Those descriptions of a sense of flow, of cooperating with the universe—in the creative process, in extraordinary athletic performances, and sometimes in everyday life—do they signify our union with the source?

The experiences reported so often on the Aquarian Conspiracy questionnaires, the hours and even months of "grace," when it seemed one was cooperating with the life source itself—were these instances of being in harmony with the primary level of reality? Millions are experimenting with the psychotechnologies. Are they creating a more coherent, resonant society, feeding order into the great social hologram like seed crystals? Perhaps this is the mysterious process of collective evolution.

The holographic model also helps explain the strange power of the *image*—why events are affected by what we imagine, what we visualize. An image held in a transcendental state may be made real.

Keith Floyd, a psychologist at Virginia Intermont College, said of the holographic possibility, "Contrary to what everyone knows is so, it may not be the brain that produces consciousness—but rather, consciousness that creates the appearance of the brain, matter, space, time, and everything else we are pleased to interpret as the physical universe."

Access to a domain transcending time and space might also account for the ancient intuitions about the nature of reality. Pribram points out that Leibniz, the seventeenth-century philosopher and mathematician, had postulated a universe of *monads*—units that incorporate the information of the whole. Interestingly, Leibniz discovered the integral calculus that made the invention of holography possible. He maintained that the exquisitely orderly behavior of light—*also* crucial to holography — indicated an underlying radical, patterned order of reality.

Ancient mystics also correctly described the function of the pineal gland centuries before science could confirm it. "How did ideas like this arise centuries before we had the tools to understand them?" Pribram asked. "Maybe in the holographic state—the frequency domain—four thousand years ago is the same as tomorrow."

Similarly, Bergson had said in 1907 that the ultimate reality is an underlying web of connection and that the brain screens out the larger reality. In 1929, Whitehead described nature as a great expanding nexus of occurrences beyond sense perception. We only imagine that matter and mind are different, when, in fact, they are interlocking.

Bergson maintained that artists, like mystics, have access to the *élan vital*, the underlying creative impulse. T. S. Eliot's poems are full of holographic images: "The still point of the turning world" that is neither flesh nor fleshless, neither arrest nor movement. "And do not call it fixity, where past and future are gathered. Except for the point, the still point/There would be no dance, and there is only the dance."

The German mystic Meister Eckhart had said that "God becomes and disbecomes." Rumi, the Sufi mystic, said, "Men's minds perceive second causes, but only prophets perceive the action of the First Cause."

Emerson suggested that we see "mediately, not directly," that we are colored and distorted lenses. Perhaps our "subject lenses" have a creative power, he said, and there are no real objects outside ourselves in the universe: the play and playground of all history may be only radiations from ourselves. A booklet published by the Theosophical Society in the 1930s described reality as a living matrix, "every mathematical point of which contains the potentialities of the whole...."

Teilhard believed that human consciousness can return to the point "where the roots of matter disappear from view." Reality has a "within," he said, as well as a "without." In the Don Juan books, Carlos Castaneda describes two dimensions that sound like the holographic primary and secondary dimensions: the powerful *nagual*, an indescribable void that contains everything, and the *tonal*, a reflection of that indescribable unknown filled with order.

In *The Man Who Gave Thunder to the Earth*, Nancy Wood's retelling of the Taos stories:

The Second World is the true center of life, the Old Man said. It is where anything can happen, for all things are possible there. It is a world of perhaps and why not.... One Way is always there and One Hand is always there. ... The Second World is a world of untying the knot ... the world of having no name, no address.... It is where there are no answers even though new questions are always asked.

Arthur Koestler described "reality of the third order," which contains phenomena that cannot be apprehended or explained on either a sensory or a conceptual level, "and yet occasionally invade them [these levels] like spiritual meteors piercing the primitive's vaulted sky."

In an ancient sutra of Patanjali, knowledge of "the subtle, the hidden, and the distant" is said to arise by looking with the *pravritti*—a Sanskrit term meaning "before the wave." This description parallels the idea of an apparently concrete world generated by interference patterns, by waves.

And, this extraordinary ancient description of a holographic reality is found in a Hindu sutra:

In the heaven of Indra there is said to be a network of pearls so arranged that if you look at one you see all the others reflected in it. In the same way, each object in the world is not merely itself but involves every other object, and in fact *is* in every other object.

The brain he was raised on was a computer, Pribram told a San Diego audience in 1976, but "the brain we know now allows for the experiences reported from spiritual disciplines."

How brain processes can be altered to allow direct experience of the frequency domain is still a conjecture. It may involve a known perceptual phenomenon—the "projection" that permits us to experience the full, three-dimensional stereophonic sound as if the sound emanates from a point midway between two speakers instead of coming from two distinct sources. Research has shown that the kinesthetic senses can be similarly affected; tapping on both hands at a particular frequency eventually causes the person to feel a third hand midway between. Pribram has suggested possible involvement of a deep brain region that has been the site of pathological disturbances, of déjà vu, and seems involved in the "consciousness without a content" of mystical experience. Some alternation of frequency and the phase relationships in these structures may be the open sesame for transcendental states.

Mystical experience, Pribram says, is no stranger than many other phenomena in nature, such as the selective derepression of DNA to form first one organ, then another. "If we get ESP or paranormal phenomena—or nuclear phenomena in physics—it simply means that we are reading out of some other dimension at that time. In our ordinary way, we can't understand that."

Pribram acknowledges that the model is not easily assimilated; it too radically overturns our previous belief systems, our commonsense understanding of things and time and space. A new generation will grow up accustomed to holographic thinking; and to ease their way, Pribram suggests that children should learn about paradox in grade school, since the new scientific findings are always fraught with contradiction.

Productive scientists must be as ready to defend spirit as data. "This is science as it was originally conceived: the pursuit of understanding," says Pribram. "The days of the cold-hearted, hard-headed technocrat appear to be numbered."

Pribram engagingly admits at times, "I hope you realize that I don't *understand* any of this." The admission generally provokes a sigh of relief in even the most scientific audiences.

The wide relevance of Pribram's synthesis of his ideas with those of David Bohm, like Prigogine's model, has stimulated excitement among social scientists, philosophers, and artists.[10] Symposia have been organized for interdisciplinary groups around the country and for government officials in Washington. In a workshop at one invitational conference, Pribram discussed the concepts with five Nobel laureates.

There is surely a message in these rapidly converging scientific revolutions: in physics, psi, the interaction of mind and body, the evolutionary thrust, the brain's two ways of knowing and its potential for transcendent awareness.

The more we learn about the nature of reality, the more plainly we see the unnatural aspects of our environment—and our lives. Out of ignorance, out of arrogance, we have been

[10]How does the holographic theory fit with the theory of dissipative structures? Pribram says the dissipative structures may represent the means of unfolding from the implicate order, the way it is manifested in time and space.

Meanwhile, Apolinario Nazarea of the University of Texas at Austin expressed "quiet optimism" that theoretical work on dissipative structures may "vindicate in its main outlines the so-called holographic theory...though from a different direction."

working against the grain. Because we have not understood the brain's ability to transform pain and disequilibrium, we have dampened it with tranquilizers or distracted it with whatever was at hand. Because we have not understood that wholes are more than the sum of their parts, we have assembled our information into islands, an archipelago of disconnected data. Our great institutions have evolved in virtual isolation from one another.

Not realizing that our species evolved in cooperation, we have opted for competition in work, school, relationships. Not understanding the body's ability to reorganize its internal processes, we have drugged and doctored ourselves into bizarre side effects. Not understanding our societies as great organisms, we have manipulated them into "cures" worse than the ailments.

Sooner or later, if human society is to evolve—indeed, if it is to survive—we must match our lives to our new knowledge. For too long, the Two Cultures—the esthetic, feeling humanities and cool, analytical science — have functioned independently, like the right and left hemispheres of a split-brain patient. We have been the victims of our collective divided consciousness.

Novelist Lawrence Durrell said in *Justine*, "Somewhere in the heart of experience there is an order and a coherence which we might surprise if we were attentive enough, loving enough, or patient enough. Will there be time?" Perhaps, at last, Science can say yes to Art.

CHAPTER 7

Right Power

There are no passengers on Spaceship Earth.
Everybody's crew.
> —MARSHALL McLUHAN

I will act as if what I do makes a difference.
> —WILLIAM JAMES

In C. P. Cavafy's poem, "Expecting the Barbarians," the populace and emperor are assembled in the public square, awaiting the invasion of the Barbarians. The legislators have abandoned the senate because the Barbarians will make the law when they come. The orators have prepared no speeches because Barbarians don't appreciate fluency and fine phrases.

But suddenly the crowd becomes solemn and despondent; the streets empty quickly. Word has come from the frontier: *The Barbarians are not coming; there are no more Barbarians.*

"And now, without the Barbarians," the poet asks, "what is to become of us? After all, they would have been a kind of solution."

An overwhelming, mysterious "they" has been the perennial excuse for apathy. Our fates will be determined by the Barbarians, the establishment, death and taxes, vested interests, red tape, machines. But something is happening to people now—a change of mind—and, as we shall see, it is disrupting the old truisms of government and politics in many ways, both subtle and dramatic. It has altered the flow of personal power: between men and women, parents and children, doctors and

189

patients, teachers and students, employers and employees, "experts" and lay people.

"A new science of politics is indispensable to a new world," Tocqueville said. The Aquarian Conspiracy assumes that the reverse is also true. A new world—a new perspective on reality—is indispensable to a new politics. "A turning of the mind," Huxley called it. The very sense of reality must be transformed, Theodore Roszak said. It has variously been called a new metaphysic, "the politics of consciousness," "New Age politics," "the politics of transformation."

This chapter is about politics in the broadest sense. It is about the emergence of a new kind of leader, a new definition of power, a dynamic power inherent in networks, and the rapidly growing constituency that can make all the difference.

As a culture, we have been ambivalent about power. We use phrases like power-mad, power-crazed, power-hungry, power brokers. Those with power are seen as ruthless, single-minded, lonely.

Yet clearly power—which derives from the Latin *potere*, "to be able"—is energy. Without power there is no movement. Just as personal transformation empowers the individual by revealing an inner authority, social transformation follows a chain reaction of personal change.

In the spirit of the Eightfold Path of Buddha, with its injunctions about Right Livelihood, Right Speech, and so on,[1] we might also think in terms of Right Power—power used not as a battering ram or to glorify the ego but in service to life. *Appropriate* power.

Power is a central issue in social and personal transformation. Our sources and uses of power set our boundaries, give form to our relationships, even determine how much we let ourselves liberate and express aspects of the self. More than party registration, more than our purported philosophy or ideology, personal power defines our politics.

"The new person creates the new collectivity," said political scientist Melvin Gurtov, "and the new collectivity creates—is— the new politics." The changing political paradigm concedes that you cannot sort out the individual from the society, nor can you separate "politics" from the people who engage in it.

The person and society are yoked, like mind and body. Arguing which is more important is like debating whether oxygen or hydrogen is the more essential property of water. Yet the debate has raged on for centuries. After tracing the philosophical

[1]The eight: Right Belief, Right Intention, Right Speech, Right Action, Right Livelihood, Right Endeavoring, Right Mindfulness, Right Concentration.

history of the self-versus-society issue, ranging from Plato to Kant, Hegel, and Marx, Martin Buber pointed out that one can never choose. Self and society are inseparable. *Eventually, anyone concerned with the transformation of the individual must engage in social action.*

"If we attempt to grow alone," Gurtov said, "we ensure that the oppressiveness of the system eventually will close in around us. If we grow together, the system itself must change."

POLITICAL CRISIS AND TRANSFORMATION

The new political paradigm is emerging in a growing consensus described by a Canadian social analyst, Ruben Nelson, as "the literature of crisis and transformation." Although this literature expresses the situation in a variety of metaphors and with varying degrees of desperation, its essence is as follows:

The Crisis: Our institutions—especially our governing structures—are mechanistic, rigid, fragmented. The world isn't working.

The Prescription: We must face our pain and conflict. Until we quit denying our failures and muffling our uneasiness, until we confess our bewilderment and alienation, we can't take the next and necessary steps.

The political system needs to be *transformed*, not *reformed*. We need something else, not just something more. Economist Robert Theobald said, "We are engaged, if the transformational thinker is correct, in a process which has no parallel in human history—*an attempt to change the whole of a culture through a conscious process.*" In a report commissioned by the Office of Technology Assessment, an advisory arm of Congress, Theobald said, "It is impossible to change one element in a culture without altering all of them."

More quickly than we can comfortably manage, we are called upon to devise, discover, and refine new alternatives. How much easier it is to calculate the wrong turns we have made than to spy out truer roads!

Our insights into human needs and capacities have changed more rapidly, especially through science, than our social structures. Were we to suddenly confront extraterrestrial beings, we would no doubt be awed, wondering how to communicate with them and what they want of us. In this case, it is the image of a new human being that is alien. Seeing patterns and possibilities we have not seen before, we are restless.

AUTARCHY—THE GOVERNING SELF

If we had to restructure a society with the old tactics (organization, propaganda, political pressure, reeducation), it would seem a hopelessly large task, like reversing the spin of the planet. Yet personal revolutions can change institutions. Individuals, after all, *are* the components of these institutions. Government, politics, medicine, and education are not actual things but the ongoing actions of people—making laws, running for office, voting, lobbying, seeking and giving medical treatment, planning curricula, and so on.

Autarchy is government by the self. The idea that social harmony springs ultimately from the character of individuals appears throughout history. According to Confucian writings, wise individuals, wanting good government, looked first within, seeking precise words to express their hitherto-unvoiced yearnings, "the tones given off by the heart." Once they were able to verbalize the intelligence of the heart they disciplined themselves. Order within the self led first to harmony within their own households, then the state, and finally the empire.

The discoveries of transformation inevitably alter our perceptions of power. The discovery of freedom, for instance, means little if we are not empowered to act, to be free *for* something, not just *from* something. As fear falls away, we are less afraid of power's Siamese twin, responsibility. There is less certainty about what is right for others. With an awareness of multiple realities, we lose our dogmatic attachment to a single point of view. A new sense of connection with others promotes social concern. A more benign view of the world makes others seem less threatening; enemies disappear. There is a commitment to process rather than programs. It matters a great deal how we accomplish our ends. We can now translate intention into action, vision into actuality, without intrigue or manipulation.

Power flows from an inner center, a mysterious sanctuary more secure than money, name, or achievement. In discovering our autonomy, we become very busy for a while, like a newly solvent musician who had hocked his instruments at pawnshops all over town and can't even recall their addresses. We are astonished to find out how freely, even absent-mindedly, we had surrendered so much that really matters, and, conversely, how often we trespassed on the autonomy of others. The power over one's life is seen as a birthright, not a luxury. And we wonder how we could ever have thought otherwise.

THE POLITICS OF FEAR AND DENIAL

"He had won the victory over himself," says the concluding line of George Orwell's grim novel, *1984*. "He loved Big Brother." Just as hostages sometimes become fond of their abductors, we become attached to the factors that imprison us: our habits, customs, the expectations of others, rules, schedules, the state. Why do we give away our power or never claim it at all? Perhaps so that we can avoid decisions and responsibility. We are seduced by pain-avoidance, conflict-avoidance.

In Colin Wilson's science-fiction novel, *The Mind Parasites*, the protagonist and his associates discover that human consciousness has been victimized, dragged down, and intimidated by a strange parasite that has been feeding on it, sapping its power, for centuries. Those who become aware of the existence of these mind parasites can get rid of them—a dangerous, painful undertaking, but possible. Free of the mind parasites, they are the first truly free human beings, elated and enormously powerful.

Just so, our natural power is sapped by the parasites of the centuries: fear, superstition, a view of reality that reduces life's wonders to creaking machinery. If we starve these parasitic beliefs they will die. But we rationalize our fatigue, our inertia; we deny that we are haunted.

Sometimes an individual's sense of impotence is justified; certainly there are vicious cycles of deprivation and lack of opportunity that make it difficult for some to break free. But most of us are passive because our awareness is constricted. The energy of our "passenger" consciousness is continuously drained off to divert us from all we feel too frightened to handle consciously. So we acquiesce, deny, conform.

"Our choice," said Ruben Nelson in *Illusions of Urban Man*, published by the Canadian government, "is between the painful but confidence-instilling process of coming to know who and where we are ... and the immensely appealing but finally empty alternative of continuing to drift, of acting as if we know what we are doing when both the mounting evidence and our most honest fears indicate that we do not.... In government, as in other relationships, we have the capacity to deceive ourselves, to shape the realities by which we live, so that our prime focus is on our comfort rather than the truth...."

Government itself is an awesome strategy for avoiding pain and conflict. For a considerable price, it relieves us of responsibilities, performing acts that would be as unsavory for most of us as butchering our own beef. As our agent, the government can bomb and tax. As our agent, it can relieve us of the responsibilities once borne face to face by the community: caring for the young, the war-wounded, the aged, the handicapped. It extends our impersonal benevolence to the world's needy, relieving our collective conscience without uncomfortable first-hand involvement. It takes our power, our responsibility, *our consciousness*.

Warren Bennis, former president of the University of Cincinnati, told of coming to work one day to find his office crowded with distraught students. Two beautiful trees had been chopped down to widen a campus driveway.

He followed the trail of blame: The man who cut the trees worked for a local contractor who was hired by the landscape architect to carry out the design of the landscape architect; the architect worked for the director of planning, whose boss was the head of the physical plant, supervised by the vice-president for management and finance, responsible to the university building committee, which reports to the executive vice-president. "When I called them all together, they numbered twenty, and they were innocents all. All of us. Bureaucracies are beautiful mechanisms for the evasion of responsibility and guilt."

Bennis categorized such evasions as "the pornography of everyday life." Just as pornography is a mechanical, distant substitute for loving sex, so a bureaucrat's fragmented decision-making is removed from reality. Our leaders "sound like they are talking through a plate-glass window."

The failure of other social institutions has caused us to heap even more responsibility on government, the most unwieldy institution of all. We have relinquished more and more autonomy to the state, forcing government to assume functions once performed by communities, families, churches—*people*. Many social tasks have reverted to government by default, and the end result has been creeping paralysis—unreality.

Tocqueville regarded the surrender of responsibility in a democracy as a danger. "Extreme centralization of government ultimately enervates society," he said over a century and a half ago. The very benefits of a democracy, its freedoms, can lead to a kind of privatization of interests. Inhabitants of a democracy lead such busy, excited lives, "so full of wishes and work, that hardly any energy remains to each individual for public life."

This dangerous tendency not only leads them to avoid participation in government but also to dread any perturbation of the peace. "The love of public tranquility is frequently the only passion which these nations retain. . . ." A democratic government will increase its power simply by the fact of its permanence, Tocqueville predicted. "Time is on its side. Every incident befriends it. . . . The older a democratic community is, the more centralized will its government become."

These bureaucracies would create their own gentle tyranny, he warned, one that had never before existed in the world. "The thing itself is new. Since I cannot name it, I must attempt to define it." When a great multitude seek largely after pleasures, they act as if their own children and close friends are the whole of mankind. They become strangers to their fellow citizens. No matter how physically close they may be, they do not see or touch those outside their immediate circles. Each citizen then exists in and for himself and his close kindred alone; *he has lost his country*.

Above the citizens stands an immense, mild, paternal power that keeps them in perpetual childhood. A hundred years before Orwell, Tocqueville foresaw Big Brother:

> [It] is the sole agent of happiness; it provides for their security, foresees and supplies their necessities, facilitates their pleasures, manages their principal concerns, directs their industry, regulates the descent of property, and subdivides their inheritances—what remains, but to spare them all the care of thinking and the trouble of living?
>
> Thus every day renders the exercise of free agency less useful . . . it circumscribes the will within a narrower range.
>
> It covers the surface of society with a network of small complicated rules, minute and uniform, through which the most original minds and the most energetic characters cannot penetrate. . . . The will of man is not shattered but softened, bent, and guided.
>
> Such a power does not tyrannize but it compresses, enervates, extinguishes, and stupefies a people. The nation is nothing better than a flock of timid and industrious animals of which the government is the shepherd.

Tocqueville had anticipated the paternal role of government and our other large hierarchical institutions (corporations, churches, hospitals, schools, labor unions). By their very structure, these institutions breed fragmentation, conformity, amorality. They expand their powers while losing sight of their original mandate. Like a great linear half-brain, amputated from feeling, they are unable to see whole. They leech the life and significance from the body politic.

Whether the rationale is capitalism, socialism, or Marxism, the focusing of great central power in a society is unnatural, neither flexible enough nor dynamic enough to respond to the fluctuating needs of people, especially the need for creative participation.

Sometimes, as George Cabot Lodge said, we also engage in a kind of nostalgic wishful thinking. We pretend to live by our lost myths like competition and Manifest Destiny and frontier individualism and Gross National Product. But on another level, we experience cognitive dissonance. We know desperately well that all nations are interdependent, that self-sufficiency is a hollow threat. We know, too, that corporations have evolved into powerful, semi-regulated little states bearing almost no resemblance to the "free enterprise" we say we cherish. Politicians, labor, and management struggle with economic realities on the one hand and deny them barefaced on the other, like the split-brain patients in the laboratory, caught between two worlds.

POLITICAL PARADIGM SHIFTS

The pending transformation from a seventeenth-century sociopolitical paradigm to a new framework is an earthquake for our institutions, Lodge said, for their legitimacy dies with the dying ideology.

Thinking about the crisis of our institutions in terms of an impending sociopolitical paradigm shift can be reassuring and even illuminating, for it places our current stress and trouble in the perspective of historic transformation.

A community of people—a *society*—runs its affairs within an agreed-upon form, a *government*. Just as the established scientific paradigm provides for "normal science," so the government and prevailing social customs provide for the normal transactions of a society. *Politics* is the exercise of power within this consensus.

Just as scientists inevitably come across facts that contradict the existing paradigm, so individuals within a society begin to experience anomalies and conflicts: an unequal distribution of power, an abridgement of freedoms, unjust laws or practices. Like a community of established scientists, the society at first ignores or denies these inherent contradictions. As tension arises, it tries to reconcile them within the existing system by elaborate rationales.

If this conflict is too intense or focused to be suppressed, a revolution eventually occurs in the form of a *social movement*. The old consensus is broken, and freedoms are extended. In American history this is best seen in the expansion of the paradigm of suffrage. First, enfranchisement was extended to propertied white males, then to all white male citizens, then to male citizens of all races, eventually to citizens of both sexes over the age of twenty-one, and then to all citizens over the age of eighteen.

A political paradigm shift might be said to occur when the new values are assimilated by the dominant society. These values then become social dogma to members of a new generation, who marvel that anyone could ever have believed otherwise. Yet in their midst new conflicts and ideas will arise, and they will be denied, ignored, even repressed, and on and on.

The irrational pattern of human behavior repeats itself again and again, individually and collectively. Even when our old forms are failing miserably, even when they cannot handle the problems of the day, they are fiercely defended; those who challenge them are derided.

Generation after generation, humankind fights to preserve the status quo, maintaining "better the devil you know than the devil you don't know," a bit of folk cynicism that assumes the unknown to be dangerous. We use "enemy skills" against change—to borrow Virginia Satir's phrase—failing to see that all growth depends on the capacity to transform. Amidst the flux of the natural world, we cling to the familiar and resist transformation. "Faced with having to change our views or prove that there is no need to do so," John Kenneth Galbraith said, "most of us get busy on the proof."

If we are to break out of this pattern, if we are to be liberated from our personal and collective history, we must learn to identify it—to see the ways of discovery and innovation, to overcome our discomfort with and resistance to the new, and to recognize the rewards of cooperating with change.

Thomas Kuhn was by no means the first to point out this pattern. It was discussed very specifically a century earlier by the English political philosopher, John Stuart Mill. Every age, he said, has held opinions that subsequent generations found not only false but absurd. He warned his nineteenth-century contemporaries that many ideas then prevalent would be rejected by future ages. Therefore they should welcome the questioning of all ideas, even those that seemed most obviously true, like Newton's philosophy! The best safeguard of ideas is "a standing invitation to the whole world to prove them unfounded."

If all of mankind minus one held an opinion, he said, and that one believed otherwise, the others would have no more right to silence him than he would to silence the majority. Mill emphasized that his point was not moral but practical. A society's suppression of new ideas robs the society itself. "We must neglect nothing that could give the truth a chance of reaching us."

He took issue with those who maintained that it did no harm to persecute ideas because—if they were true—nothing could obscure their rightness. Mill pointed out that many important ideas had surfaced several times and their exponents had been persecuted before they were rediscovered in a more tolerant age. Although historically, Europe advanced only when it broke the yoke of old ideas, most people continued to act as if "new truths may have been desirable once, but we have quite enough of them now." These new truths—"heresies"—smoldered among the few, Mill said, rather than blazing into the whole culture. Fear of heresy is more dangerous than heresy, for it deprives a people of "the free and daring speculation which would strengthen and enlarge minds."

Many political philosophers pondered this problem of popular resistance to new and strange ideas. They called it "the tyranny of the majority," the tendency of societies, even the most liberal, to suppress free thinking. This is the paradox of freedom: Anyone who comes to treasure autonomy must grant it to others, and the only means of collective self-determination is majority rule, which may then endanger freedom itself.

Revolutionary thinkers do not believe in single revolutions. They see change as a way of life. Jefferson, Mill, Tocqueville, and many others were concerned about creating an environment hospitable to change within a relatively stable political system. They wanted governments in which healthy unrest would make for continuous renewal, in which freedoms would be continually enlarged and extended. Thoreau, for example, looked for a form of government beyond democracy, one in which individual conscience would be respected by the state as "a higher and different power," the context for all authority.

Society puts its free spirits in prison, he said, when instead it should "cherish its wise minority." But there is a way out: Anyone who discovers a truth becomes a majority of one, a qualitatively different force from the uncommitted majority. In their unwillingness to practice the virtues they preached, Thoreau found the inhabitants of his town "a distinct race from me." Jailed for refusing to pay taxes because he opposed the war against Mexico, Thoreau observed that even behind walls of stone and mortar he was freer than those who had jailed him. "I was not born to be forced. I will breathe after my own fashion. They only can force me who obey a higher law than I."

If all of those who opposed slavery or the war would refuse to pay their taxes, he said in his famous essay on civil disobedience, the state—faced with full jails and diminishing funds—would have to relent. This would create a peaceful revolution.

"Cast your whole vote, not a strip of paper merely, but your whole influence. A minority is powerless while it conforms to the majority . . . but it is irresistible when it clogs by its whole weight. . . . Let your life be a counter friction to stop the machine."

Gandhi carried the concept of the powerful committed minority into the twentieth century, first gaining recognition of the rights of Indians living in South Africa and then achieving India's independence from British domination. "It is a superstitious and ungodly thing to believe that an act of a majority binds a minority," he said. "It is not numbers that count but quality. . . . I do not regard the force of numbers as necessary in a just cause."

The revolutionary principle introduced by Gandhi resolves the paradox of freedom. He called it *satyagraha*, "soul force" or "truth force." Satyagraha was essentially misunderstood in the West, described as "passive resistance," a term Gandhi disavowed because it suggests weakness, or "non-violence," which was just one of its components. As educator Timothy Flinders said, to call satyagraha passive resistance is like calling light nondarkness; it does not describe the positive energy in the principle.

Satyagraha derives its power from two apparently opposite attributes: fierce autonomy and total compassion. It says, in effect: "I will not coerce you. Neither will I be coerced by you. If you behave unjustly, I will not oppose you by violence (body-force) but by the force of truth—the integrity of my beliefs. My integrity is evident in my willingness to suffer, to endanger myself, to go to prison, even to die if necessary. But I will not cooperate with injustice.

"Seeing my intention, sensing my compassion and my openness to your needs, you will respond in ways I could never manage by threat, bargaining, pleading, or body-force. Together we can solve the problem. *It* is our opponent, not each other."

Satyagraha is the strategy of those who reject solutions that compromise the freedom or integrity of any participant. Gandhi always said it is the weapon of the strong because it requires heroic restraint and the courage to forgive. He turned the whole idea of power upside down. When he visited the mountain hideout of Indian militants and saw their guns, he said, "You must be very frightened."

Satyagraha, by whatever name, is an attitude that removes politics from the old territory of confrontation, deal-making, seduction, and game-playing, into a new arena of candor, shared humanness, a search for understanding. It transforms conflict at its source, the hearts of the participants. It is an environment of acceptance in which people can change without feeling defeated. Those who use it must be vigilant and flexible, looking for truth even in the position of the opponent.[2] Erik Erikson said of Gandhi that he "could help others discard costly defenses and denials.... Insight and discipline can disarm, or give a power stronger than all arms."

[2]The alliances of groups protesting nuclear power have adapted Gandhi's ideas to their cause. Those who wish to participate in their demonstrations undergo a weekend training seminar in nonviolent political action, then are assigned to small "affinity groups." These groups, typically comprised of five men and five women, are free to create their own form of protest within the larger demonstration.

Satyagraha requires an openness to the truth in whatever form it may appear. A brochure of the Alliance for Survival notes that "truth and the sense of justice reside in every person. We are not the incarnation of good while Pacific Gas & Electric Company officials are the incarnation of evil. Just as we have injustice in us, so they have justice in them."

All actions must be free of the attempt to humiliate, injure, or subjugate, the leaflet warns. "Such actions only serve to harden and justify the opposition's position against us. That is why the nonviolent take upon themselves suffering and hardships. By so doing we open the heart of our adversary and stir the conscience of the indifferent." The goal must be more than winning the fight against nuclear power. "Our goal must be a thorough cultural revolution. So we must be careful not to sacrifice what we believe to be good in order to stop nuclear power."

The spirit of nonviolence must be reflected in leaflets, interviews, the tone and phrasing of publications, relations with utility officials, the running of meetings, interpersonal relationships. "All signs of defiance and contempt defeat our purpose. The closed-fist salute, obscene or nearly obscene chants, and rhetorical diatribes against the government: are these really anything more than signs of our own frustration and impotence? The strong-hearted have no need for anything more than love."

Satyagraha works silently and apparently slowly, Gandhi said, "but in reality, there is no force in the world so direct or so swift." It is an old idea, as old as the hills, he said, and he and his friends had merely experimented with it. "Those who believe in the simple truths I have laid down can propagate them only by living them." Start where you are, he told his followers. Thoreau had said the same thing: "It matters not how small the beginning may seem."

LEADERSHIP AND TRANSFORMATION

James MacGregor Burns, political scientist and Pulitzer-prize-winning historian, used Gandhi as an example of "transforming leadership," leadership as a process of continuous change and growth. The true leader, as Burns defined it, is not a mere "power wielder" eager to accomplish personal objectives. *The true leader senses and transforms the needs of followers*.

> Keep in mind that I have a different view of followers than most people do. I don't see followers simply as persons holding a collection of static opinions. I see them as having levels of needs.... The effective leader mobilizes new, "higher" needs in his followers.
> The *truly* great or creative leaders do something more— they induce new, more activist tendencies in their followers. They arouse in them hopes and aspirations and expectations.... Ultimately they arouse *demands* which are easily politicized and even turned back onto the leaders who arouse them.

In this engagement with their followers, the leaders are also transformed. They may even reverse roles with followers, as teachers learn from students.

By Burns's definition, dictators cannot be true leaders because, by suppressing the feedback from followers, they interrupt the dynamics of the relationship. No longer transformed by the changing needs of the people, dictators cannot foster further growth. Leader-follower relationships include parent and child, coach and athlete, teacher and student, and so on. Many parents, coaches, and teachers are not true leaders but only power wielders. Transforming leadership cannot be a one-way street.

Historically, leaders have sometimes inspired a surprisingly high-minded response from constituents. Burns cites as an example the state conventions in the 1780s that ratified the United States Constitution. Despite a poorly educated populace and poor communications, the conventions focused on such issues as the need for a bill of rights, questions of the distribution of power, representation. "That is a superb example of the capacity of leaders *and* followers to rise above the belly, to the level of the brain or perhaps even the soul," Burns said.

Many revolutions succeeded despite limited popular support in the beginning, he said, "because the leaders engaged their followers so intensely that attitudes were transformed, consciousness was aroused." True leadership not only helps satisfy our present needs. . . . It awakens us to deeper dissatisfactions, hungers. By definition, you can only "raise consciousness" about something that is true. Propaganda, on the other hand, can be a lie. The difference between an authentic leader, making us aware of inarticulate needs and conflicts, and a power wielder is like the difference between a guide and a hard-sell advertiser.

The true leader fosters a paradigm shift in those who are ready. But transforming leaders know that you cannot "teach" or "help" others to higher awareness in the same way you might teach them to prepare tax forms. You can seduce people into direct experiences, you can embody freedom and aliveness as an example, but you cannot *convince* anyone to change.

Nor do the most effective leaders take credit for changes they help to elicit. As Lao-tse said, leadership is best when the people say, "We did it ourselves."

As soon as power is localized, as soon as attention centers on an individual, the coherence and energy in a movement is diminished. Sensing when to assume leadership and when to pull back is not easy. Like learning to ride a bicycle, it takes some falling over and a constant readjustment of balance. But people *can* coalesce into self-organizing groups to powerful effect. And they are devising ways to govern themselves without determining a boss or establishing a clear agenda. Such self-organizing groups are the fabric of the Aquarian Conspiracy. Even individuals accustomed to running large institutions can easily fit into such a format.

For example, a meeting at a country retreat in a southern state in early December 1978: The fourteen men and six women who attended included a congressman; the heads of founda-

tions in Washington, New York, and California; a former presidential speechwriter; the dean of an Ivy League college; the
retired dean of a medical school; a Canadian policymaker; the
owner of a major-league baseball team; the director and the
assistant director of a famous think tank; an artist; a publisher;
and three federal policymakers. Most did not know each other.

They had been invited by a letter that explained that, despite
their diverse backgrounds, they had something in common:

> We tend to share a conviction that this nation, and indus-
> trialized society in general, is experiencing profound trans-
> formation. We perceive that the next decade could be
> perilous if we fail to understand the nature and tran-
> scendent potential of the transformation.
>
> We agree that at the heart of this transformation is a
> change in the basic social paradigm, including fundamen-
> tal beliefs and values underlying the present form of the
> industrial economy. In our own positions in government,
> business, education, or professional life, we sense a deep
> need for the society to find its spiritual moorings, its sense
> of destiny, of right direction.
>
> We seek the support and comradeship of others of like
> mind, confident that when minds are joined in common
> search and purpose, the effect is amplified. We recognize
> that our country was guided in its initial decades by this
> kind of joining of minds in common purpose.
>
> It is in keeping with these shared convictions that the
> meeting be quite unstructured. There will be no chairper-
> son. There is no agenda. There will be no speeches. Simply
> come prepared to share your deepest hopes and concerns.
> We have no specific expectations for what may emerge
> from this meeting.

After dinner the first evening, the attendees were asked to
introduce themselves one by one. What had started as a simple
formality became the agenda for that night and part of the
following morning; the process became the program. Almost
like tribal storytellers around a fire, they told their tales of
power and of transformation, intensely personal and moving
narratives. Defenseless and matter of fact, they talked about
their fears and successes, their despair and disillusionment, the
ways in which life's blows had often proved blessings, turning
them toward a more rewarding path. Strangers who trusted

each other immediately, they recounted the ways in which the society's most sought-after prizes had failed them. At some point each had experienced a profound shift in perception, often at a time of personal trauma. Each was overtaken by deeper, more intense needs. Life became a spiritual quest, a joyful, mysterious search for meaning, marked in most cases by an accelerating occurrence of coincidences, events that seemed significant in their timing—synchronicities.

Each had come to feel strangely like an instrument of evolution, following a path that was only lighted step by step; they were feeling their way into this new reality, testing their inner gyroscopes. Clearly these odysseys followed the same form, with the same landmarks here and there. And the participants had concluded, independently, that they must join others to make a world in which such journeys were less lonely. They must conspire.

Over the next three days they talked about cooperating to a particular end or purpose, but again and again drew back from anything like a "master plan." They knew they could effect changes in the society—action was their forte—but they were concerned about imposing a specific vision, afraid that they might be tempted to "play God" despite their best intentions. There was honest conflict, self-inquiry, resolution. Twos and threes joined for long conversations, long walks. Many hours were spent searching the further reaches of that most difficult of power issues, close personal relationships.

Occasionally they all joined hands for ten or fifteen minutes and "listened" in silence. At times, when a silent interval followed urgent debate or confrontation, several were in tears, having experienced a release of tension and often a shaking insight into themselves or into the perspective of someone else.

Here and there, without a master plan, the joining of purpose happened. Linkages were formed: friendships, plans for meetings, joint projects, introductions to mutual friends. Four of the participants met afterward on the East and West Coasts to set up a new international foundation for peace. Soon they were presenting small seminars on the new consciousness for generals at the U.S. Army War College and in the offices of the International Communications Agency. Within the month, several in the group mobilized to intervene successfully on behalf of the academic freedom of the dean when his research was judged too controversial by the president of his university. Those who lived in proximity (Washington, New York City, the

Bay Area) pooled their connections and enlarged their networks. The congressman enlisted the aid of participants in his
effort to obtain testimony and funding for research into altered
states of consciousness.

"People," Robert Theobald once remarked, "are the organizing principle."

EXPERIMENTS IN SOCIAL TRANSFORMATION

At first glance, social transformation seems a foolhardy, even
perilous ambition for any group to undertake. There is a necessary and critical chain of events. First, profound change in individuals who care deeply about social change, who find each
other, and who acquaint themselves with the psychology of
change, with insights into our universal fear of the unknown.
They must then devise ways to foster paradigm shifts in others;
they must perturb, awaken, and recruit. This aligned minority,
knowing that changes of heart and not rational argument alone
sway people, must find ways of relating to others at the most
human and immediate level.

If they are not to fall into the old traps (power plays, desperate compromises, self-aggrandizement), they must live by their
principles. Knowing that means must be as honorable as ends,
they go into political battle stripped of conventional political
weapons. They must discover new strategies and new well-
springs of power.

And this aligned, principled, sophisticated, committed, and
creative minority must also be irrepressible. It must make
waves large enough to set off a reordering of the whole
system—fluctuations, in the language of the theory of dissipative structures. Difficult? Impossible? Seen another way, the
process cannot fail *because it is also the goal.*

That's why the new collective *is* the new politics. As soon as
we begin to work for a different kind of a world, the world
changes for us. The networks of the Aquarian Conspiracy —
self-organizing forms that allow both autonomy and human
connection — are at once both the tools for social change and
the models of a new society. Every collective struggle for
social transformation becomes an experiment in social transformation.

The goal recedes; whether or not the whole of society
changes, and however long that process may take, individuals

are finding joy, unity, and purpose in their mutual efforts.
They are engaged in meaningful, and therefore adventurous,
work. They know that the cynics must have their grim world,
too. As Thoreau said, the minority need not wait to persuade the majority. And the vision, as we shall see, is self-
propagating.

The transformative effect of social movements on both participants and society can be seen in the effects of the protest
and counterculture of the 1960s. A counterculture is living,
breathing theory; speculation about the society's next phase. At
its worst, it can seem lawless and strange, an experiment that
fails to bridge the old and new. At its best, it is a transforming
leadership, deepening the awareness of the dominant culture.
The first colonists to dissent from British rule were a counterculture; so were the Transcendentalists.

Like a play within a play, the transformation of the counterculture and the protest movements is instructive; a pendulum
change that has become paradigm change. Like generations of
activists and reformers before them, the counterculturists tried
at first to change the political institutions. It was only as they
struggled among themselves and in frustrating confrontation
with the establishment that they discovered the real vanguard
of revolution: the "front" within.

Jerry Rubin, one of the Chicago Eight, who made headlines
as a radical social activist in the sixties, later said, "It's the
spiritual movement that's truly revolutionary. Without self-
awareness, political activism only perpetuates cycles of
anger. . . . I couldn't change anybody until I changed myself."
Laurel Robertson recalled her years as a student in Berkeley:

> I really wanted to help people, to change things for the
> better. One summer I was involved in a very constructive
> non-violent education program about the Vietnam war.
> Everybody who was working on it had selfless motives,
> but by the end of the summer the whole thing fell apart
> because we couldn't get along with each other. I had to
> face the fact that you cannot make the world nonviolent
> and loving unless you make yourself nonviolent and
> loving.

In retrospect, the inward turn of this revolution seems almost
inevitable. A former protestor, now on the faculty of a state
medical school, said, "Despite the violence, the protest of the

1960s basically reflected *human* concerns—peace, minority rights, relevance in education—rather than traditional political issues."

Philosophically, if not always practically, the movements of the 1960s focused on a new kind of power, personal rather than collective. Dorothy Healy, who was then chairman of the Communist party in Southern California, said years later, "A new generation was marching, moving, and the party was not into it, did not understand it. What was happening did not proceed according to classical Marxism as we understood it. The working class was not in the vanguard, and the basic issues were not economic."

With failures and partial successes behind them, many of the leading activists went in a direction that greatly troubled their supporters in the conventional Left. They became involved in their own transformative process. This turn of events confused the media and many social scientists into thinking the revolution had dissolved. Lou Krupnick said:

> We stayed in the streets through tear gas and billy clubs and went inside only when holy people whispered Sanskrit mantras into our eager ears. We went inward for several years, trying to generate alternatives to the madness. . . .
>
> We're entering a new period. Now we're beginning to synthesize the creative and organizing drives that are part of our heritage.

In "Notes on the Tao of the Body Politic," Michael Rossman remarked, "When I look through the political lens now, I see that all I do is an essential test of holiness, politically speaking." Democracy, as one of the radicals said, is not a political state but a spiritual condition: "We're parts of a whole."

The attempt to find and foster wholeness, to be social healers, has given new life to the old concerns. Ex-militants have successfully run for office around the country and have received major political appointments as well. For example, Sam Brown, organizer of the War Moratorium protest against the Vietnam conflict, successfully reformed banking practices as the state treasurer of Colorado and was later appointed by Carter to head the agency that administers VISTA and the Peace Corps. Brown said, "Social change isn't going to come as quickly as any of us would like it to come. Building a community is a more subtle, delicate, long-term process. . . ."

In the 1960s most of the serious social activists disapproved of the easy-going counterculture, with its interest in psychedelics, camaraderie, a spontaneous lifestyle. Writing in 1976 in *Focus/Midwest*, a radical journal, Harold Baron said:

With a different mind-set we could react differently. We could feel comradeship, sense new possibilities. . . . Perhaps hope for the humanized urban future lies not with the technocrats but with the community-builders. If this is true, we must make one last bow in the direction of the counterculturists; at the very least they were asking the right questions. We shall all be asking them again.

Initially the activists of the 1960s, like generations of political reformers before them, tried force and persuasion; they wrote, demonstrated, sermonized, scolded, lobbied, proselytized, argued. But they began to realize the truth of Thoreau's injunction: *Live* your beliefs, and you can turn the world around.

The emphasis on building community and on action in small groups represents the major shift in radical political thinking. Another former social activist, Noel McInnis, said recently, "I'm convinced that society will be changed only by events, not institutions. Meaningful change can only be implemented at the level of the person, the neighborhood, the small group. At a recent reunion of the SDS [Students for a Democratic Society], most who showed up had come to the same conclusion and restyled their activism accordingly."

James MacGregor Burns said that greatness in leadership is most likely to arise from "creative local circumstances." Just as the American people, with so much going against them in the 1770s and 1780s, were challenged by their leaders to rise to greatness in the state constitutional conventions, so may we transcend our present crisis. He predicted that the leaders of the future are likely to emerge from those who were involved in the conflicts of the 1960s—"a leadership corps in exile, people now in their thirties and forties who could burst onto the national scene."

Because the leadership of the future is coming out of organizations close to people, Burns said, social critics who rely only on the central media will miss this revolution in the making. Expressions of ferment are more evident in hundreds of thousands of small publications and in the statements of groups.

Tom Hayden, a co-defendant of Rubin in the Chicago trial,

later a California Democratic candidate for the United States Senate, said of himself and his fellow activists, "Our time is coming, but not as quickly and not necessarily in the same way we once wished." They had not abandoned the barricades so much as they had now taken their struggle into specific service: political, ecological, consumerist, spiritual. Hayden wrote in 1979:

> As spiraling energy costs aggravate the economic picture, more and more Americans will be competing for less and less in the "land of opportunity." Hope, the force that motivates people to become involved in life—may burn low or even out, especially for the young.
>
> I can think of only one long-term alternative, and I still see it coming. What began in the 1960s—a rising demand for a voice in the decisions controlling our lives—will spread to every sphere. . . .
>
> The political activists of the '60s, having now fully cut their teeth, will be back again and again with the same philosophy but expressed through new roles. If the '60s brought our birth and development, the '80s and '90s will be our years of maximum influence and maturity.
>
> My point is simple: the '60s created what can be called leadership for the future . . . a new generation of dedicated and politicized people. In our fathers' time, democracy was threatened from abroad, our own institutions were basically sound, affluence appeared to most to be guaranteed, America was No. 1.
>
> In our time we have received a different world view. Democracy has been threatened by "plumbers" operating from the White House, our institutions are troubled, affluence is hardly guaranteed, and being No. 1 in bombs hasn't made us No. 1 in the quality of life.
>
> The reappearance in years ahead of the '60s activists . . . will be misread by many. Some will not recognize us, and some will believe we have "settled down" too much. We will not be a protesting fringe, because the fringe of yesterday is the mainstream of tomorrow. We will not be protesting but proposing solutions: an energy program emphasizing renewable resources . . . democratic restructuring of large corporations . . . technology to decentralize decision-making and information. . . .
>
> Those who filled the streets in the '60s may yet fill the halls of government in the '80s, and if we do, I don't be-

lieve we will forget our roots. When I was being sentenced by Judge Julius Hoffman at the end of the Chicago trial, he looked bemusedly at me and said, "A smart fellow like you could go far under our system."

Who knows, Your Honor, perhaps I will. . . .

THE EMERGENT PARADIGM OF POWER AND POLITICS

Obviously there are many heresies in the emergent paradigm. It denies that our leaders are our betters, that money can solve many problems, that more and better can solve problems, that loyalty outranks inner authority. The new paradigm avoids head-on confrontation, political poles. It reconciles, innovates, decentralizes, and does not claim to have the answers. If we were to summarize the paradigms, we would find the following contrasts:

ASSUMPTIONS OF THE OLD PARADIGM OF POWER AND POLITICS	ASSUMPTIONS OF THE NEW PARADIGM OF POWER AND POLITICS
Emphasis on programs, issues, platform, manifesto, goals.	Emphasis on a new perspective. Resistance to rigid programs, schedules.
Change is imposed by authority.	Change grows out of consensus and/or is inspired by leadership.
Institutionalizes help, services.	Encourages individual help, voluntarism, as complement to government role. Reinforces self-help, mutual-help networks.
Impetus toward strong central government.	Favors reversing trend, decentralizing government wherever feasible; horizontal distribution of power. Small focused central government would serve as clearinghouse.

ASSUMPTIONS OF THE OLD PARADIGM OF POWER AND POLITICS	ASSUMPTIONS OF THE NEW PARADIGM OF POWER AND POLITICS
Power *for* others (care taking) or against them. Win/lose orientation.	Power *with* others. Win/win orientation.
Government as monolithic institution.	Government as consensus of individuals, subject to change.
Vested interests, manipulation, power brokerage.	Respect for the autonomy of others.
Solely "masculine," rational orientation, linear model.	Both rational and intuitive principles, appreciation of nonlinear interaction, dynamic systems model.
Aggressive leaders, passive followers.	Leaders and followers engaged in dynamic relationship, affecting each other.
Party- or issue-oriented.	Paradigm-oriented. Politics determined by worldview, perspective of reality.
Either pragmatic or visionary.	Pragmatic *and* visionary.
Emphasis on freedom from certain types of interference.	Emphasis on freedom for positive, creative action, self-expression, self-knowledge.
Government to keep people in line (disciplinary role) or as benevolent parent.	Government to foster growth, creativity, cooperation, transformation, synergy.
Left versus Right.	"Radical Center"—a synthesis of conservative and liberal traditions. Transcendence of old polarities, quarrels.

ASSUMPTIONS OF THE OLD PARADIGM OF POWER AND POLITICS	ASSUMPTIONS OF THE NEW PARADIGM OF POWER AND POLITICS
Humankind as conqueror of nature; exploitive view of resources.	Humankind in partnership with nature. Emphasis on conservation, ecological sanity.
Emphasis on external, imposed reform.	Emphasis on trans-formation in individuals as essential to successful reform.
Quick-fix or pay-later programs.	Emphasis on foresight, long-range repercussions, ethics, flexibility.
Entrenched agencies, programs, departments.	Experimentation encouraged. Favors frequent evaluation, flexibility, ad hoc committees, self-terminating programs.
Choice between best interest of individual or community.	Refusal to make that choice. Self-interest and community interest reciprocal.
Prizes conformity, adjustment.	Pluralist, innovative.
Compartmentalizes aspects of human experience.	Attempts to be interdisciplinary, holistic. Searches for interrelationships between branches of government, liaison, cross-fertilization.
Modeled after Newtonian view of the universe. Mechanistic, atomistic.	In flux, the counterpart in politics of modern physics.

NETWORKS—A TOOL OF TRANSFORMATION

A revolution means that power changes hands, of course, but it does not necessarily mean open struggle, a coup, victor and vanquished. Power can be dispersed through the social fabric.

While most of our institutions are faltering, a twentieth-century version of the ancient tribe or kinship has appeared: the network, a tool for the next step in human evolution.

Amplified by electronic communications, freed from the old restraints of family and culture, the network is the antidote to alienation. It generates power enough to remake society. It offers the individual emotional, intellectual, spiritual, and economic support. It is an invisible home, a powerful means of altering the course of institutions, especially government.

Anyone who discovers the rapid proliferation of networks and understands their strength can see the impetus for worldwide transformation. The network is the institution of our time: an open system, a dissipative structure so richly coherent that it is in constant flux, poised for reordering, capable of endless transformation.

This organic mode of social organization is more biologically adaptive, more efficient, and more "conscious" than the hierarchical structures of modern civilization. The network is plastic, flexible. In effect, each member is the center of the network.

Networks are cooperative, not competitive. They are true grass roots: self-generating, self-organizing, sometimes even self-destructing. They represent a process, a journey, not a frozen structure.

As Theodore Roszak said, the old revolutionary mass movements offered no more refuge to the person than did capitalist societies. "We need a class smaller than a proletariat.... The new politics will speak for the millions—one by one."

Interestingly, H. G. Wells had predicted in his 1928 blueprint for a new society that the Open Conspiracy would have no "ordinary" adherents—no pawns, no cannon fodder. The form of the conspiracy would not be a centralized organization but, rather, small groups of friends and coalitions of such groups. This is a radical idea. For all its claims of grass-roots support, traditional politics has always been applied from the top down; influential political scientists, economists and miscellaneous power brokers decided the issues and passed the word to blocs of voters.

As the benefits of linkage and cooperation become more visible, networks have coalesced for just about every imaginable purpose. Some focus on personal development, spiritual search, or rehabilitation of members; others address themselves primarily to social issues. (Some are strong special interest groups and apply political pressure in fairly conventional ways; they are the most vulnerable to conversion to conventional hierarchical organizations.)

Whatever their stated purpose, the function of most of these networks is mutual support and enrichment, empowerment of the individual, and cooperation to effect change. Most aim for a more humane, hospitable world.

In its rich opportunities for mutual aid and support, the network is reminiscent of its forebear, the kinship system. Yet the "family" in this case has formed on the basis of deeply held values and shared assumptions, bonds thicker than blood.

The network is a matrix for personal exploration and group action, autonomy and relationship. Paradoxically, *a network is both intimate and expansive*. Unlike vertical organizations, it can maintain its personal or local quality while ever growing. You don't have to choose between involvement on a community or global scale; you can have both.

Networks are the strategy by which small groups can transform an entire society. Gandhi used coalitions to lead India to independence. He called it "grouping unities" and said it was essential to success. "The circle of unities thus grouped in the right fashion will ever grow in circumference until at last it is coterminous with the whole world." Edward Carpenter's turn-of-the-century prophecy spoke of the linking and overlapping of networks to create "the finished, free society."

Informally, as well as with computers and directories, networks are connecting those with complementary skills, interests, goals. Networks promote the linkage of their members with other people, other networks.

Art historian Jose Arguelles compared such networks to the biological force of syntropy—the tendency of life energy toward ever greater association, communication, cooperation, awareness. The network is like a collective bodymind, he suggested, like the brain's left and right hemispheres, intellect and intuition. "The network is tremendously liberating. The individual is at the center...."

Comparing the network to the human nervous system is more than a handy metaphor. In a very real sense, the brain and a network operate similarly. The brain is more coalitional than hierarchical in its structure. Meaning in the brain is generated by dynamic patterns, coalitions of groups of neurons and interaction between groups. Power in the brain is decentralized.

In the most expanded and coherent states of consciousness, as we have seen, energy is the most widely available and ordered. The brain is *wholly awake*. Just so, the network is an alert, responsive form of social organization. Information moves in a nonlinear fashion, all at once, and in a meaningful way.

As the creative person makes new connections, juxtaposing unlikely elements to invent something new, so the network connects people and interests in surprising ways. These combinations foster invention, creativity. A network formed to assure a more psychologically healthy environment for babies cooperates with a humanistically oriented organization for old *E.T.* people. The old people, otherwise feeling useless and lonely, *Centres* help love and nurture babies and toddlers in a day-care center.

Synergy, the bonus of energy that results from cooperation in natural systems, is there for us, too. As we begin to discover it in relationship with others in our small group, potential benefits for society become evident. As physicist John Platt put it:

> Whenever even two people start giving to each other and working for each other, these qualities and rewards immediately appear—greater mutual benefit, greater ease, and greater individual development at the same time. They appear as soon as a couple begins to work together, or a family, or a neighborhood, or a nation. The great creative teams of American scientists exhibit them. The European Common Market exhibits them.
>
> By mutual giving with those around us, we begin to make a kind of local Utopia where the benefits are so obvious.

Once you have seen the power inherent in human alignment, you cannot think about the future in old terms. The explosion of networks in the past five years has been like a conflagration in a fireworks factory. This spiraling linkage—individuals with each other, groups with groups—is like a great resistance movement, an underground in an occupied country on the eve of liberation.

Power is changing hands, from dying hierarchies to living networks.

Alfred Katz of the University of California, Los Angeles, School of Public Health, who organized an international conference in Dubrovnik, Yugoslavia, to discuss mutual-aid networks, called them "a dynamic social force in the latter half of the Twentieth Century." This is our healthy response to the remoteness of modern institutions, Katz said. Networks have "a powerful and refreshing impact on social policy.... They represent a spontaneous social resistance to massive bureaucratic trends."

He suggested that one reason networks have been little noticed is that no one has figured out how to spend large amounts of money on something so simple and powerful.

"Mutual-help networks reflect a shift of both action and consciousness in great numbers of people. The consequences should not be underestimated."

California governor Jerry Brown called self-reliance and mutual help in the private sector the first new idea to emerge in politics in twenty years. The idea of neighbors cooperating to build an open and equal society is "both human and visionary."

Luther Gerlach and Virginia Hine, anthropologists who have studied social-protest networks since the 1960s, have christened the contemporary networks SPINs (Segmented Polycentric Integrated Networks). A SPIN gains its energy from coalitions, from the combining and recombining of talents, tools, strategies, numbers, contacts. It is Gandhi's "grouping of unities." Like a brain, the SPIN is capable of simultaneous connection at many points. Its segments are the small groups, which hang together loosely on the basis of shared values. Occasionally, by a kind of friendly fission, the SPIN has a spin-off. The multiplicity of groups strengthens the movement.

Whereas a conventional organization chart would show neatly linked boxes, the organization chart of a SPIN would look like "a badly knotted fishnet with a multitude of nodes of varying sizes, each linked to all the others, directly or indirectly." These cells or nodes, in the social-protest movement, are local groups ranging from a handful of members to hundreds. Many form for a single task and are here today, gone tomorrow.

Each segment of a SPIN is self-sufficient. You can't destroy the network by destroying a single leader or some vital organ. The center—the heart—of the network is everywhere. A bureaucracy is as weak as its weakest link. In a network, many persons can take over the function of others. This characteristic is also like the brain's plasticity, with an overlap of functions so that new regions can take over for damaged cells.

Just as a bureaucracy is less than the sum of its parts, a

network is many times greater than the sum of its parts. This is a source of power never before tapped in history: multiple self-sufficient social movements linked for a whole array of goals whose accomplishment would transform every aspect of contemporary life.[3]

These networks, Gerlach has suggested, produce valuable local mutations. News of successful experiments travels swiftly across the movement linkages, and they are widely adopted.

When the anthropologists first observed the networks, they thought they were leaderless. In reality, Gerlach said, "There is not a dearth of leadership but an embarrassment of riches." The leadership passes from person to person, depending on the needs of the moment.

Because SPINs are so qualitatively different in organization and impact from bureaucracies, Hine said, most people don't see them—*or think they are conspiracies*. Often networks take similar action without conferring with each other simply because they share so many assumptions. It might also be said that the shared assumptions *are* the collusion.

The Aquarian Conspiracy is, in effect, a SPIN of SPINs, a network of many networks aimed at social transformation. The Aquarian Conspiracy is indeed loose, segmented, evolutionary, redundant. Its center is everywhere. Although many social movements and mutual-help groups are represented in its alliances, its life does not hinge on any of them.

It cannot be disengaged because it is a manifestation of the change in people.

What do the networks want? Many different things, of course. Not only are no two networks alike; a single network changes over time because it reflects the fluctuating needs and interests of its members. But the essential intent is the redistribution of power.

The environmentalist groups, for example, want humankind to "live lightly on the earth," stewards of nature rather than exploiters or dominators. Spiritually and psychologically oriented networks are seeking the power that flows from in-

---

[3]The League of Nations and the United Nations, Hine said, "failed because they were built upon the very form of social organization they were designed to supersede—the nation-state." Their creators were unable to break out of the cultural assumption that all organizations must be bureaucratic. The anthropologists found a parallel between the networks for social change and the emerging supranational web of corporations. Another anthropologist, Alvin Wolf, had suggested that this new economic network transcends the nation-states. Ironically, it might do more to eliminate war than all the direct peacekeeping efforts in history.

ward integration, reclaiming authority for disenfranchised parts of the self. Educational networks are trying to empower the learner by identifying resources. Health networks want to shift the old power balance between institutionalized medicine and personal responsibility. Other groups rechannel economic power by boycotts, barter, cooperative buying, and business practices.

From the simplest neighborhood or office networks (food co-ops, car pools, shared child care) people tend to move to more ephemeral or abstract sharing, such as expertise or information. Mutual-help and self-help networks are more intimate and therefore a more powerful transformative force. According to the National Self-Help Clearinghouse associated with the City University of New York, around fifteen million Americans now belong to networks in which people help each other deal with such diverse problems as retirement, widowhood, overweight, divorce, child abuse, drug abuse, gambling, emotional disorders, handicaps, political action, environmentalism, the death of a child. Such groups carefully keep from becoming too "professionalized" for fear that a hierarchy of authority may develop and their whole purpose would be defeated. For the mutuality is essential. It is in helping others that one is helped.

The British Broadcasting Corporation created a television series, "Grapevine: The Self-Help Show," to help people find appropriate networks. There are national and state clearinghouses for self-help networks, associations of self-help groups, and recently a self-help fair was held in Boston. Among the groups mentioned in a single issue of *Self-Help Reporter* were networks for unemployed persons over forty, parents of prematures, women recovering from mastectomies, families and friends of missing persons, and the survivors of suicide victims.

The formation of these groups, said anthropologist Leonard Borman, director of the Self-Help Institute in Evanston, Illinois, "represents in part a desire by people who face similar problems to assume responsibility for their own bodies, minds, and behavior—and to help others do the same."

Self-help networks, one assessment noted, are usually supported internally rather than by appeals to the public; they have no professional leadership, they are inclusive (no strict guidelines for membership), local, innovative, nonideological; and they emphasize greater self-awareness and a fuller, freer emotional life. Such organizations prove the potential of even the most vulnerable members of society, as in the remarkable success of the ex-junkies at Delancy Street in San Francisco helping other addicts rehabilitate themselves.

One network, the Linkage, started by Robert Theobald, is international, computerized, and primarily conducted by correspondence. Its members introduce themselves via statements about their work and interests. These statements are reproduced by Theobald's service, Participation Publishers, and circulated by mail from Wickenburg, Arizona, for a small yearly fee. "Our operating assumption," Theobald said, "is that we are right now in the middle of a stress period caused by the ever more rapid collapse of the industrial era. We are looking for ways to aid in the necessary transformation. Many people would like to make this transformation.... We are trying to find ways to help people make the required shift."

Personal statements that went out in a single mailing suggest the variety of backgrounds. Included were a military communications analyst, two political scientists, a nurse, two doctors, a historian, a Presbyterian minister, an educator, a nuclear physicist, an engineer. Their concerns included paradigm shifts, radical social transformation, personal mystical experiences, appropriate technology, decentralization, the bridging of East and West, intentional communities, voluntary simplicity, organization models built on trust and communication, "creative ways we can help each other," "conscious technology," power and freedom in relationships, "making a difference."

One participant spoke of allies he found in his own community: "Having seen ourselves as loners, we're forming a network with new visions for this city." One described the linkage as "a sea-anchor, moderating the effects of other forces."

A clergyman sent a list of publications and organizations in England, in case anyone in the network should visit there and wish to find "like-minded people." Two described their own extensive networks. An educational consultant said, "In our frenetic world, I want to learn how to hear whispers again, with my family and others who are searching." From Nebraska:

We are moving into a new age, requiring an entirely different way of looking at things.... The modern age is over. But civilization needs new lines of demarcation. Can we etch in new forms fast enough?

Linkage offers a starting point. For the first time in history, can people who have never met become a "we" just because they want to?

A professor of business management wrote, "On my mind is a larger question of using the wealth and resources of business to support the transformation rather than work against it."

In summer 1979 Linkage mail increased dramatically. Members were expressing a growing need to communicate their transformative vision beyond the network. Theobald wrote the members of his sense that "we are moving into the time when further activities could be catalyzed." Significantly, many members were asking for "sub-linkages," names of others in their geographical area with whom they could work on specific projects. This need for action in small groups is characteristic of the Aquarian Conspiracy.

Theobald is what the *Open Network News*, published in Denver, calls a "weaver," a person who designs open networks, who sees patterns and connections, making the network more effective. Not only are individuals weavers, but so are some publications and even businesses.

Another network that functions primarily through the mails, like Linkage, is the Forum for Correspondence and Contact, founded in 1968 by such luminaries as Viktor Frankl, Arthur Koestler, Roberto Assagioli, Ludwig von Bertalanffy, Abraham Maslow, Gunnar Myrdal, E. F. Schumacher, and Paolo Soleri. The Forum's purpose, as expressed in a recent invitation to membership:

> We have identified persons associated with some of these vital new clusters of activity (human-centered, future-oriented) and are trying to stimulate various explorations.... They are all central to what is variously described as new ways of humankind, transformation of man and society, holistic growth, etc.

The Association for Humanistic Psychology offers a networking service. Any member may propose a networking project—compiling a directory of those interested in a particular subject, publishing a newsletter for that interest group, creating a workshop.

Some networks, like the Renascence Project in Kansas City and Briarpatch in Northern California, link entrepreneurs. These will be discussed further in Chapter 10. A network in

San Jose, California, the Mid-Peninsula Conversion Project, was founded to find alternative production for defense industries, a practical step toward disarmament. People Index in Fairfield, California, calls itself "a human switchboard helping people find others with the same goals.... We want people to connect more directly with each other. Got a project you can't do alone? Are you a resource for others? What future do you want to be a part of—and help create? Join the network of people for a new world."

And there are countless informal alliances, crisscrossing every institution and organization — for example, groups of sympathetic nurses and doctors in a hospital, faculty members and students in a university. Ready-made networks emerge from existing organiztions, sometimes as "special interest groups" given subdivision status in professional associations, but more often just an informal alliance of those whose thinking has shifted into a larger paradigm. Humanistically oriented psychologists in the American Psychological Association, World Future Society members more interested in consciousness than hard technology, and social-transformation advocates within the Association for Humanistic Psychology have formed effective informal internal networks. They often succeed in changing the emphasis in the larger organization's official publication; they bring in more innovative speakers for programs, run for office, and otherwise break the hold of the thinking of the old guard. The collusion is so low-key that no one notices, and there is usually no significant struggle among network members for offices or honors.

OTHER NEW SOURCES OF POWER

Some political scientists have speculated on the formation of a "centrist" party, one that might reflect both humanistic principles and economic freedom. Because political parties are precisely the kind of conventional social structure that is not working well, it seems unlikely that any will emerge from the Aquarian Conspiracy or from any of the social movements now afoot. The energy expended to launch a new party and field candidates against entrenched parties would divert energy from enterprises with a better pay-off.

There are new, more imaginative and rewarding sources of the power needed for social transformation. We have already talked about *the power of the person*, inherent in the transformative process—the discovery that any of us is "the difference in the world." We have talked about *the power of the network*, the form of catalyzing and mobilizing people all over the world.

The power of paying attention, of discovering what works, of facing and transforming conflict, gives one the advantage of being wide awake even in the company of those hooked on our social painkillers: distraction, denial, cynicism. The deliberate transformation of stress is a new factor in history.

So is *the power of self-knowledge*. Until technology freed us from the struggle to survive, few had the time or opportunity to look within to explore the psyche. Self-knowledge leads to a profound change in the individual's definition of power. As the ego diminishes, so does the need to dominate, to win. *Not engaging in power games becomes a kind of natural power.* There is a liberation of the energy formerly channeled into anxious competition: *the power of letting go*.

The power of flexibility allows the potential opponent to become part of the solution to the problem, much as the practitioner of aikido flows with the energy of an opponent. This political aikido channels energy into an intended direction, in part by identifying the needs of potential adversaries. It helps these adversaries make the transition, whereas frontal attack hardens their position.

In his 1967 book, *Step to Man*, John Platt proposed the use of natural strategies for effecting social transformation. Work with the grain, he said. Find the focus of power. Work out the path of least dislocation. Be a catalyst. Too often vocal minorities expend their energies on firm friends or firm opponents rather than on those ripe for persuasion. "The main business of an enlightened minority is not fighting the majority but showing them how."

Any minority that understands the power of the seed crystal, of amplifying an idea, can quickly assume influence beyond its numbers. Work *with* technology and natural social forms, not against them, Platt urged. Be flexible. A brittle system will allow stresses to build until some part of the structure breaks down suddenly or dangerously.

Matt Taylor, founder of the Renascence Project, compared social reordering to the turning of a ship. In the past, people have tried to put the rudder on the front of the ship when tackling social issues, applying direction and pressure at the wrong places. "You can steer a large organization with subtle input."

The power of communication, growing all the time, enables the rapid transmission of new ideas, a contagion of visions, good questions, experiments, images. Economist Kenneth Boulding once said that a change which might take a generation to accomplish in a nonliterate society can occur in days in a culture with mass communication.

The power of decentralization derives from the flow of new images, ideas, and energy to all parts of the body politic. Concentrations of power are as unnatural and deadly as a blood clot or an ungrounded electrical line.

Aldous Huxley saw decentralization as the alternative to Left and Right. In a letter to a friend at the close of World War II, he wrote:

> As H. G. Wells once remarked, the mind of the Universe is able to count above two. The dilemmas of the artist-intellectual and of the political theorist have more than two horns. Between ivory towerism on the one hand and direct political action on the other lies the alternative of spirituality. And between the totalitarian fascism and totalitarian socialism lies the alternative of decentralism and cooperative enterprise—the economic-political system most natural to spirituality.
>
> The majority of intellectuals at the present time recognize only two alternatives in their situation and opt for one or the other....

With typical insight, Huxley had written earlier to his brother Julian that social transformation—"a direction of the power of the state, self-government, decentralization" — could best be accomplished by simultaneous attack along all fronts: economic, political, educational, psychological. H. G. Wells also insisted that change must occur in all parts of society at once, not one institution at a time.

This view parallels transformation in natural systems, the sudden change of the dissipative structure. The jump into a new order is sudden, all or nothing. Even at the most simple-minded level, we can see that any aspect of social transformation has a ripple effect. The individual who has learned to take responsibility for his own health is likely to become more interested in political aspects of medicine, environment, the role of learning in health and disease, the beneficial or deadly aspects of relationships and work, and so on. This is *the power of a new paradigm*, a perspective that politicizes even those who have had no interest in conventional politics.

"A radical consciousness," said Gurtov, "based on shared feelings and needs, is far more likely to hold than radical ideology." You can't defect from an insight; you can't unsee what you have seen.

The power of process recognizes that the very act of reclaiming our autonomy is transformative. Every step we take on the road of freedom and responsibility makes the next step easier. Goals, programs, and timetables are less important than the engagement itself. As Gandhi put it, "The goal ever recedes from us. . . . Salvation lies in the effort, not in the attainment. Full effort is full victory."

The power of uncertainty makes it easier to innovate, experiment, risk. As Theobald said, "There is no riskless route into the future; we must choose which set of risks we wish to run." Writing in a network journal, philosopher Jay Ogilvy coined the term "parapolitical" to describe the avocational involvement in politics that comes from commitment to a new vision:

> If we wish to break out of the iron cage of a totally administered society, then our imaginations must be free enough to make mistakes. If we want to play, some games we will lose. But the stakes are nothing less than the flickering life of the human spirit; so some of us would risk losing rather than not play at all.

We become less surprised when surprising things happen. After all, in a creative universe, even an apparent disaster may prove to be serendipity. This viewpoint is comfortable with ambiguity. It assumes that most issues are tricky and does not pretend to resolve once and for all that which is in perpetual flux. The politician or citizen willing to acknowledge uncertainty is free to learn, err, adapt, invent, and go back to the drawing board again and again.

The power of the whole gathers in all the power lost by fragmentation and ignorance. It enhances our collective options by drawing on the talents and ideas of those who might not have been noticed or appreciated in the past. A society that rewards the diversity and gifts of all its citizens will reap a richer harvest than a conformist society.

The power of the alternative lies in recognizing that we have more choices than we once thought. By imagining new possibilities, we can say no to the suffocating, unacceptable options we confronted in the past. And just as personal change comes from becoming conscious of our own thought processes, seeing that we can choose how to react in a given situation, awakening to the influences of our conditioning, a society can discover collectively that "it doesn't have to be that way." A culture can become aware of itself, its own conditioning.

Too often it did not even occur to us that we had a choice. In discussing what he calls "alternativism," Erich Fromm said that most people fail because "they do not wake and see when they stand at a fork in the road and have to decide."

As increasing numbers of people come to a sense of autonomy, they respect the choices of others. At the 1977 Women's Year convention, many debates died away as the audience began to chant: "Choice, choice, choice...." Even if you don't want a particular lifestyle or philosophy for yourself, they were saying, you can allow others their options.

We are all surrounded by limits of a kind, Tocqueville said, "but within that circle we are powerful and free."

The power of intuition can be extended from the individual to a group. A conference brochure invited,"Come, let us drink at the well of collective intuition." Groups of the Aquarian Conspiracy often listen for inward guidance, like Quakers seeking inner light at a meeting. Rather than charting their activities exclusively by logic, they seek a kind of consensual intuition. They report a sense of finding their direction as a group rather than inventing it. It is as if teams of archeologists were digging not for the past but for the future.

The power of vocation is a kind of collective sense of destiny— not a mapped-out myth but a search for meaning, a tacit understanding that people and leaders believe in something beyond material success, beyond nationalism, beyond quick gratification.

As spiritual and humanistic values are coming to the fore, a few politicians are struggling to articulate this shift.

The power of withdrawal, psychological as well as economic, comes from the recognition that we can take back the power we have given others. Teilhard said, "We have become aware that, in the great game being played, we are the players as well as the cards and the stakes. Nothing can go on if we leave the table. Neither can any power force us to remain."

Ingenious economic boycotts are devised. Large national organizations attempt to influence policy (as in the ratification of the Equal Rights Amendment) by threatening not to hold their annual meetings in certain locales. Nutrition-oriented groups boycott the products of manufacturers who aggressively market infant formulas in developing countries where infant mortality is worsened by artificial feeding. Community groups protest red-lining — the refusal of lenders to grant mortgages in certain areas — by withdrawing their savings from neighborhood banks and savings and loan companies until they agree to invest a specific dollar amount in the community.

All our high priests—doctors, scientists, bureaucrats, politicians, churchmen, educators—are being defrocked at once. Rushing in where angels fear to tread, we are challenging old laws, proposing new ones, lobbying and boycotting, wise now to the hidden powers of democracy. "We are challenging the legitimacy of entire systems," said Willis Harman. "The citizen grants legitimacy to any institution—or withholds it."

THE POWER OF WOMEN

"Women hold up half the sky," says a Chinese proverb. Women represent the greatest single force for political renewal in a civilization thoroughly out of balance. Just as individuals are enriched by developing both the masculine and feminine sides of the self (independence and nurturance, intellect and intuition), so the society is benefiting from a change in the balance of power between the sexes.

The power of women is the powder keg of our time. As women enlarge their influence in policymaking and government, their *yin* perspective will push out the boundaries of the old *yang* paradigm. Women are neurologically more flexible than men, and they have had cultural permission to be more intuitive, sensitive, feeling. Their natural milieu has been complexity, change, nurturance, affiliation, a more fluid sense of time.

The shift from militant feminism is evident in recent statements like that of Patricia Mische in a monograph, *Women and Power*. Instead of asking for a piece of the pie men have had all along, she said, "we should be trying to create quite another pie." Human affairs will not be advanced by the assimilation of more and more women into a literally man-made world. Rather, women and men together can create a new future. Women have been torn between their fear of powerlessness on the one hand and a fear of the capacity for destruction on the other: "We tend to block out both fears—the one because powerlessness is too painful to confront, the other because we associate power with evil drives."

Women are now learning to use their power openly, she

said, exercising what Rollo May called "integrative power" rather than the coy or manipulative ways of the past.

> Integrative power recognizes that men as well as women have been the victims of history and narrowly defined roles.... It is a caring form of power—power aligned with love.
>
> Work for social justice, for peace, for overcoming poverty and alienation, for building a more truly humanizing future...is not even possible without a combination of love and power. Love itself is not possible without power or self-assertion. And power without love is easily reduced to manipulation and exploitation.
>
> We cannot make somebody else's contribution to the ongoing shaping of history. Nor can anyone else make ours. Each of us is here for a purpose, each life has significance and meaning. This meaning—whatever it is—cannot be realized if we abdicate our powers....
>
> The values that have been labeled feminine — compassion, cooperation, patience—are very badly needed in giving birth to and nurturing a new era in human history.

Lou Harris of the Harris Poll said that women are far ahead of men in pushing for basic human qualities; they are more dedicated to peace and opposed to war, more concerned over child abuse, deeply moved by what he called "the pall of violence. Women are playing for keeps and are a formidable new part of the political scene."

If we redefine leadership, we can think differently about women in leadership roles. James MacGregor Burns called it a "male bias" that sees leadership as mere command or control, whereas it is properly the engagement and mobilization of human aspirations. As we become more aware of the true nature of leadership, he said, "women will be more readily recognized as leaders, and men will change their own leadership styles."

Thinking itself will be transformed, poet Adrienne Rich said. Women can bring to the society the very qualities necessary to alter life, a more deeply sustaining relationship to the universe. "Sexuality, politics, intelligence, power, motherhood, work, community, intimacy, will develop new meanings."

The idea that women might rescue a failing society is not new. As early as 1890 Havelock Ellis saw a coming "invasion" of women into leadership as a source of renewal comparable to that new life a wave of barbarians brings to an effete and degenerate civilization. Masculine approaches to social organization had reached a dead end, he said. Women, with their greater sensitivity to relationships and social form, might devise ways to transcend conflict and confrontation.

"The rise of women to their fair share of power is certain," Ellis said. "... I find it an unfailing source of hope."

In 1916 psychologist George Stratton of the University of Southern California was describing the inherent superiority of female brains in seeing the whole. Writing on "Feminism and Psychology" in *Century Magazine* he expressed the hope that women would dispel masculine illusions when they took their rightful place in society. Men, he said, tend to fix on cogs instead of flesh and blood. Beginning with a generous wonder at nature, they end up with fascination for the tool—the scientific instrument. They establish governments to give order to life, then end up coveting the functions of government *more* than life."The masculine genius for organization," Stratton said, "needs women's sense of the heart of things, not the trappings."

Recently a woman psychologist suggested that human survival may require that the private virtues of women go public. "Perhaps the women's movement is part of an evolutionary process that will keep us from going the way of the dinosaur and the dodo."

Wherever the Aquarian Conspiracy is at work, perpetrating holistic health or creative science or transpersonal psychology, women are represented in far greater numbers than they are in the establishment. For example, one-third of the founding members of a new holistic medical organization were women, compared to the percentage of women physicians in the United States (8.3 percent). Men in such organizations are not only comfortable with women in leadership roles but openly emulate such yin qualities as integration, empathy, reconciliation. They see in women a greater sensitivity to time and season, intuition about direction, an ability to wait. "If satyagraha is to be the mode of the future," Gandhi once said, "then the future belongs to women."

THE POWER OF RADICAL CENTER

The political perspective of the Aquarian Conspiracy is best described as a kind of Radical Center. It is not neutral, not middle-of-the-road, but a view of the whole road. From this vantage point, we can see that the various schools of thought on any one issue—political or otherwise—include valuable contributions along with error and exaggeration.

As it was expressed in an editorial in the British journal, *The New Humanity*:

> We are neither right nor left but uplifted forward. *The New Humanity* advocates a new kind of politics. . . . Governance must develop a framework, not a rigid structure, and we must find unity within our immense and wonderful diversity.
>
> At this point in human evolution there can be no way out of the global political stalemate unless there is first, and fast, a new humanity with a changed psychology. That new psychology is developing, a new humanity is emerging.

Most historical movements have written their last will and testament along with their manifesto. They have known more surely what they oppose than what they are. By taking a firm position, they trigger an inevitable countermotion, one that will disorient their fragile identity almost at once. Then rapid metamorphosis and self-betrayal: pacifists who become violent, law-and-order advocates who trample law and order, patriots who undo liberties, "people's revolutions" that empower new elites, new movements in the arts that become as rigid as their predecessors, romantic ideals that lead to genocide.

Anthropologist Edward Hall lamented our cultural inability to reconcile or include divergent views within one frame of reference. We are so indoctrinated by our right/wrong, win/lose, all/nothing habits that we keep putting all our half-truths into two piles: truth versus lies, Marxism versus capitalism, science versus religion, romance versus realism—the list goes on and on. We act as though either Freud or B. F. Skinner had to be right about human behavior, as Hall noted, when in fact "both work and are right when placed in proper perspective."

Partial viewpoints force us into artificial choices, and our lives are caught in the crossfire. Quick, choose! Do you want your politician to be compassionate or fiscally responsible? Should doctors be humane or skillful? Should schools pamper children or spank them?

The rare successful reforms in history—the durable Constitution, for example—synthesize. They blend old and new values. Dynamic tension, in the form of the system of checks and balances, was built into the paradigm of democracy. Whatever its flaws, the framework has proved amazingly resilient.

When nearly two hundred of the most effective Aquarian Conspirators were asked to categorize themselves politically on a questionnaire, many expressed great frustration. Some checked off every box — radical, liberal, centrist, conservative — with apologies. Some drew arrows across the spectrum. Others wrote marginal notes: "Liberal but . . ." "Radical on some issues, conservative on others." "These categories don't apply." "Radical but not in the usual sense." "Choices too linear." "Old categories are useless."

One, a British-born economist, drew a circular spectrum, saying that the United States has a reservoir of flexibility in its political system. "It has not yet polarized into the sterile left-right axis now compounding Britain's problems. The forces in the United States are circular: corporations, trade associations, smaller businesses, cults, environmentalists, etc."

Politicians of the Radical Center are easily misunderstood and unusually vulnerable to attack, regardless of their accomplishments, because they don't take strident positions. Their high tolerance of ambiguity and their willingness to change their minds leave them open to accusations of being arbitrary, inconsistent, uncertain, or even devious.

Traditionally, we have wanted to identify our friends and enemies. Lobbies, political realities, and the media, playing both sides against each other, usually force politicians into taking black-and-white positions. But sooner than we may suppose, Radical Center will be a viable point of view. The rising number of new movements, all demonstrating and pressuring, combined with traditional special-interest lobbies, may finally force politicians to seek a middle way through the mine field. Politicians may finally have no choice but to transcend the either-or dilemma.

Historian Henry Steele Commager urged a restoration of the traditional meanings to the terms "conservative" and "liberal." We can all work to save that which is of value, and we can all be free to innovate and change. "How fortunate if we could accept once again that we are all republicans, we are all democrats . . . we are all conservatives, we are all liberals." Willis Harman emphasized that the concept of a transcendental, ultimately responsible self is central to the entire theory of democratic government. Under those values the nation can become reconciled. "Conservatives will insist that we keep and respect our national precepts. Radicals will insist that we live up to them."

It is hard, often impossible, to implement a new political perspective in an old system crisscrossed with old alliances, debts, and enmities and riddled with interests desperately guarding the status quo. The first politicians groping for the Radical Center, like scientists who make "premature discoveries," may fail or have only a small impact. But they are a beginning.

In the long run, it is the evolving Radical-Center constituency that will engender increasing numbers of candidates and elect some of them to office. This new constituency will support those who seem likely to create and conserve. It will admire them for refusing to make simplistic choices. It will encourage them to foster the kind of growth that charts and figures cannot measure. As in the model of Burns, the followers will help transform the leaders—those leaders who sense the shift to higher needs.

During the 1976 presidential primaries, political commentators observed that both Jimmy Carter and Jerry Brown drew on "protest of the center" constituencies and seemed to sense an unarticulated trend. Brown once remarked, "We're going to go left and right at the same time," and the *Los Angeles Times* called him "our liberal-moderate-conservative-governor," both pragmatist and visionary. Unfortunately, the apparent paradox in the approaches of both Brown and Carter was more often attacked than supported, and both began to resort more and more often to politics as usual.

In his study of cultural awakenings, William McLoughlin said that Carter is subject to too many countervailing pressures to undertake an effective restructuring; consensus must first be reached at grass roots. "Some elements of [his] world view may indeed be part of the new consensus—his casual style, his recognition that America must restrain its power, his sense of common humanity, his concern for ecology, his recognition that the 'American way of life' is culturally limited and needs to be judged by some transcendent values." But our political leaders have never been the prophets of new light, in McLoughlin's judgment. "They may implement it but they do not originate it."

He foresees that at some future point, no earlier than the

1990s, a consensus will emerge that will thrust into political leadership a president with a platform committed to fundamental restructuring. It will reflect the new belief system, with its greater respect for nature, for others, for craftsmanship, and for success measured in terms of friendship and empathy, not money or status.

> The reason an awakening takes a generation or more to work itself out is that it must grow with the young; it must escape the enculturation of the old ways. It is not worthwhile to ask who the prophet of this awakening is or to search for new ideological blueprints in the work of the learned. Revitalization is growing up around us in our children, who are both more innocent and more knowing than their parents and grandparents. It is their world that has yet to be reborn.

A commitment to Radical Center doesn't work as a sometime thing.

SELF DETERMINATION

Predictably, citizen involvement in the "politics of transformation" is more evident in California than elsewhere, and a number of legislators have participated in consciousness-oriented conferences and networks. In 1976 a coalition of state legislators, members of Congress, and citizens formed a statewide organization, Self Determination. The founders of this "personal/political" network said in their invitation to join:

> Self Determination proposes a practical and powerful alternative to cynicism: changing both ourselves and society by transforming the most basic myth by which we live— our assumptions about our nature and potential. . . .
> *Such a transformation is already happening in America.* Many are now living a positive vision of self and society. We want now to give it vital public visibility. We are developing principles of social action and institutional change based upon a faithful vision of who we are and who we can be.
> Much of life is self-fulfilling prophecy. The citizen who takes responsibility for his/her own self-awareness and

self-determination will become visionary, energetic, and enduring. . . .

The network does not lobby, does not focus on particular issues, but promotes interaction between persons and institutions "to empower." Psychologist Carl Rogers pointed out that Self Determination is significant "whether it succeeds or falters. . . . A totally new type of political force is being born. Even in its process, it is person-centered. No one person is in charge, no big name. . . . It is not a drive for power."

The new power manifests itself through the emergence of a new kind of person, "a pattern which has not been seen before except perhaps in rare individuals." This is a new phenomenon, Rogers said. "We've had a few Thoreaus, but never hundreds of thousands of people, young and old alike, willing to obey some laws and disobey others on the basis of their own personal moral judgment." These new people refuse to put up with order for order's sake. They take action quietly, without fanfare, "openly but without defiance." They act in small, nonhierarchical groups to humanize institutions from the inside. They ignore meaningless rules, exhibiting what Rogers calls "an Elizabethan quality of adventure—everything is possible. . . . These emerging persons are neither power-hungry nor achievement-hungry. When they seek power, it is for other than purely selfish purposes."

These are not frightening trends but exciting ones, he said. "In spite of the darkness of the present, the culture may be on the verge of a great evolutionary-revolutionary leap."

John Vasconcellos, a California state assemblyman from San Jose, was instrumental in the founding of Self Determination. To many, not only in California but elsewhere, Vasconcellos has come to represent a prototype of the new politician. But he would be the first to warn that there is no such creature. "The politics we do is who we are," he has frequently said. Your life makes your political statement, and each is different.

He has been responsible for an impressive body of California legislation aimed at humanizing education and medicine, but he is as quick to point out the failures and disappointments of each legislative session as the successes. There is none of the self-congratulation one expects from politicians. The emergent paradigm of power and politics is evident in Vasconcellos's public statements:

You could change all the political leaders, rules, and institutions tomorrow, but if we don't change ourselves—if we keep carrying all our fears, denials, and self-repression in our minds and bodies—then we would live no differently.

Government is *us*—and it is as we choose it to be. We elect leaders who are close to where we are in terms of vision. We need to see to it that our institutions, including government, become peopled by those who share our struggle, our vision about this human transformation.

Two hundred years ago the major public issue in America was freedom from political bondage, from being owned as a nation by another nation. A century later the Civil War was fought for freedom from physical bondage. "In the last fifteen years we have witnessed a third type of revolution—the liberation of one's body, mind, feelings. There are literally millions saying, 'I want to be who I am, and I want to be whole.'"

The once-silent majority learned lessons in power from the student uprisings of the 1960s, Vasconcellos believes.

The real political revolutionary act is to enable someone to see something he has not been able to see before.

There is a great movement on. I think it is unstoppable. When you add together all those in this country who are attempting to become more aware and whole, you realize there are *millions* involved in this new revolution. Yet we have not yet seen a clear enough statement or theory to help us understand the signficance of this event—to help it along.

At a conference on holistic health, Vasconcellos urged participants to descend en masse on Sacramento. "We're not giving our power away any more," he said. "We're moving from 'mystique' and expertise." Citing evidence of "consciousness in the Capitol," he quoted new state educational guidelines emphasizing the uniqueness and potential of each child, the importance of self-esteem and self-awareness. The state has funded research on left- and right-brain perceptual modes as they relate to education, pilot projects on humanizing the workplace, the feasibility of hospices (humane centers for the care of the terminally ill). Vasconcellos brought obstetrician Frederick Leboyer, author of *Birth Without Violence*, to Sacramento to meet legislators and urge the study of more appropriate birth practices in the state. He urged Brown and David Saxon, president of the University of California, to establish a series of conferences on the nine campuses of the university, to address the transformation of thinking about health care, aging, education, death and dying, birth, and other topics.

When Brown expressed an interest in learning more about holistic medicine, Vasconcellos arranged for a group to meet with him to discuss the new medical paradigm; a dozen people talked in Brown's apartment until early morning about the possibilities. Later Brown issued the formal invitations to a state conference on the new concepts in medicine which Vasconcellos helped organize.

The invitation to the conference, "Health Care: Whose Responsibility?" reflected the need to disperse power from paternal agencies to the community:

> New and better forums are needed to work on these vital questions—interdisciplinary forums where leaders of government, directors of foundations, representatives of health professions associations, university researchers, philosophers, educators, providers, bureaucrats, and humanists can reason together, working through agreements and disagreements toward the emergence of new health policies more directly related to today's changing social values and needs.

Vasconcellos was chief author of a 1979 bill establishing the California Commission on Crime Control and Violence Prevention, whose charge is to study and analyze the research relating to the origins of mental health.

CONSPIRACY IN GOVERNMENT

In bureaucracies, in every corner of government, human beings conspire for change. An Aquarian Conspirator at the cabinet level of the United States government helped foster departmental change by setting up staff workshops in human development, saying, "If you want to change bureaucracies, you have to first change bureaucrats."

In April 1979 representatives of the United States Departments of Commerce, Energy, and the Interior met with leaders of the Association for Humanistic Psychology to discuss the implications of changing values and the prospects for social change, a meeting praised by the *Washington Post* as an effort by bureaucrats to enlarge their vision.

A government, after all, is not a "they." In a bureaucracy there are many individuals with creative programs and new paradigms in their peddler's packs, just waiting for a responsive administration or the opportune moment. One veteran bureaucrat at the National Institute of Mental Health said, "There are a lot of us in the woodwork." He was referring to a loose coalition of conspirators in agencies and on Congressional staffs. Within the Department of Health, Education and Welfare, innovators have created informal rap groups to share their strategies for slipping new ideas into a resistant system and to give each other moral support.

Concepts that might otherwise appear "far out" can be given legitimacy by a single federally funded program. The grant-making apparatus of government determines fashion in some research fields. This aura of legitimacy is fostered here and there by conspirator-bureaucrats.

Government represents an incalculably large source of energy: people, money, authority. Political aikido, the power that comes from turning a potential opponent's energy to one's own advantage, can include the use of government funds, even defense grants, for humanistically oriented research and pilot projects. There are several strategies for obtaining such funding. Sometimes an attractive alternative is proposed, a more effective or economical medical treatment. Often the project is nominally orthodox, but a daring question has quietly been incorporated into the research design. Sometimes the project originates with a sympathetic conspirator-bureaucrat who recommends how the proposal should be written and what is likely to be approved. Conspirator-politicians sometimes apply gentle pressure for the agency funding of such programs.

Research projects on meditation, biofeedback, psychic phenomena, and alternative medical approaches have been funded by the Department of Defense. One example of the sophisticated use of government energy and authority is a project started by Jay Matteson, a civilian consultant to the United States Navy.

His undertaking was foreshadowed by an earlier project that had apparently failed. Several years ago Admiral Elmo Zumwalt, then head of United States naval operations, proposed a "human goals" program that met considerable resistance from old-timers in the service. In 1975 a similar program, renamed Leadership and Management Training, was introduced. Admirals and the chief of naval education and training were among the attendees, and they endorsed the idea that all company commanders receive instruction in human-behavior areas. A crackdown on covert maltreatment of recruits was under way at the time.

Under a human-resources management contract let by the navy in San Diego, Jay Matteson helped organize an appropriate course. Matteson knew that he could never get away with teaching meditation to the navy. He knew that he was also unlikely to get approval for teaching the relaxation-response technique adapted by Herbert Benson of Harvard from Transcendental Meditation. After all, who wanted a relaxed military? But he was convinced that the technique would be the most powerful way to engender both the sensitivity to human behavior that the navy wanted in its officers and the awareness of their rights that it wanted to instill in its recruits. Matteson got the course approved as "Dynamic Methods of Coping."

The timing was perfect. Another consultant joined him in teaching the course, and they also brought in a Florida swim coach who had used the technique to train a university team. The meditative technique, cleansed of ideology, was a smash. Feedback from the company commanders was so favorable that the material was incorporated into instructional guides written by Matteson and his colleagues.

The guides have since been adopted for use throughout the armed services. Because of the reported value of meditative techniques in preventing and treating drug abuse, all basic training programs must now include mention of relaxation and meditation as alternatives to drug use. A videotape demonstrating the relaxing technique is available to all instructors.

Matteson said later that the acceptability of meditation was underscored by the increasing percentage of recruits already familiar with the technique.

With the total program, you see changes happening. Every recruit now gets twenty-two hours of human-resource management training, including the coping classes. . . . The group dynamics includes freely expressing feelings. The recruits can tell what they don't like about the Navy.

They're given a course in "rights and responsibilities" where they're taught problem-solving, generalization, and other skills. The Navy is saying, let's take more time, give them skill development so they can be critical thinkers instead of robots. As the skill development progressed, more people at higher levels began to buy into the program.

The recruits are told about the Special Request Chit, a grievance form, and reminded that their superiors must forward such complaints upstairs. The recruit can see that he has power.

Power has been used to empower others.

Economist Stahrl Edmunds, in an article in *The Futurist*, proposed possible scenarios for the economic future of the United States, suggesting the probable outcomes if we should follow the patterns of various governments—the Romans, the Greeks, the medieval societies, industrial democracies, the sovietization of capitalism (government effort to control the economy through spending and taxation)—and, finally, "an original American play," a more hopeful alternative enlightened by the mistakes of the past.

In the latter scenario, the American president in the 1990s (who had been a member of the youth movement of the 1960s) speaks out for the ratification of new amendments to the Constitution:

> Two great merits in these amendments commend themselves—the facility for change and the dispersal of power. As a president who has wielded massive amounts of power, I can say to you that the temptation to retain power is great. But the opportunity to recover authority over your own lives comes rarely in history. Seize it, my friends, seize it as it stands, whatever your reservations, lest the opportunity slip from you forever.

In 1930 the India Congress party challenged the British protectorate by raising a flag of independence. As tension grew throughout the country, everyone looked to Gandhi for a new campaign. As Eknath Easwaran tells it in his stirring memoir, *Gandhi the Man*:

> Finally, after weeks of deliberation, the answer came to Gandhi in a dream. It was breathtakingly simple. The government had imposed a law forbidding Indians to make their own salt, making them dependent on a British monopoly for what is, in a tropical country, a necessity of

life. To Gandhi it was the perfect symbol of colonial exploitation. He proposed to march with seventy-eight of his
most trusted followers to the little coastal town of Dandi,
some two hundred forty miles away, where salt from the
sea lay free for the taking on the sand. When he gave the
signal, everyone in India was to act as if the salt laws had
never been enacted at all.

    ... It was an epic march, with the attention of news aud-
iences everywhere riveted on every stage of the way....
By the time he reached Dandi, twenty-four days later, his
nonviolent army had swelled to several thousand.

    Throughout the night of their arrival Gandhi and his
followers prayed for the strength to resist the violence
which might easily sweep away so large a crowd. Then, at
the moment of dawn, they went quietly down to the water, and Gandhi, with thousands of eyes watching every
gesture, stooped down and picked up a pinch of salt from
the sand.

    The response was immediate. All along India's coastline
huge crowds of men, women, and children swept down to
the sea to gather salt in direct disobedience of the British
laws. Their contraband salt was auctioned off at premium
prices to those in the cities who could break the law only
by buying. The whole country knew it had thrown off its
chains, and, despite the brutality of the police reprisals,
the atmosphere was one of nationwide rejoicing.

No one can grant freedom to anyone else. Gandhi's act,
however symbolic and inspiring, only liberated those who had
the courage to take action of their own.

    Like the salt on India's shores, our power is there for the
taking. It is free, inherent in nature. By the simplest gesture we
can reclaim it. To the extent that rules and precedents strangle
our ability to become all we can be, each of us must commit our
own form of civil disobedience.

    Plato once said that the human race would have no rest from
its evils until philosophers become kings or kings become
philosophers. Perhaps there is another option, as increasing
numbers of people are assuming leadership of their own lives.
They become their own central power. As the Scandinavian
proverb says, "In each of us there is a king. Speak to him and
he will come forth."

    It is the new worldview that gives birth to new politics; new
power relationships between individuals, between citizens

and individuals. We shift as we discover what is real, what is fair, what is possible. This is the long-awaited "turning of the mind."

"Start here, now, with yourself," John Platt said in *Step to Man*. "Start here, at this place in the human network. You don't have to be rich or influential or brilliant; even fishermen can turn the world upside down. If they can, you can.... All of the evolving potentialities of the future are contained in the world at this instant."

Individuals and groups are translating inner discoveries into action. The Nobel Peace Prize for 1977 was awarded to "ordinary men and women"—to the Peace People in Northern Ireland and Amnesty International. "Our world is rushing toward disaster," said Mairead Corrigan of the Peace People, "but it's not too late to prove the power of love...." From California come announcements of new, politically oriented groups: Groundswell, "an association of people primarily from the consciousness/growth movement, who feel it's time to join forces ... to generate social action"; members of a group in Sacramento describe themselves as "bureaucrats and academicians who want to coalesce California's transpersonal political network" for the rewriting of the state constitution; and New Age Caucus urges "decentralized, responsive government."

Lone consumer activists and free-lance reformers around the country, having discovered their power to investigate, publicize, petition, and sue, find themselves on the evening news and in the Sunday newspaper features. If there is hope for a new society, our politics will have to be based on *information*. Democracy can work well only if the populace is informed. By informing ourselves and urging others to do the same, we can be the people for whom democracy was designed.

"If there is a new politics," said one Aquarian Conspirator, the co-founder of a preventive-health network and a treatment center for disturbed youngsters, "it thoroughly transcends all the old labels. It is a spiritual-bio-psycho-social perspective with powerful implications."

Politics of spirit, body, mind, society.... The new political awareness has little to do with parties or ideologies. Its constituents don't come in blocs. Power that is never surrendered by the individual cannot be brokered.

Not by revolution or protest but by autonomy, the old slogan becomes a surprising fact: *Power to the people*. One by one by one.

8

Healing Ourselves

Complete health and awakening are really the same.
—*TARTHANG TULKU*
Something we were withholding made us weak
Until we found it was ourselves.
—*ROBERT FROST*

The hope for real social transformation need not rest on circumstantial evidence. One major arena, health care, has already begun to experience wrenching change. The impending transformation of medicine is a window to the transformation of all our institutions.

Here we can see what happens when consumers begin to withdraw legitimacy from an authoritarian institution. We see the rise of the autonomous health seeker, the transformation of a profession by its leadership, the impact of the new models from science, the way decentralized networks are effecting wide geographic change.

We can see the power of an aligned minority to speed up a paradigm shift, the power of the media and informal communications to alter our image of health and our expectations, the value of "aikido politics" rather than confrontation or rhetoric, the exploitation of existing sources of power, the potential of the psychotechnologies, and a fresh appreciation for intuition, human bonds, inner listening.

The autonomy so evident in social movements is hitting the old assumptions of medicine hard. The search for self becomes a search for health, for wholeness—the cache of sanity and wisdom that once seemed beyond our conscious reach. If we respond to the message of pain or disease, the demand for adaptation, we can break through to a new level of wellness.

For all its reputed conservatism, Western medicine is undergoing an amazing revitalization. Patients and professionals alike are beginning to see beyond symptoms to the context of illness: stress, society, family, diet, season, emotions. Just as the readiness of a new constituency makes a new politics, the needs of patients can change the practice of medicine. Hospitals, long the bastions of barren efficiency, are scurrying to provide more humane environments for birth and death, more flexible policies. Medical schools, long geared to skim the cool academic cream, are trying to attract more creative, people-oriented students. Bolstered by a blizzard of research on the psychology of illness, practitioners who once split mind and body are trying to put them back together.

No one had realized how vulnerable the old medical model was. Within a few short years, without a shot's being fired, the concept of holistic health has been legitimized by federal and state programs, endorsed by politicians, urged and underwritten by insurance companies, co-opted in terminology (if not always in practice) by many physicians, and adopted by medical students. Consumers demand "holistic health," a whole new assortment of entrepreneurs promise it, and medical groups look for speakers to explain it.

Taking its own pulse, American medicine has voiced the need for reform—for training in values, ethics, human relations. Most physicians, for example, have had little or no training in coping with death—not only in counseling patients and relatives, but in their own feelings of defeat and fear.

Articles on the human context of medicine appear with increasing frequency in the trade press. A former editor of the *Journal of the American Medical Association* described his own use of touch—a pat on the back, a warm handshake. He said that modern practitioners may be better listeners to organs than the good clinicians of early times, but the old-timers were better listeners to *people*. "I suspect that some atrophy of our diagnostic senses occurred when subjective observation was replaced by objective laboratory data." Another medical publication expressed editorial concern about "the elusive skills"—the need for new doctors to recognize the psychological, social, and spiritual aspects of illness.

I-THOU MEDICINE

We seem to have gone through a period of unleavened medical "science," and now we are getting the heart back. Physicians themselves are writing and speaking of the lost dimension in healing. A guest editorial in *American Medical News* decried medicine's crisis of human relations:

> Compassions and intuitions are waylaid. . . . Physicians must recognize that medicine is not their private preserve but a profession in which all people have a vital stake. . . . It will take great medical statesmanship to correct a major failure—the patient's sense of unrequited love.

An article in a dentistry journal quoted Teilhard: "Love is the internal, affectively apprehending aspect of the affinity which links and draws together the elements of the world. . . . Love, in fact, is the agent of universal synthesis."

In *Modern Medicine* a physician wrote bitterly about "the Laying Off of Hands." Bartenders, he said, make people feel better, but we physicians usually make them feel worse. Warmth and palliation have been relinquished to other practitioners, many of them outside mainstream medicine. "Physicians are left with their diagnostic requisition slips and their prescription pads to pursue their increasingly automated, slick, scientific, impersonal 'art.'"

A poignant account of a surgeon-essayist described the physician to the Dalai Lama making the rounds of an American hospital. The Tibetan physician did a pulse diagnosis on a patient:

> For the next half hour he remains thus, suspended above the patient like some exotic golden bird with folded wings, holding the pulse of the woman beneath his fingers, cradling her hand in his. All the power of the man seems to have been drawn down into this one purpose. . . . And I know that I, who have palpated a hundred thousand pulses, have not truly felt a single one.

The Tibetan, he said, accurately diagnosed a specific type of congenital heart disorder solely on the basis of the pulse.

William Steiger, chairman of the department of medicine of a Virginia hospital, told a group of physicians that their empathy is what Martin Buber called *I-Thou* and the necessary objective examination and testing is *I-it*. He quoted Buber's statement that "knowledge is an autopsy upon the corpse of real living." If you count something, Steiger said, it goes away. "The *I-it* is a monologue, the *I-Thou* is a dialogue. They're complementary." When a medical problem persists, the doctor usually pursues more *I-it*, more lab tests, when what is needed at that point is a deeper human understanding, more *I-Thou*.

"The therapeutic attitude should be, 'What can I do to help?' We should offer warmth and succor *before* we order the first tests."

THE CRISIS IN HEALTH CARE

Neither tact nor conspiracy could have triggered such rapid change if medicine had not been beset by crisis—in economics, in performance, in credibility.

Like the foil wrap on a disappointing gift, the shiny technology has dealt stunningly with certain acute problems, as in inoculations and sophisticated surgical procedures, but its failures in chronic and degenerative disease, including cancer and heart disease, have driven practitioners and the public to look in new directions.

We have been alienated by costs that soared beyond the means of all but the well-insured or wealthy; by specialization and the cold, quantifying approach that brushes past human concerns, and by the growing despair that comes from spending without regaining health.

Health care (including medical insurance) is now the third largest industry in the United States; medical costs are roughly 9 percent of the Gross National Product. Federal health costs are over fifty billion dollars. Neighboring hospitals duplicate expensive equipment, doctors order unnecessary laboratory tests to protect themselves from malpractice suits ("defensive medicine"). Even a simple office call now represents a major expenditure to the average person. Runaway costs, especially hospital charges, have made it all but impossible to enact any sort of national health plan.

Even those to whom cost is no problem may only buy technological failures. A British study of three hundred and fifty random coronary patients, for example, found that the death rate for those in intensive-care units was higher than for those convalescing at home. A federal spokesman recently referred to the so-called war on cancer as "a medical Vietnam." The billions spent, the onslaught of technology, have yielded little. The mortality rate for most major cancers has not changed significantly in twenty-five years, despite more public education, new drugs, more sophisticated radiation and surgery techniques. It has been estimated that as many as a million hospital admissions per year are related to some form of drug reaction and that illness caused by the side effects of treatment adds perhaps eight billion dollars per year to the total medical bill.

Brilliant new operations are taken up like intellectual fashions. Thousands had coronary bypass operations before the belated studies reported that most candidates benefited as much from drugs as from the dangerous, expensive surgery. The pathos of the technological dream is especially plain in our hundred years' fruitless search for a powerful, nonaddictive painkiller.

One of the most prevalent medical problems of our times is *iatrogenic* illness. It means—literally—"doctor-caused." Iatrogenic illness results from surgical complications, wrong medication, side effects of drugs or other treatments, and the debilitating effects of hospitalization.

Not long ago, when physicians represented the pinnacle of status and humanitarian service, proud mothers spoke of "my son, the doctor." Pity the poor doctor now: thirty to a hundred times likelier than the general population to be addicted to drugs. Likelier to suffer from coronary disease. Likelier to be a problem drinker, with an estimated 5 to 6 percent of all physicians said by professional-organization surveys to be totally incapacitated by emotional disorders, including alcoholism. More often sued—and suicidal.

A recent Gallup poll disclosed that 44 percent of the public does *not* believe physicians to be "highly ethical and honest"—a low blow to a group that had long been venerated. "MDs Take It on the Chin," read a medical newspaper headline; the article noted that thirteen of fifteen physicians running for national office in 1976 lost their elections. Physicians commented in their professional publications that malpractice suits seem to reflect disappointment or hostility and that doctors with good patient rapport are unlikely to be sued, no matter what.

A Senate subcommittee on health reported growing consumer disenchantment:

The problem of dehumanization in health care is of increasing concern to health professionals. . . . Medicine is at the interface between humanity and technology, but the former has been so relatively disregarded in recent decades that medicine is in danger of losing a great deal of its relevance. The Committee sees as a priority national health need that health personnel at every level deliver care in a humanistic way.

Especially in the light of new scientific findings, we see in retrospect some of the tragic wrong turns of twentieth-century medicine—not surprisingly, the same mistakes that plague us in our other social institutions. We have oversold the benefits of technology and external manipulations; we have undersold the importance of human relationships and the complexity of nature.

THE EMERGENT PARADIGM OF HEALTH

The new paradigm of health and medicine enlarges the framework of the old, incorporating brilliant technological advances while restoring and validating intuitions about mind and relationships. It explains many heretofore puzzling phenomena. Its coherence and predictive powers are superior to those of the old model. It adds the fire and poetry of inspired science to the prose of workaday science.

"Holistic," when that adjective is properly applied to health care, refers to a qualitatively different approach, one that respects the interaction of mind, body, and environment. Beyond the allopathic approach of treating the disease and symptoms of disease, it seeks to correct the underlying disharmony causing the problem. A holistic approach may include a variety of diagnostic tools and treatments, some orthodox, some not. A much-simplified comparison of the two views:

ASSUMPTIONS OF THE OLD PARADIGM OF MEDICINE	ASSUMPTIONS OF THE NEW PARADIGM OF HEALTH
Treatment of symptoms.	Search for patterns and causes, plus treatment of symptoms.
Specialized.	Integrated, concerned with the whole patient.

ASSUMPTIONS OF THE OLD PARADIGM OF MEDICINE	ASSUMPTIONS OF THE NEW PARADIGM OF HEALTH
Emphasis on efficiency.	Emphasis on human values.
Professional should be emotionally neutral.	Professional's caring is a component of healing.
Pain and disease are wholly negative.	Pain and disease are information about conflict, disharmony.
Primary intervention with drugs, surgery.	Minimal intervention with "appropriate technology," complemented with full armamentarium of non-invasive techniques (psychotherapies, diet, exercise).
Body seen as machine in good or bad repair.	Body seen as dynamic system, context, field of energy within other fields.
Disease or disability seen as thing, entity.	Disease or disability seen as process.
Emphasis on eliminating symptoms, disease.	Emphasis on achieving maximum wellness, "meta-health."
Patient is dependent.	Patient is (or should be) autonomous.
Professional is authority.	Professional is therapeutic partner.
Body and mind are separate; psychosomatic illness is mental, may be referred to psychiatrist.	Bodymind perspective; psychosomatic illness is province of all health-care professionals.
Mind is secondary factor in organic illness.	Mind is primary or coequal factor in *all* illness.
Placebo effect shows the power of suggestion.	Placebo effect shows the mind's role in disease and healing.

A IDS

ASSUMPTIONS OF THE OLD PARADIGM OF MEDICINE	ASSUMPTIONS OF THE NEW PARADIGM OF HEALTH
Primary reliance on quantitative information (charts, tests, dates).	Primary reliance on qualitative information, including patient's subjective reports and professional's intuition; quantitative data an adjunct.
"Prevention" largely environmental: vitamins, rest, exercise, immunization, not smoking.	"Prevention" synonymous with wholeness: work, relationships, goals, body-mind-spirit.

Notice the parallels between the assumptions of the new paradigm and the scientific discoveries discussed in Chapter 6: dynamic systems; the transformation of stress; the bodymind continuum; a new appreciation of qualities, not just quantities.

THE MATRIX OF HEALTH

Edward Carpenter condemned the medical thinkers of his day for their single-minded preoccupation with disease. They should try, rather, to understand health, he said. Health is a governing harmony, just as the moon governs the tides. We can no more manipulate the body into health by external ministrations than we can manage the ebb and flow of the tides by "an organized system of mops." The greatest outside effort cannot do "what the central power does easily and with unerring grace and providence."

Well-being cannot be infused intravenously or ladled in by prescription. It comes from a matrix: the bodymind. It reflects psychological and somatic harmony. As one anatomist put it, "the healer inside us is the wisest, most complex, integrated entity in the universe." In a sense, we know now, there is always a doctor in the house.

"You can't deliver holistic health," one practitioner said. It originates in an attitude: an acceptance of life's uncertainties, a willingness to accept responsibility for habits, a way of perceiving and dealing with stress, more satisfying human relationships, a sense of purpose.

We honor the invisible matrix of health as we lose our uneasiness about it. As science becomes more spacious in its thinking, wider in its synthesis, old puzzles begin to make sense. Although we don't know *how* beliefs and expectations affect health, we know clearly that they do. Two hundred years ago the French Academy threw Mesmer out, declaring that hypnosis was a fraud, "nothing but imagination." "If so," said a dissident member, "what a wonderful thing imagination must be!"

After decades of trying to "explain" one mystery by invoking another, medical science is now coming to terms with the unavoidable and critical influence of the patient's expectations. "Placebo effect" now refers to more than the inactive substance (sugar pill, salt-water injection) given to difficult patients. The doctor's reputation, the mood of the hospital staff, the fame of the medical center, the mystique of a particular treatment—any of these can contribute to healing by coloring the patient's expectations. There is also a "nocebo effect," the opposite of placebo. When laboratory subjects were given an inactive substance and told it would give them a headache, two-thirds got a headache.

The placebo activates a capacity that was in the mind all along. As noted earlier, research has shown that placebo pain relief is apparently due to the brain's release of a natural analgesic. Yet most doctors and nurses still treat the placebo as a trick that works on people whose suffering is not "real," a misunderstanding that rests on a naive idea of reality and ignorance of the role of the mind in creating experience.

The belief of the healer can also alter the efficacy of the treatment. In a set of experiments described by Jerome Frank, an authority on the placebo effect, patients were given either a mild painkiller, a placebo, or morphine. When the *doctors* thought they were administering morphine, the placebo was twice as effective as when they thought they were giving a mild analgesic! In a similar study, psychotic patients were given either a mild tranquilizer, a major tranquilizer, or a placebo. The placebo's effects were far greater when the doctors thought they had given the powerful drug rather than the mild one.

Rick Ingrasci, a physician and co-founder of a Boston-area network, Interface, said that the placebo effect offers dramatic proof that *all* healing is essentially self-healing:

As the placebo effect so vividly demonstrates to us, changing our expectations or fundamental assumptions can profoundly affect our experience of health and well-being. Healing comes as a direct result of perceiving ourselves as whole . . . when we reestablish our sense of balanced relationship with the universe, through a *change of mind*—a transformation in attitudes, values, beliefs.

Ingrasci said that his experiences with patients have convinced him that once negative mindsets are released, healing takes place automatically. "It's as if there is a life force or ordering principle ready to reestablish our natural state of wholeness and health if we can just drop the barriers of negative expectations." If we relax, however briefly, these positive expectations can produce positive effects. "To start, we must first learn to get past the psychological barriers—cynicism, mistrust, fear— that prevent us from even trying. . . . The long-term effects may prove truly transformative for ourselves and society."

ATTENTION: CHANGING THE MATRIX OF DISEASE

People promoting holistic health are fond of pointing out that dis-ease is a lack of harmony or ease. Clearly, it is more important to teach people how to change the matrix of their illness— the stress, conflict, or worry that helped bring it about—than to trick them with placebos.

The role of altered awareness in healing may be the single most important discovery in modern medical science. Consider, for example, the extraordinary range of illnesses treated by biofeedback: high blood pressure, seizures, ulcers, impotence, incontinence, ringing in the ears, paralysis after stroke, tension headaches, arthritis, cardiac arrhythmia, hemorrhoids, diabetes, cerebral palsy, grinding of teeth.

Attention itself is the key. Several years ago researchers at the Menninger Foundation reported that patients could abort headaches by raising the temperature of their hands. They conjectured that drawing blood from the head to increase hand temperature might relieve congested blood vessels causing the headache. Temperature biofeedback became a popular and successful method for treating migraine. But then biofeedback clinicians discovered that some patients can stop their migraines by *lowering* hand temperature—or by lowering it on one occasion and raising it on another.

It is not a simple physical change but rather the state of mind that is the key to health. This state has been called "restful alertness," "passive volition," "deliberate letting." Like the ice breaking free in a spring thaw, cumulative stresses seem to melt under this paradoxical attention, restoring natural flow to the bodymind whirlpool.

Stress cannot be sidestepped. New information, noise, tension, congestion, personal conflict, and competition add up to the stress-related diseases that plague the twentieth century.

Or *is* stress the culprit? Perhaps what we really have are change-avoidance diseases. Our vulnerability to stress appears to be due more to our interpretation of events than their inherent seriousness. F.D.R.'s famous remark, "The only thing we have to fear is fear itself," relates to the bodymind as well.

Kenneth Pelletier, a psychologist at the University of California School of Medicine in San Francisco who has spent most of the past decade teaching people to deal with stress, points out that the body is literal. It can't tell the difference between a "real" threat and a perceived one. Our worries and negative expectations translate into physical illness because the body feels as if we are endangered, even if the threat is imaginary.

We can handle short-term stress naturally because of the body's rest-and-renewal response, its parasympathetic reaction. But long-term stress—the "one damned thing after another" typical of modern existence—takes its toll because there is no opportunity for rebound between stresses. When Pelletier studied meditators in the laboratory, he found not only highly integrated responses but the ability to shift the body into a parasympathetic phase. "The yogis have learned to let go of those excess levels of self-stressing neurophysiological activity and simply quiet themselves down."

Most of us suffer from what he called a "cumulative destructive cycle. The secret is paying attention, investing your life with attention." Paying attention to stress in a relaxed state transforms it. Meditation, biofeedback, relaxation techniques, autogenic training, running, listening to music—any of these can help elicit the body's recovery phase.

Refusal to acknowledge stress means that we pay double; not only does our alarm not go away but it goes into the body. This was evident in a recent laboratory experiment. The threat of an imminent painful electric shock caused strikingly different body changes in individuals, *depending on whether they decided to confront it or avoid thinking about it*. The confronters tried to understand the situation. They actively focused their attention on the coming shock and wanted to get it over with. They thought about events in the laboratory environment or directed attention to their bodies.

The avoiders, on the other hand, used a host of strategies to distract themselves. They tried to think about nonstressful subjects, matters outside the laboratory; or they fantasized. Whereas the confronters felt they could do something about the stress situation, if only to prepare for it, the avoiders tended to feel helpless and tried to escape through denial.

Muscle activity increased in the confronter—an appropriate physiological response. The avoiders had significantly higher heart rates, suggesting that their stress was pushed back to another, more pathological level.

Denial can follow us to the grave. Not only does the mind have strategies for walling off psychological conflict; it can also deny the illnesses that result from the first round of denial. The pathological effect of this refusal to face facts was evident in a cancer study at the University of Texas. Those patients who showed the greatest denial in response to questions about their disease were likeliest to have a poor prognosis when they were followed up two months later.

Conflict not dealt with consciously can wreak its physical damage in almost as many ways as there are people. One of the Aquarian Conspirators, who had worked in a medical setting, expressed her belief that ill people should not be told, "You'll be your old self again."

> Very often they don't want to go back to being the way they were, doing the things they were doing. My daughter-in-law, who had a stroke recently, conceded that she hadn't faced the fact that she wanted to change her life. So the stroke changed her life.
>
> Another man I know of was a car dealer in partnership with a lazy brother. He carried the whole load of work without saying anything. When he had a stroke, his brother had to take over. He said later that he was *glad* he'd had the stroke.

If we learn to pay attention to such inner conflicts, we can resolve them in ways less drastic to our health.

THE BODY'S MIND

As more is learned in brain research, the connection between mind and illness becomes more understandable. The brain masterminds or indirectly influences every function of the body: blood pressure, heart rate, immune response, hormones, everything. Its mechanisms are linked by an alarm network, and it has a kind of dark genius, organizing disorders appropriate to our most neurotic imaginings.

The old saying, "name your poison," applies to the semantics and symbols of disease. If we feel "picked on" or someone gives us a pain in the neck, we may make our metaphors literal—with acne or neck spasms. People have long spoken of a "broken heart" as the result of a disappointing relationship; now research has shown a connection between loneliness and heart disease. In animal research, heart disease has been caused by the prolonged stimulation of a brain region associated with strong emotion. The same region is connected to the immune system. So the "broken heart" may become coronary disease; the need to grow may become a tumor, the ambivalence a "splitting headache," the rigid personality arthritis. Every metaphor is potentially a literal reality.

All illness, whether cancer or schizophrenia or a cold, originates in the bodymind. On his deathbed Louis Pasteur acknowledged that a medical adversary of his had been right in insisting that disease is caused less by the germ than by the resistance of the individual invaded by the germ. "It is the terrain," he conceded.[1] As Lewis Thomas pointed out in *The Lives of a Cell*, our bodies often respond hysterically to harmless germs, as if the intruder evokes ancient memories and we react to a kind of propaganda. "We are, in effect, at the mercy of our own Pentagons most of the time."

The body's ability to make sense of new information, to transform it, is health. If we are flexible, able to adapt to a changing environment, even a virus or damp air or fatigue or spring pollens, we can withstand a high level of stress.

A recent and radical concept of the immune system can help us understand how the "inner physician" maintains health—and how it fails. The body, via the immune system, seems to have its own way of "knowing," parallel to the way the brain knows. This immune system is linked to the brain. The "mind" of the immune system has a dynamic image of the self and a drive to transform environmental "noise," including viruses

---

[1]This is not to disregard the role of genetic susceptibility or environmental influences such as smoking. Illness or health originates in a milieu. The translation of unresolved conflict or change into a particular disease is partially influenced by genetic vulnerability, which biases us toward particular disorders. One whose family history includes a high incidence of allergy, diabetes, schizophrenia, or cardiac disease is somewhat likelier to experience these disorders than, say, cancer under stress.

and allergens, into sense. It does not reject certain substances or react to them violently because they are foreign, as was believed in the old paradigm, but because they are *nonsense*. They cannot be fitted into the orderly system.

This immune system is powerful and plastic in its ability to render sense out of its environment, but since it is tied into the brain it is vulnerable to psychological stress. Research has shown that stressful mental states like grief and anxiety alter the immune system's capability. The reason we sometimes "get" a virus or have an "allergic reaction" is because the immune system is functioning under par.

This immune system has a memory whose subtlety was demonstrated in animal research. If an innocent drug is paired with an immunosuppressant—a drug that suppresses the immune system—the body learns to suppress its immune system when it gets *only the innocent drug*, even if it is months later. In just this way, stressful periods of our lives can be paired with innocent cues in the environment (for example, allergens or events that remind us of other events) to cause chronic illness, long after the original source of stress has been removed. The body "remembers" to be sick.

Cancer, of course, represents a failure of the immune system. At various points in our lives, most of us have malignant cells that do not become clinical cancer because the immune system efficiently disposes of them. Of the psychological factors implicated in cancer, the most conspicuous is bottled-up emotion. One researcher remarked that many cancer patients exhibit the stolid faces of the famous Grant Wood painting, *American Gothic*.

Cancer patients have more difficulty remembering their dreams than patients found not to have cancer, fewer marital changes (separations, divorces), fewer symptoms of illnesses known to reflect psychological conflict (ulcers, migraine, asthma).[2] Various studies have found that cancer patients tend to keep their feelings to themselves, and most have not had close relationships with their parents. They find it difficult to express anger. One study reported that they are conforming and controlled, less autonomous and spontaneous than those whose tests later prove negative. One cancer therapist said of

[2]In most such studies, personality assessments *precede* the diagnosis. Those later found to have cancer are then compared to those whose tests were negative. In some studies, large groups have been followed for decades to determine whether those who eventually develop cancer have distinguishing personality characteristics or similar life stresses.

her patients, "They have typically experienced a gap in their lives—disappointment, expectations that didn't work out. It's as if the need for growth becomes a physical metaphor."

Unexpressed grief may trigger pathology by depressing the immune system. One study showed that the death of a spouse resulted in lower immune function during subsequent weeks. A Boston project found a 60 percent miscarriage rate in women who got pregnant just after losing a baby to the Sudden Infant Death syndrome. The report urged that such bereaved women "should wait until the body is no longer feeling the effects of grief."

THE BODY AS PATTERN AND PROCESS

Over the years our bodies become walking autobiographies, telling friends and strangers alike of the minor and major stresses of our lives. Distortions of function that occur after injuries, like a limited range of motion in a hurt arm, become a permanent part of our body pattern. Our musculature reflects not only old injuries but old anxieties. Poses of timidity, depression, bravado, or stoicism adopted early in life are locked into our bodies as patterns in our sensorimotor system.

In the vicious cycle of bodymind pathology, our body's tight patterns contribute to our locked-in mental processes. We cannot separate mental from physical, fact from fantasy, past from present. Just as the body feels the mind's grief, so the mind is constricted by the body's stubborn memory of what the mind *used to feel*, and on and on.

This cycle can be interrupted by "bodywork"—therapies that deeply (and often painfully) massage, manipulate, loosen, or otherwise change the body's neuromuscular system, its orientation to gravity, its symmetry. Changing the body in this way can affect the whole bodymind loop profoundly. The late Ida Rolf, whose structural integration method (Rolfing) is one of the best-known approaches, quoted Norbert Weiner, the founder of cybernetics: "We are not the stuff that abides but patterns that perpetuate themselves."

Just as some psychotechnologies increase the fluctuation of energy through the brain, enabling new patterns or paradigm shifts to occur, bodywork alters the flow of energy through the body, freeing it of its old "ideas" or patterns, increasing its range of movement. Structural integration, the Alexander method, Feldenkrais, Applied Kinesiology, Neurokinesthetics, bioenergetics, Reichian therapy, and hundreds of other systems initiate transformation of the body.

John Donne's famous line, "No man is an island," is as true of our bodies as of our social interdependence. Belatedly, half a century after we should have taken the hint from physics, Western medicine is beginning to recognize that the body is a process—a bioelectric whirlpool, sensitive to positive ions, cosmic rays, trace minerals in our diet, free electricity from power generators.

Picturing the body at its dynamic level helps us to make sense of otherwise puzzling controversies. For example, orthomolecular psychiatry, which treats mental disturbances with megadoses of vitamins and trace minerals, bases its approach on the effect of these nutrients on the brain's bioelectrical activity. Electrical stimulation hurries the healing of slow-mending bones, perhaps by creating large enough fluctuation of energy to bring about regeneration. Direct current has been measured at the acupuncture points.

Acupuncture and acupressure, which stimulate particular points on precise meridians, show how even remote parts of the body are connected. The more we see of the effects of acupuncture, the better we understand why treating symptoms alone seldom alleviates disease.

We are oscillating fields within larger fields. Our brains respond to the rhythm of sounds, pulsations of light, specific colors, tiny changes of temperature. We even become biologically entrained to those close to us; couples who live together, for example, have been shown to share a monthly temperature cycle. When we engage in conversation, even if we are only listening, we enter into a subtle "dance" with the other person, synchronous movements so small they can only be detected by examining movie film frame by frame.

Stimulation in the environment affects the growth and connections of the plastic human brain from its earliest critical periods to its last days—its weight, nutrients, the number of cells. Even in the elderly, the physical brain does not lose a measurable number of cells if the environment is stimulating.

If the bodymind is a process, so disease is a process.... And so is healing, whole-making, with seven million of our red blood cells blinking out of existence every second, replaced by seven million more. Even our bones are fully rebuilt over a period of seven years. Just as in the dance of Shiva, we are continuously creating and destroying, creating and destroying.

Wallace Ellerbroek, a former surgeon now a psychiatrist, said:

> We doctors seem to have a predilection for nouns in naming diseases (epilepsy, measles, brain tumor), and because these things "deserve" nouns as names, then obviously they are things—to us. If you take one of these nouns— measles—and make it into a verb, then it becomes, "Mrs. Jones, your little boy appears to be measling," which opens both your mind and hers to the concept of disease as a process.

Ellerbroek has successfully treated a number of diseases by teaching the patient to *confront* and *accept* the process—to pay attention to it. In one well-known experiment, he instructed chronic acne patients to react to any new outbreak of pimples with nonjudgmental attention. They might look into the mirror and say, in effect, "Well, pimple, there you are, right where you belong at this moment in time." They were urged to accept the acne rather than resisting it with negative emotions.

All participants had had their acne for fifteen or more years without relief. The results of the experiment were stunning. Several patients were completely clear within weeks. An active process—fear, resentment, denial—had been *maintaining* the acne.

Health and disease don't just happen to us. They are active processes issuing from inner harmony or disharmony, profoundly affected by our states of consciousness, our ability or inability to flow with experience. This recognition carries with it implicit responsibility and opportunity. If we are participating, however unconsciously, in the process of disease, we can choose health instead.

HEALTH AND TRANSFORMATION

Illness, as Pelletier and many others have said, is potentially transformative because it can cause a sudden shift in values, an awakening. If we have been keeping secrets from ourselves— unexamined conflicts, suppressed yearnings—illness may force them into awareness.

For many Aquarian Conspirators, an involvement in health care was a major stimulus to transformation. Just as the search for self becomes a search for health, so the pursuit of health can lead to greater self-awareness. All wholeness is the same. The proliferating holistic health centers and networks have drawn many into the consciousness movement. A nurse said, "If healing becomes a reality with you, it's a lifestyle. Altered states of consciousness accompany it, increased telepathy. It's an adventure."

One woman sought biofeedback instrumentation to see if she could lower her intraocular pressure and cure her glaucoma. She succeeded, but more importantly, she discovered that her states of consciousness affected her entire life, not just her vision. An MD, concerned about the abusive doses of Valium he was taking for his headaches, tried biofeedback...which led to inner attention...which led to meditation and wrenching change, including a far different career in medicine. A prominent attorney came to believe that there was a valuable purpose in his progressive loss of eyesight:

> I felt called, not to fight against the sudden impairment of outer vision but to cooperate with it as a way to enhance my own life process. Looking back over the past fifteen months, I'm convinced it would have been a great loss if by some chance, miracle, or effort of will, the process had been reversed at once.

A conspirator-bureaucrat said he discovered health as a by-product of meditation. After several years of Transcendental Meditation he found it easy to give up his compulsive drinking and soon thereafter his compulsive overeating. "At an age when I should be going downhill, I'm healthier than I was five years ago and getting healthier all the time."

A psychologist, a national leader in holistic medicine, wandered into the field by way of a T'ai Chi instructor who interested him in acupuncture. He has now successfully integrated alternative medical approaches into the curriculum of a major medical school and has arranged lecture series on holistic approaches for a group of medical schools. "When you develop liaisons," he said, "it's critical that you speak the right language. If I talked yin and yang to most neurosurgeons, they wouldn't hear me. I talk the sympathetic and parasympathetic nervous systems. If we want to help people change, it's important that we don't push them or pull them—just walk together."

A former political activist—now on the faculty of a medical school—who teaches courses on the biology of the bodymind, said, "This revolution says that we're all basically all right and that the return to health is natural. It's anti-elitist. Professionalism, the degree on the wall, is eroding as a symbol of authority. Love is the most irresistible power in the universe. Caring—that's what healing is all about."

A New York MD, all but paralyzed from chronic back pain after an automobile accident, discovered that pressure at acupuncture points on her foot relieved her agony. "I believe my acumassage worked because of my readiness and perspective at that time and the treatment itself which redirected the flow of energy. Through that experience I became interested in learning more about hypnosis, biofeedback, and meditation."

A clergyman who responded to the Aquarian Conspiracy questionnaire opened a holistic health and meditation center after finding relief from chronic pain through meditation. A New Mexico MD said she began using a spiritual network as a counseling adjunct for patients who were slow to get well. Several respondents said they had been drawn into the psychotechnologies by their curiosity about healing phenomena they saw as medical professionals.

THE AQUARIAN CONSPIRACY IN MEDICINE

The new way of thinking about health and disease, with its message of hope and its charge of individual responsibility, is widely communicated by the Aquarian Conspiracy, as in a 1978 Washington conference, "Holistic Health: A Public Policy," cosponsored by several government agencies and private organizations. Agencies from the Department of Health, Education and Welfare were represented. So was the White House staff. Insurance companies, prepaid health-plan organizations, and foundations sent representatives—in many cases, their top executive officers. Politicians, physicians, psychologists, traditional healers, spiritual teachers, researchers, futurists, sociologists, and health policymakers shared the platform. The assistant surgeon-general opened the conference; principal speakers included Jerome Frank on the placebo effect, California legislator John Vasconcellos, meditation teacher Jack Schwarz, Buckminster Fuller on human ecology.

Topics included public-health policy, implementation of holistic health centers, crosscultural healing practices, systems theory, the holographic theory of mind and reality, yoga, music and consciousness, acupuncture and acupressure, Buddhist meditative techniques, electromedicine, alternative birth approaches, bodywork, biofeedback, guided imagery, homeopathy, nutrition—and "the changing image of man."

This inclusive program typifies the new paradigm, which sees many nontraditional healing systems as complementary to Western medicine. Whether we understand how they work or not, they can be put to our service, just as conventional medicine uses aspirin, digitalis, and electroconvulsive shock without knowing why they are effective.

It was in 1970 that the first group of scientists and physicians — friends — gathered in a public forum to assert their interest in spiritual realities and alternative approaches to health. The standing-room-only program at De Anza College in Cupertino, California, was underwritten by Lockheed Aircraft. Six months later a similar cast of characters staged twin weekend programs at UCLA and Stanford, emphasizing the role of the mind in disease, telling of "new" therapies: meditation, visualization, biofeedback, acupuncture, hypnosis, psychic healing, folk healing. Within a few years, variations on this scientific-spiritual mating dance had been performed on the campuses of most major universities in the country, including Yale, Harvard, New York University, New York Institute of Technology, every branch of the University of California system, and the Universities of Massachusetts, Miami, Michigan, and Illinois. The Rockefeller, Ford, and Kellogg foundations funded programs exploring the interface of mind and health.

In October 1975 Roy Menninger of the Menninger Clinic said at a Tucson conference, "The traditional ideas about medicine and the new concept of man are on a collision course." Other speakers foresaw confrontation and resistance in the realm of health-care reform.

But even then, at the Tucson meeting, detente had begun. Take the case of Malcolm Todd. Todd, then president of the conservative AMA, gave a somewhat defensive recounting of the technological wonders of modern medicine. His talk was not an audience pleaser, but everyone agreed that his willingness to appear on the platform along with unorthodoxy was significant.

Less than a year later, appearing on a similar, larger program in San Diego, Todd endorsed the concept of a "humanistic medicine" that deals with the "bodymind." Nine months later he urged a heavily medical audience in Houston to take an active role in the integration of these holistic approaches into the system. Wisely used, he said, they promise an exciting rejuvenation of Western medicine. "The spectrum of components might range from biofeedback and the psychology of consciousness to paranormal phenomena, psychic healing...."

The conspiracy has understood that potential opponents should be listened to, not shouted down. And they should be given first-hand experience of the larger context. In 1975 and 1976 Rick Carlson, an attorney specializing in health policy, and others organized small conferences at Airliehouse, Virginia, near Washington, to acquaint government officials and legislative aides with the power of holistic concepts and alternative medicine.[3] Those who attended had an opportunity to try biofeedback, meditation, imagery, relaxation, and other psychotechnologies. Those meetings were quietly funded by Blue Cross-Blue Shield.

In 1976 "the Blues," the Rockefeller Foundation, and the University of California-San Francisco cosponsored a meeting at the Waldorf-Astoria Hotel in New York City, where two hundred top policymakers were introduced to alternative health approaches, emphasizing the importance of the "inner physician." Two months later a similar meeting was held, this time with an additional sponsor, the Institute of Medicine.

The conspirators moved around the country like circuit riders, preaching a perspective, not a dogma; launching an educational program here, a pilot project there, promoting and publicizing the work of others in the network, forging new links. Some worked at changing their local and state professional organizations. Others alerted foundations and the press to the possibilities of a wider paradigm.

The most successful strategies were gentle persuasion and first-hand experience. The wooing of influential policymakers has been an effective way of shaking the status quo. For example, some conferences served a dual purpose, enlightening the paying participants and seducing partially committed speakers into full alliance.

Like a promise, a litany, a manifesto for wholeness in a broken society, are the gatherings. And they are materializing all across the national landscape, more quickly than they can be counted: symposia and conferences, workshops and seminars,

[3]Actually, the Airliehouse meetings had been preceded by a ten-day London "human-potential workshop" in May 1975 in which various speakers—Moshe Feldenkrais, Rick Carlson, Fritjof Capra, Werner Erhard, and others—had brainstormed potential social change under the theme, "Frontiers of Medicine and Science."

retreats, fairs and festivals, giant expositions. Among them: *Ways of Healing, Healing East and West, New All-American Bi-Centennial Medicine Show, Annual Healing Arts Camp and Fair, Health Expo, New Age Expo, Toward Tomorrow Fair, New Physics and New Medicine, Meditation-related Therapies, Human Ecology, Human Energy, Common Ground, Body Faire, The Mind Can Do Anything, It's All in the Mind, Holistic Health Retreat, Holistic Life University, Celebration of Health, New Perspectives on Medicine, New Prescriptions for American Medicine, Physician of the Future, Healing Center of the Future, Cultural Perspectives in Healing, Native American Healing, Natural Resources for Health, Self and Body, Body-Mind-Spirit, Stress Without Distress, Stress and the Psychology of Cancer, Biofeedback and Behavioral Medicine, Reintegrating the Body-Mind Split in Psychotherapy, Chinese Total Health for Body and Mind, New Dimensions in Health Care, Touch for Health, A Holistic Affair.*

And the organizations: The Center for Integral Medicine, The Institute of Humanistic Medicine, The Association for Holistic Health, numberless "holistic-health centers" and "holistic-health clinics."

The conspiracy concedes that there is strength in numbers and certainly strength in cooperation, but not in centralization. One tentative effort to weld a single body of practitioners in 1977 was vigorously resisted. Despite its powerful national alliances and coalitions, the movement is determined to stay grass-roots and decentralized.[4]

The networks are SPINs, classic examples of the self-sufficient, multicentered groups described in Chapter 7. Caucuses have been formed in many of the older professional organizations, and, at every national convention, panels and workshops are devoted to topics relating to alternative medicine: altered states of consciousness, acupuncture, hyp-

---

[4]Any wide-open, fuzzy field like "holistic health" offers abundant opportunity for fraud and overpromise. Ground rules include making sure that the unorthodox procedures are used only to complement proven conventional treatments rather than subjecting consumers to needless risk. Consumers are warned against practitioners who make unwarranted promises or charge outrageous fees.

There have been some calls for licensure, but the debates usually come to this: Holistic health is a perspective, not a specialty or discipline. You can't license a concept. And you can't even know for sure what works. As Marshall McLuhan once said, "Mysticism is just tomorrow's science, dreamed today." The line between quackery and crazy-new-paradigm is not always easy to establish.

nosis, meditation, biofeedback. The body-mind-spirit slogan of these sessions may take its place as a revolutionary motif with "liberty, equality, fraternity." A number of holistic-health centers, conferences, and networks have also emerged from churches or church-affiliated foundations.

One newsletter said, "At this time holistic medicine is very much a 'people field' rather than an institutional field, depending on a communications pattern which links a global informal network.... As in many emerging disciplines, this informal network *is* the field of holistic health." Just as the new collective was said to *be* the new politics, so the health networks are the new paradigm of wellness—living and breathing examples of a better way.

The conspiracy also recognizes the importance of semantics to bridge the old and the new. For example, the protocols for a landmark study of unconventional healing were approved by participating hospitals under the title "therapeutic touch" because it seemed less esoteric than "the laying on of hands." A researcher prepared a grant proposal to study "The Psychobiology of Health." It was rejected. Knowing that the funding agencies are more oriented to pathology than wellness, he retitled his proposal "The Psychobiology of Disease" and it was promptly accepted.

By 1977 there were weekly "rap groups" at the National Institute of Mental Health (NIMH), informal discussions of shamanic healing, meditation, aura diagnosis. A working conference in California, sponsored by NIMH, produced a book of commissioned papers on alternative medicine for the express purpose of giving legitimacy to the concepts. Federal grants supported the study of bodymind changes produced by the psychotechnologies. NIMH also contracted for the preparation of an annotated bibliography on holistic medicine. In its work request, the agency eloquently defined the need:

During the last two decades many physicians and mental health professionals have begun to discover the limitations in the paradigms and practices of western allopathic medicine.... The focus on pathology and disease rather than prevention, the destructiveness of so many pharmaceutical and surgical remedies, the too-rigid separation of physical and emotional problems, the assumption of an asymmetrical relationship between an all-powerful physician and a submissive patient... have all prompted clini-

cians and researchers to look for answers in other traditions and techniques.

This search has led many to seek out traditions in which
body and mind are regarded as one, in which therapeutics
are directed at aiding natural healing processes. . . . Some
workers have turned their interest to forms of traditional
medicine—acupuncture, homeopathy, herbalism, meditation, psychic healing; others, to such new techniques as
guided imagery and biofeedback.

"The war is over," Norman Cousins, publisher of *Saturday
Review*, said in 1978. "We have allies out there, a lot of doctors
who believe as we do but need encouragement." Cousins had
reason to know of the "allies out there." He had recounted in
the *New England Journal of Medicine* his own dramatic recovery
from critical illness using an unorthodox approach when conventional medicine was at a loss. He prescribed his own
treatment—a marathon of Marx Brothers movies and old
"Candid Camera" shows, along with massive intravenous
doses of Vitamin C. What had appeared to be a fatal cellular
disease was reversed.

The response to his article was phenomenal. Seventeen medical journals asked to reprint it, thirty-four medical schools included it in their course materials, and Cousins was invited to
address medical schools around the country. More than three
thousand physicians from many countries wrote him apprecia-
tive, enthusiastic letters. Later in 1978 Cousins joined the faculty of the UCLA Medical School.

THE TRANSFORMATION OF A PROFESSION

Cousins also addressed the 1977 convention of the American
Medical Students Association (AMSA) in Atlanta. The convention theme, "Alternative Roles in Health—a New Definition of
Medicine," made it increasingly clear that the paradigm shift is
happening in medical schools. Around the country, students
and sympathetic faculty have started informal discussion
groups on consciousness and holistic approaches to medicine.
These groups meet regularly at such medical schools as UCLA,
the University of Texas in Galveston, Baylor in Houston, Johns
Hopkins in Baltimore.

A national network, Goldenseal, grew out of the Johns Hopkins group; one of its founders was then vice-president of

AMSA. From its two founding members it grew to a membership of two hundred fifty in its first year.

The AMSA official magazine, *New Physician*, devoted an entire issue in 1977 to alternative practices and has a regular department on humanistic medicine. Laurel Cappa, 1976 president of AMSA, told a physicians' convention of the students' interest in family practice and in nontraditional approaches such as meditation and Gestalt psychology. Medical students were saying that they want to be partners, not authority figures to their patients.

In 1978, the AMSA immediate past president, Doug Outcalt, was invited to Denver to address the founding conference of a new organization of physicians, the American Holistic Medical Association. He urged the members to serve as models for those students looking for a more open, humanistic approach to health care.

Medical students, he said, can be roughly divided into thirds: the Traditionalists, content to pursue medicine as it was practiced by their fathers; the Dues-payers, who don't approve of the system but can't imagine that it will change; and the Searchers, those actively interested in alternatives. "You can help us," Outcalt said. "Infiltrate the admissions committees. Infiltrate the curriculum committees. Get on the clinical faculties at the medical schools."

Conspiracy and crisis are indeed changing medical schools. A number of those who filled out Aquarian Conspiracy questionnaires are on the faculties of medical schools, not only offering the students a more generous paradigm but also organizing continuing medical-education programs for licensed physicians. (Many states require physicians to update their training with a minimum number of hours' training each year.)

In Sacramento, the medical-affairs committee of the California legislature was considering whether changes in medical-school curricula were in order. A conspirator-psychologist and friend of the committee chairman announced himself—"I represent the non-physicians of the state of California"—and proceeded to make recommendations for humanizing the education of future doctors.

When the medical-college deans protested that the suggested changes would be too difficult and complicated, he said mildly, "I agree. Innovation probably *is* too difficult for our medical schools." The deans backtracked at once. Well, maybe it wasn't *that* difficult.

But above and beyond the conscious assistance of the Aquarian Conspiracy, the implosion of knowledge and the failure of "rational medicine" are inexorable forces for change.

Life has not been easy for most doctors caught in the paradigm shift. They are between generations, not young enough to move smoothly into the new concepts, not old enough to have died with the technological dream and the mystique of the doctor.

Many health-care professionals around the country have been serving as the kind of "transforming leadership" described by James MacGregor Burns (see Chapter 7). In a way, they are trying to break their own cultural trance, for Western medical training is a narrow subculture, what one medical anthropologist called "the harsh Galenic tradition."

The holistic ideal is hardly new. In the prestigious journal *Science*, in an essay titled "The Need for a New Medical Model," George Engel pointed out that the approach had been attempted at Johns Hopkins medical school before 1920. In *The Will to Live* (1950), Arnold Hutschnecker, a physician, made a vigorous case for bodymind medicine. The physician's preoccupation with disease and the psychoanalyst's preoccupation with the mind would be synthesized, for the truth is not a monopoly of either branch of medicine. "They will meet and fuse, and their fusion will be found most profoundly in the general practitioner."

What Hutschnecker could not have foreseen was the rapid disappearance of the general practitioner. In 1950 nearly 90 percent of the graduates of medical school went into family practice. By 1970 that figure had dropped to *less than 10 percent*. Mind and body were not only treated by separate camps but every part of the body became somebody's turf.

Specialization was the understandable, perhaps even inevitable, result of an increasing reliance by medical schools on the Medical College Admissions Test (MCAT). According to Harrison Gough, a psychologist at the University of California, Berkeley, who has been studying medical students since 1951, the test shaped a generation of American medicine by selecting students of a particular temperament. As higher scores were required for admission, the test eliminated many "doers and good workers" in favor of those with a strong academic orientation. These scholarly types tended to go into research or into specialties like radiology and anesthesiology. "Reliance on the test produced a generation of doctors who didn't want to talk to a patient about how his stomach hurt."

Gough discovered over the years that the most creative medical students were the likeliest to drop out. "It's not that they weren't fit to be doctors. They just couldn't tolerate the chain gang—the highly scheduled lockstep program of medical school."

Especially in recent years, many of the best potential doctors did not even make it to the dropout stage. Increasingly intense competition for relatively few spaces meant that spectacular grade averages were prerequisite to admission. Warmth, intuition, and imagination are precisely the characteristics likely to be screened out by the emphasis on scholastic standing and test scores. The right brain, in effect, was being denied admission to medical school. There were no quotas for creativity.

In April 1977, nearly thirty thousand applicants took a dramatically different MCAT for 1978-79 entry to medical school. By its very nature, the new test blunted the sharp competitive edge that once favored science majors. It enabled non-science majors to qualify for admission. Furthermore, it screened for characteristics never before tested: the ability to synthesize, to see *patterns*, to extrapolate, to ignore irrelevant data. There were few cut-and-dried answers.

The new MCAT was the first truly new test for medical school admission since 1946. The American Association of Medical Colleges, which had commissioned the test at a cost of one million dollars, has begun actively considering strategies for evaluating the kinds of human traits likely to make a good doctor. A spokesman said, "Everyone agrees that the traits not tapped by cognitive tests are important—perhaps more critical than a candidate's knowledge of medicine."

The medical colleges are also assessing the impact of the curriculum itself on the student's personality. A former dean of the Harvard Medical School remarked that "there is less intellectual freedom in the medical course than in almost any other form of professional education in this country." Howard Hiatt, dean of the Harvard School of Public Health, urged the broadening of medical education, too long "isolated from the richness of the university's mainstream."

The new test, by requiring only knowledge from first-year science courses, is expected to encourage pre-med students to take courses in the humanities. In fact, there is a small but significant trend among medical schools to encourage the applications of non-science majors. At McMaster University in Hamilton, Ontario, entering medical students are about evenly divided between science and humanities majors.

Medical students are starting to demand (and even organize) courses in nutrition, psychosomatic medicine, biofeedback, acupuncture, and other nontraditional alternatives.

In a lecture to the faculty and alumni of the University of California-San Francisco medical school, an intern, Scott May, urged the respect and nurturance of feminine principles. He listed examples of the exaggerated masculine orientation: the medical schools' pushing students to ignore the exhaustion of their own bodies, the "objectification" of the patient which keeps the doctor from understanding his own feelings, the lack of compassion, the suicides and breakdowns and drug abuse among doctors. "Value, don't deprecate, those students who are less thick-skinned, less distant from their own feelings and those of the patients. Look for them on the admissions committee." He urged his classmates, "Remember your heart. . . ."

A Yale medical student, Tom Ferguson, launched a successful publication, *Medical Self Care*, offering articles on nutrition, psychology, exercise, psychotechnologies, herbs, drugs, assorted alternatives. Ferguson also started an adult-education program, saying, "The way the medical-school curriculum is set up now, people interested in medicine for very humanistic reasons are put into situations where they're kept away from patients for two, three, or even four years." To get human contact, frustrated students at the University of Louisville School of Medicine set up their own free clinic.

Younger doctors see themselves in partnership with non-physicians. Their view was typified in a letter to the *American Medical News* editor protesting an article that had characterized chiropractors as cultists. The student said, "Let's work *with* chiropractors." Old issues of power (who has the expertise, who deserves more authority) are fading. Psychologists are as influential as MDs in a number of innovative medical programs. In California, a doctorate in mental health is being experimentally offered—a blend of psychiatry, psychology, and social-work courses. Old hierarchical distinctions fall away: Psychiatrists seek advice from psychologists, orthopedists from chiropractors, ophthalmologists from optometrists. Nurse-practitioners, midwives, family counselors, lay counselors, clergymen, folk healers, body therapists, physicists, medical engineers—anybody can contribute to holistic medicine. As an anatomist at a California medical school put it, "We all have a piece of the truth. Nobody has it all." Harvard's Hiatt said:

The days of the physician as the sole central figure in the

health arena are over. No matter how able the doctor is . . . we need other professionals involved in the system because medical care, no matter how well delivered, is not the sole solution to most of the health problems that confront us.

These issues demand input from law and economics, Hiatt said, as well as from the biological sciences, mathematics, public policy, business, journalism, ethics, education.[5]

WAYS OF LIVING, DYING, HEALING

Everything of importance is already known, a sage said—the only thing is to rediscover it. Much of the current excitement about healing is a kind of collective remembering, a homecoming to the old wives and old doctors. Hippocrates, with his insistence on the importance of mind and milieu, could have warned us of the consequences of medical pigeonholing.

Scientific discoveries about the richness and complexity of nature reveal the poverty of our usual approaches to health, especially our efforts to deal externally, forcefully, and invasively with systems whose delicate balance can only be corrected if the inner physician is recruited. Just as outer reforms have limited effect on the body politic, external treatments are insufficient to heal the body if the spirit is in conflict.

In many instances traditional ways are being re-adopted, not out of nostalgia but because we recognize that our "modern" approaches have been an aberration, an attempt to impose some sort of clumsy order on a nature far more ordered than we can imagine. For example, the twentieth century gave us four-hour bottle feedings of infants, induced labor of childbirth and Caesarian-section deliveries for the convenience of hospitals and doctors, birth and death segregated into isolated, sterile environments empty of human consolation.

In a typical modern delivery, drugged babies are taken from drugged mothers, pulled into a shock of bright lights and loud noises, tied up, wrapped, and placed in plastic boxes. Their

[5]In late 1979, in response to lawsuits and government pressure, the AMA began circulating a new code of ethics allowing physicians to cooperate with nonphysicians. Psychologists were also challenging physicians' groups and insurors in the courts, demanding their right to be included in health-care payments.

fathers see them through glass, their siblings not at all. Yet we know now that mothers and infants become physically and emotionally "bonded" if given time enough together immediately after birth: The eye contact, touching, smiling, and feeding seem to have a long-term effect on their rapport and the child's later development. Practices from other cultures and revived customs from our own show us the startling benefits of *natural* behavior toward the newborn: a mother's cuddling, a father's play, human milk furnishing substances crucial to development, the human voice triggering micromovements in the infant.

The importance of bonding has been quantified by crosscultural studies that have shown strong correlations between bonding and the mother's later sensitivity, the child's long-term IQ, and reduced instances of abuse or neglect. There seems to be a paternal bonding as well. Swedish fathers allowed to handle their babies in the hospital were much more involved with them three months later. Long-range studies have shown greater social competence in children whose fathers were involved in their infant care.

At first the interest in bonding was dismissed by the medical profession. Capitulation, when it came, was sudden and unexpected. In 1978 the AMA announced its endorsement of obstetric approaches that consider the importance of mother-infant bonding.

Obviously, modern hospitals were not designed for family childbirth, a factor that caused an enormous wave of home births in recent years. At first this trend was looked on with alarm by the medical profession, but the first major evaluation of safety was a shocker. Studying nearly twelve hundred cases of home childbirth, the California State Department of Health found them safer than the state average *on every count*. (The mothers, who had been screened for major risk, were not quite representative of the general population.) More than twice as many babies died in the hospital deliveries, and midwives outperformed physicians when it came to handling complications! (For example, the midwives' techniques kept lacerations to around 5 percent, compared to 40 percent in physician deliveries.)

In the face of consumer revolt, a growing number of hospitals have attempted to compete. The obstetric ward is "a home away from home," a humane environment with access to emergency facilities. In the New Life Center at Family Hospital in Milwaukee, the Alternative Birth Centers at San Francisco

General and Hollywood Presbyterian, parents and other children are together in homelike quarters, listening to music, visiting during the mother's labor, sharing meals.

Many hospitals have adopted the delivery method of French obstetrician Frederic Leboyer. The baby is born into a dimly lit environment in silence and then gently welcomed, massaged, placed in a warm bath. A physician at Rush-Presbyterian St. Luke's Medical Center in Chicago remarked on the "almost universal smile" that appears as the baby stretches. A Florida physician told his colleagues, "It's a concept, not a procedure."

Leboyer has described his gradual discovery of the awareness and intelligence of the newborn, a phenomenon he had been educated against in his medical training. "A *person* is there, fully conscious, deserving of respect." A French experiment studied one hundred and twenty babies delivered by the Leboyer method, all from working-class mothers who knew nothing of the method when they arrived at the hospital for delivery. These babies scored higher on psychomotor scales than the average infant, had superior digestion, walked earlier, and were surprisingly likely to be ambidextrous!

Leboyer was among the speakers at a 1978 Los Angeles conference organizing Our Ultimate Investment, a foundation devoted to "conscious childbirth," sponsored by Laura Huxley, widow of Aldous Huxley. Strong convictions about the spiritual and psychological aspects of childbirth, infant care, and bonding have led to the formation of a network, NAPSAC (the National Association of Parents and Professionals for Safe Alternatives in Childbirth). Widespread interest around the country has inspired conferences, seminars, books, and informal mutual-support networks. It has greatly increased support for established natural approaches to birth, like the Lamaze method, and the La Leche League, a mutual-help network for women wishing to breastfeed their babies.

A woman who filled out the Aquarian Conspiracy questionnaire described the birth of her child at home as "a drugless psychedelic high, a peak experience." Her husband, who delivered the baby, also ranked the birth as a high point in his life, "being born a parent." The mother said she was grateful to all the women who had preceded her "in bearing children in their own way, reclaiming birth from the field of medicine and giving it back to parents and children, to whom it belongs."

And just as increasing numbers of prospective parents are demanding home births or homelike settings, many of the dying are coming home to die or are seeking out the few available hospices, which are humane centers for the terminally ill modeled after St. Christopher's in London. Advocates of the hospice movement have described it as "a concept rather than a specific place," just as the Leboyer method was called a concept rather than a technique. "The hospice movement," said a *Science* report on a two-day meeting on hospices at the National Institutes of Health, "far from being a separate and specialized phenomenon, supplies a model for getting the whole health system back on the track."

"It is ultimately the concept of *life*, not the concept of death, which rules the question of the right to die," remarked Hans Jonas, a professor of philosophy at the New School for Social Research. "The trust of medicine is the wholeness of life. Its commitment is to keep the flame of life burning, not its embers glimmering. Least of all is it the infliction of suffering and indignity." The technology of slow death—tubes, respirators— can now be rejected in many states in the name of "the right to die."[6]

The Shanti Project in Berkeley employs lay and professional counselors for the loving guidance of the dying and their families. At the Center for Attitudinal Healing in Tiburon, California, psychiatrist Gerald Jampolsky supervises a group of children with life-threatening illnesses like leukemia. They meet in each other's homes once a week to share their fears, meditate together, and convey healing thoughts to those among them in crisis. A grant from Pacific Bell has made it possible for the center to sponsor a telephone support network so that children around the country can talk to each other about their shared experiences of dangerous illness.

Of all the self-fulfilling prophecies in our culture, the assumption that aging means decline and poor health is probably the deadliest. Although research has demonstrated that there are many ways to age, we set ourselves up for senility or death. We draw the aging away from meaningful work: The elderly rich are tempted into sunny, childless ghettos and the elderly poor are left in neighborhoods long since abandoned by families. Even the ambulant ill are often segregated in nursing homes.

[6]One indicator of turnabout in medicine: Twenty years ago only 10 percent of the physicians polled believed patients should be told that they have cancer, whereas a recent survey found that 97 percent favor telling them.

But revolution is upon us. Not only is a vocal minority chanting, "Hell, no, we won't go," but sympathetic younger generations are likely to be even more militant. Maggie Kuhn of the Gray Panthers typifies the Radical Center of the new views toward aging:

> Let's not pit ourselves against the young. We don't want to be adversaries. And you young people—together, we will conspire. We need radical social change, a new agenda. Such an agenda would include age-integrated housing, an end to mandatory retirement.
>
> Together we can devise holistic health centers—to challenge and change, to point the way to large institutional change.
>
> We're experiencing a new kind of humanness and our corporate power to change society.
>
> I'm sorry when my peers put all their efforts into obtaining services, like reduced utility rates. Services are Novocain. They dull the pain but they don't solve the problem.
>
> We can be coalition builders. And we can experiment. Those of us who are old can afford to live dangerously. We have less to lose.

Kuhn urges her peers to take college courses, to become involved in self-actualizing activities, to launch imaginative enterprises. A group of Gray Panthers in one city jointly purchased several old houses to renovate, occupy, and rent.

The national SAGE program—Senior Actualizations and Growth Explorations—combines spiritual and body therapies: acupuncture, meditation, T'ai Chi, music, even opportunities for barter. A recently founded National Association for Humanistic Gerontology is comprised of professionals interested in fostering alternative approaches to aging. Individuals of any age may join chapters of the Phenix Club founded by Jerome Ellison. The activities and mutual support are designed to make the second half of life a creative, spiritual adventure.

Predictably, there are also new approaches to treating psychiatric disorders. Medical science is less sure these days of the efficacy of its conventional methods, including the major tranquilizing drugs. The new drugs greatly increased the number of hospitalized patients who could resume functioning in the world, but they did little for the inner dissonance that helped trigger psychosis.

Psychiatry in the West is beginning to respect the insight of those societies that view madness as an attempt to break through to new vision. Acute psychosis may be a feverish strategy to transcend conflict, a sometimes valuable natural process rather than a symptom to be quickly eradicated. Sanctuary and understanding are often more effective than the powerful but temporary chemical adjustment usually given to psychotic individuals. In one California study young male schizophrenics who were not given drugs recovered from their acute psychoses about two weeks later than those given Thorazine, but they were far less often readmitted over the course of the next year.

Psychiatry means, literally, "doctoring the soul." It is unlikely that great doses of tranquilizing drugs can heal a fractured soul; rather, they interrupt the pattern of distress and conflict by altering the brain's disturbed chemistry. Remembering that the brain can either deny or transform conflict, we can understand Karl Menninger's observation that many individuals who recover from madness become "weller than well." They have reached a new level of integration, another example of stress driving individual evolution.

Some communities have established retreats so that stressed persons can find rest and support before their conflict becomes more than they can handle. A few retreats, now closed, even handled psychotic disturbances. Diabasis House in San Francisco and Crossing Place in Washington, were pilot projects that showed the value of residential structures even for acutely psychotic patients. They cost less to operate than psychiatric hospitals.

All through history the fear of creative behavior and mystical states—of the intuitive side of human experience—has led to witch-hunts too various to name. Psychiatrist R. D. Laing blames this on the ambivalence of the society toward inner hungers, the consensus of denial of spiritual needs on which artists and mystics throughout history have been shipwrecked. Now increasing numbers of former mental patients have joined forces to oppose what they consider insensitive treatment of mental illness and to promote a greater reliance on such noninvasive therapies as biofeedback, meditation, nutrition, and sanctuary rather than drugs and electroshock. One such network is the Bay Area Association for Alternatives in Psychiatry. Many psychiatrists are looking at alternative therapies.

There is also a growing interest in traditional and folk healing systems. Physicians, nurses, psychologists, and anthropologists are looking into the shamanic (native healing) practices of many cultures: Chinese, Native American, Tibetan, African, Japanese. Insurance companies are now reimbursing the visits of Alaskan Eskimos to their shamans and Arizona Navajos to their medicine men. Shamanic healers help the sick look for meaning in the illness and see it in the context of their families or communities. Traditional healing systems view illness as a disturbance of the individual's harmony with others and with nature.

Brazil's popular medicine, sometimes called *cura* ("curing"), may be a preview of the synthesis taking place in some parts of the world. Cura blends Western medicine, spiritual healing, herbalism, homeopathy, Amerindian and African healing traditions. Some sixty million Brazilians are estimated to partake of cura, with rapidly growing numbers among the well-educated and middle class. Cura involves body, emotions, soul. There is a great respect for the "moral ascendancy" of the healer as well as the expertise of formally trained physicians. Cura emphasizes whatever works and establishes a support group for the individual in need of healing.

THE HEALING EFFECT

"I am convinced that there is such a thing as healing power," Jerome Frank said at a New York conference on alternative medical approaches. But he expressed doubt that it will be evaluated clearly enough in the near future for full acceptance by Western scientists.

Actually there is already something of a scientific grid through which we can understand a healing resonance between people. Bell's theorem, the Bohm-Pribram holographic theories, and other radical proposals offer a model for understanding the connectedness between persons. The image of the body as a responsive field of energy, predominant in Eastern philosophy, coincides with evidence that the acupuncture meridians are a reality and that the chakras of Buddhist lore may indeed have a basis in fact. Dolores Krieger, a professor of nursing at New York University, elegantly demonstrated changes in hemoglobin values in patients treated with a kind of "scanning" healing, in which practitioners do not actually touch the body but attempt to sense field changes—heat, cold, a tingling sensation—as their hands pass over particular regions of the body.

There is other evidence of a healing effect: unusual brain-wave patterns in persons attempting to heal, enzyme changes, EEG shifts in the "healee," inexplicable tumor remissions, and other rapid cures. Medical interest is high. Krieger's method, for example, has been taught in day-long therapeutic touch workshops to thousands around the country, mostly nurses, and Krieger herself has been invited by several New York hospitals to teach the method to their entire nursing staffs. A number of doctors are now using similar methods.

Unorthodox healers like Rolling Thunder, Olga Worrall, Paul Solomon, and Jack Schwarz have lectured to medical schools and conducted workshops for doctors and medical students.

While psychic healing may prove a useful adjunct to medicine in the future, it is unlikely to become a primary mode of treatment—for a simple reason. A "healer" is ministering in much the same way as a doctor, doing something *to* the patient. Shamanic healers—the *curanderos* of South America, for instance—tell those they treat that they can affect the symptoms but they cannot change the inner process that produces disease. The symptom may disappear for a time but too often the deeper matrix of disease has not been changed. Only the individual can effect a healing from within.

A healing state of mind has specific benefits for the healer, however, and for the rapport between therapist and sufferer. A British scientist has observed a particular configuration of brain rhythms in most of the spiritual healers he has tested. (England has thousands of licensed healers, and they are permitted to work in hospitals.) One anxious physician wired to the brain-wave device did not show that pattern. Finally the sympathetic researcher said, "Imagine you are about to treat a patient. You have no medicine, no equipment. *You have nothing to give but your compassion*." Suddenly the physician's brainwave activity shifted into the "healing state" pattern.

Robert Swearingen, a Colorado orthopedist, tells of finding himself with an emergency-room patient in intense pain because of a dislocated shoulder. The rest of the clinic staff was attending to a more critical emergency, so he could not call for a nurse to deliver tranquilizers and anesthetic.

At that moment I felt overwhelmed by a sense of impotence, of dependence on technology. Partly to reassure the patient, partly to calm myself, I began urging him to relax. Suddenly I felt the shoulder let down—and I knew that with the patient's cooperation I could slip it into place without pain or pain medication.

The experience changed his entire career, not only because he was then able to teach the painless procedure to nearly anyone, but also because he discovered the crucial importance of the human element in medicine. He also found that he could achieve a nonverbal rapport with patients, a kind of "listening" that led to intuitive diagnosis beyond anything his technology had given him.

A famous psychologist once remarked privately that biofeedback is the ultimate placebo, an intermediate step for those clinicians and patients reassured by "hard" science, who have not yet noticed that all the action is in a soft brain and vanishes into whirling particles on closer inspection. "It's all in the imagination," he said. We can have it as we imagine and as we will.

In the sixteenth century Paracelsus observed that the physicians of his day "know only a small part of the power of will." Yet on another level, we always knew that you can die of a broken heart, that a woman's prolonged distress can disturb her unborn baby, that old people don't grow senile if they maintain an interest in life.

Surely historians will marvel at the heresy we fell into, the recent decades in which we disregarded the spirit in our efforts to cure the body. Now, in finding health, we find ourselves.

CHAPTER 9

Flying and Seeing: New Ways to Learn

I would like to be able to fly if everyone else did, but otherwise it would be kind of conspicuous.

—Twelve-year-old girl quoted by
DAVID RIESMAN in *The Lonely Crowd*

*'Tis ye, 'tis your estranged faces,
That miss the many-splendored thing.*

—*FRANCIS THOMPSON*

We are in the early morning of understanding our place in the universe and our spectacular latent powers, the flexibility and transcendence of which we are capable. The scientific breakthroughs are throwing out a challenge: If our memories are as absorbent as research has demonstrated, our awareness as wide, our brains and bodies as sensitive; if we can will changes in our physiology at the level of a single cell; if we are heirs to such evolutionary virtuosity—how can we be performing and learning at such mediocre levels? If we're so rich, why aren't we smart?

This chapter is about learning in its broadest sense. It's about our surprising capacities, new sources of knowledge, mastery, creativity. It's about the learner within, waiting to be free.

And it's about how the learner came to be unfree...about our culture's great learning disability, an educational system that emphasizes being "right" at the expense of being open. We begin to see the unease and disease of our adult lives as elaborate patterns that emerged from a system that taught us young how to be still, look backward, look to authority, construct certainties. The fear of learning—and transformation—is the inevitable product of such a system.

This is the poignant human paradox: a plastic brain capable of endless self-transcendence, equally capable of being trained into self-limiting behavior. It is evident even in newborn babies, who have been shown by modern research techniques to be incredibly sensitive, seeking out patterns, reacting to subtle emotions in the human voice, attracted to faces, discriminating between colors. But science has also shown how easily newborns can be programmed. They can be conditioned to respond to a light or a bell not unlike the salivating dogs in Pavlov's famous experiments. Both Teilhard and Skinner were right: We are capable of evolutionary leaps *and* conditioning in boxes.

You can only have a new society, the visionaries have said, if you change the education of the younger generation. Yet the new society itself *is* the necessary force for change in education. It's like the old dilemma: You can't get a job without experience, but you can't get experience because no one will give you a job.

Schools are entrenched bureaucracies whose practitioners do not compete for business, do not need to get re-elected or to attract patients, customers, clients. Those educators who would like to innovate have relatively little authority to change their style.

The consumer cannot simply boycott this institution. Private schools are beyond the reach of most families and may not be an improvement over public schools. Yet some parents are now saying that deliberate withdrawal of their children from compulsory schooling—an illegal act in most states—is not unlike draft resisting in an immoral war.

Of the Aquarian Conspirators surveyed, more were involved in education than in any other single category of work. They were teachers, administrators, policymakers, educational psychologists. Their consensus: Education is one of the *least* dynamic of institutions, lagging far behind medicine, psychology, politics, the media, and other elements of our society.

They are, as one expressed it, "in peaceful struggle" within the system. There are heroes in education, as there have always been heroes, trying to transcend the limits of the old structure; but their efforts are too often thwarted by peers, administrators, parents. Mario Fantini, former Ford consultant on education, now at the State University of New York, said bluntly, "The psychology of becoming has to be smuggled into the schools."

Yet there are reasons for optimism. Our error has been in assuming that we had to start with the schools. Schools are an effect of the way we think—and we can change the way we think.

"The fallacy of the back-to-basics movement and the vast majority of educational reform efforts in this country," said John Williamson, former director of planning and policy development for the National Institute of Education, "has been the failure of our common-sense point of view." We have overlooked the critical variables, he said—the limiting personal beliefs of our students, the consciousness of our educators, the intention of our communities.

Beliefs. Consciousness. Intention. We can see why piecemeal reform is hopeless, for the problems are mired in our old notions of human nature, and they are intricately related. The inability of conventional education to teach basic skills and the failure to foster self-esteem are part of the same deep mismanagement and misperception.

Perhaps the back-to-basics movement could be channeled deeper—to bedrock fundamentals, the underlying principles and relationships, real "universal" education. Then we can reclaim our sense of place.

Only a new perspective can generate a new curriculum, new levels of adjustment. Just as political parties are peripheral to the change in the distribution of power, so the schools are not the first arena for change in learning.

Subtle forces are at work, factors you are not likely to see in banner headlines. For example, tens of thousands of classroom teachers, educational consultants and psychologists, counselors, administrators, researchers, and faculty members in colleges of education have been among the millions engaged in *personal transformation.* They have only recently begun to link regionally and nationally, to share strategies, to conspire for the teaching of all they most value: freedom, high expectations, awareness, patterns, connections, creativity. They are eager to share their discoveries with those colleagues ready to listen.

And many *are* ready, veterans of earlier, partially successful movements to humanize the schools. They have learned a lot. Much as social activism moved in recent years from confrontation to cooperation and from external to internal healing, educational reformers are shifting their emphasis. And there is power in the new alignment of parents and educators. Teachers, administrators, and sympathetic school-board members are working together rather than confronting one another.

These networks have an ally in *scientific research*. We are beginning to realize, with appalling clarity, how unnatural many of our educational methods have been and why they worked poorly, if at all. Research in brain function and consciousness demonstrates that teaching must change if we are to tap our potential.

Another strong force for change: *crisis*. All the failures of education, like a fever, signal a deep struggle for health. The business of the Aquarian Conspiracy is calm diagnosis of that illness—to make it clear that synthesis is needed—paradigm change rather than pendulum change.

If the streambed of education is being enlarged, one formidable force altering its contours is *competition*. Learning is where you find it: on "Sesame Street," in inner games of tennis and the Zen of everything, in teaching and learning cooperatives, in computers, on FM radio, in self-help books, in magazines, cassettes, and television documentaries.

The most potent force for change, however, is the growing recognition of millions of adults that their own impoverished expectations and frustrations came, in large measure, from their schooling.

PEDOGENIC ILLNESS

If we are not learning and teaching we are not awake and alive. Learning is not only like health, it *is* health.

As the greatest single social influence during the formative years, schools have been the instruments of our greatest denial, unconsciousness, conformity, and broken connections. Just as allopathic medicine treats symptoms without concern for the whole system, schools break knowledge and experience into "subjects," relentlessly turning wholes into parts, flowers into petals, history into events, without ever restoring continuity. Or, as Neil Postman and Charles Weingartner observed in *Teaching as a Subversive Activity*:

English is not History and History is not Science and Science is not Art and Art is not Music, and Art and Music are minor subjects and English, History and Science major subjects, and a subject is something you "take" and when you have taken it, you have "had" it, and if you have "had" it, you are immune and need not take it again. (The Vaccination Theory of Education?)

Worse yet, not only is the mind broken, but too often, so is the spirit. Allopathic teaching produces the equivalent of *iatrogenic*, or "doctor-caused," illness—teacher-caused learning disabilities. We might call these *pedogenic* illnesses. The child who may have come to school intact, with the budding courage to risk and explore, finds stress enough to permanently diminish that adventure.

Even doctors, in their heyday as godlike paragons, have never wielded the authority of a single classroom teacher, who can purvey prizes, failure, love, humiliation, and information to great numbers of relatively powerless, vulnerable young people.

Dis-ease, not feeling comfortable about ourselves, probably begins for many of us in the classroom. One biofeedback clinician remarked that the correlation between stressful memories and arousal of the body can be demonstrated. If a biofeedback subject is asked to think about school memories, the feedback shows immediate alarm. In one PTA workshop, every adult asked to write about a remembered school incident described a negative or traumatic event. Many adults describe nightmares of being in school again, late for class or having failed to turn in an assignment.

Most of us seem to have considerable unfinished business with school. This residue of anxiety may intimidate us yet on some level of consciousness; it may forever pull us back from challenges and new learning.

In Chapter 8 we noted the impressive research associating personality characteristics with diseases—the cancer patient's difficulty in expressing grief or anger, for example, or the heart patient's obsession with schedules and achievements. Is it possible that our authoritarian, achievement-geared, fear-inducing, clock-watching schools have helped set us up for the illness of our choice? Were we discouraged from expressing honest anger, sorrow, frustration? Were we urged to compete, strive, fear tardiness and deadlines?

Noel McInnis, an educator concerned with the physical environments for learning, described the process: For twelve years we confine the child's body to a limited territory, his energy to a limited activity, his senses to limited stimulation, his sociability to a limited number of peers, his mind to limited experience of the world around him. "What will he learn?" McInnis asked. "To *don't* his own thing."[1]

Whereas the young need some sort of initiation into an uncertain world, we give them the bones from the culture's graveyards. Where they want to do real things, we give them abstract busywork, blank spaces to fill in with the "right" answers, multiple choices to see if they can choose the "right" answers. Where they need to find meaning, the schools ask memorization; discipline is divorced from intuition, pattern from parts.

If wholeness is health, the violence done to both meaning and self-image by most of our educational institutions is a major source of disease in our culture—a force that fragments even the child from a secure and loving home. The trauma of Humpty Dumpty begins with the first denials of feeling, the first suppressed questions, the muted pain of boredom. No home can fully undo the effects of what Jonathan Kozol, describing his experiences teaching ghetto children, called *Death at an Early Age*.

Buckminster Fuller once remarked that neither he nor anyone else he knew was a genius: "Some of us are just less damaged than others." Like Margaret Mead, Fuller was essentially home-taught. Studies have shown that an impressive proportion of great, original achievers were educated at home, stimu-

---

[1]The wasted potential was dramatically illustrated in the Milwaukee Project, an experiment in the sixties sometimes known as Operation Babysnatch. Psychologists at the University of Wisconsin arranged for special attention to be given to babies born to a group of borderline feeble-minded women (IQs of 70 or less). Normally, by the time they are sixteen, such children show intelligence as low as their mothers. Presumably, a dull mother cannot stimulate a baby's mind very much.

Forty babies were picked up at their homes and taken to a university center where they were played with, sung to, and otherwise stimulated. Later they learned in small groups of toddlers. By the time they were four, these children scored a mean IQ of 128 on one test, 132 on another—in the range psychologists label "intellectually gifted." These experimental children were brighter than the typical child from a superior, middle-class home. Forty children of comparable circumstances who had *not* received the extra attention scored IQs of 85 (very low normal) by age four. The magic of human interaction had made all the difference.

lated by parents or other relatives from infancy, borne up by high expectations.

LEARNING FOR A NEW WORLD

Why have our schools routinely punished and diminished the young? Perhaps it's because schools as we know them were designed long before we had any understanding of the human brain and for a society long since superseded. Furthermore, they were designed to impart a fairly specific body of knowledge, from a period when knowledge seemed stable and bounded.

It was enough to master the content of certain books and courses, learn the tricks of the trade, and you were finished. The student learned what he needed for his "field." The journeyman knew his job. Knowledge kept in its proper compartments, people in their departments. In the very short history of mass education—not much more than a century—schools went from teaching simple piety and fundamental literacy to eventual instruction in the arts and social sciences. Education became "higher" and "higher" in terms of elaboration and sophistication.

But schools were always presumed to be carrying out the mandate of the society, or at least giving it their best effort. They taught for obedience or productivity or whatever trait seemed appropriate at the time, producing teachers for teacher shortages, scientists after we began worrying that we were falling behind the Soviet Union scientifically after the launching of Sputnik.

If now, as polls and some educators are saying, the society prizes *self-actualization* above all else . . . how do you teach?

Millions of parents are disenchanted with conventional education, some because their children are not acquiring even simple literacy, some because the schools are dehumanizing. One recent Oregon survey showed that the community gave equal weight to the importance of fostering self-esteem and teaching basic skills.

A revision in the education code of California, authorizing all school districts to provide for alternative schools, emphasized the importance of developing in students "self-reliance, initiative, kindness, spontaneity, resourcefulness, courage, creativity, responsibility, and joy"—a tall order. A study commissioned for the National Education Association, "Curriculum

Change Toward the Twenty-first Century," noted that we are entering a period of great discontinuity, change, and interdependence of people and events.

Ironically, because their structure itself tends to paralyze them, school systems have responded slowly, if at all, to (1) new scientific findings relating to the mind and (2) changing values in the society. Knowledge in general moves very slowly into the schools; textbooks and curricula are typically years, even decades, behind what is known in any given field. Except at the level of university graduate schools, education is not a party to grapevines, speculation, breakthroughs, front-line research.

A society shaken by an implosion of knowledge, a revolution in culture and communication, cannot wait for a creaking educational bureaucracy to sanction its search for meaning. What we know of nature now has broken through the artifices of disciplinary boundaries; technology is accelerated so that traditional careers vanish and new opportunities materialize suddenly. New information is rushing together, dovetailing across disciplines.

The educational establishment has been nightmarishly slow in responding to our changing needs, slower than any other institution. At an increasingly high cost (nearly 8 percent of the Gross National Product, compared to 3.4 percent in 1951), the old forms are not working. New hardware and refurbished curricula are not enough.[2]

LEARNING: THE EMERGENT PARADIGM

Innovations in education have crisscrossed the sky like Roman candles, and most sputtered quickly out, leaving only the smell of disenchantment in the air. Too often they addressed themselves to only partial aspects of human nature, setting off skirmishes: cognitive versus affective (emotional) learning, free versus structured settings. Max Lerner observed that theorists at both ends of the spectrum have long viewed American schools with an almost theological fervor. The other side is always charged with having destroyed the heavenly city.

[2]An example of the misuse of educational funds: In 1972 Edith Green, a member of Congress, revealed that 60 percent of the first year's budget of the federal Right-to-Read program had been misspent in unauthorized architectural and office decorating expenses, public relations, and salaries.

Who killed our Eden? The humanists blame the technologists, the behaviorists blame the humanists, the secularists the churches, the churches blame the lack of religious education, the fundamentalists blame the progressives, and on and on.

In truth, we never had a heavenly city. Our public schools were designed, fairly enough, to create a modestly literate public, not to deliver quality education or produce great minds.

The Radical Center of educational philosophy—the perspective typical of the Aquarian Conspiracy—is a constellation of techniques and concepts sometimes called *transpersonal education*. The name derives from a branch of psychology that focuses on the transcendent capacities of human beings. In transpersonal education, the learner is encouraged to be awake and autonomous, to question, to explore all the corners and crevices of conscious experience, to seek meaning, to test outer limits, to check out frontiers and depths of the self.

In the past most educational alternatives have offered only pendulum change, pushing discipline (as in fundamental schools) or affective/emotional values (as in most free schools).

In contrast to conventional education, which aims to adjust the individual to society as it exists, the "humanistic" educators of the 1960s maintained that the society should accept its members as unique and autonomous. Transpersonal experience aims for a new kind of learner and a new kind of society. Beyond self-acceptance, it promotes self-transcendence.

Merely humanizing the educational environment was still something of a concession to the status quo. In too many cases the reformers were afraid to challenge the learner for fear of pushing too hard. They assumed old limits. (As we shall see in the next chapter, early efforts at "humanizing the workplace" also ran into the problem typical of partial solutions: They may be rejected before their full value is realized because they promised more than they can deliver.)

Transpersonal education is more humane than traditional education and more intellectually rigorous than many alternatives in the past. It aims to aid transcendence, not furnish mere coping skills. It is education's counterpart to holistic medicine: education of the whole person.

One of the Aquarian Conspirators remarked, "Transpersonal education is the process of exposing people to the mysterious in themselves—and then getting out of the way so you don't get run over." But he warned against overselling to educators, who are understandably skeptical. "Schools have had so many 'revolutions' over the past few years. The battleground is scarred. Don't promise miracles, even if you expect them."

Phi Delta Kappan, the influential journal for school administrators, observed that transpersonal education holds potential for solving grave social crises, like juvenile crime, as well as enhancing learning. "Ill defined though it is," the journal said, "this movement is perhaps the dominant trend on the educational scene today and presages a momentous revolution."

Like holistic health, transpersonal education can happen anywhere. It doesn't need schools, but its adherents believe that the schools need *it*. Because of its power for social healing and awakening, they conspire to bring the philosophy into the classroom, in every grade, in colleges and universities, for job training and adult education.

Unlike most educational reform in the past, it is *imbedded in sound science*: systems theory, an understanding of the integration of mind and body, knowledge of the two major modes of consciousness and how they interact, the potential of altered and expanded states of consciousness. It emphasizes the continuum of knowledge, rather than "subjects," and the common ground of human experience, transcending ethnic or national differences. It aids the learner's search for meaning, the need to discern forms and patterns, the hunger for harmony. It deepens awareness of how a paradigm shifts, how frustration and struggle precede insights.

Transpersonal education promotes friendly environments for hard tasks. It celebrates the individual and society, freedom and responsibility, uniqueness and interdependence, mystery and clarity, tradition and innovation. It is complementary, paradoxical, dynamic. It is education's Middle Way.

The larger paradigm looks to the nature of learning rather than methods of instruction. Learning, after all, is not schools, teachers, literacy, math, grades, achievement. It is the process by which we have moved every step of the way since we first breathed; the transformation that occurs in the brain whenever new information is integrated, whenever a new skill is mastered. Learning is kindled in the mind of the individual. Anything else is mere schooling.

The new paradigm reflects both the discoveries of modern science and the discoveries of personal transformation.

ASSUMPTIONS OF THE OLD PARADIGM OF EDUCATION	ASSUMPTIONS OF THE NEW PARADIGM OF LEARNING
Emphasis on *content*, acquiring a body of "right" information, once and for all.	Emphasis on learning how to learn, how to ask good questions, pay attention to the right things, be open to and evaluate new concepts, have access to information. What is now "known" may change. Importance of *context*.
Learning as a *product*, a destination.	Learning as a *process*, a journey.
Hierarchical and authoritarian structure. Rewards conformity, discourages dissent.	Egalitarian. Candor and dissent permitted. Students and teachers see each other as people, not roles. Encourages autonomy.
Relatively rigid structure, prescribed curriculum.	Relatively flexible structure. Belief that there are many ways to teach a given subject.
Lockstep progress, emphasis on the "appropriate" ages for certain activities, age segregation. Compartmentalized.	Flexibility and integration of age groupings. Individual not automatically limited to certain subject matter by age.
Priority on performance.	Priority on self-image as the generator of performance.
Emphasis on external world. Inner experience often considered inappropriate in school setting.	Inner experience seen as context for learning. Use of imagery, storytelling, dream journals, "centering" exercises, and exploration of feelings encouraged.

ASSUMPTIONS OF THE OLD PARADIGM OF EDUCATION	ASSUMPTIONS OF THE NEW PARADIGM OF LEARNING
Guessing and divergent thinking discouraged.	Guessing and divergent thinking encouraged as part of the creative process.
Emphasis on analytical, linear, left-brain thinking.	Strives for whole-brain education. Augments left-brain rationality with holistic, nonlinear, and intuitive strategies. Confluence and fusion of the two processes emphasized.
Labeling (remedial, gifted, minimally brain dysfunctional, etc.) contributes to self-fulfilling prophecy.	Labeling used only in minor prescriptive role and not as fixed evaluation that dogs the individual's educational career.
Concern with norms.	Concern with the individual's performance in terms of potential. Interest in testing outer limits, transcending perceived limitations.
Primary reliance on theoretical, abstract "book knowledge."	Theoretical and abstract knowledge heavily complemented by experiment and experience, both in and out of classroom. Field trips, apprenticeships, demonstrations, visiting experts.
Classrooms designed for efficiency, convenience.	Concern for the environment of learning: lighting, colors, air, physical comfort, needs for privacy and interaction, quiet and exuberant activities.

ASSUMPTIONS OF THE OLD PARADIGM OF EDUCATION	ASSUMPTIONS OF THE NEW PARADIGM OF LEARNING
Bureaucratically determined, resistant to community input.	Encourages community input, even community control.
Education seen as a social necessity for a certain period of time, to inculcate minimum skills and train for a specific role.	Education seen as lifelong process, one only tangentially related to schools.
Increasing reliance on technology (audiovisual equipment, computers, tapes, texts), dehumanization.	Appropriate technology, human relationships between teachers and learners of primary importance.
Teacher imparts knowledge; one-way street.	Teacher is learner, too, learning from students.

The old assumptions generate questions about how to achieve norms, obedience, and correct answers. The new assumptions lead to questions about how to motivate for lifelong learning, how to strengthen self-discipline, how to awaken curiosity, and how to encourage creative risk in people of all ages.

LEARNING IS TRANSFORMING

Think of the learner as an open system—a dissipative structure, as described in Chapter 6, interacting with the environment, taking in information, integrating it, using it. The learner is transforming the input, ordering and reordering, creating coherence. His worldview is continually enlarged to incorporate the new. From time to time it breaks and is reformed, as in the acquiring of major new skills and concepts: learning to walk, speak, read, swim, or write; learning a second language or geometry. Each is a kind of paradigm shift.

A learning shift is preceded by stress whose intensity ranges across a continuum: uneasiness, excitement, creative tension, confusion, anxiety, pain, fear. The surprise and fear in learning are described in *The Teachings of Don Juan* by Carlos Castaneda:

He slowly begins to learn—bit by bit at first, then in big chunks. And his thoughts soon clash. What he learns is never what he pictured, or imagined, and so he begins to be afraid. Learning is never what one expects. Every step of learning is a new task, and the fear the man is experiencing begins to mount mercilessly, unyieldingly. His purpose has become a battlefield. . . .

He must not run away. He must defy his fear, and in spite of it he must take the next step in learning, and the next, and the next. He must be fully afraid, and yet he must not stop. That is the rule! And a moment will come when his first enemy retreats. Learning is no longer a terrifying task.

The transforming teacher senses readiness to change, helps the "follower" or student respond to more complex needs, transcending the old levels again and yet again. The true teacher is also learning and is transformed by the relationship. Just as Burns pointed out that a dictator is not a true leader because he is not open to input from his followers, a closed teacher—the mere "power wielder"—is not a true teacher.

The closed teacher may fill the student with information. But the learner forfeits his participation. The students, like the citizens of a dictatorship, are unable to feed their needs and readiness back to the one who is supposed to facilitate their growth. It is like the difference between a loudspeaker and an intercom.

The open teacher, like a good therapist, establishes rapport and resonance, sensing unspoken needs, conflicts, hopes, and fears. Respecting the learner's autonomy, the teacher spends more time helping to articulate the urgent *questions* than demanding right answers.

Timing and nonverbal communication are critical, as we shall see. The learner senses the teacher's perceptions of his readiness, the teacher's confidence or skepticism. He "reads" the teacher's expectations. The true teacher intuits the level of readiness, then probes, questions, leads. The teacher allows time for assimilation, even retreat, when the going gets too heavy.

Just as you can't "deliver" holistic health, which must start with the intention of the patient, the true teacher knows you can't impose learning. You can, as Galileo said, help the individual discover it within. The open teacher helps the learner discover patterns and connections, fosters openness to strange new possibilities, and is a midwife to ideas. The teacher is a steersman, a catalyst, a facilitator—an agent of learning, but not the first cause.

Trust deepens over time. The teacher becomes more attuned, and more rapid and powerful learning can take place.

A teacher clear enough for such attunement obviously must have a healthy level of self-esteem, little defensiveness, few ego needs. The true teacher must be willing to let go, to be wrong, to allow the learner another reality. The learner who has been encouraged to hear inner authority is tacitly welcome to disagree. Submission to outer authority is always provisional and temporary. As the Eastern wisdom puts it, "If you see Buddha on the road, kill him."

Like the spiritual teacher who enlarges or heals the self-image of the disciple, awakening him to his own potential, the teacher liberates the self, opens the eyes, makes the learner aware of choice. We only learn what we always knew.

We learn to walk through fears that held us back. In the transformative relationship with a teacher, we move to the edge, our peace is disturbed, and we are challenged by what psychologist Frederick Perls called "a safe emergency."

The optimum environment for learning offers security enough to encourage exploration and effort, excitement enough to push us onward. Although a humanistic environment is not a sufficient condition for transformation/education, it engenders the necessary trust. We trust the teachers who give us stress, pain, or drudgery when we need it. And we resent those who push us for their own ego, stress us with double binds, or take us into the deep water when we're still frightened of the shallow.

Yet appropriate stress is essential. Teachers can fail to transform if they are afraid to upset the learner. "True compassion," said one spiritual teacher, "is ruthless." Or, as the poet Guillaume Apollinaire put it:

Come to the edge, he said.
They said: We are afraid.
Come to the edge, he said.
They came.
He pushed them . . . and they flew.

Those who love us may well push us when we're ready to fly.

The too-soft teacher reinforces the learner's natural wish to retreat and stay safe, never venturing out for new knowledge, never risking. The teacher must know when to let the learner struggle, realizing that "help" or comfort, even when asked, can interrupt a transformation. This is the same good sense that knows the swimmer must let go, the bicyclist must achieve a new, internal equilibrium. Even in the name of love or sympathy, we must not be spared our learnings.

Risk brings its own rewards: the exhilaration of breaking through, of getting to the other side, the relief of a conflict healed, the clarity when a paradox dissolves. Whoever teaches us this is the agent of our liberation. Eventually we know deeply that the other side of every fear is a freedom. Finally, we must take charge of the journey, urging ourselves past our own reluctance and misgivings and confusion to new freedom.

Once that happens, however many setbacks or detours we may encounter, we are on a different life journey. Somewhere is that clear memory of the process of transformation: dark to light, lost to found, broken to seamless, chaos to clarity, fear to transcendence.

To understand how we learn fear and mastery, risk and trust, we have to look past the schools to our first teachers. Parents are our models of exploration. From them we learned to retreat or advance. We were imbued with their expectations. Too often, we inherited second-generation fears, anxieties we sensed in them. And—if we are not conscious of the cycle—we are all too likely to pass their fears and our own on to our children. That is the heritage of uneasiness, bequeathed from generation to generation: fears of losing, falling, being left behind, being left alone, not being good enough.

Recent studies of the "fear of success," a fairly common syndrome, revealed that its likeliest cause is the parent's communication of the fear that the child will not be able to master the tasks at hand. The child realizes simultaneously that (1) the task is considered important by the parent, and (2) the parent doubts that the child can do it unassisted. That individual establishes a lifelong pattern of sabotaging his own successes whenever he is on the verge of real mastery.

Most parents, it seems, don't mind if their children are better than they at certain things: schoolwork, athletics, popularity. There is vicarious satisfaction in a child's extending one's ambitions. But most parents do not want their children to be *different*. We want to be able to understand them, and we want them to share our values. This fear of an alien offspring appears in myth and in science-fiction tales of children who leap into new modes of being and are no longer subject to their parents' frailty or their mortal limits, as in Arthur Clarke's *Childhood's End*.

If as parents we are afraid of risk and strangeness, we warn our children against trying to beat the system. We do not acknowledge their right to a different world. In the name of adjustment, we may try to spare them their sensible rebellion. In the name of balance, we try to save them from intensity, obsessions, excesses—in short, from the disequilibrium that allows transformation to occur.

A parent who shows confidence in the child's capacity to learn, who encourages independence, who counters fear with humor or honesty, can break the ancient chain of borrowed trouble. As increasing numbers of adults have undergone their own transformative process in the decade just ending, they have become aware of this tragic bequest, and they are a powerful force for change—a historically new factor.

WHOLE-BRAIN KNOWING

Another development is unprecedented. Once mind became aware of evolution, Teilhard said, humankind entered a new phase. It was only a matter of time until we would see evidence of a worldwide expansion of consciousness.

The deliberate use of consciousness-expanding techniques in education, only recently well under way, is new in mass schooling. Never before has a culture undertaken to foster whole-brain knowing in the general populace. The transcendent state in which intellect and feeling are fused, in which higher cortical judgment makes peace with the intuitions of the old limbic brain, was the province of the few: the Athenian philosopher, the Zen master, the Renaissance genius, the creative physicist. Such heroic stuff was not for "normal" people. And it was certainly not the business of the schools!

But there is no longer reason to confine whole-brain knowing to an elite. Both science and personal transformative experiences of great numbers of people demonstrate that it is an innate human capacity, not just the gift of artists, yogis, and scientific prodigies. The brain of each of us is capable of endless reordering of information. Conflict and paradox are grist for the brain's transformative mill.

We need only pay attention. By creating what psychologist Lester Fehmi called "open focus," the psychotechnologies amplify awareness. They boost memory, accelerate the rate of learning, help integrate the functions of the two cortical hemispheres, and promote coherence between the old and new brain regions. They also allow greater access to unconscious anxieties that may be standing in our way.

They help the learner, old or young, to become centered—to create, connect, unify, transcend.

And it soon becomes obvious that our underestimation of the brain's capacity and our ignorance of its workings led us to design our educational systems upside-down and backward. Leslie Hart, an educational consultant, described schools as "brain-antagonistic":

> We are obsessed by "logic," usually meaning...tight, step-by-step, ordered, sequential (linear) effort.... But the human brain has little use for logic of this kind. It is a computer of incredible power and subtlety, but far more analog than digital. It works not by precision but probabilistically, by great numbers of often rough or even vague approximations.

The brain's calculations do not require our conscious effort, only our attention and our openness to let the information through. Although the brain absorbs universes of information, little is admitted into "normal" consciousness, largely because of our habits and wrong assumptions about how we know what we know.

Discoveries about the nature of the mind, unfortunately, have been like the slow-spreading news of armistice. Many die needlessly on the battlefield, long after the war is over. Young minds are dampened and diminished every day in numbers too great to bear thinking about, forced through a system that stunts the capacity for a lifetime of growth. In contrast to insects, as someone said, human beings start out as butterflies and end up in cocoons.

Brain science was long absent from the course work in most colleges of education—understandably, since it tends to be swathed in technical language. The discoveries about the specialization of the right and left hemispheres, however oversimplified, have offered education a provocative new metaphor for learning.

The scientific validation of "intuition," our term for knowing that can't be tracked, has shaken science and is just now having its impact on education.

On the common-sense level, we try to trace ideas from point to point, like hard wiring or a "train of thought." A leads to B leads to C. But nonlinear processes in nature, like crystallization and certain brain events, are A–Z, all at once. The brain is not limited to our common-sense conceptions, or it would not function at all.

The dictionary defines intuition as "quick perception of truth without conscious attention or reasoning," "knowledge from within," "instinctive knowledge or feeling associated with clear and concentrated vision." The word derives, appropriately, from the Latin *intuere*, "to look upon."

If this instant sensing is disregarded by the linear mind we should not be surprised. After all, its processes are beyond linear tracking and therefore suspect. And it is mediated by the half of the cortex that does not speak — our essentially mute hemisphere. The right brain cannot verbalize what it knows; its symbols, images, or metaphors need to be recognized and reformulated by the left brain before the information is wholly known.

Until we had laboratory evidence of the validity of such knowledge and some inkling of the nonlinear process, it was hard for our one-track selves to accept this knowing, much less trust it. We now know that it derives from a system whose storage, connection, and speed humble the most brilliant investigators.

There is a tendency to think of intuition as separate from intellect. More accurately, intuition might be said to encompass intellect. Everything we have ever "figured out" is also stored and available. The larger realm knows everything we know in our normal consciousness—and a great deal more. As psychologist Eugene Gendlin put it, the dimension we used to call the unconscious is not childish, regressive, or dreamy but very much *smarter* than "we" are. If its messages are sometimes garbled, that is the fault of the receiver, not the sender.

"Tacit knowing" has always had its defenders, including many of our greatest and most creative scientists and artists. It has been the essential, silent partner to all our progress. The left brain can organize new information into the existing scheme of things, but *it cannot generate new ideas. The right brain sees context—and, therefore, meaning*. Without intuition, we would still be in the cave. Every breakthrough, every leap forward in history, has depended on right-brain insights, the ability of the holistic brain to detect anomalies, process novelty, perceive relationships.

Is it any wonder that our educational approach, with its emphasis on linear, left-brain processes, has failed to keep pace with the times?

In a way, it makes sense that evolving human consciousness eventually came to over-rely on that hemisphere in which language primarily resides. Some theorists think, based on the research data, that the left brain behaves almost like a separate, competitive individual, an independent mind that inhibits its partner.

Our plight might be compared to the long, long journey of twin sailors. One is a verbal, analytical fellow, the other mute and sometimes dreamy. The verbal partner earnestly calculates with the aid of his charts and instruments. His brother, however, has an uncanny ability to predict storms, changing currents, and other navigational conditions, which he communicates by signs, symbols, drawings. The analytical sailor is afraid to trust his brother's advice because he can't imagine its source. Actually, the silent sailor has wireless, instantaneous access to a rich data bank that gives him a satellite perspective on the weather. But he cannot explain this complex system with his limited ability to communicate details. And his talkative, "rational" brother usually ignores him anyway. Frustrated, he often stands by helplessly while their craft sails head-on into disaster.

Whenever their convictions are in conflict, the analytical sailor stubbornly follows his own calculations, until the day he stumbles onto the schematics for his brother's data bank. He is overwhelmed. He realizes that by ignoring his twin's input, he has been traveling through life half-informed.

Jerome Bruner, one of the leading scientists interested in the realm of learning, remarked that the young child approaching a new subject or an unfamiliar problem—like the scientist operating at the edge of his chosen field—would be paralyzed without intuition. We do not "figure out" how to balance, for example. More often than we realize, we feel our way. The A–Z computer fine-tunes its guesses, and we move.

If we are to use our capacities fully and confidently, Bruner said, we must recognize the power of intuition. Our very technology has generated so many options that only intuition can help us choose. And because our technology can handle the routine, the analytical, we are free to refine the attention that gives us access to holistic knowing.

Now we realize that the right brain sees relationships, recognizes faces, mediates new information, hears tone, judges harmonies and symmetries. *The greatest learning disability of all may be pattern blindness*—the inability to see relationships or detect meaning. Yet no school district has remedial programs to overcome this most basic of handicaps. As we have seen, our educational system aggravates and may even cause it.

Research confirms what observant parents and teachers have always known: We learn in different ways. Of our assorted brains, some are left-dominant, some are right-dominant, some are neither. Some of us learn better by hearing, others by seeing or touching. Some visualize easily, others not at all. Some recall odometer readings, telephone numbers, dates; others remember colors and feelings. Some learn best in groups, others in isolation. Some peak in the mornings, others in the afternoon.

No single educational method can draw the best from diverse brains. Findings about the specialties of the two hemispheres and the tendency of individuals to favor one style or the other also helps us understand why we differ so much in how we see and think.

Brain research is also revolutionizing our understanding of differences in the ways males and females perceive. The sexes vary markedly in some aspects of brain specialization. The left and right hemispheres of the male brain specialize at a much earlier age than those of the female brain, which gives them certain advantages and disadvantages. Male brains are superior at certain types of spatial perceptions, but they are less flexible, more vulnerable than female brains to deficits after injury. One recent study found almost no language loss in women who had suffered injury to the left brain and subnormal language in males with the same type of trauma. Vastly more males than females suffer from dyslexia (reading difficulty).

Dyslexia, which afflicts at least 10 percent of the population, seems to be associated with a dominance by the right cerebral hemisphere in the reading process. Those with a strong holistic perception are often handicapped by our educational system with its emphasis on symbolic language and symbolic mathematics. They have initial difficulty in processing these symbols. Yet this neurological minority may also be unusually gifted. They typically excel in the arts and in innovative thinking. Ironically, their potential contribution to society is frequently diminished because the system undermines their self-esteem in their first school years.

Schools have taught and "graded" a kaleidoscope of individual brains by a single program, a single set of criteria. They have overrewarded and conditioned some skills to the exclusion of others, "failing" those whose gifts are not on the culture's most-wanted list, thus convincing them for life that they are unworthy.

Individually, and as a society, we have urgent needs that can only be met if we think differently about learning.

THE NEED FOR INNOVATION

Synthesis and pattern-seeing are survival skills for the twenty-first century. As culture grows more complex,[3] science more all-encompassing, choices more diverse, we need whole-brain understanding as we never needed it before: the right brain to innovate, sense, dream up, and envision; the left to test, analyze, check out, build constructs and supports for the new order. Together they invent the future.

Novelist Henry James anticipated brain science when he observed that there are two major kinds of people: those who prefer the emotion of *recognition* and those who prefer *surprise*. The left hemisphere seems to specialize in processing highly structured stimuli, like a click, whereas the right integrates novel, diffuse information, like a light flash. The left essentially recognizes the relationship of the stimulus to what it already knows. The right handles material for which there has been no previous experience.

The hemispheres are conservative and radical, traditional and innovative. Experiments suggest that in addition to understanding relationships and excelling at depth perception, the right also perceives better through gloom and dimness. This seems poetically appropriate in view of its peering into the unknown, its penchant for the mystical.

Free-floating right-brain knowledge is like a borrowed book, a snatch of melody heard in passing, a vague memory. If the felt idea—the stranger—is not given a name, a definition, an outline, it is lost to full consciousness. It goes to wisps and tatters like a half-remembered dream. It is not realized. Without the left brain's ability to recognize, name, and integrate, all the imagination that could rejuvenate our lives remains in limbo.

The psychotechnologies ease the emergence of the stranger.

---

[3]Sociologists calculated recently that an individual in Western society receives sixty-five thousand more pieces of stimuli each day than did our forebears one hundred years ago.

In a state of diffuse attention, complex feelings and impressions come forth to be recognized by the analytic left brain. The real mystery is in this sudden integration, when the inchoate clicks into place. Then the whole brain knows. It's like the light bulb that appears over the head of a cartoon character who has a "bright idea."

We are living in a time of rapid readjustment in everyday life and radical revisioning of science. Multiple levels of reality, new notions about the physical world, expanded states of awareness, staggering technological advances — these are neither science fiction nor a curious dream. They will not go away.

Most schools have been especially inhospitable to creative and innovative individuals in the past. Innovators jolt, they disturb the drowsy status quo. They dissent from the comfort of consensus reality, assorted Hans Christian Andersons marveling at the emperor's gleaming nakedness.

Hermann Hesse wrote of "the struggle between rule and spirit" that repeats itself year after year, from school to school:

> The authorities go to infinite pains to nip the few profound or more valuable intellects in the bud. And time and time again the ones who are detested by their teachers and frequently punished, the runaways and those expelled, are the ones who afterwards add to society's treasure. But some—and who knows how many?—waste away with quiet obstinacy and finally go under.

Inadvertently, we may push people to the extremes of their innate tendencies by the bias of our schools. The rebel-innovator diverges more and more, perhaps to become antisocial or neurotic. The timid child who wishes to please is shaped into an even more conformist position by the authoritarian structure. In their study comparing high schools to prisons, Craig Haney and Philip Zimbardo commented that the real tragedies are not the troublemakers or even the dropouts, but "the endless procession of faceless students who go through the school system quietly and unquestioningly, unobtrusively and unnoticed."

Fear can keep us from innovating, risking, creating. Yet we settle for only the illusion of safety. We prolong our discomfort, and we are troubled in our sleep. On one level we know that we are in danger, avoiding change in a changing world. The only strategies imaginative enough to rescue us will come from listening to our "other" consciousness. We must open and reopen the issues, we must break and reform the structures again and again.

Alvin Toffler suggested in *Future Shock* (1970) that we need "a multiplicity of visions, dreams, and prophecies—images of potential tomorrows...." Conjecture and visions become as coldly practical as "realism" — both feet on the floor — was in an earlier time. "We must create sanctuaries for social imagination."

Tomorrow is likely to bring thrilling, scary, even cataclysmic surprises. An educational system that pushes "right answers" is scientifically and psychologically unsound. And by demanding conformity, in either belief or behavior, it inhibits innovation and asks for scorn in an increasingly autonomous age.

"The present educational paradigm assumes that the only questions worth asking are those for which we already have the answers," said Ray Gottlieb, an optometrist specializing in learning. "Where, then, can one learn to live with the uncertainties of the real world?"

We are beginning to realize that we must educate for the uncertainty of freedom beyond frontiers. The ability to shift perspectives is a distinct aid to problem solving. In one experiment, psychologists trained students to reframe problems or to visualize them more vividly. Students who learned to reformulate had to enlarge their definition of the problem and check their assumptions to see if they were all true and necessary. The reframers dramatically outscored the visualizers! The experimenters remarked that perhaps you can be clear about the wrong thing, achieving "crystal clearness where there is none."[4]

Imaginative leaps, curiosity, synthesis, spontaneity, the flash of insight—these should not be the franchise of a favored minority. Educator John Gowan, whose special concern is creativity, said:

> Heretofore we have harvested creativity wild. We have used as creative only those persons who stubbornly remained so despite all efforts of the family, religion, education, and politics to grind it out of them....
>
> If we learn to domesticate creativity—that is, to enhance it rather than deny it in our culture—we can increase the

---

[4]For example, subjects were asked to design a clock that has no moving parts on its face or any feature that changes visibly during normal use. The answer: an *auditory* clock. Trying too hard to *see* a clock trapped most people into assuming that the clock must give visual readout.

number of creative persons [to the point of] critical mass. When this level is reached in a culture, as it was in Periclean Athens, the Renaissance, Elizabethan England, and our own Federalist period, civilization makes a great leap forward. We can have a golden age of this type such as the world has never seen. ... A genius is always a forerunner; and the best minds of this age foresee the dawn of that one.

Having no alternative, we were born creative. Our first sights and sounds were fresh, new, and original. We explored our small universes, named things, and knew them intimately in the I-Thou sense. Then, abruptly, formal education interrupted this contemplation, forcing us into another, more anxious kind of attention, shattering the state of consciousness necessary for good art and good science.

For the first time, if we're very lucky, education may undertake to foster that richer, more fluent consciousness. Our schools may gradually stop trying to row sailboats.

THE NEED FOR CONNECTION

Meaning emerges from context and connectedness. Without context, nothing makes sense. Try to imagine checkers without a checkerboard, language without a grammar, games without rules. The right brain, with its gift for seeing patterns and wholes, is essential for understanding context, for detecting meaning. "Learning to learn" includes learning to see the relationships between things. "Unfortunately our schools are no help," anthropologist Edward Hall said, "because they consistently teach us *not* to make connections. ... There should be a few people at least whose task is synthesis — pulling things together. And that is impossible without a deep sense of context."

Context ... literally, "that which is braided together." We are looking now at the ecology of everything, realizing that things only make sense in relation to other things. Just as medicine began to look at the context of disease, the milieu and not just symptoms, education is beginning to acknowledge that the interrelationship of what we know, the web of relevance, is more important than mere content. Content is relatively easy to master, once it has been given a framework.

Preschoolers, in one experiment, for example, learned to read words more readily than individual letters, apparently because they associated meaning with the words. The word *heavy*, which includes the letter *e*, was easier to learn than the letter *e* alone. However, if the letter was given a meaning rather than just a name or sound—if the children were told that *e* meant "taxi"—it could be learned as easily as a word. The researchers remarked on what a powerful factor meaning is and what a relatively minor influence visual complexity has if meaning is part of the equation.

Under the Title I program designed to help culturally deprived children, educational consultants from Synectics, a Cambridge, Massachusetts firm, have taught thousands of elementary-school children how to make connections—in effect, how to think metaphorically.[5] Initially, most of the children cannot make meaningful connections if the teacher asks, "How is the growth of a seed like the growth of an egg?" Typical responses of third-graders before training: "The flower is best." "The chick can walk." "The chicken is smaller." "There are no feathers on the flower."

After several hours of group exercises in connection-making, the children are asked again about the seed and the egg. All can now generalize some aspect of the similarities: growth, changing form, and so on. Their metaphors are often striking. In a program in Lawrence, Massachusetts, one child said, "Only the egg and the seed know what they'll be when they grow up. . . . Something inside must tell them. It's like 'Mister Rogers' on TV. He tells a story, and only he knows how it'll come out." One said that both a seed and an egg start small and get surprisingly big, like father's anger. "When he's mad, it starts out a little mad—and gets madder and madder." One compared the cracking of the seed and egg to the cracking of water pipes by expanding ice.

When the children in the Lawrence schools were tested one year after their training in metaphorical thinking, first graders showed a *363 percent* increase in knowledge of letters and sounds, a *286 percent* increase in aural comprehension, a *1038 percent* increase in word reading. Kindergartners showed year-to-year increases of *76 percent* on a picture-vocabulary test. Third graders showed an increase of nearly *40 percent* in reading scores.

William J. J. Gordon, the originator of the Synectics ap-

---

[5]Synectics exercises are also used for adults, especially in training for creativity.

proach, believes that learning is based on making connections that relate the new to the familiar, an ability that has been discouraged in many people.

Among the questions in Synectics exercises: "What needs more protection, a turtle or a rock?" "Which weighs more, a boulder or a heavy heart?" "Which grows more, a tree or self-confidence?" Metaphor builds a bridge between the hemispheres, symbolically carrying knowledge from the mute right brain so that it may be recognized by the left as being *like* something already known. Synectics also asks for examples of repulsive attraction, delicate armor, frozen haste, disciplined freedom—exercises in transcending paradox.

In the midst of a wealth of information, we may be moving toward an economy of learning—a few powerful principles and theories making sense across many disciplines.

The elements of the world cannot be understood except in terms of the whole, as our best thinkers keep trying to tell us. "Nature is one wonderful unit," Albert Szent-Gyorgyi said. "It is not divided into physics, chemistry, quantum mechanics...." Kenneth Boulding, economist and president of the American Association for the Advancement of Science, spoke of the "profound reorganization and restructuring of knowledge" taking place in our time: "The old boundaries are crumbling in all directions." Note that he said *restructuring*, not adding onto. It is the shape and form of what we know that is changing.

People must learn to accommodate "the whole brain in a whole world," said Joseph Meeker, speaking of what he called "ambidextrous education":

Left-brained linear thinkers are in for some hard times. Those who persist in believing that they live in a garden will find their carrots veering off to join or intersect the lettuce, while weeds and animals from the forest insinuate themselves through the slackening fencewire. No one thing can any longer be treated in isolation...Life in such a wilderness will require all the brain there is, not just that part that thrives on analytical divisions.

In its 1977 report, the Carnegie Foundation for the Advancement of Teaching said, "We have been through a period when knowledge was fragmented, but dreams of coherence survived.... Field by field, individuals have sought to recreate an intellectual whole after a long period of fission. We seem to be entering a period of new attempts at synthesis." From fission to fusion... As the report noted, this coming-together of knowledge is more evident at the graduate level of education because "the expanding edges of fields, where new research takes place, are closer to each other than are the central cores of fields."

It's hard to visualize the far edges of our various fields of knowledge coming together. We might more easily think in terms of depth: the penetration of human inquiry, from whatever direction, seems to be taking us to certain central truths or principles.

Indeed, at the level of graduate education, synthesis is evident. The National Endowment for the Humanities is sponsoring a five-year teaching and research effort in conjunction with San Francisco State University, the Science-Humanities Convergence Program. The newly formed National Humanities Center near Duke University, funded by private foundations and corporations, aims to encourage interdisciplinary research by providing support for scholars. Law schools, medical schools, and other centers of professional training are enriching and broadening their curricula.

THE NEED TO TRANSCEND CULTURE

Not only are we learning to connect information, but we are connecting with each other as well. We are increasingly aware that no one culture and no period in history has had all the answers. We are gathering our collective wisdom, from the past and from the whole planet.

"We have been the benefactors of our cultural heritage," said psychologist Stanley Krippner, "and the victims of our cultural narrowness." Our concepts of the possible are mired in the heavy materialism, the obsolete mind-body dualism, of our cultural perspective.

Just as medical innovators have drawn upon insights about health from other cultures—curanderismo, shamanism, acupuncture—we are now discovering and adapting traditional teaching systems, tools, and perspectives.

One such tool is the Indian Medicine Wheel, or the Cheyenne Wheel of Knowledge. In contrast to the way we compartmentalize information, the Cheyennes and other American Indian tribes attempt to show the circular, connected nature of reality by mapping knowledge on a wheel. For instance, the wheel may be divided into four seasons, the "four corners of the earth," or the seasons of one's life. Or, it may demonstrate patterns and relationships between social groups or crops, like a round flow chart. Educators at the Harvard School of Education have adapted the wheel to illustrate relationships between disciplines.

And just as the advocates of holistic medicine have resurrected relevant statements from Plato and other Greek philosophers, so educators are belatedly examining a holistic Greek concept, the *paidea*. The paidea referred to the educational matrix created by the whole of Athenian culture, in which the community and all its disciplines generated learning resources for the individual, whose ultimate goal was to reach the divine center in the self.

Euphenics, a recent idea in genetics, suggests that there is a scientific basis for such learning approaches as paidea. Whereas eugenics promoted the breeding of certain traits and selecting against other traits, euphenics takes the view that the environment can be optimized to bring out potential traits. In human terms, we might say that everyone is gifted, in the sense of having special potentials in the genetic repertoire, but that most of these gifts are not elicited by the environment. If the learning environment is stimulating and tolerant, a great array of skills, talents, and capacities can be developed.

Another native system offers a new way to introduce relevance. Students have often complained that there is little point to the information offered by schools. A number of American educators have adapted the idea of the "walkabout," a prolonged and dangerous journey into the wilderness required for male Australian aborigines at about age fourteen. Knowing that they are preparing for a life-or-death initiation gives immediacy to the aborigines' tribal education. In some schools, urban youngsters are now creating their own programs of study in preparation for a great task they choose, their version of the walkabout.

There is growing excitement among educators about old myths and symbols, oral history, earth festivals, primitive rites of passage and customs, extraordinary abilities documented in cultures less linear than our own.

As our view changes, the world changes: It becomes smaller, richer, more human, like McLuhan's Global Village, the jewel-like planet of the *Whole Earth Catalog*, Buckminster Fuller's *Spaceship Earth*. What is it to see subtle patterns in a terrain of snow or sand, to navigate from island to island, to dance on coals, to try to exorcise sickness? What can human beings do? What are all the things we collectively know? "None of us," says a poster in an alternative school, "is as smart as *all* of us."

We discover that we, too, can create myths, an age-old strategy for cultures engaged in transformation.

In the accounts of life-changing, shaking experiences included in the Aquarian Conspiracy questionnaires, several individuals mentioned cultural shock—moving to another country, another part of the world.

There are powerful lessons for us in other cultures. Primitive initiations, for instance, teach the initiate about pain, identity, confrontation. An Eskimo child who feels tense is encouraged to stare at a bird or a fish, temporarily withdrawing from a disturbing situation as a bird might take flight or a fish might swim rapidly away. The child is also taught to return to the problem after this respite, just as the bird and the fish return.

The Plains Indians of North America teach their children about "the twinness" in man, the existence of conflicting selves that can be made whole. An old chief quoted by Hyemeyohsts Storm in *Seven Arrows* compared this twinness to the forked branches of a tree. "If One Half tries to split itself from the Other Half, the Tree will become crippled or die.... Rather than taking this barren way, we must tie together the paradoxes of our Twin Nature with the things of the One Universe."

Our culture has needed its Cheyenne Wheel of Knowledge— a cosmology into which it can order information and experience: our place on the planet; our sequence in the pageant of evolution and history; our relationship to the infinitely small electron and the immense galaxies; our environments for birth, death, work, families. All of these are contexts. We cannot understand ourselves, each other, or nature without seeing whole systems: the tissue of events, the web of circumstances, multiple perspectives.

THE NEED FOR HIGH EXPECTATIONS

"What we thought was the horizon of our potentials turns out to be only the foreground," Tom Roberts, an Illinois educator, told a group of teachers interested in transpersonal education. A proposed project in the federal mills, "The Limits of Human Educability," recommended that researchers identify some of the *outer* limits: "The very task of identifying those limits serves to focus energy on going toward or beyond them. Focusing on the outer reaches of human educability creates a different perspective. . . ."

The transpersonal view encourages the learner to identify with those who transcended "normal" limits. What we think of as intellectual giftedness is potential in every normal brain, as research has shown, yet most of us fall tragically short of our birthright.

Experiments have also demonstrated the power of the self-image: the high or low expectations held by one's parents, one's teachers, oneself. A recent study of men from the same low socio-economic class revealed that those who were upwardly mobile had one critical ingredient the others lacked: parents who had expected them to succeed.

Teachers have been trained to expect little. In a famous experiment in the 1960s, Robert Rosenthal of Harvard and Lenore Jacobson, a San Francisco educator, demonstrated what they called the Pygmalion effect—the finding that teachers unintentionally communicate their expectations of what a student can do, thus setting in motion a self-fulfilling prophecy. Those youngsters expected to do well usually thrive, *even if the teacher's expectations are based on bogus information*. On the other hand, one study showed that teachers give little *negative* feedback to students of whom they expect little, making it difficult for the students to correct what they're doing wrong. Not only has the Pygmalion effect been replicated in hundreds of experiments; it turns out that teachers also have measurable biases based on the sex, race, and physical attractiveness of their students.

When Abraham Maslow asked a college class whether anyone there had expectations of achieving greatness, no one responded. "Who else, then?" he asked drily. A master teacher in Great Britain tells all the students she trains, "Do you realize when you stand before that class that you have there the Einsteins, the Picassos, the Beethovens of the future?"

We must stop fragmenting our image of high achievement, making separate labels for intelligence, creativity, giftedness, leadership, morality. As educator Barbara Clark put it in *Growing Up Gifted*:

> When we have integrated our focus, changed and extended our view of reality, and established the underlying connectedness of each to all, we will then have a new meaning of giftedness. The gifted, the talented, the "intuned," and the illuminated will then be merged. . . .

There is an impetus in education to develop "values clarification," a curriculum for moral development. Lawrence Kohlberg and others have reported that children become sensitive to moral issues if they are led to think about them. Actually, the teacher's character can inspire cooperation, altruism, and service in students—or hypocrisy, put-downs, and competitiveness. As someone has pointed out, all teachers teach values, consciously or unconsciously.

The possibilities are staggering—haunting, if we consider the human waste, the lost potential. But the very fact that we are now discovering this potential and communicating our concern offers hope. We live in the age of the *Guinness Book of World Records*. We can look to Olympic athletes who break their own barriers, folk heroes who pull people from burning cars, television human-interest stories like that about a crippled ghetto father who propelled his wheelchair eight miles to a hospital to get help for the fevered baby in his lap.

This is *living* moral education, teaching for transcendence. Because of travel and communications, the interaction that once produced "schools" of artists and clusters of great physicists and writers can now be accomplished in surprising measure on a global scale.

THE TRANSFORMATION OF TEACHERS

Reform after reform, some no doubt promising, failed because too many teachers disliked the key concepts or misunderstood them. As Charlie Brown in *Peanuts* remarked, "How can you do new math with an old-math mind?"

You can no more reform education by decree than you can heal by what Edward Carpenter called "external ministrations." Teachers have to understand new ideas from the inside out if they are to benefit from them. As one educator said, "Teachers who do a bad job with old tools are likely to do a worse job with strange new tools."

Some teachers are what Bruner called "dream killers," what Aldous Huxley called "bad artists" whose shortcomings can affect whole lives and destinies. Just as medical colleges have tended to select for the academically sharp, good memorizers rather than those best suited to care for people, so the colleges of education have constructed an obstacle course of jargon and course work dull enough to discourage all but the most stubborn of the creative candidates.

If the bright, imaginative individual survives the training marathon, the system itself is chilly to change. The creative teacher who hires into an experimental program frequently experiences burn-out—exhaustion and depression from the prolonged struggle to keep innovation alive amidst paperwork, constraints, attack.

We have put the lowest premium on talent and sensitivity in the profession most critical to the society's mental health.

Long after the original Pygmalion experiments, Rosenthal and his associates at Harvard developed a 200-item audiovisual test, "Profile of Non-verbal Sensitivity" (PONS), to measure the ability of an individual to perceive the emotions and intentions of others without the aid of verbal cues.

As a group, teachers were relatively low scorers. Students, on the other hand, were quite perceptive. Those who believe that others can be manipulated—who score high on the "Machiavellian scale"—are relatively insensitive to nonverbal cues.

The testmakers categorized the high scorers as Listeners, the low scorers as Speakers. On the whole, teachers are accustomed to telling, not hearing. Or, as one book title put it, *The Geranium on the Window Sill Just Died, but Teacher You Went Right On.* Meanwhile, students, in their sensitivity to all that is unsaid—the teacher's looks, postures of disapproval or rejection —learn what they must to survive the system.

Until recently, education has had it backward, caring little about the teacher, who is a kind of context for learning, and enormously about the content. Yet a gifted teacher can infect generations with excitement about ideas, can launch careers—even revolutions. Carl Cori, for example, a Nobel laureate professor and researcher at Washington University in St. Louis, supervised the work of *six* scientists who later won Nobel prizes.

The lifelong impact of a single first-grade teacher was reported in *Harvard Educational Review.* Two-thirds of the former pupils of "Miss A," all educated in a poor neighborhood in Montreal, had achieved the highest level of adult status, and the remainder were classified as "medium." None was in the "low" group.[6]

[6]As established on a comparative basis in the group studied, not in the society as a whole. Remember, these individuals lived in a low socioeconomic neighborhood, and "highest group" includes college instructor, successful businessman, etc.

Miss A was convinced that all children would read by the end of first grade, regardless of background. She impressed upon her students the importance of education, gave extra hours to the slow learners, stayed after school to help them, shared her lunch with students who had forgotten theirs, and remembered them by name twenty years later. She adjusted to new math and innovative techniques for teaching reading, but her real secret, former students and colleagues said, was that she "taught with a lot of love."

Educator Esther Rothman, author of *Troubled Teachers*, attributes poor teaching not only to ineptitude but also to unconscious conflicts, needs, and motives in the teacher. Violence, sarcasm, power games, permissiveness, low expectations leading to low achievement, especially in minority children—all these contribute mightily to the failures of education, she said. Budgets, school environments, and techniques are of secondary importance.

As teachers allow their deepest feelings and motivations to emerge, as they go inward to seek self-awareness and to free themselves emotionally, they are beginning to move outward to change the social structure. *Then* the teacher-idealist, the "undercover reformer," makes a mark, Rothman said.

> Many teachers are already crusading rebels in the best sense of the word; some are in the process of becoming. . . . Only then, when aggression, love, and power are used constructively in the classroom, can education really succeed. . . . Education, like the neurons of the brain, would then be an expressively aggressive process, dynamic and explosive.

Voices in education have proclaimed this need. "Education can transform culture, but only insofar as educators are transformed," said Diane Watson, a member of the Los Angeles school board.

Recently, within education's policymaking circles, the "facilitative behaviors" movement has focused attention on teachers as human beings who can kill or nurture learning. "Most school districts have concluded within the past five years that they can't improve education if they don't change teachers," one consultant said.

This movement sounds simple: It aims to awaken teachers to their classroom behavior and their attitude toward themselves and others. By rating teachers in the classroom or by having them rate themselves on videotape, the facilitative-behaviors approach calls attention to positive and negative acts.

Research has shown that children learn best from adults who are spontaneous, creative, supportive, physically fit . . . who look for meaning rather than just facts . . . who have high self-esteem . . . who see their job as liberating rather than controlling the slow learner. Good teachers are more interested in the process of learning than in achieving specific goals. They admit their own mistakes, entertain radical ideas by students, discuss feelings, foster cooperation, encourage students to help plan their work, provide resources beyond the call of duty. Humiliation, lining up, punishment, and rulemaking inhibit learning.

Project Change in Los Angeles is just one example of the training programs around the country designed to increase teachers' sensitivity. "Without exception," one trainer said, "the teachers tell us that the greatest benefits were in their personal lives, total changes in perspective. They say they're now aware of talents they didn't realize they had, and many experience a real explosion of creativity in the classroom. They're more open to others—less critical, more apt to see what others have to offer. There's a correspondence between this growth and the teacher's productivity. They write more lessons, there are self-reports of more energy, and the students rate them higher."

Educators engaged in transpersonal and humanistic methods have begun linking in national networks and centers; there are also local networks, like Lifeline in Los Angeles, sponsored by the Association for Humanistic Psychology, whose intention is the establishment of a new paradigm in education "co-existing with other, more traditional paradigms."

Beverly Galyean, consultant on "confluent education" for the Los Angeles city schools, expressed the network's conspiratorial, Radical Center intentions at a 1978 meeting:

> We meet as professional humanistic educators, expert in traditional methodology, wise enough to know what works and is to be retained, yet humble enough to seek new solutions.

> Around Los Angeles hundreds of people are practicing this kind of education, but fear permeates the environment because of a call for "fundamentals," discipline, control. . . . The individual humanistic teacher, counselor, administrator, parent, or student is left wondering how to merge a philosophy of love, openness, trust, belief in pro-

cess and learning from within, creative expression, personal responsibility, and group consensus with a tradition that seems its opposite.

Our answer: *Take the need where it is.* Provide creative alternatives to those programs that no longer work. If your district wants "back to basics," improved reading scores, and better attendance, show them how your humanistic program, or the program of your colleagues, accomplishes these goals. You can use traditional subject matter to provide students with processes for self-reflection. . . .

Or, if your district wants discipline, tell them about programs that operate on the principle of internal control. . . . Perhaps hyperactivity is a problem at your school. Use natural methods for calming over-active energies: yoga, meditation, massage, movement, nutrition.

No one can learn when the environment is distracting, fragmented. Learn how to lead focusing activities, group meditations, and relaxing techniques. . . .

The crises now facing most school districts can be the springboard for your own humanistic experiments. When people hurt they ask for help. Education is hurting and is asking for help. Let's not be shy in responding.

Even a tiny minority of committed teachers, counselors, and administrators can set off seismic shocks with programs that work.

THE NEW CURRICULUM

Because the emergent educational paradigm encompasses a great deal more than the old, experimental programs often fall short of their own ambitions. These are, after all, innovations and experiments, by definition not yet refined or streamlined. It is no small undertaking to humanize schools and challenge students at the same time.

The new school community is very close, more a family than a school, complete with occasional family fights. Teachers, parents, and students jointly decide important issues of policy and curriculum and hire new staff members. Students address teachers by first name and view them more as friends than authoritarian figures.

Age groupings are usually flexible, not the lockstep structure of traditional education. Most innovative educational programs eventually learn to include enough structure to remind students of their responsibility and to prepare them for some old-paradigm expectations when they leave school. Letter grades are available for those who need a record for college entry.

The new curriculum is a rich and subtle tapestry, constrained only by school bureaucracy and budget and the limits of the teacher's energy. Virtually no subject is too difficult, controversial, or offbeat to think about.

In most states, of course, some components of the curriculum are prescribed by law. Even so, educators integrate many academic subjects with "right-brain" activities (music, gymnastics, the arts, sensory stimulation) or present it dramatically, as in the reenactment of historic trials so that students will think freshly and with interest about the issues. Students experience other historic periods and other cultures by staging fairs and festivals, by learning the crafts and music of other times and places.

They use their mathematics to build domes. They use the community for their campus. Parents and "experts" from the community are volunteer teachers for special subjects, and the students also tutor each other. Typically the curriculum includes a sophisticated dose of the arts and humanities; students may learn calligraphy and batik dying, stage a Broadway play, write and perform their own television scripts. They learn the uses and sources of political power by attending school board and city council meetings. They learn biology by caring for animals, botany while planting gardens.

They learn about conditioning. They learn to recognize their own patterns of behavior, how to identify fear and conflict, how to act responsibly, how to communicate what they need and what they feel.

Altered states of consciousness are taken seriously: "centering" exercises, meditation, relaxation, and fantasy are used to keep the intuitive pathways open and the whole brain learning. Students are encouraged to "tune in," imagine, identify the special feeling of peak experiences. There are techniques to encourage body awareness: breathing, relaxation, yoga, movement, biofeedback.

Students are encouraged to think about semantics—how labels affect our thinking. They study topics that would be considered too controversial for most classrooms—birth and death, for instance. Foreign language may be taught by techniques like the Silent Way, a method in which the teacher says little and the student is challenged to use the language right away; or Suggestology, the accelerated-learning method that originated in Bulgaria, which employs music and rhythmic breathing to engage the right hemisphere. There are courses in ecology, in discriminating between junk food and good nutrition, in being an intelligent consumer.

Students are pushed to think about paradoxes, conflicting philosophies, the implications of their own beliefs and actions. They are reminded that there are always alternatives. They innovate, invent, question, ponder, argue, dream, agonize, plan, fail, succeed, rethink, imagine. They learn to learn, and they understand that education is a lifelong journey.

Students of all ages play games: educational games, math games, board games of fantasy, history, space exploration, social issues. Rather than fiercely competitive physical games, they may play "New Games," an ever-expanding collection of activities, some of them ancient sport, that fit the slogan of the New Games Foundation: "Play hard, play fair, nobody hurt."

Competition, status, and popularity contests play a relatively small part in the dynamics of such schools. Most students attend voluntarily because they and their families favor this educational approach. Such families tend to de-emphasize social striving and competition and to emphasize excellence for its own sake. The curriculum and teacher behavior also reinforce autonomy, empathy, and mutual support in students. Squabbling is more in the vein of transient sibling disputes rather than the deep patterns of "in" and "out" groups typical of conventional schools.

A major ambition of the curriculum is autonomy. This is based on the belief that if our children are to be free, they must be free even from us—from our limiting beliefs and our acquired tastes and habits. At times this means teaching for healthy, appropriate rebellion, not conformity. Maturity brings with it a morality that derives from the innermost self, not from mere obedience to the culture's mores.

As modern history has tragically shown, obedience based on fear is not morally selective. Psychologist Stanley Milgram, in a series of now classic experiments, ordered experimental subjects to administer what they believed to be painful shocks to another person. (Actually, the victim, a confederate of the experimenter, only pretended to be in pain.) Most subjects, although visibly anguished over what they were being asked to do, were incapable of saying no to the "authority," a psychologist in a white coat. *Sixty-five percent* of these ordinary people were willing to inflict severe, possibly permanent, damage by pushing the bogus lever of the apparatus to its highest setting. Even when they heard terrible screaming from the other room, they could not bring themselves to walk out on the experimenter. This phenomenon—Milgram calls it "obedience to authority"—crosses all cultures and age groups, with children slightly more susceptible than adults.

Most people conform in exchange for the world's acceptance. If we already feel at home in the world, deeply related and comfortable, if we are unafraid, we do not have to strike this kind of bargain. The autonomous learner navigates by an inner gyroscope, obeying an internal authority. Sarah McCarthy, a Pittsburgh schoolteacher, urged that educators introduce remedial programs for "overly obedient" children, teaching them a kind of creative, appropriate disobedience as an antidote to the Milgram effect.

BEYOND SCHOOLS

Although the rise in educational alternatives has been relatively dramatic, most families do not have access to innovative schools, open classrooms, and the kinds of teachers who can make it work—who resonate, celebrate, initiate.

Help is at hand—not a uniformed cavalry to the rescue, but volunteers, renegades, advance scouts. There are new places to learn, new ways to learn, new people to teach, new abilities to master, new connections to be made. We are moving into a period of learning without boundaries, age limits, prerequisites, flunking. The larger educational matrix draws heavily on the community and on entrepreneurs who have discovered the thirst for learning, for transformative technologies, for useful skills and knowledge.

Achieving paidea, the Radical Center, the heavenly city; "teaching both halves of the brain"—this is no small ambition. *No school can do it. No school has ever done it.* Only a community can offer holistic education, and only a whole person can take it. Simultaneous personal and social transformation can take us into what Confucius called "the great learning," compared to the "little learning" imparted by the schools. "The university will most likely not grow into the size of a city," said William Irwin Thompson in *The Edge of History*. "It will shrink as it realizes that it is the city itself (and not the campus) that is the true university."

The greatest re-form of education may be *decentralizaton*, the dismantling of the windowless walls that have closed off school from community, from the milieu of real life. Ronald Gross, an educator, said:

My hope is that through the gradual weakening of the constraints of schooling, we will so loosen its fabric and so strengthen the opportunities to learn from other sources, that it will become impossible to separate learning from life, and student and teacher from friends learning together. For this we need a real flowering of other options....

A top-level government policymaker for education speculates that we may eventually have the equivalent of the GI Education Bill in lieu of compulsory curricula—an allotment to be spent by the individual for whatever learning, specialized or general, he seeks: "funding the student and not the institution." The idea of educational vouchers in lieu of compulsory public education has appeal across the political spectrum, however starkly different the radical and conservative rationales may be.

Demystification, decentralization, despecialization are the order of the day. Most of the exciting changes and successes in education's new incarnation reflect its return to its proper keepers, the community and the learner. Just as medicine's turnabout was instigated not only by reformer-doctors but also by biofeedback clinicians, nutritionists, psychologists, journalists, brain scientists, and those from dozens of other disciplines; so new partnerships in education mean new life.

The learning process has opened up: universities without walls, "free universities," mobile schools, work-study projects even for young children, medieval-style tutoring programs, community-run schools, elderly volunteers in the schools and youngsters in real work environments, field trips, adult education, an explosion of crafts and self-teaching literature for skills, life-experience credit toward college degrees, private instruction, peer teaching, skill-sharing, student-service and restoration projects in the community. And technological aids are getting cheaper and more accessible—tape-cassette instruction, for example, and computer kits.

Teaching and learning are now cottage industries. The home-start projects for disadvantaged children, community-run public schools, parent-created learning and play groups for preschoolers and after school, learning networks, the successes of Jesse Jackson's PUSH program urging pride and literacy among ghetto kids—all are essentially independent of the system.

Part of the transformative process is becoming a learner

again, whatever your age. When we were children we had little choice about what and how we learned. In this sense, most of us remain passive children for the rest of our lives, never aware that we can choose, never aware that learning — transformation — takes place. We grow up, whatever our age, whenever we take over the process, when we become conscious learners rather than accidental learners.

"All of us," said Jerry Fletcher of the Office of the Assistant Secretary of Education, "even those apparently most fully functioning, have areas of our lives in which we are blocked, unable to fully experience and develop." True education, he said, strengthens the capacity to continue to make sense of one's life as it develops.

> A change in cultural expectations will do a lot. One of the things that will change the cultural climate most rapidly is a carefully worked-out description of the levels that are possible above what most adults now attain. If our description of this becomes accepted as legitimate in the culture, we are on our way.

An example of the openness to lifelong learning is the Elderhostel program, a network of residential study programs for adult learners on two hundred college campuses. Similar programs are in effect in France, Switzerland, Belgium, Poland, and Canada. The participants, primarily older people, need not have had a formal education. Mental and physical stimulation are provided in college-level classes and physical activities, lectures, and round tables.

"Free universities" first appeared in the mid-sixties as part of the student rebellion. Now nearly two hundred independent free universities around the country offer a potpourri of noncredit courses in every imaginable subject. Seventeen thousand attended Denver Free University's summer session in 1979. The state of Kansas is offering the free schools funding assistance in the hope that they may create a sense of community in rural areas.

In 1971 a consortium of twenty-five colleges and universities formed the University Without Walls (UWW) program, which they administer as the Union of Experimenting Colleges and Universities. Similar programs, many with less firm accreditation than the UWW, have been developed all over the country, some modeled on Britain's Open University.

Jose Arguelles said of such networks:

What the networking model suggests is a common paradigm linking together the physical and psychological, the intellectual and the intuitive, the left hemisphere and the right hemisphere. . . .

Just as the human being goes from childhood to puberty and sexual awareness, so the idea of educational networking must . . . take its place in the great and fertile context of ideas and social values which comprise the evolutionary thrust of humanity.

We give each other the courage to move into the unknown, to risk in each other's company and with each other's blessings. We are constantly engaged in what someone has called "mutual education." One who has become involved in his own education again needs the company of others on that journey. When we say we've "outgrown" someone or someone has outgrown us, we mean that one of us in interested in learning and the other is not.

It is characteristic of the Aquarian Conspirators to describe as their teachers not only formal educators but also their friends, children, spouses, former spouses, parents, colleagues — and life events. If you are noncompetitive and nonhierarchical in defining masters and learners, then everyone is a teacher, every experience a lesson, every relationship a course of study. "Even the stone is a teacher," said the Sufi, Idries Shah.

The intense intellectual and spiritual sharing of the Aquarian Conspiracy, the joint expeditions into new territory, the pooling of the wealth, create the kind of mutual inspiration John Gowan described. The almost sexual interplay of ideas, yin and yang, old and new, East and West, results in a kind of collective synthesis: a creative community, hospitable to risk and imagination.

CHILDREN OF THE NEW PARADIGM

Long before Thomas Kuhn observed that new ideas may have to wait for a new generation's acceptance, folk wisdom made this bittersweet point. A Hebrew proverb warns, "Do not confine your children to your own learning, for they were born in another time."

Karl Pribram once commented that a new generation will learn about paradox in the early grades and will grow up understanding concepts of primary and secondary levels of reality. Not long thereafter, coincidentally, a junior-high student, John Shimotsu of Los Angeles, tried his hand at interpreting for his fellow eighth graders the holographic model of reality proposed by Pribram and physicist David Bohm. In conclusion, he said:

> Why can't you perform actions that we consider paranormal? I think it is because you do not think you can. You may say you wish to, or may sincerely want to, but that will not change what you subconsciously think. Our culture says that those actions would not be possible, so that is what you think is real. *To change your reality, you would have to alter your innermost thoughts*. The holographic idea is fascinating. What is theory today may be fact tomorrow.

All over the world, children and young people are being exposed, via the communications revolution, to such ideas. They are not limited to the parochial beliefs of a single culture.

Paul Nash likened this shift in realities to the gap between an immigrant couple and their children. "The children usually learn the language and adopt the local mores more easily than do the older folks, who become dependent on the children as guides to the 'new world.'"

Variations on this theme, the powers of the child and the primitive, appear in recent writings like Joseph Chilton Pearce's *Magical Child* and Lyall Watson's *Gift of Unknown Things*. A generation in love with Tolkien's fantasy and Castaneda's sorcerer are ready for magic in themselves and in their young children.

Entry into this new world is suggested by the titles of conferences on transpersonal learning and childrearing: *Children of the New Age, Celebration of the Child, Nurturing the Child of the Future, The Metaphoric Mind, The Conscious Child, Transpersonal Frontiers, Infinite Frontiers*.

If education cannot be mended, perhaps it can metamorphose. As someone pointed out, trying to explain the difference between reform and transformation, we have been trying to attach wings to a caterpillar. Our interventions in the learning process to date have been almost that crude. It is high time we freed ourselves of attachment to old forms and eased the flight of the unfettered human mind.

10

The Transformation of Values and Vocation

*If the nature of the work is properly appreciated
and applied, it will stand in the same relation to the higher
faculties as food is to the physical body.*

—J.C. KUMARAPPA, *philosopher and economist*

If there is power in the transformative experience, it must inevitably shake our values and, therefore, the total economy—the marketplace, the factory, corporations, the professions, small business, social welfare. And it must redefine what we mean by words like "rich" and "poor"; it must make us rethink what we owe each other, what is possible, what is appropriate. Sooner or later, the new paradigm changes the individual's relationship to work; part-time transformation is inherently impossible.

Making a life, not just a living, is essential to one seeking wholeness. Our hunger turns out to be for something different, not something more. Buying, selling, owning, saving, sharing, keeping, investing, giving—these are outward expressions of inward needs. When those needs change, as in personal transformation, economic patterns change. For example, spending

323

is an opiate to many people, a balm to disappointments, frustrations, emptiness. If the individual transforms that inner distress, there is less need for drugs and distractions. Inner listening makes clearer to us what we really want, as distinct from what we have been talked into, and it might not have a price tag. We may also discover that "ownership" is in some sense an illusion, that holding on to things can keep us from freely enjoying them. Greater awareness may give us new appreciation for simple things. And quality becomes important—the much-talked-about "quality of life." If work becomes rewarding, not just obligatory, that also reorders values and priorities.

We will look at the evidence for a new paradigm, based on *values*, which transcends the old paradigm of economics, with its emphasis on growth, control, manipulation. The shift to the values paradigm is reflected in changing patterns of work, career choice, consumption . . . evolving lifestyles that take advantage of synergy, sharing, barter, cooperation, and creativity . . . the transformation of the workplace, in business, industry, professions, the arts . . . innovations in management and worker participation, including the decentralization of power . . . the rise of a new breed of entrepreneurs . . . the search for "appropriate technology" . . . the call for an economics congruent with nature rather than the mechanistic views that have propelled us into our present crises.

CRISIS AND DENIAL

We have proved that you can't eat yourself slim. Trying to consume our way to prosperity, we have been exhausting our resources. High production costs, scarcities, inflation, and severe unemployment have become our regular diet.

Because the economy is such a political issue it is propagandized, rationalized, lied about. Because our beliefs about the economy affect it, as in the "confidence index," business and government try to buffer the reaction of investors and consumers to unnerving economic news.

And because divergent viewpoints are loudly argued, you can choose whom to believe:

Nuclear power is essential/deadly.

Solar energy will be cheap/impractical.

Fossil fuel is plentiful/exhausted.

We should consume/conserve.

Full employment is feasible/impossible.

Automation/environmentalism do/do not undermine jobs and growth.

There are illusions of rescue by technology, by the reshuffling of moneys and resources. But our temporary easing of this chronic illness—scarcities, dislocated markets, unemployment, obsolescence — is as dangerous as the medical treatment of symptoms when the cause of disease is unknown. Our intervention in the body economic, like intervention by drugs and surgery, often leads to severe side effects requiring further and deeper intervention.

The crisis is evident in the chronic nature of unemployment and underemployment: the technological obsolescence that has overtaken millions of specialized skilled workers, increasing numbers of the highly educated vying for too few white-collar jobs, increasing numbers of teenagers and women trying to enter the work force.

A United States Department of Labor study found "true unemployment"—including those working but with earnings below the poverty level—more than *40 percent*. Fewer jobs, more applicants. Proportionately fewer interesting jobs. Technological ingenuity that doubles the productivity of worker A so that B can be laid off so that A can grumble about paying taxes to help support a demoralized B. Affirmative-action programs that often just redistribute the unfairness and bitterness to a different group.

Labor and management savage each other periodically, like crazy Siamese twins who don't know that their lifeblood is the same.

The indices of our economy are often misleading. For example, the Gross National Product figures include the expenditures for treating disease, repairing wrecked automobiles, and eliminating factory pollution; that is, we are measuring activity, not true production. It is increasingly evident that our efforts to control, explain, and understand the economy are wholly inadequate.

The economy is alive and integrated, more an organism than a machine. It has qualities as well as quantities. Like the weather, it cannot be repaired. It won't be still long enough and is predictable only in patches. Even its "laws" are only descriptions of the past. "The truth is," said David Sternlight, chief economist for the Atlantic Richfield Company, "there are no facts about the future."

It is fashionable to assume that any economic prediction is better than none, E. F. Schumacher said in 1961. "Make a guess, call it an assumption, and derive an estimate by subtle calculation. The estimate is then presented as the result of scientific reasoning, something far superior to mere guesswork." Colossal planning errors result because this method offers "a bogus answer where an entrepreneurial judgment is required."

The unexamined assumption of the old paradigm—dominant since the days of John Locke—is that human beings are most deeply motivated by economic concerns. Yet, beyond a certain level of material sufficiency, other strong needs clearly take precedence: the desire to be healthy, to be loved, to feel competent, to participate fully in society, to have meaningful employment. And even if Locke were right about our economic motives, we would have to change: Our civilization cannot go on escalating its manufacture and consumption of non-renewable resources.

Assessing the New York City financial crisis in the mid-seventies, Julius Stulman of the World Institute said that our greatest mistake is that we continue to relate everything to the past, "the steps we have laboriously climbed for six thousand years—brick by brick, hand over fist, in singular, linear fashion. However necessary those steps may have been to our evolution, that stage has ended. *We cannot cope until we think differently.*"

Our best hope now is to pay attention, to recognize the ways in which our lives and livelihood have been influenced, even run, by outmoded structures. Our ideas about work, money, and management grew out of an old stable social order irrelevant to present flux and were based on a view of humankind and nature long since transcended in science. The real world turns on different principles than those imposed by our partial economic philosphies.

THE EMERGENT PARADIGM:
VALUES, NOT ECONOMICS

The economic systems of the modern world take sides in the old argument: individual versus society. When we are polarized, we are arguing about the wrong issue. Rather than debating whether capitalism is right in its emphasis on opportunities for the individual or socialism in its concern for the collective, we should reframe the question: Is a materialistic society suited to human needs? Both capitalism and socialism, as we know them, pivot on material values. They are inadequate philosophies for a transformed society.

The failures of our economic philosophies, like the failures of our political reforms, can be attributed to their emphasis on the external. Inner values, like inner reform, precede outward change. In synthesis may be our salvation—the path between right and left Aldous Huxley called "decentralism and cooperative enterprise, an economic and political system most natural to spirituality."

Just as health is vastly more than medicine, just as learning transcends education, so a system of values is the context for the workings of any economy. Whatever our priorities—self-aggrandizement, efficiency, status, health, security, recreation, human relationships, competition, cooperation, craftsmanship, material goods—they are reflected in the workings of the economy. A society that prizes external symbols will want showy automobiles, whatever the cost. A family that values education may make considerable sacrifices to pay tuition for a private school. One who values adventure may give up a financially secure job to sail around the world.

Most importantly, when people become autonomous, their values become *internal*. Their purchases and their choice of work begin to reflect their own authentic needs and desires rather than the values imposed by advertisers, family, peers, media.

Louis Mobley, former director of executive training for IBM, suggested that the turn inward marks a cultural reversal. Having concluded an era in which we looked only outward and denied our inner realities, we are now making value judgments. "And that's why the answers escape economists." The 1978 Nobel laureate in economics, Herbert Simon, criticizes the classic "rational" assumptions of economists and their consequent failure to deal with changing values and expectations.

Societies, as Ilya Prigogine pointed out, are the strangest and most unstable of dissipative structures. The complexity of our modern pluralistic society and the increasingly autonomous values of its people have created vast economic uncertainty. Now we need an approach to the economy comparable to the wise uncertainty of the physicist.[1]

The two paradigms might be summarized as follows:

[1]Max Planck once said that he had started out as a student of economics; finding it too difficult, he took up physics.

ASSUMPTIONS OF THE OLD PARADIGM OF ECONOMICS	ASSUMPTIONS OF THE NEW PARADIGM OF VALUES
Promotes consumption at all costs, via planned obsolescence, advertising pressure, creation of artificial "needs."	Appropriate consumption. Conserving, keeping, recycling, quality, craftsmanship, innovation, invention to serve authentic needs.
People to fit jobs. Rigidity. Conformity.	Jobs to fit people. Flexibility. Creativity. Form and flow.
Imposed goals, top-down decision-making. Heirarchy, bureaucracy.	Autonomy encouraged. Self-actualization. Worker participation, democratization. Shared goals, consensus.
Fragmentation, compartmentalization in work and roles. Emphasis on specialized tasks. Sharply defined job descriptions.	Cross-fertilization by specialists seeing wider relevance of their field of expertise. Choice and change in job roles encouraged.
Identification with job, organization, profession.	Identity transcends job description.
Clockwork model of economy, based on Newtonian physics.	Recognition of uncertainty in economics.
Aggression, competition. "Business is business."	Cooperation. Human values transcend "winning."
Work and play separate. Work as means to an end.	Blurring of work and play. Work rewarding in itself.
Manipulation and dominance of nature.	Cooperation with nature; taoistic, organic view of work and wealth.

ASSUMPTIONS OF THE OLD PARADIGM OF ECONOMICS	ASSUMPTIONS OF THE NEW PARADIGM OF VALUES
Struggle for stability, station, security.	Sense of change, becoming. Willingness to risk. Entrepreneurial attitude.
Quantitative: quotas, status symbols, level of income, profits, "raises," Gross National Product, tangible assets.	Qualitative as well as quantitative. Sense of achievement, mutual effort for mutual enrichment. Values intangible assets (creativity, fulfillment) as well as tangible.
Strictly economic motives, material values. Progress judged by product, content.	Spiritual values transcend material gain; material sufficiency. Process as important as product. Context of work as important as content— not just what you do but *how* you do it.
Polarized: labor versus management, consumer versus manufacturer, etc.	Transcends polarities. Shared goals, values.
Short-sighted: exploitation of limited resources.	Ecologically sensitive to ultimate costs. Stewardship.
"Rational," trusting only data.	Rational and intuitive. Data, logic augmented by hunches, feelings, insights, nonlinear (holistic) sense of pattern.
Emphasis on short-term solutions.	Recognition that long-range efficiency must take into account harmonious work environment, employee health, customer relations.

ASSUMPTIONS OF THE OLD PARADIGM OF ECONOMICS	ASSUMPTIONS OF THE NEW PARADIGM OF VALUES
Centralized operations.	Decentralized operations wherever possible. Human scale.
Runaway, unbridled technology. Subservience to technology.	Appropriate technology. Technology as tool, not tyrant.
Allopathic treatment of "symptoms" in economy.	Attempt to understand the whole, locate deep underlying causes of disharmony, disequilibrium. Preventive "medicine," anticipation of dislocations, scarcities.

THE "ETHEREALIZATION" OF AMERICA: NEW VALUES

In the nineteenth century John Stuart Mill saw past the early materialist promises of the Industrial Age: "No great improvements in the lot of mankind are possible until a great change takes place in their mode of thought." In the 1930s historian Arnold Toynbee spoke of "etherealization"—the development of higher, intangible riches as the ultimate growth of a civilization.

There seems to be growing sympathy, if not a mandate, for reversing the materialist trend. Maybe the etherealization is happening. A 1977 Harris poll showed an astounding preponderance of persons—79 percent—favoring better use of basic essentials rather than reaching higher material standards of living. A similar percentage preferred spending more time on human interaction rather than improved technological communication and hoped to see the society appreciate human values over material values. The idea of developing bigger and more efficient ways of doing things was less attractive than "breaking up big things and getting back to more humanized living."

A majority said they preferred finding inner rewards from work rather than increasing productivity, and they wanted to see their children's education directed more toward such intangible rewards than toward a higher material standard of living.

Most people living in the United States today have sampled the fruits of at least a little affluence. We have been free of the desperate survival needs that haunted generations of human history and still haunt whole populations. Still there is hunger, of a different kind, and still we are not free. Beyond our compulsive, addictive behavior, we can discover what we want; we can pay attention to the unfocused questions inside us. Now we are asking, *What matters?*

Our prehistoric ancestors helped lay the groundwork for this anticipation, in a sense, when they stopped being hunters and gatherers and became farmers, cooperating with nature's major cycles. Perhaps that is where we got our "agribusiness" minds, plowing and planning, concerned for the coming harvest. Perhaps we may become hunters and gatherers of a sort again, living for the day's treasures as well as for the long growing season.

Perhaps, as one report put it, we are living in a "post-extravagant society." We seem to be hunting for meaning, for a transcendent vision like that of our founding fathers.

The etherealization was expressed by one of the Aquarian Conspirators, a teacher:

> I have been influenced by knowing and sharing with persons who have no major needs (financially well-to-do) and with persons who voluntarily adopt poverty (religious vows). It is mainly in terms of these associations that I have been able to order my values: authentic *vs.* inauthentic, must-haves *vs.* nice-to-haves, permanent *vs.* immediate, happiness *vs.* pleasure.

Autonomous human beings can create and invent. And they can change their minds, repudiating values they once held. Business analysts are now looking realistically at the creeping effects of what were once the values of the counterculture. They see the coming of age of a generation less impressed by the old toys and symbols.

A Bank of America economist said in 1977 that the demand for durable goods was likely to level off permanently as more and more Americans see national and personal consumption as wasteful. Goods would increasingly be purchased as replacements rather than as symbols of conspicuous consumption or because of style and model changes. The pendulum would swing back to the virtues of thrift, integrity, and high moral values, he predicted. The primary population growth over the next decade, those twenty-five to thirty-four years old, will place a high value on the quality and social implications of their purchases.

A young truck driver with a liberal arts degree answered the frequent question about what he intended to do with his education:

> I will practice living. I will develop my intellect, which may incidentally contribute to the elevation of the esthetic and cultural levels of society. I will try to develop the noble and creative elements within me. I will contribute very little to the grossness of the national product.

His five-year struggle to earn a living intensified his appreciation and respect for his education, he said. The environment in which he worked was so hostile to imagination that his books and art were especially exciting and vital to him. "I work alongside people who attempt to secure meaning for their lives by pursuing the tawdry baubles American industry has to offer. . . ."

THE VALUE OF SYNERGY: NEW WEALTH

However many wars and weapons we may have devised, human beings are a biologically social, cooperative species. We have survived by helping each other. Even our prehistoric ancestors exhibited tenderness, lining their children's slippers with fur, caring for their cripples; recent archeological evidence suggests that they buried their dead with flowers.

The whole is richer than its parts. This synergy has opened the way for new sources of goods and services: cooperatives, barter, mutual-help networks. Pooled resources make everyone richer, pooled information makes everyone smarter, and nothing is lost in the dispersal.

Older than money, ancient economic shortcuts like cooperatives, credit unions, and barter give leanness to the cumbersome distribution system, for they involve only that which people want and have to offer, in contrast to the ever-accelerating production of items people have to be persuaded to buy or "invest in."

There are modern urban counterparts of quilting bees, barn-raisings, and farmers' co-ops. Carpools, learning networks, food cooperatives, and shared childcare create a sense of community as well as an economic boost.[2]

Popular women's magazines have begun publishing articles on how to start networks and cooperatives. Low-income people formed the Oregon Urban-Rural (OUR) credit union, in the tradition of the drought-poor villagers in southern Germany who started the first credit union in the mid-nineteenth century. Around the country, labor pools and service collectives have coalesced. Free for All in Los Angeles was organized for the bartering of services. Commerical barter companies like Trade-Americard, Executive Trade Club, Charge-a-Trade, and Business Exchange swap and credit goods and services to their members through sophisticated bookkeeping. One barter company does a yearly business of around one hundred million dollars in reciprocal trade agreements, recycling surpluses and mistakes, advertising space, and hotel rooms. About seventy-five bartering groups in the United States are franchised under the International Trade Exchange.[3] They use computers to facilitate the transactions among member businesses, tradespeople, and professionals. Trading, as the owners of one exchange remarked, helps beat inflation. Barter is likely to boom in a recession. *New Age* observed:

In a time when the little metal and paper tokens we call wealth are becoming increasingly isolated from the craft or toil which they are supposed to represent, the business of barter seems a healthy trend indeed. "Payment in kind," the original mode of economic transaction, is grounded on

[2]Immigrants to California established similar networks, according to sociologists. James Q. Wilson described a version of urban labor-swapping in California in the 1950s that foreshadowed today's extensive bartering: "The Southern California equivalent of the eastern uncle who could get it for you wholesale was the Los Angeles brother-in-law who would help you put on a new roof or paint the garage, or lend you (and show you how to use) his power saw. A vast, informally organized labor exchange permeated the region, with occasional trades of great complexity running through several intermediaries—the friend who would ask his brother, the plumber, to help you, if you would ask your uncle with the mixer to lay concrete in front of somebody's sister's home. Saturday saw people driving all over the county, carrying out these assignments."

[3]Barter is also big business these days among trading corporations within the Soviet Union and among multi-national companies that trade raw materials for finished products.

cooperation more than competition; rather than the ac-
cumulation of money for its own sake, it stresses the quality of human work.

The founders of Provender, a natural-food cooperative in the
Northwest, wrote of the self-reliance and regional unity they
sensed when they joined forces: "Fellow cooperators, we can
celebrate the birth of a network...."
The reward transcends the mere economics involved, as can
be seen by some of the statements of purpose of such networks:

...The Community Soap Factory and the co-ops were
started, not because of the promise of commercial success
—by those standards they are risky—but by the beliefs in
an ideal, a vision of how society might be.... If we can
formulate a cogent, communitarian ideology, many more
people will be moved to create and support alternative
structures.

* * *

We focus on right attitude and right timing. This opening
up and transformation of the power dynamic is the very
stuff which will move us into a new age of compassion and
self-empowerment.

* * *

The work of our communities is to lay the foundation, the
groundwork...to develop the models, designs, and archetypes of a new civilization.

* * *

The Community Memory Project will help people connect
to others of similar interests and will add exchange of
goods, resources, and ideas. This network is nonhierarchical and interactive—that is, the information in the system
is created and shared by the people who use it, not "broadcast" from a central authority.

Cooperative ventures include intentional communities and
shared housing. In some cases several families have collectively
developed apartment houses and condominiums. Some have
acquired clusters of private residences and established specific
communal activities like shared gardens and shared weekly
meals. The commune comprised of middle-class profession-

als is becoming increasingly commonplace. In fact, the 1980 census was designed with a special category for communal households.

One example of an established large communal household is Ramagiri, a center whose members came together in 1971 after experimentation in smaller groups. There are now forty members (including ten married couples, four pairs of siblings) living on a 250-acre California farm that was once a small Catholic seminary. Ramagiri has its own sustaining businesses, but most of the residents work outside as teachers, health professionals (nurses, physical therapists, nutritionists), secretaries. Two young medical residents plan to open a practice together. A garden, office, and kitchen are communally operated. The commune has published several successful books by Eknath Easwaran, the Indian teacher around whom its members originally coalesced, and a best-seller, *Laurel's Cookbook*.

Members of Movement for a New Society, a Philadelphia group, live in fourteen communally operated houses. They run a media training group, seminars, an organization for older women, and a "transit collective" for shared transportation. They publish *Resource Manual for a Living Revolution* and other literature on nonviolent cultural change.

A group in the making, Cooperative College Community, has been coordinating the efforts of teachers and artists from East Coast colleges to live together on a large tract of land, already acquired, and operate a small liberal arts college. Its organizers stated:

> We conceive of this enterprise as an experiment in human values. It is an attempt to demonstrate that a rich and dignified life can be sustained in an economically limited community, [by] sharing labor and political responsibility, choosing to restrict accumulation and consumption of material wealth, and making efficient use of natural resources.... We do not presume to be presenting either a social panacea or an easily replicable paradigm for every existing social institution. But we do believe we are realizing one possible alternative, thus concretely challenging prevailing conceptions of social and economic organization.

One participant in a communal project said, "We are not land developers, we are community discoverers. We do not offer a dream home but an opportunity to create a new life more satisfying than the one we are leaving behind."

From a newsletter:

> One of our objectives is to demonstrate that it is possible for a group of ordinary human beings to come together and to create a "new-age" community. New-age communities are not going to be built by big governments or by big corporations, and it probably wouldn't be a good idea for that to happen anyhow. We think it is desirable for people to take charge of their own lives, to become self-reliant (as groups)....We want to show that life can be lived more simply, in harmony with nature, within the constraints of nature, cooperatively, creatively, humanly....We hope to see a network of New Age communities, sharing, working, helping each other.

Some of the larger communities have indeed established ties; they are not competitive, and however different the expression, their visions have much in common. A magazine published for cooperative communities praised the networking between the larger ones, such as Arcosanti (Arizona), Another Place (New England), Auroville (India), and Findhorn (Scotland): "An important element of this sense of world community is the reaching beyond our idiosyncrasies, getting at the essence of what we are trying to do. Our work must be translatable to be usable."

An ever-changing portion of the population is living a shared dream in the midst of the wreckage of the old dream. One observer said, "Communes have been no less successful than the mundane American Dream. We judge them more harshly because they attempted to be more." We also judge them too often by the values of the old paradigm: economic success and stability.

Another Place, a rural collective and network in New Hampshire, welcomes people involved in politics, alternative schools, meditation, holistic health—"creative alternatives to the dominant society." It takes its name from a poem by Wendell Berry, whose book, *The Unsettling of America*, is influential among community builders:

> ...the mind turns, seeks a new
> nativity—another place,

simpler, less weighted
by what has already been.

Another place
it's enough to grieve me—
that old dream of going,
of becoming a better man
just by getting up and going
to a better place.

The mystery. The old
unaccountable unfolding.
The iron trees in the park
suddenly remember forests.
It becomes possible to think of going.

The new life begins, not with action but with a new awareness,
when it first becomes possible to think of going.

In community, in human exchange, there is a qualitatively
different kind of wealth.

THE VALUE OF KNOWING WHAT YOU WANT

Our values come consciously out of our understanding—or unconsciously, out of our conditioning. As we become aware of
once-unconscious motives, we may awaken to what we really
want and what our options are.

Just as the public has withdrawn considerable legitimacy
from its other institutions, it has become increasingly suspicious of the consumption ethic—the mystique of things. The
consumer movement, for one thing, raised awareness about
shoddy business practices and deceptive merchandise. The
ecology movement raised questions about environmental
quality and exploitation of resources. Our growing sophistication has made us less susceptible to the glossy fictions of
advertising.

Our problems are often the natural side effects of our successes. For example, increasing efficiency in production meant
that fewer people could produce the basics of life, so we were
trained over the decades to "need" more (or better, or different). People were there to serve the economy, prodded by government as well as by business, teased by gimmickry, tricked
by obsolescence.

We all know the feeling of being offered food when we are

not hungry. Now, as consumers, we may find that our appetites are changing. Knowing what we want, we may spend less, we may spend more, or we may spend differently. In 1936 Richard Gregg, a political philosopher, coined the term *voluntary simplicity* to describe a lifestyle in which one avoids clutter and focuses one's energies on what really matters. "The degree of simplification," Gregg said, "is a matter for each individual to settle for himself." A person living a life of voluntary simplicity might choose to own a costly and sophisticated quadraphonic sound system, for example, and drive an old car.

Voluntary simplicity is an attitude, not a budget: thoughtful consumption, resistance to artificially created "needs," sensitivity to the limits of natural resources, a more human scale for living and working. According to a Stanford Research Institute (SRI) report, adherents of voluntary simplicity want to realize "higher human potential, both psychological and spiritual, in community with others."

The report, which provoked more reprint requests from the business community than any other publication in the history of the think tank, warned business interests that a different social order may be in the making, one aimed more toward material sufficiency than material abundance. Its values would favor enlightened self-interest rather than competition, cooperation rather than rugged individualism, and both rational and intuitive judgments. An ever-growing segment of the population cares little for status or fashion, is willing to recycle durable goods and pay for products that are healthful, nonpolluting, authentic, esthetically pleasing. Many of these products and the services likely to become popular are as easily furnished by entrepreneurs and local businesses as by multinational giants. The report was not an economic forecast to cheer General Motors and General Electric.[4]

Laurence Peter, author of *The Peter Principle*, related how he and his wife determined not to let their possessions possess them. Their move toward deliberate simplicity was "not an attempt to live cheaply but rather to achieve a better balance between the material and nonmaterial components of life." Each new acquisition, whether esthetic or practical, was chosen for its quality and permanence as well as for its real need.

---

[4]A three-year, one-million-dollar study of changing consumer values, released by SRI in 1979, predicted a continuing shift away from conventional materialistic values by individuals across the economic spectrum.

Until I replaced our cheap power lawnmower with the highest quality hand mower obtainable, I would not have believed what a big step forward I was taking. The hand mower costs more but is a delight to operate. It never runs out of fuel. It never tests my patience getting it started. It emits no pollutants. It provides me with healthful exercise. I can stop and start it with ease. I feel in control. I feel relieved of the nervous strain, the safety hazards, and the inevitable mechanical problems and responsibilities that power equipment entails.

For most of its adherents, voluntary simplicity is neither altruistic nor a sacrifice. It can even be hedonistic. Simple lifestyles can become a pleasure in themselves.

One advocate called it "the only way to be rich." Usually it is embedded in larger changes: a deepened appreciation of ordinary pleasures, a keen sense of living in the moment, the company of affectionate, like-minded friends. One of the profound rewards of the transformative process is the discovery of how much we really have. Enhanced attention reveals all the valuables we have misplaced, forgotten, or—blinded by habit— failed to notice: books, records, people, pets, vistas, lost arts, neglected hobbies, abandoned dreams. "I'm not at all contemptuous of the comforts," economist E. F. Schumacher once said, "but they have their place, and it is not first." The less you need, he remarked, the freer you become. In Thoreau's terms, "You must live within yourself and depend on yourself, always tucked up and ready for a start."

"A realm of intimate personal power is developing," said the statement of purpose of the *Whole Earth Catalog*, "the power of the individual to conduct his own education, find his own inspiration, shape his own environment...." Kits, manuals, tools, books, and other resources in the catalog were geared to another vision of life, one rich in options.

The originators of an environmental fair, the New Earth Expo, announced their eagerness to reach all those who assume there is no hope: "There are many things people can do to regain control over their own lives." Increasing self-sufficiency is one.

Many businesses are already trying to respond to the coming wave of "conscious consumptions." In an SRI report Willis Harman said, "Humanistic and transcendental values aren't a luxury imposed on economic values. They're the measure of the *appropriateness* of economic values.... We can choose either to understand and move with the tides of history, whatever they may be—or try to resist them.[5]

"Upon that choice may rest in great measure the state of business in 1990—and beyond."

THE TRANSFORMATION OF BUSINESS

Increasing numbers of business leaders are trying to articulate a new perspective. One Aquarian Conspirator who works with top management people around the country refers to the new "businessmen-philosophers" who talk to each other until three in the morning about their own changing values and their discoveries of human potential. Business executives may be the most open-minded group in the society, far more open than scholars and professionals, because their success depends on their being able to perceive early trends and new perspectives.

Robert Fegley of General Electric described "a new breed of top executives" taking charge of American corporations, broader and deeper than most of their predecessors, more current, literate, articulate, open. Between 1976 and 1978, he said, the amount of time spent on public issues by chief executives of the top thousand corporations doubled—from 20 to 40 percent. "There is a deep interest in public attitudes and a desire to do something—not only to communicate 'our side of the story' but also to re-examine company policy and change it where necessary...."

The president of Trans World Airlines, C. E. Meyer, Jr., expressed the sense of transformed values in an editorial in the airline's magazine in July 1978. The most important change of the past decade was not technological advancement, he said, but "the virtual revolution that has occurred in our collective social awareness." After the turbulence, violence, and confrontations of the late sixties came a period of looking inward, "as if our whole people, shocked and deeply sobered by those years of uproar ... began working quietly to sort out the merits of all those causes." We have tried to heal divisions, both with in-

[5]One example of big business cooperating with social trends: Hofmann-LaRoche, the pharmaceutical company, began furnishing complimentary tapes on holistic medicine to physicians in the early 1970s and more recently sponsored symposia on such topics as alternatives to drug therapy. In 1979, with increasing numbers of people turning to vitamins and nutrition rather than drugs, Hofmann-LaRoche announced its plans to build an immense Vitamin C plant.

sight and with effort, resulting in a qualitative change in our national attitude—our concern for the environment, job security for the work force, dignity for the handicapped, enhanced purpose for the aged, and higher regard for the consumer. These causes are no longer considered controversial but "society's unfinished business," he said.

Big business, in its need to understand the potential impact of the new paradigm, is becoming aware of the networks of the Aquarian Conspiracy as resources. This was the subject of a "preliminary document on emerging trends" published under the Diebold Corporate Issues Program in 1978: *The Emergence of Personal Communications Networks Among People Sharing the New Values and Their Possible Use in Sensitizing Operating Management*. Its authors urged that management try to "plug into" such networks, where new concepts were developed and experimented with before moving into the marketplace.

Such networks are submerged, of low visibility, "yet much of our future originates there." The report compared them to the committees of correspondents that helped design the American Revolution and to the "invisible college," the secret network of scientists in England before scientific research was legally sanctioned by King James II in 1663.

In a section titled "Why We Do Not See Them," the report pointed out that groups emerging from the underground always fear attack; and, being essentially creative, they shun formal organization in favor of flexibility and new forms.

> Before we can discuss these networks, we have a cultural problem to overcome. . . . Important organizational forms may exist which have none of the characteristics we usually associate with organizations. But their impact in originating the ideas that are shaping our times is undisputed, and increasingly they are so pervasive that we are surrounded by them. It seems to me there is a common thread. . . . In one sense, it's a more idealistic, more humane outlook—a feeling that such goals possess, by being so clearly morally right, an unarguable kind of authority.
>
> That's part of it, but in another sense, it's a supremely pragmatic and realistic view they take of such things— recognizing that change of this kind, being irresistibly right, is also therefore inevitable, and that those who try to stand in its way can only dissipate their energies and substance in a futile effort to hold back the tide.

As an example, the report describes one such underground network, whose main orientation is radical science and transpersonal psychology and whose photo-copying is furnished by the vice-chairman of American Telephone and Telegraph.

Changing Image of Man, the now-classic report issued by SRI in 1972, described a new transcendental social and business ethic characterized by self-determination, concern for the quality of life, appropriate technology, entrepreneurship, decentralization, an ecological ethic, and spirituality. The report urged a rapid corporate understanding of this emergent order, "probably the most important observation of our time."

The new order offers as exciting a challenge as the great geographical expeditions and technological breakthroughs of history, the report said.

THE VALUE OF VOCATION

The contemporary individual's struggle to find that higher purpose—to find meaning in work—was discussed at length in *The Gamesman*, Michael Maccoby's composite portrait of the new corporate rebel. The gamesman is more innovative and playful than his predecessor, the "organization man," but still judges wins and losses by left-brain, manipulative rules. In a section titled "The Head and the Heart," Maccoby explored the uneasiness and frustration felt by many gamesmen, who acknowledged that they found little opportunity in their work to develop compassion, openness, humanness:

> People think of the qualities of the heart as opposite to those of the head. They think heart means softness, feeling, and generosity, while head means toughness, realistic thought. But this contrast itself is symptomatic of a schizoid culture in which the heart is detached from the rest of the body. In pre-Cartesian traditional thought, the heart was considered the true seat of intelligence. . . . The head can be smart but not wise.

In the new paradigm, work is a vehicle for transformation. Through work we are fully engaged in life. Work can be what Milton Mayerhoff called "the appropriate other," that which requires us, which makes us care. In responding to vocation— the call, the summons of that which needs doing—we create and discover meaning, unique to each of us and always changing.

That famous transition, the mid-life crisis, may be due in part to the cumulative effect of decades of denial, the sudden thrust into consciousness of pain that can no longer be sedated. One sensitive observer of the phenomenon said that it manifests as "either a cry or a call"—a cry of disappointment or the stirring call to new purpose—to vocation—experienced by one who has been engaged in introspective, transformative processes for some time.

However intently the person with a vocation may pursue his purpose, he should not be confused with a "workaholic." The workaholic, like an alcoholic, is indiscriminate in his compulsion. He attempts to find meaning by working. The individual with a vocation, on the other hand, finds meaningful work. A vocation is not a job. It is an ongoing transformative relationship.

The participants in the Aquarian Conspiracy questionnaire represented nearly every vocational field: education, psychology, medicine, business, publishing, television, research, government, law, dentistry, the clergy, anthropology, sociology, nursing, the arts, theater, music, the military, political science, economics. There were a few whom a census taker might have considered unemployed: retired persons, housewives, independently wealthy persons—all leading busy lives, pursuing vocations that defy easy description.

In many instances, the individuals defined themselves unconventionally, often in terms of how they actually function, rather than the narrow specialty in which they were trained. A physician described herself as a teacher, a teacher as a futurist.

In a gentle prod toward helping others transform work and wealth, some Aquarian Conspirators actively engage in a kind of institutional rehabilitation — counseling corporations, smoothing the way for new experiments, new jobs, new products; making professional assessments of coming change. Others are models of change, having invented or transformed their own livelihoods. For them Right Livelihood is, more than a Buddhist ideal, a component of mental health.

Some of the sharpest internal conflict reported in the survey was in the struggle to reconcile the old work with the new perspective. During what we have termed the entry-point stage of the transformative process, the new ideas do not seem to threaten work and relationships. During the second stage, exploration, there is the uneasy hope that this new interest will be no more than an intensive avocation. By the third stage, integration, it becomes apparent that the transformative process can't be compartmentalized. As one businessman said:

It will impinge on your work, or your priorities change. The new consciousness affects the way you function in your job. It usurps every waking moment. You look at the world through a different grid, with different eyes.

It's easy for the work to become less important. It's hard to keep making widgets after you've seen the sun. If your job can expand with your vision, you're lucky.

At this critical juncture, the discoveries that accompany transformation are like a compass. The sense of *vocation*, of having discovered a meaningful direction, strengthens the resolve to bring work in alignment with belief, head with heart. The new respect for *intuition*, tacit knowing, encourages risk taking. Security, in the conventional sense, is an illusion. Success itself is redefined. A businessman-conspirator said:

> I used to define myself in terms of specific accomplishments. Success might be an *A* in school—later it was business deals. Now success has to do with living my life in harmony with the universe. It's a question of context and content. You can see individual events, "successes" and "failures," as content. But in the context of life there isn't winning or losing—only the process.
>
> When you experience life as broader, richer, more complex, the events manifest differently.

Conventional goals of success are like a blueprint drawn up by an architect who does not yet know the terrain, who has outlined a structure too rigid for nature. Vocation has more the quality of an inner summons to move in a particular direction, feeling one's way, or of a vision, a glimpse of the future that is more preview than plan. A vision can be realized in many ways...a goal, in only one. The transformative process enables us to be the artists and scientists of our lives, creating and discovering as we go. There is the awe and excitement of cooperating with the life process, of becoming more sensitive to its clues, nuances, promises.

The clearer sense of *self* transcends job categories and roles. You are not primarily your job—carpenter, computer programmer, nurse, lawyer. When the respondents to the questionnaire were asked whether or not they regularly read literature "outside your field," many replied that they considered everything to be in their field.

The *wholeness* experienced through the transformative process says that there doesn't have to be a break between work and pleasure, between convictions and career, between personal ethics and "business is business." Fragmentation becomes increasingly intolerable to the person moving toward greater awareness. As the anesthesia wears off, one feels the tearing of flesh and spirit. And it becomes hard to ignore the *context* of one's work. Products and services don't exist in a vacuum, after all. They reverberate through a whole system.

The experience of greater *connectedness*, of unity with others, generates new ways of thinking about problems: joblessness, forced retirement, poverty, fixed incomes, makework, welfare cheating, exploitation. A policy analyst said, "If we think we are a large family, rather than a large factory, we will deal with these problems differently."

The growing network of support—the Aquarian Conspiracy itself—encourages the individual in the lonely enterprise of changing jobs, starting a business, changing the practice of a profession, revitalizing institutions. It is a do-it-yourself revolution, but not do-it-*by*-yourself. For example, friends in Washington, D.C., started a "go-for-it-group" to encourage each other in their vocational goals. They counseled, inspired, and prodded each other, ruthlessly pointing out the rationalizations and delaying tactics each was using to postpone the risk of a new step. Within a year, several had begun to realize their dreams. A librarian had started her own acting company, an attorney had opened a center for the study of psychology in law, another member turned her farm into an artists' colony, and a bureaucrat resigned his job to go into business with friends.

New attitudes change the very experience of daily work. Work becomes a ritual, a game, a discipline, an adventure, learning, even an art, as our perceptions change. The stress of tedium and the stress of the unknown, the two causes of work-related suffering, are transformed. A more fluent quality of attention allows us to move through tasks that once seemed repetitious or distasteful. We make fewer judgments about what we're doing ("I hate this," "I like this"). Boredom diminishes, just as pain abates when we drop our futile resistance to it.

When the ego is no longer running the show, we make fewer value judgments about the status of the job at hand. We see that meaning can be discovered and expressed in any human service: cleaning, teaching, gardening, carpentry, selling, caring for children, driving a taxi.

The stress of the unknown is transformed by an attitude of

trust and patience; when we have learned that breaking apart and reordering are the nature of things, we are less unsettled by the need to change our way of working, to develop a new product, to learn a new skill, to reorganize a task or even a company. The need to innovate becomes a challenge, not a threat.

Carla Needleman, writing of her experience as a craftsman, described this paradox, the goal that betrays the process:

> The attitude of the achiever is so fixed in us that we can scarcely envision a different way of our lives.... The fact of our lives is uncertainty, and we crave certainty. The fact of our lives is change, movement: We long to "arrive."
>
> ...I had come to realize that the solidly entrenched attitude toward results—"success"—poisoned all my efforts, and that I could not change it. I wanted to make beautiful pottery, and that desire, which is a kind of avarice, prevented me.
>
> The need for success is a constrictive force that bars me from immediate participation in the moment as it appears, that prevents the all-important conversation with the material of the craft, prevents openness of relationship, prevents a kind of quickness of response much swifter than the cautions of the mind. The need for success distorts pleasure.

A new understanding of success and failure shifts the emphasis in work from the product—"getting there"—to the process itself. Focusing on the goal is a kind of artificial certainty that distracts us from the possibilities inherent in our work. To work creatively and meaningfully, we have to be alert to the moment, willing to change our plans as events show us new possibilities. We need to risk, cooperate with new developments, reconcile conflicts.

THE TRANSFORMATION OF WORK

Work also becomes a medium through which the individual can express the vision of the Aquarian Conspiracy. A New England professor said, "One of my joys in life is passing along the word of the coming transformation to students hearing it for the first time." Composer Harry Chapin said, "After a while, you've got to find a way to plug in. Most of us lack perspective on our own lives. I try to write about that in my music—ordinary people going through extraordinary moments in their lives."

Paolo Soleri, who has attempted through his Arcosanti architecture to "build a bridge between matter and spirit," traces his inspiration to Teilhard. "I became very excited about a book of his I found in the late sixties. I realized that in a very clumsy way, I was translating what he was saying into environmental terms. Eventually I developed my model, which is probably parallel to his."

There are lawyers trying to find less adversarial ways to practice their profession, who see a new role for the law as mediator. A 1978 Columbia University seminar on humanistic law for deans of law schools looked at the implications of the new paradigm, especially its emphasis on cooperation and collaboration.

Calvin Swank, an assistant professor of criminal justice at the University of Alabama, predicted that even police departments will be affected "as more and more people become absorbed in their own growth and potential." "Self-actualized cops" will question the usual conformity to authority. They will trust their own judgment, based on experience and intuition, and police departments will be unable to cling to their antiquated ways in the face of changing social values.

In many ways the military, with its guaranteed financial base, has more opportunity to fund innovation than any other institution. Jim Channon, then a lieutenant colonel in the army's public affairs office in Los Angeles, created a hypothetical "First Earth Battalion," a futurist vision of what a transformed military might be like. The soldiers of the First Earth Battalion seek nondestructive methods of conflict resolution. Their first loyalty is to the planet. After Channon introduced the notion at an army think tank in Virginia he was inundated with requests for more information. He created a packet of material and a T-shirt decal to send out in response to calls from army personnel all over the country. The army's Task Force Delta authorized him to prepare a multimedia presentation on the First Earth Battalion, an idea that seems to generate the response William James called "the moral equivalent of war," a sense of purpose as urgent as the confrontation of danger but without violence.

Task Force Delta itself, the army's tool for innovation and transition, includes systems theorists, semanticists, and specialists in personal growth and the psychology of stress; the structure of the organization was circular rather than the conventional pyramid of a hierarchy.

The constellation of transformative values—wholeness, flow, community—can give meaning to many different kinds of work. And transformation also changes work relationships: between worker and manager, worker and product, worker and consumer.

NEW WORKING RELATIONSHIPS

"It would seem," Tocqueville observed in the mid-nineteenth century, "as if rulers of our time sought only to use men in order to make things great; I wish that they would try a little more to make great men; that they would set less value on the work and more upon the workman; that they would never forget that a nation cannot be strong when everyone belonging to it is individually weak."

In the same way that a gifted teacher releases capacities in the learner, a gifted manager helps workers realize potential skills, enterprise, creativity. The transformative manager encourages self-management in others.

We are entering a period of real change in work relationships. A growing number of managers prefer to be catalysts rather than just power wielders, and an emergent breed of autonomous employees gives service but not subservience. This shift is causing not a little discomfort to those who are not changing. Some employees would rather be passive than take on new responsibilities or create their own work plans, which can frustrate the manager who is no longer a traditional boss. One executive commented that his own changes caused him to want not only a new set of friends but a new set of co-workers. On the other hand, autonomy in employees has proven stressful to many traditional managers.

A report from the University of Michigan Institute for Social Research warned that traditional management styles will have to give way. Recognizing the growing autonomy of employees, American Telephone and Telegraph arranged weekend retraining sessions for seventeen hundred managers in 1977 and 1978.

The traits of highly successful managers are strikingly similar to the traits of good teachers discussed in Chapter 9. One study of sixteen thousand managers found success associated with a trusting attitude, concern for the personal fulfillment of employees, a lack of ego, willingness to listen to subordinates, risk-taking, innovation, high expectations, collaboration, and the ability to integrate ideas. IBM, hoping to uncover the traits of chief executive officers (CEOs) in order to design a test to screen management talent, found no overall pattern but a constellation of attitudes about change. CEOs saw systems as open rather than closed, change as organic rather than mechanical. They focused on process more than on goals. And they were creative.

A McGill University report described successful managers as unusually open to the complex and mysterious, interested in "soft" and speculative information (facial expression, tone of voice, gestures, hunches, intuitions). Another study portrayed the successful manager as "scanning the environment, perceiving, brainstorming, intuiting, daydreaming." Executives seemed to call more often than most people on right-hemisphere processes, judging from an EEG study, whereas corporate analysts relied on left-brain strategies, such as qualification.

Ron Medved of the Pacific Institute, a Seattle organization that stages personal development seminars for large institutions, envisioned the coming change:

> The New American Working Machine is founded on the philosophy of working smarter, not harder—*from the bottom up*. (The Japanese have taught us that those who do the work seem to know more about how to do it than anyone else.) There will be a fresh emphasis on innovation and streamlining, for there is no security in our current levels of national productivity.
>
> The New American Working Machine will enjoy a different organizational structure. Bureaucratic dinosaurs with level upon level of decision-making won't survive the competition from new-form management styles both here and abroad....
>
> New American Managers will be recognizable not because they have all the right answers but because they know how to ask the right questions....
>
> The New American Worker seems to be in for the biggest change of all...a new vision of himself or herself.
>
> The New American Working Machine looks different than many of the worlds you and I work in. While it promises a better world, it challenges us to do a whole lot of growing and changing to get there....In a very real way,

the New American Working Machine is banking on the sleeping genius in every one of us.

"Sleeping genius," human potential—whatever term they use, new management theorists are interested in the latent capacities that can unfold, given motivation. For instance, workers in the Lucas Aerospace plants in England, threatened in 1974 with the consolidation of their seventeen factories, organized to brainstorm ideas for socially useful products their employer could manufacture. They inventoried their skills, everything from engineering to manual labor, and assessed the company's equipment. Then they issued a questionnaire to the entire work force asking, "What do you think you should be making?" One hundred and fifty viable ideas were translated into designs, specifications, and analyses. Although Lucas's management had been slow to take on the new products, by 1979 the company had manufactured some prototypes and was working with the employee group.

The workers were nominated for the 1979 Nobel Peace Prize by international peace groups and by several members of the Swedish parliament in recognition of their grass-roots effort to convert military into nonmilitary production.

C. Jackson Grayson of the American Productivity Center in Houston, whose research is supported by two hundred of the nation's top corporations, blames the bureaucratic structure of business for suppressing the desire and abilities of individuals to feel they contribute. Contrary to what's being said, "People haven't lost the work ethic," he said.

There is a definite trend toward decentralizing power in companies—dismantling the pyramid, as one consultant put it. According to Frank Ruck, who became vice-president of Chicago Title and Trust, "Making organizational changes in work can make people happier, as well as enhancing productivity—a double payoff."

Increasingly, professional management theorists are urging the use of flexible structures, work arrangements that shape themselves to human needs, that tap latent potential. The need for drastic action is evident in the slowdown of American productivity. Despite accelerated technology, the output per man-hour of work in the United States increased only 21 percent between 1970 and 1977. That compared to 41 percent in West Germany, 42 percent in France, 41 percent in Japan, 38 percent in Italy.

"Job enrichment" and "humanizing the workplace" were integrated into management philosophy in many companies in recent years. Semi-autonomous work teams were formed. Higher pay was awarded on the basis of proficiency tests, not job description. Signed time sheets replaced time clocks, those infernal symbols of dehumanization and lack of trust. Assembly lines were broken into smaller components. Some companies adapted consensual management ideas from Japan, Norway, and Sweden. By 1976 more than a thousand United States companies and government agencies were experimenting with "flex-time," a procedure that allows employees to choose their work schedule within certain limits, built around a core period: 6:00 A.M. to 2:00 P.M., for instance, or 11:00 A.M. to 7:00 P.M.

The American Council of Life Insurance trend-analysis program reported in 1979 on "The Changing Nature of Work": a new breed of employee seeking work consistent with personal values; greater flexibility of hours and type of work; more cooperation between management and employees; non-hierarchical organizational structures; a work environment increasingly compatible with physical and mental health.

A Labor Day advertisement by the Communications Workers of America emphasized the concern for meaningful work:

> This Labor Day finds masses of American workers searching for the self-esteem that comes with an interesting, challenging, and productive job. A national public opinion firm has been polling young people for several years. They find that regardless of sex, race, or type of employment, people under thirty want jobs that are meaningful and offer a chance for personal growth.... [They are] seeking improvement in what is broadly called "the quality of life.'"

THE VALUE OF PERSONAL DEVELOPMENT

These external changes have been fruitful, but they are not enough. Now those concerned about productivity and people have taken the inner route, turning to methods designed for self-actualization. *Personal development* has become the complement to job enrichment and a humane workplace. And, as one management trainer observed, "We turned to these techniques for pragmatic reasons, and a lot of us got hooked."

Werner Erhard once used the term "high intention" to describe an attitude that contributes to the marked superiority of some workers in any organization:

People who have no intention just go through the motions. They make mistakes, they can't handle things, nothing around them works, they don't do things completely, they complain all the time. What gives people superiority at a task is true intention. That makes you attuned to everything. You handle everything, and your mind doesn't give you reasons for not noticing and not handling things. I don't enjoy people who have low intention. I don't enjoy playing for low stakes.... I want the person with whom I am interacting to have something at stake.

High intention cannot coexist with a low self-image. Only those who are awake, connected, and motivated can add to the synergy of an organization. Everyone else adds to entropy, randomness. To achieve major changes in worker attitudes, management is turning increasingly to training techniques drawn from consciousness research.

Trainers are now talking about cultural trance, the fear of transformation, alternative realities, paradigm shifts, insights, the importance of individuals learning to "see through new eyes." A two-part article in *Training*, a professional journal, said, "As trainers we cannot afford to ignore what is happening in the human-potential movement." It quoted a bank executive on the awakening of his staff through personal-growth seminars: "For my money, these soul-searchers are our future."

Personal-growth training doesn't and shouldn't promise more widgets per hour, fewer grievances, less overtime, or more sales—"but then neither does your liability insurance." Mostly people will begin to feel better about who they are and what they're doing about their lives. "There is no accounting entry headed 'number of people who feel good about themselves.' But perhaps, just perhaps, that's an outcome much too big and important for inclusion on a mere profit and loss statement."

Many companies have undertaken stress-reduction training programs for their employees, biofeedback training, programs to enhance creativity. Some have set aside quiet sites for rest and meditation. Indeed, the health aspects of the transformative technologies are a major rationale for corporate support. A fully functioning employee with a healthy self-image is money in the bank—at any rate, that was the original rationale, but now many companies seem to consider the development of employee potential as part of their social responsibility.

General Electric has sponsored conferences on right- and left-brain research relevant to creativity. Menninger Foundation seminars on "The Other Self" have been staged for many corporate groups. "Companies are caught in a 'revolution of rising expectations' of what it takes to be fully human," said Layne Longfellow of Menninger. "Somebody raised the ante. We face an aspiration gap between what we are and what we're beginning to consider normal."

Intuition need not be the exclusive province of executives, Jay Mendell, a business futurist, said in *Planning Review*. Millions of workers, having discovered new capacities through the psychotechnologies, are eager to develop their intuition and creativity on the job.

Much as the new paradigm of education sees in all of us the creative potential we once attributed only to geniuses, management trainers are beginning to look at all employees as potential self-managers who can begin to think like entrepreneurs.

THE NEW ENTREPRENEUR

In the communication to members of the Linkage network in the summer of 1979, Robert Theobald cited the many letters from those longing to move more strongly toward a new society. He asked:

What is holding us back in Linkage and throughout the society? I believe we are afraid of recognizing how fundamentally our lives would have to be changed if we should choose to work out of this vision. We are caught in old models, and most of us owe our survival to the fact that we straddle the "functioning" present world and the new universe which we should like to bring into existence.

The paradox is that the new world promises to be both personally and professionally more rewarding if we would take the leap of faith to embrace it.

For many, entrepreneurship—being in business for oneself— is a natural sequel to the transformative process. Armed with a greater sense of self and vocation, a new willingness to risk (and be poor for a time), emotional support from the network, a sturdier trust in their own creativity and will, they make their own work. These new enterprises are characterized by the Buddhist ideal of Right Livelihood: work that serves society and does not harm the environment.

Briarpatch, a Bay Area network of three hundred or so

businesses, artists, and nonprofit organizations, is a mutual-help medium for entrepreneurs "trying to reveal and uncover principles that can help us reconnect with our community and society rather than exploit them." Dick Raymond, Briarpatch founder, described the stress of translating one's new philosophy into practice:

> Crossing this river is difficult: it means leaving behind some of your old ideas about work and jobs. . . . Most of us (including myself) try to tiptoe around the pain, but it's important to talk about some of the agonies one is apt to confront. We're not talking about simply trading one job for another, or getting from one company into a more suitable one. When you start abandoning your old beliefs or values, some very primal circuits get ignited. . . . You may be stuck on the threshold for two or three years. Before moving on, you have to clear away all your cherished beliefs.
>
> The people I know who have successfully made this transition are the most joyful, the most outgoing, the most well-rewarded people I know. As I meet more every day, their existence sustains my sanity.

Entrepreneurship fills many of the needs of transformation. Richard Gunther, a successful real-estate developer, described to a group of would-be entrepreneurs the confluence of work and enjoyment, socially constructive aims pursued in fellowship with congenial people, a sense of "conscious" and creative enterprise.

Training programs have been developed to prepare those setting out on their own. Based in part on his growing interest in the phenomenon and his weekend School for Entrepreneurs, Bob Schwartz, founder of Tarrytown (New York) Executive House, has characterized the new breed as catalysts who may transform the marketplace:

> The emerging entrepreneur is a more truly thoughtful person who is changing products and services to fill the needs of a more thoughtful and caring audience than the world has previously known. . . . This is what the young are saying: Don't make me an adjunct to the process; make me inherent in it.
>
> The new reality is that products are not going to be a

major part of the American scene. Production is rapidly moving downhill as a factor in the American economy, and services are moving in.

Entrepreneurs, Schwartz said, are "the poets and packagers of new ideas, both visualizers and actualizers." Historically, in a time of cultural change, a new type of entrepreneur emerges to embody the vision with services and products.

He pointed to the burgeoning demand for human-development courses as an example of service needs little known a decade ago. The new entrepreneurs have moved from a manipulative I-it to an I-Thou philosophy, relating to both consumer and product in immediate, personal ways. They and their customers "are the most potent revolutionary force that America furnishes to the world. The entrepreneur is the new non-violent Change Agent."

The Renascence Project in Kansas City, a network of entrepreneurs, demonstrated that alternatives can be both cost effective and profitable. Among its activities: renovation of properties at a key Kansas City location into an eight-million dollar business complex, the establishment of learning networks, an educational program for the "whole person," a self-supporting alternative high school, restoration of a historic dance hall, restoration of a large house by a partnership of residents, and development of a master plan for Kansas City calling for block-by-block renovation of neighborhoods along an eleven-mile pedestrian mall.

In an article titled "The Coming Entrepreneurial Revolution," Norman McRae, the editor of the British publication *The Economist*, suggested that the creeping giantism in American industry has opened the door for the emergence of entrepreneurship patterns even within large industry. Small enclaves in big companies may be run by these "intrapreneurs." The article also predicted that big-business corporations, in their present form, may disappear by the year 2010.

The new entrepreneurs refuse to separate good-for-business from good-for-people. Mo Siegel, co-founder of the Celestial Tea Company in Boulder, Colorado, has articulated this view for his two hundred and thirty employees: "All department leaders will be held accountable for their people development as well as business results." Achievement, Siegel said, is just a by-product of living an ideal. "In this age of transition, we're learning to retain the good aspects of the culture while discarding negative ones."

THE RE-EVALUATION OF TECHNOLOGY

The problem with technology, Robert Pirsig observed in *Zen and the Art of Motorcycle Maintenance*, is its noncoalescence between reason and feeling. Technology has not been connected with matters of the spirit and of the heart, "and so it does blind, ugly things quite by accident and gets hated for that."

In the emergent paradigm technology is not seen as negative, just abused and in need of rehumanization. Our technology promised us power but it became our master in too many areas of our lives. Little wonder many of the "new" political and economic perspectives look to the past in their preference for decentralization, their sensitivity to natural harmonies and concern for stewardship of the land, their desire for "creative simplicity," spiritual and cultural enrichment, the celebration of nonmaterial values.

A society's consciousness should be the context for its work and consumption; its technology, only the content: tools that create products and services the people value. E. F. Schumacher's original title for the book that became famous as *Small Is Beautiful* was *Economics As If People Mattered*. He particularly deplored the effects of big, unconscious applications of technology: centralization, urbanization, the depletion of resources,[6] the dehumanization of workers. Particularly in developing countries, turbines, dams, and earth-moving machines can disrupt social patterns to the detriment of both environment and people. Schumacher's Radical-Center response to applied science gone berserk was what he called "appropriate technology."

"Intermediate" or appropriate technology offers a third way: tools more advanced than a primitive shovel but more practical and human-scaled than a bulldozer. With superior but manageable tools people can improve their lot without going to urban factories.

"Before we choose our tools and techniques," said an editorial in *Rain: The Journal of Appropriate Technology*, "we must choose our dreams and values, for some technologies serve them, while others make them unobtainable."

Schumacher's ideas have had a worldwide influence. An article on appropriate technology in *Foreign Affairs* in late 1977

---

[6]The United States, with 6 percent of the world's population, consumes more than 30 percent of its energy resources.

resulted in the biggest reprint request in that publication's history.

Many countries and some states have set up offices of appropriate technology. The United Nations is establishing a global network of institutions to further the idea. Appropriate technology has been endorsed by the International Labor Organization, the World Bank, the president of the Philippines, the Ford and Rockefeller Foundations. In the two years preceding his death Schumacher was the guest and advisor of presidents, prime ministers, and kings.

Schumacher's economic philosophy reflected intense spiritual values he discussed more fully in the posthumously published *Guide for the Perplexed*. Spiritual values, indeed, are at the base of much of the ecological concern in our time, a quickening sense of the whole earth, respect for the matrix of our evolution, the nature in which we are embedded. Fittingly, Lao-tse is quoted in the brochure of California's Office of Appropriate Technology: "These are my treasures. Guard them well."

THE VALUE OF CONSERVATION

Environmental concerns have a growing impact on lifestyle and consumption. A study conducted in the state of Washington in 1976, published in 1978, polled householders drawn randomly from the telephone directories of every community. The researchers found evidence of surprising adherence to "a new environmental paradigm."

A majority of those polled expressed concern about the abuse of the environment and uncontrolled population growth. They saw earth as a spaceship with limited room and resources. They favored a steady-state economy with control of industrial growth. They opposed the idea of human dominance over nature. In every particular, the general public supported the views of environmentalists in their state.

Behavior is not necessarily consistent with beliefs, the researchers noted, and conceded that many of the respondents might resist personal sacrifice.

> ... We nonetheless must stress what we believe to be the rather remarkable nature of our results. When we consider that just a few short years ago, concepts such as "limits to growth" and "spaceship earth" were virtually unheard of,

the degree to which they have gained acceptance among the public is extremely surprising. This acceptance is all the more surprising when one realizes how dramatically the new environmental paradigm departs from our society's traditional worldview. . . . Indeed, in a society which has always taken abundance, growth, progress, etc., for granted, the rise of the new paradigm represents a revolutionary occurrence . . . we cannot help but be impressed by its rapid ascendance.

The shift to an environmental view involves vastly more than a concern for redwoods. Nowhere is the connectedness of all life more evident than in our awakened ecological conscience. Care of the planet joins economic, legal, political, spiritual, aesthetic, and medical issues. It extends to our purchases, choice of family size, recreation. The youngest school child is aware of the controversies — military defoliation, nuclear power, carcinogens, supersonic transports, dams flooding Indian burial grounds, population growth, propellant gases that may destroy the ozone layer. The young fear the slow death of Earth as a previous generation feared the atomic bomb.

Ecotopia, a novel by Ernest Callenbach, launched something of a cult, especially in the western United States. Originally issued by a small press, the book became an underground best-seller and was republished as a mass-market paperback in 1978. Ecotopia is a fictional new country created by the secession of Washington, western Oregon, and Northern California. Ecotopians employ alternative technology and are hyperconscious of environmental issues.

Ecotopia enthusiasts have designed a flag, created a magazine, named schools and streets after the book, and even celebrated Ecotopia Day in Eugene, Oregon. Callenbach was invited to Sacramento to confer with the California governor and his advisers. However far-fetched the premise of a new country—a new beginning—the book's mass appeal tells us something.

Sim Van der Ryn, first director of California's Office of Appropriate Technology and former state architect, insists that Ecotopian communities are possible right now, at least "the construction of some modest first examples." He urged enlightened entrepreneurs and politicians to commit themselves to an idea that could bring credit to business and government alike. "The seeds of ecological design *are* beginning to sprout, and many of the hardware components to create an ecologically stable urban community have already been developed and are working. What we have yet to do is bring together all the threads and weave them into a single coherent design for a new community."

A sound environmental approach will revitalize urban design, retaining the best of the high-technology culture "while renewing people's sense of place." It will translate the old linear understanding into systems thinking, an awareness of the complex interactions of people and environmental elements.

Another urbanologist called this "the age of recovery" for many American cities; a time of new understanding of urban amenities, a sense of historic continuity, the need for energy efficiency, and new insights on how people want to live, including more humanly scaled architecture. "We have begun to settle down, finally, to seek a sense of place."

Well-known architects surveyed in 1979 described a new paradigm of urban design: more human, with a richer mix of housing and community facilities, places to walk, heightened concern about public transportation, the creation of festive malls and squares, the planting of more trees, a sense of "the commons." An emergent technology will draw increasingly on wind, sun, tidal forces, natural lighting, and natural ventilation.

We may be on our way to regaining the intimate connection and awareness of our place in nature. This neo-medieval trend is evident in another phenomenon: environments of celebration — fairs, expositions, and festivals. In medieval Europe fairs were set up at crossroads, in neutral territory, so that warring people could drop their hostilities long enough to barter, juggle, mime, eat, drink, make music. They were one in celebration — playful, curious, unself-conscious. We are recreating spontaneous community in our tens of thousands of art and craft exhibits, music festivals, environmental and new-age "expos," and period celebrations like Renaissance fairs, medieval games, Dickensian bazaars.

People are improvising new ways to observe old holidays, like a July Fourth "Interdependence Day" celebrated by the Friends Meeting of Palo Alto, California. After sharing food, music, crafts, and games, they concluded by lighting candles and singing "Let There Be Peace on Earth." One participant said, "Celebrations like this come from ourselves. They need not be confined to traditional holidays. They can acknowledge other meaningful events in our lives. . . . What if we really gave ourselves the opportunity to explore our imaginations—if we let go of prefabricated forms of creativity?"

IMAGINATION AS A SOURCE OF WEALTH

Here and there are cheerful insurrections by citizens of the new commonwealth, early drafts of its constitutions, its declaration of interdependence. If you know what to look for, you can detect the architecture of invisible cathedrals and theaters and lending libraries, universities without walls, the society whose individuals are its institutions and whose awakening sense of fraternity is its highest law.

The true source of wealth, Eugen Loebl concluded while brooding about economics during his fifteen years as a political prisoner in Czechoslovakia, is not its productivity, its Gross National Product, its tangible assets. Creative intelligence is the wealth of a modern society. "If we see gain as a function of man's ability to think, and if we recognize the importance of the intellectual level on which the economy is based, then our prime interest will be oriented toward the development of this level. ... We can change our reality toward the goals we desire."

On his historic visit to the United States, Tocqueville sailed down the Ohio River. On one hand was Ohio, a free state; on the other Kentucky, a slave state. On the Ohio side of the river he observed industrious activity, rich harvests, handsome homes. The Ohioan could enter any path fortune might open to him. He might become a sailor, a pioneer, an artisan, a laborer. On the Kentucky side Tocqueville saw only indolence. Not only were the slaves half-hearted in their labors, but the masters themselves were enslaved. They could not work their own land because that would demean their status. A few crossed over to Ohio to work, but most turned for excitement to "the passionate love of field sports and military exercises ... violent bodily exertion, the use of arms...."

We have passed into other cultural ages, each with its own forms of economic and psychological enslavement. For too long, like the Kentucky slaveholders, we have turned our best energies toward the pursuit of secondary excitement, hoping to find in such distractions the reward that comes only from vocation. But we have a choice; now we can emigrate to a freer state, finding there new heart, new enterprise, and values that match our deepest needs.

CHAPTER 11

Spiritual Adventure: Connection to the Source

Behind the night . . . somewhere afar
Some white tremendous daybreak.
—RUPERT BROOKE

In its early stages, transformation may seem easy, even fun, not at all stressful or threatening. We may enjoy an intensified sense of connection, vocation, freedom, peace. We *use* the process as we might use a tape recorder. We visit altered states of awareness as we would drop into a health club for the Jacuzzi. Biofeedback cures our headaches, meditation eases tension. An imagery technique dissolves a learning block.

But all the transformative technologies also train our attention. Gradually there is a sense that we have been betraying some sort of harmonious inner universe by our attitudes, behavior, and beliefs. A realm of exquisite order, intelligence, and creative potential begins to reveal itself. Meditation is now doing *us*. Reality breaks through into larger, richer spaces. Now it is not just a matter of seeing things differently but of seeing different things. Language fails, symbols fail. This territory is too unlike anything we have known, too paradoxical, a dimension we may speak of as deep or high, as helpless as the Square in Flatland trying to describe the Third Dimension to his disbelieving countrymen. "One can only grasp it by experiencing," said Master Hakuin, a Zen sage, "as one feels for oneself cold and hot by drinking water. It is to melt all space in a wink and to look through all time, from past to future, in one thought."

Consciousness is not a tool. It is our being, the context of our lives—of life itself. Expanding consciousness is the riskiest enterprise on earth. We endanger the status quo. We endanger our comfort. And if we do not have the nerve to resolve the ensuing conflicts, we endanger our sanity. We may have been uncomfortable at earlier points in the transformative process, as when we took responsibility for our health, but this is much bigger: the transformation of the transformative process itself.

In Chapter 6, we explored scientific discoveries about the underlying unity of nature, the role of consciousness in constructing the world of appearances, the brain as an interpreter of patterns emerging from a primary reality, the transcendence of time and space, the thrust of evolution, the reordering of living systems at levels of ever greater intricacy and coherence.

Spiritual or mystical experience, the subject of this chapter, is the mirror image of science—a direct perception of nature's unity, the inside of the mysteries that science tries valiantly to know from the outside. This way of understanding predates science by thousands of years. Long before humankind had tools like quantum logic to describe events that ordinary reason could not grasp, individuals moved into the realm of paradox through a shift in consciousness. And there they know that what cannot be *is*. Millions living today have experienced transcendent aspects of reality and have incorporated this knowledge into their lives.

A mystical experience, however brief, is validating for those attracted to the spiritual search. The mind now knows what the heart had only hoped for. But the same experience can be deeply distressing to one unprepared for it, who must then try to fit it into an inadequate belief system.

Inexorably, direct experience of a larger reality demands that we change our lives. We can compromise for a time, but eventually we realize that ambivalence is like deciding to recognize the law of gravity only sometimes and in certain places. This transformation of transformation, with its acceleration of connections and insights, can be a frightening period. Eventually, in stages, there is action. We must make our lives congruent with our consciousness. "A condition of utmost simplicity," said T. S. Eliot, "costing not less than everything."

By radically altering one's values and perceptions of the world, mystical experience tends to create its own culture, one with wide membership and invisible borders. This parallel culture seems to threaten the status quo; as Alexander Solzhenitsyn said, Western society is outraged if an individual gives his soul as much daily attention as his grooming. The statements and behavior of those in the emergent culture are judged by a belief system as irrelevant to their experience as the warnings of the Flat Earthers were to Columbus. Critics call them narcissistic, not knowing the thoughtful nature of their inward search; self-annihilating, not knowing the spaciousness of the Self they join; elitist, not knowing how desperately they want to share what they have seen; irrational, not realizing how much further their new worldview goes toward resolving problems, how much more coherent it is with everyday experience.

THE SEARCH FOR MEANING

The spiritual quest begins, for most people, as a search for meaning. At first this may be only a restless desire for something more. The prescient Tocqueville remarked on the coexistence in America of a strong religious spirit and material ambition. But perhaps, he said, this was a precarious balance. "If ever the faculties of the great majority of mankind were exclusively bent upon the pursuit of material objects, it might be anticipated that an amazing reaction would take place in the souls of some. I should be surprised if mysticism did not soon make some advance among a people solely engaged in promoting its own worldly welfare."

Indeed, our vigorous appetite for the material has led us to satiation. Zbigniew Brzezinski, chairman of the United States Security Council, spoke of an "increasing yearning for something spiritual" in advanced Western societies where materialism has proven unsatisfying. People are discovering, he said, that 5 percent per annum more goods is not the definition of happiness.

Traditional religion, he conceded, does not provide a substitute:

This is why there is a search for personal religion, for direct connection with the spiritual.... Ultimately, every human being, once he reaches the stage of self-consciousness, wants to feel that there is some inner and deeper meaning to his existence than just being and consuming, and once he begins to feel that way, he wants his social organization to correspond to that feeling.... This is happening on a world scale.

In a public poll conducted by Yankelovich, Skelly, and White, 80 percent of the respondents expressed a strong interest in "an inner search for meaning." In 1975 the National Opinion Research Corporation reported that more than 40 percent of the adults polled believed they had had a genuine mystical experience. These experiences were characterized by joy, peace, a need to contribute to others, the conviction that love is at the center of everything, emotional intensity, knowledge impossible to articulate, unity with others, and the imminence of a new world. A 1974 Roper poll found that 53 percent believed in the reality of psi, with stronger belief correlated with higher income and education. A 1976 Gallup poll reported that 12 percent were involved in a mystical discipline.

A Gallup poll released in February 1978 reported that ten million Americans were engaged in some aspect of Eastern religion, nine million in spiritual healing. Those involved in Eastern religions tended to be younger adults, college-educated, living on either of the two coasts, about equally men and women, Catholic and Protestant. "Although [they] are not as likely to be church-goers . . . they are just as likely to say that their religious beliefs are 'very important' in their lives."

Spiritual experience moved beyond the borders of the establishment so quietly that only the poll takers have measured the change. Addressing fellow scholars and historians in the field of religion, Jacob Needleman remarked ironically in 1977 that these ideas and practices are now—"without our prior permission, so to speak—entering the real lives of real people, causing trouble, having real effects on marriages, careers, politics, goals, friendships."

But the spiritual shift is not readily uncovered by sociological methods. It's an individual phenomenon, William McCready of National Opinion Research said. "If you try to gauge it by membership in groups, you won't see it. Because they aren't much for joining, the people involved in this inner search are hard to pin down statistically."

In early 1979 Ram Dass observed that his audiences had

changed considerably. "For the most part it's the middle class these days, and the ages are broadening incredibly. Where I was working with a ten-year age span out of the alternative cultures five or six years ago, I'm now seeing a fifteen-year span out of the mainstream of society—what used to be called straight. Now there are hundreds of thousands for whom spiritual awakening is a reality. I can go to Omaha, Idaho City, Seattle, Buffalo, or Tuscaloosa, and everywhere thousands of people are ready to hear. They are growing spiritually in their daily lives, without putting on far-out clothes and wearing beads around their necks. Their spiritual awakening grows from within."

An Aquarian Conspirator at a famous think tank said, "There is a whole new tolerance for the search for transcendence. I'm surrounded by colleagues who are going in the same direction, who value the same kinds of explorations. . . . A person is no longer an oddball because he is known to be on a spiritual quest. And he's even envied a little, which is quite a change over the last fifteen years."

A Washington lobbyist for an organization promoting international peacemaking called the mutual recognition of these seekers "the small mysticism":

> It was not sought or wanted but asserted itself in my life . . . something was growing, emerging. These little events added up; they began to fit together. I began to find God in others, then a sense of God in me, then a bit of myself in others with a sense of God, then others and myself in God—a mysterious and complex set of transactions. The curious side-effect was that there is recognition of this sort of unitarianism among the small mystics. We sense each other.
>
> Even my political work . . . benefited. Small mystics in politics quickly "smell" my secret stance, and a certain fellowship occurs, scarcely ever explicit but nonetheless effective.
>
> I do not know yet how common this sort of closet small mysticism is, but it seems to me to be easier in the last five years or so to confess with some expectations of recognition. . . .

Western psychologists like William James, Carl Jung, Abraham Maslow, and Roberto Assagioli focused their mature powers on trying to understand transcendent needs and the irrepressible hunger for meaning. Jung compared the spiritual impulse to sexuality in its urgency.

Although there is reason to believe that we all have an innate capacity for mystical experience—direct connection—and although about half the population reports having had at least one spontaneous experience, never before has this capacity been explored by people in great numbers. Historically, even in those parts of the world where the most sophisticated techniques were available—India, Tibet, China, Japan—only a tiny minority undertook the systematic search for spiritual understanding.

Among the millions now engaged in this search, many, if not most, were drawn in almost unawares, like the good-natured Hobbits drawn into cosmic quests in J. R. R. Tolkien's *Lord of the Rings*. Quite innocently they found themselves beyond their familiar haunts. Sy Safransky, the editor of a North Carolina literary magazine, described his departure from common-sense reality:

> I'm a journalist whose ability to take notes and ask the right questions evaporated years ago on a sunny beach in Spain, when I suddenly became aware that the whole world was alive...I saw the earth breathe, I felt its rhythms, and I discovered a missing part of myself. Finding corroboration neither in the *New York Times* or the *New Republic* but only in literature I'd hitherto shunned as religious (then an epithet) or plainly bizarre, I began the long, slow drift away from the radical mainstream towards shores for which I've yet to find a name.

Pianist Arthur Rubinstein struggled to define what he called "this thing in us, a metaphysical power that emanates from us." He had often felt it in his concerts, he said, this tangible energy reaching out into the audience. "It is something floating, something unknown that has no place to disappear to."

In his Nobel prize acceptance speech novelist Saul Bellow said, "The sense of our real powers, powers we seem to derive from the universe itself, also comes and goes.... We are reluctant to talk about this because there is nothing we can prove, because our language is inadequate, and because few people are willing to risk talking about it. They would have to say, 'There is a spirit,' and that is taboo."

The unnamed shores, the power, the spirit—these are the subject of this chapter. We will look at the spiritual experience in contemporary America, an experience that has little to do with religion as our culture has known it. It also has little to do with exotic cults and practices. The grass-roots movement is taking place quietly, manifesting itself in ways unique to *this* time and place. Most of its adherents are incognito to those looking for conventional symbols of religiousness.

FROM RELIGION TO SPIRITUALITY

The emergent spiritual tradition is not new in American history, according to Robert Ellwood, a scholar of Oriental religions at the University of Southern California. Rather, it is the revitalization of a stream "going back as far as Transcendentalism." Adherents prefer direct experience—what Ellwood calls "excursion" to an inner world whose vision then infuses all of life—to any form of organized religion.

With its periodic Great Awakenings, the United States has always attracted mystics and evangelists. Long before the spiritual revolution we see now, Eastern and Western mystics influenced mainstream American thought. Their ideas were daily bread to the American Transcendentalists and the "beat generation." Yet, as Ellwood pointed out, all these exports are filtered through the American psyche and experience. Zen, Swedenborgianism, Theosophy, or Vedanta in the United States are not what they were in Japan, eighteenth-century England, or nineteenth-century India. American adherents may sometimes use Eastern symbols, but their essential spiritual life is better understood through the American lineage of Emerson, Thoreau, Whitman, the Shakers, and others. "Down-home Zen" is the term Rick Fields used to describe the Zen center in the heart of the Wilshire business district of Los Angeles.

Needleman said Westerners were moving away from the form and trappings of Judaism and Christianity, "not because they had stopped searching for transcendental answers to the fundamental questions of human life but because that search has now intensified beyond measure."[1] They were looking to

---

[1]Although the Aquarian Conspirators are by no means representative, being both more spiritually involved and more iconoclastic than most, their questionnaire responses show a pattern that may be a harbinger of more general change. Ninety-five percent had some early religious background, however token (55 percent Protestant, 20 percent Jewish, 18 percent Catholic, 2 percent other, 5 percent "none"). Only 19 percent consider themselves active in that tradition in any way, a percentage that includes several clergy, exclergy, and theologians.

Eastern traditions to see what they might offer "our threatened society and our tormented religions."

We turn East for completion. Whitman called it "the voyage of the mind's return. . . . Passage to more than India." Hesse spoke of "the eternal strivings of the human spirit toward the East, toward Home." The East does not represent a culture or a religion so much as the methodology for achieving a larger, liberating vision. In that sense, the "East" has existed in Western mystical traditions.

In January 1978, *McCall's* magazine published a survey of sixty thousand readers showing an overwhelming skepticism about organized religion, even among churchgoers. A poll commissioned by Protestant and Catholic groups and released in June 1978 revealed what Gallup summarized as "a severe indictment of organized religion." Eighty-six percent of the "unchurched" and 76 percent of the churchgoers agreed that individuals should arrive at their beliefs outside organized religion. About 60 percent of the churchgoers agreed with the statement, "Most churches have lost the real spiritual part of religion."

Formal religion in the West has been shaken to its roots by defections, dissent, rebellions, loss of influence, diminishing financial support. Unlike the schools, churches are not mandated by law and their bureaucracies are not directly tax supported; they cannot pass bond issues or raise property taxes. If they cannot find new roles in a rapidly changing society, they may go the way of the railroads—without Amtrak.

A Catholic theologian, Anthony Padovano, remarked at a 1976 conference on meditation:

> The religious response that has occurred in the Western world—a revolution that has made us more sensitive to the religions of the Orient—is an understanding that whatever answers there are must come from ourselves. The great turmoil in the religions is caused by the spirit demanding interiority. Faith is not dying in the West. It is merely moving inside.

That most authoritarian of religious institutions, the Catholic church, has suffered what historian John Tracy Ellis called "a shattering of its fixity," a trauma apparent in the new variety of doctrine and discipline among American Catholics. "No one group has full authority nor the ability to impose it on other groups," Ellis said. The American church is "shaken and uncertain in an anxious, uncertain time." Laypeople are urging reforms, evangelizing and participating in pentecostal and charismatic movements; by 1979 one-half million Catholics were estimated to have become charismatics, speaking in tongues and engaging in healing practices. The number of nuns and priests declined dramatically during the seventies, theologians were dissenting from papal authority, parochial school populations were declining. Similar rebellions have been taking place in nearly every organized religious body in the country.

A convocation of spiritual leaders read a statement to the United Nations in October 1975:

> ... The crises of our time are challenging the world religions to release a new spiritual force transcending religious, cultural, and national boundaries into a new consciousness of the oneness of the human community and so putting into effect a spiritual dynamic toward the solutions of the world's problems. ... We affirm a new spirituality divested of insularity and directed toward planetary consciousness.

An increasing number of churches and synagogues have begun to enlarge their context to include support communities for personal growth, holistic health centers, healing services, meditation workshops, consciousness altering through music, even biofeedback training.

Cultural awakenings, as historian William McLoughlin noted, are preceded by a spiritual crisis, a change in the way human beings see themselves in relationship to each other and to the divine. During "great awakenings" there is a shift from a religion mediated by authorities to one of direct spiritual experience. Not unexpectedly, some religious groups see the emergent spiritual tradition as a fearful threat to the Judeo-Christian tradition. The fundamental Berkeley Christian Coalition, sponsor of the Spiritual Counterfeits Project, devoted its August 1978 journal to this threat:

> At this point in Western cultural history, it is an understatement to say that Eastern metaphysics and the New Consciousness have gained a significant following in our society. Just ten years ago the funky drug-based spirituality of the hippie and the mysticism of the Western yogi were restricted to the counterculture. Today, both have

found their way into the mainstream of our cultural mentality. Science, the health professions, and the arts, not to
mention psychology and religion, are all engaged in a fundamental reconstruction of their basic premises.

The coalition blames the rise of New Age spirituality on the
timidity of the Christian church in America:

> Eastern metaphysics and the New Consciousness, on the
> other hand, derive their popularity in part from the fact
> that they directly challenge the oppressive assumptions of
> technocratic Western mentality. They have not been afraid
> to charge our rationalist, materialist, mercantile culture
> with depleting the quality of human life.... Leaders of
> these movements have stepped into the vacancy created
> by the church's prophetic silence. They call plastic plastic
> and poison poison in a society whose economy is built on
> convincing people that both are good for them. Moreover
> the followers ... are hard at work developing workable al-
> ternatives to the death-dealing culture they condemn.

The SCP expressed concern about the increasing legitimacy of
the spiritual movement in the eyes of the medical establishment and its ability to draw on and consolidate support from
many other groups: humanistic psychology, secular
humanism, Eastern mysticism, authors like George Leonard,
noted medical personalities like Jonas Salk. At every hand the
Berkeley Christian Coalition detected the influence of non-
Christian doctrine: the yin-yang symbol drawn by Salk at a San
Diego conference, Ruth Carter Stapleton's friendly attitude toward meditation, references by physician-speakers to the Kabbalah and chakras.

The idea of a God within was particularly disturbing: The
religious point of view embodied in the holistic health movement, said the coalition,"is an integral part of the mystical
worldview that is making a coordinated thrust into every aspect of our cultural consciousness.... It is not a fad, it will not
go away, and it is fundamentally hostile to Biblical Christianity."

Ironically, every organized religion has been based on the
claims of direct experience of one or more persons, whose rev-
elations are then handed down as articles of faith. Those who
want direct knowledge, the mystics, have always been treated

more or less as heretics, whether they were the medieval mystics within Christianity, the Sufis within the borders of Islam, or the Kabbalists within Judaism.

Now the heretics are gaining ground, doctrine is losing its authority, and knowing is superseding belief.

DIRECT KNOWING

"Mystical states," said William James, "seem to those who experience them to be states of knowledge. They are insights into depths of truth unplumbed by the discursive intellect."

The dictionary's first definition of mystical is "direct communion with ultimate reality." The second meaning: "vague or incomprehensible." Here is a central problem: Direct communion with ultimate reality is vague and incomprehensible to those who have not experienced it!

The word *mystical* derives from the Greek *mystos*, "keeping silence." Mystical experience reveals phenomena that are usually silent and inexplicable. This expanded consciousness, this whole-knowing, transcends our limited powers of description. Sensation, perception, and intuition seem to merge to create something that is none of these.

A Canadian psychologist, Herbert Koplowitz, has called this whole-knowing Unitary Operational Thinking, a stage that is two steps beyond the most advanced level of cognitive development in the theory of Jean Piaget. Piaget's stages—Sensori-Motor, Pre-Operational Thinking, Concrete Operational Thinking, Formal Operational Thinking—span the spectrum of human mental development from the diffuse world of the infant to the symbolic, abstract thought of an intellectually active young adult.

Beyond ordinary cognitive thought Koplowitz postulates a fifth stage, Systems Thinking, in which the individual understands that there are often simultaneous causes that cannot be separated. Conventional science assumes that cause and effect *can* be clearly separated and does not reach the level of Systems Thinking.

In the sixth stage—Unitary Operational Thought—we discover our own conditioning. We understand that the way we perceive the external world is only one of many possible constructs. "Opposites, which had been thought of as separate and distinct, are seen as interdependent. Causality, which had been thought of as linear, is now seen as pervading the universe, connecting all events with each other." There is no dualism, no separation of mind and body, self and others.

Having achieved a cognitive state that empowers a more coherent understanding, the Unitary Thinker is to a Formal Operational adult as that adult is to a child. "Just as mysticism is not a rejection of science but a transcendence of it," Koplowitz said, "science is not a rejection of mysticism but a precursor of it."

Unitary thought is holistic. Because it goes beyond the further reaches of our rational tools, it can only be conveyed through paradoxes, meditation, *experience*. "Mystic traditions such as Taoism may offer the most thoroughly developed bodies of Unitary Operational Thought," Koplowitz said.

To experience the domain of Unitary Knowing we must get outside our old, limited way of perceiving. As psychologist Ron Browning put it, "To grasp that which is beyond the system, you need to transcend the system. You have to get out of 'lineness' into 'squareness,' out of linearity into planes, then shift or expand into three-dimensional space-time, then four-dimensional space. . . . Change at this level is a change in the very nature of change."

As a metaphor Browning suggested that we imagine a system called "asleep." The realm lying beyond that system is called "awake." "Inside 'asleep' we can have a sign representing awake, we can have the word awake, we can have symbols and images—everything but actually *being* awake. You can dream that you have awakened, but you cannot, within that system, actually wake up."

Direct knowing gets us out of the system. It is the awakening. It reveals the context that generates our lesser reality. The new perspective alters our experiences by changing our vision.

To Jung, for example, the transpersonal perspective, what he called "the raising of the level of consciousness," enabled some individuals to outgrow problems that destroyed others. "Some higher or wider interest arose on the person's horizon, and through this widening of his view the insoluble problem lost its urgency. It was not solved logically in its own terms but faded out in contrast to a new and stronger life-tendency. It was not repressed and made unconscious but merely appeared in a different light."

Transpersonal psychology, which draws from the world's spiritual disciplines, does not aim to reduce suffering to "normal" dimensions but to transcend suffering. "Getting in touch with one's feelings" is of little value if those dark feelings are not transformed. Anger, fear, despair, resentment, jealousy, greed—these can all be changed, not just identified, through the psychologies of direct knowing.

A shift from intellectual concept to direct knowing was described by one of the Aquarian Conspirators on a questionnaire:

> One of my personal turning points came when I awoke one morning from a dream which I interpreted in a very discouraging way, and I seriously contemplated suicide. . . . The more I did that, the lower I got, until finally something somewhere somehow *clicked*. I'm not sure how else to describe it. The ideas I had written about conceptually four years before at an intellectual, left-brained level were now real at an experiential level. I realized that my choices were — as I had written, as others had written — limited only by me and my perceptions of reality.
>
> That was rough but a great turning point toward consciousness and freedom. It was almost like I had to go through midnight to get to the dawn.

Brain scientist Karl Pribram tried to describe an even greater perceptual shift:

> It isn't that the world of appearances is wrong; it isn't that there aren't objects out there, at one level of reality.
>
> It's that if you penetrate through and look at the universe with a holographic system, you arrive at a different reality, one that can explain things that have hitherto remained scientifically inexplicable: paranormal phenomena . . . synchronicities, the apparently meaningful coincidence of events.

As a way of looking at consciousness, holographic theory is closer to mystical and Eastern thought than to our ordinary perception, he said. "It will take a while for people to become comfortable with the idea that there is an order of reality other than the world of appearances." But the discoveries of science have begun to make sense of mystical experiences people have been describing for millennia. They suggest that we can tap into that order of reality *behind* the world of appearances. Perhaps mystics have hit upon a mechanism that gives them entry to the implicate, or enfolded, order: "My best hunch is that access to those other domains is through attention... that the brain can somehow abrogate its ordinary constraints and gain access to the implicate order."

Such a shift, he said, might be mediated by the brain's connection between the frontal lobe and the older limbic region, the tie between the cortex and deep brain structures. This region is a major regulator of attention. "Perhaps we can eventually discover the rules for 'tuning in,' for leaping into the timeless, spaceless domain."

Physicist Fritjof Capra recounts such an experience in which he no longer merely believed in a dynamic universe, based on his intellectual understanding, but *knew* it to be so. He recalls that he was sitting by the ocean one late summer afternoon, watching the waves, feeling the rhythm of his breathing, when he suddenly experienced the whole environment as a cosmic dance—not just as a concept of physics but as an immediate, living experience:

> I "saw" cascades of energy coming down from outer space, in which particles were created and destroyed in rhythmic pulses; I "saw" the atoms of the elements and those of my body participating in this cosmic dance of energy; I felt its rhythm and I "heard" its sound, and at that moment I *knew* this was the Dance of Shiva....

Spiritual disciplines are designed to attune the brain to that larger domain. Ordinarily the brain is unfocused and dyssynchronous. It is also busy filtering out a vast amount of information not needed for survival; otherwise we would be bombarded by awareness of electrical fields, slight temperature changes, cosmic radiation, internal physiological processes. Yet we can have access to a wider sensory realm and the mystical dimension by altering the brain's biochemistry. Meditation, breathing exercises, and fasting are among the common technologies for shifting brain function.[2]

For many people in many cultures, psychedelic drugs have offered a beginning trail if seldom a fully transformative path. Aldous Huxley, who had no illusion about drugs as permanent routes to enlightenment, pointed out that even *temporary* self-

[2]Those surveyed in the Aquarian Conspiracy questionnaire revealed experience in a variety of spiritual and meditative disciplines, including Zen Buddhism (40 percent), yoga (40 percent), Christian mysticism (31 percent), Transcendental Meditation (21 percent), Sufism (19 percent), and the Kabbalah (10 percent), along with many dozens of other systems.

transcendence would shake the entire society to its rational roots. "Although these new mind-changers may start by being something of an embarrassment, they will tend in the long run to deepen the spiritual life of the communities. . . ."

Huxley believed that the long-predicted religious revival in the United States would start with drugs, not evangelists. "From being an activity concerned mainly with symbols religion will be transformed into an activity concerned mainly with experience and intuition—an everyday mysticism."

He said that he himself had been electrified by understanding fully, under the influence of mescaline, the radical meaning of the phrase *God is love*. One of the Aquarian Conspirators said, "After many years in intellectual, left-brain pursuit of 'reality,' I learned from LSD about alternative realities—and suddenly all bibles made sense." Others have said that they seemed to experience the nature of matter, the unity of all things, life as a splendid game we are playing, a story we are telling. One reported experiencing "dynamic present time— that the world is flow and uncertainty, not static as in the concepts of our culture."

Psychiatrist Stanislav Grof, who has guided over three thousand LSD sessions and has had access to eighteen hundred records of sessions conducted by his colleagues, sees psychedelics as catalysts or *amplifiers* of mental processes. There is no element of the LSD experience that does not have a non-drug counterpart. Psychedelics seem to facilitate access to the holographic domain described by Pribram and David Bohm, Grof said.[3] The individual may experience himself as a field of consciousness rather than as an isolated entity. Past, present, and future are juxtaposed. Space itself seems multidimensional, limitless. Matter is no longer perceived as tangible but disintegrates into patterns of energy. Subjects report direct experience of microcosm and macrocosm, vibrating molecules and spinning galaxies, archetypes and deities, the reliving of early experiences, even what seems to be their own birth or uterine existence. "In the experiences of consciousness of the Universal Mind and the Void, LSD subjects . . . find the very categories of time, space, matter, and physical laws of any

[3]Compelling mystical experiences are by no means universal among psychedelics users. These are dependent on many factors: dosage, prior experiences, introspectiveness, willingness to explore states of consciousness, prior interest in spirituality, expectations, and an appropriate environment. Casual recreational use often results in little more than sensory alterations and a "high."

kind to be arbitrary and ultimately meaningless categories."
The Cartesian-Newtonian worldview becomes philosophically
untenable. It seems simplistic and arbitrary, useful for the practical purposes of everyday life but "unfit for the purpose of
philosophical speculation and understanding. . . . The universe
is [now] seen as a divine play and an infinite web of adventures
in consciousness."

If it can be demonstrated that subjects in unusual states of
consciousness have access to accurate information about the
universe, if they experience it as portrayed by quantum-
relativistic physics, "we might have to abandon the derogatory
term 'altered states of consciousness.'" At least some of these
states might be seen as a valid source of information about the
nature of the universe and the dimension of the human mind.

"The essential conflict," Grof said, "is no longer between
science and mysticism." Rather it is between the emergent
paradigm and a "coalition" paradigm: the joining of the old
mechanical model of science and ordinary or "pedestrian" consciousness. In other words, the problem is not so much contradictory data as contradictory states of consciousness—a conflict Grof feels is resolved by the holographic view.

THE SPIRITUAL ADVENTURE

In his account of a Sufi apprenticeship, Reshad Feild said:

> I suddenly understood that it is most certainly necessary to
> seek, to ask the question; rather than pushing away the
> answer by dashing after it, one must ask and listen at the
> same time. . . . At that moment I knew that I was being
> heard, that I was dissolving and becoming food for the
> great transformation process that was taking place in the
> universe. . . . At the same time that I was dying I was being
> born. . . .

Hamid said, "The Soul is a knowing substance."

In the West religious issues are customarily supposed to be
resolved by faith, but a teacher in the traditions of direct knowing encourages questions, even doubts. This spirituality asks
the seeker to drop beliefs, not add to them.

Assorted dangers await the spiritual adventurer. We have
discussed some obvious ones in an earlier chapter: regressive

behavior, unsettling experiences, fanaticism, the passive surrender to an unworthy teacher, pendulum change.

But the disciplines themselves warn of other, subtler dangers. "The Way in this world is like the edge of a blade," says a Hasidic master, and, in the Katha Upanishad, the famous caveat: "The path is narrow . . . sharp as a razor's edge, most difficult to tread."

Whereas the outsider may perceive the spiritual seeker's transient loss of internal equilibrium as alarming, a teacher might consider it a necessary step. The greater danger, in the teacher's mind, is that the student may become certain of the answers, stop there, and never reach appropriate uncertainty.

Asked to name ideas they had given up as a result of the transformative process, several of those who responded to the Aquarian Conspiracy questionnaire said "conventional Christianity," "religious dogma"—and about an equal number said "atheism" or "agnosticism."

The Radical Center of spiritual experience seems to be knowing without doctrine.

One contemporary seeker described his own experience:

> There were a number of times when I felt I really understood what it was all about. Then several years later I would have to say that was a stupid thing. . . . From a subsequent vantage point, I obviously hadn't understood a damned thing. I think this is fairly universal.
>
> . . . Every time you enlarge that knowing — or acquire more of it — you see things in a different perspective. It isn't that it was really wrong before, but it's just seen quite differently, in a different light. . . . That's the essence of transformation, reaching the part of ourselves that knows, that doesn't feel threatened and doesn't fight the metamorphosis. . . .

Teachers and techniques in the spiritual disciplines must be considered together, for the teacher does not impart knowledge but technique. This is the "transmission" of knowledge by direct experience.

Doctrine, on the other hand, is second-hand knowledge, a danger. "Stand above, pass on, and be free" is the advice of Rinzai, the same sage who advised the seeker to kill the patriarchs or the Buddha if he should encounter them. "Do not get entangled in any teaching."

Disciples are supposed to find the teacher, not vice versa.

The teacher's authority rests on personal liberation. One follows qualities, not people.

The path to direct knowing is beautifully illustrated in a series of paintings from twelfth-century China known as the ten ox-herding pictures. The ox represents "ultimate nature." At first (*Seeking the Ox*) the searcher undertakes to look for something he only vaguely apprehends. Then (*Finding the Tracks*) he sees in traces of his own consciousness the first evidence that there truly is an ox. After a time (*First Glimpse*) he has his first direct experience and knows now that the ox is omnipresent. Next (*Catching the Ox*) he undertakes advanced spiritual practices to help him deal with the wild strength of the ox. Gradually (*Taming the Ox*) he achieves a more subtle, intimate relationship with ultimate nature. In this phase, the seeker *un*learns many of the distinctions that were useful in earlier stages. "The Ox is a free companion now, not a tool for plowing the field of enlightenment," Lex Hixon, a meditation teacher, wrote in his sensitive commentary on the pictures.

In the stage of illumination (*Riding the Ox Home*) the former disciple, now a sage, realizes that disciplines were not necessary; enlightenment was always at hand. Afterward (*Ox Forgotten, Self Alone* and *Ox and Self Forgotten*) he comes even nearer to pure consciousness and discovers that there is no such person as an illuminated sage. There is no enlightenment. There is no holiness because everything is holy. The profane is sacred. Everyone is a sage waiting to happen.

In the penultimate phase (*Return to the Source*) the sage/seeker merges with the domain that generates the phenomenal world. A scene of mountains, pine trees, clouds, and waves emerges. "This waxing and waning of life is no phantom but a manifestation of the source," reads the caption. But there is a stage beyond this idyll.

The final picture (*Entering the Marketplace with Helping Hands*) evokes human compassion and action. The seeker is now shown as a cheerful peasant who wanders from village to village. "The gate of his cottage is closed, and even the wisest cannot find him." He has gone so deeply into human experience that he cannot be traced. Knowing now that all the sages are one, he does not follow great teachers. Seeing the intrinsic Buddha nature in all human beings, even innkeepers and fishmongers, he brings them to bloom.

These ideas are part of all traditions of direct knowing: the glimpse of the true nature of reality, the dangers of early experiences, the need to train attention, the eventual disassociation from ego or individual self, enlightenment, the discovery that the light was there all along, connection with the source that generates the world of appearances, reunion with all living things.

The methods for attaining liberation were likened by Buddha to a raft that takes you to the far shore. Once on the opposite bank, you have no need for the method. Similarly, the teacher is compared to a finger pointing to the moon. Once you see the moon—once you understand the *process*—there is no point in looking at the finger. Just as we need to become rich before we can discover we didn't need to be rich, we acquire techniques that teach us we didn't need techniques. The sacred takes us back to the profane, but we will never again know it as profane.

We need not still our passions, Blake said, but only "cultivate our understandings. . . . Everything that lives is holy."

FLOW AND WHOLENESS

Two key principles seem to emerge in all mystical experience. We might call them "flow" and "wholeness." The ancient Tibetan teacher Tilopa referred to them as "the principle of the nonabiding" and "the principle of nondistinction," and he warned against harming them. Our culture has indeed harmed these principles. We try to freeze the nonabiding, we try to imprison that which exists only in movement, freedom, relationship. And we betray wholeness, nondistinction, by breaking apart everything in sight so that we miss the underlying connection of everything in the universe.

In mystical experience there is the sense that "this is the way things are." Not how we wish them to be, not how we analyze them to be, not as we have been taught, but the *nature* of things—the Way.

Flow and wholeness are seen as true principles, not just in relation to work, health, or psychological growth but throughout the fabric of life. The developer of a kind of psychological aikido for dealing with conflict remarked on the way the technique of flowing with an opponent causes a gradual change in the practitioner. "It may be subtle at first, but even the most mean-spirited of people begin to relinquish their grasp on their aggression, lose their anger, and reconnect with the living force."

These mystical experiences reflect, more than just the flowing wholeness inherent in living systems (as in the theory of dissipative structures), the flow of our world from another dimension and the tendency of the universe to create ever more complex wholes. On an everyday level this knowledge shifts our time frame from temporal to eternal; we accept impermanence and cease struggling to keep the same all that must change. We experience life's blows and blessings with greater equanimity.

Our futile effort at control impedes the flow we might otherwise have in our lives. Once we get out of our own way, we can become ourselves. "I set the rivers free for all mankind," says that most ancient of mystical writings, the *Rig Veda*.

"The world is a spinning die," according to an old Hasidic passage, "...and all things turn and spin and change, for at the root all is one, and salvation inheres in the change and return of things."

Just as we must trust ourselves to the buoyancy of water if we are to swim, we can relax into that flow, turn with the spinning die. The novices in Zen monasteries are called *unsui*, cloud-water. They are meant to move freely, to form and reform spontaneously, to seek a way around obstacles. In ancient traditions, consciousness itself is pictured as an emergent wave from the source, very much like the interference patterns postulated in the holographic theory described in Chapter 6.

The second principle of *wholeness* — non-distinction — represents the connectedness, the context, of everything. Just as science demonstrates a web of relationship underlying everything in the universe, a glittering network of events, so the mystical experience of wholeness encompasses all separation. "In free space there is neither right nor left," says a Hasidic master. "All souls are one. Each is a spark from the original soul, and this soul is inherent in all souls." Buddhism maintains that all human beings are Buddhas, but not all have awakened to their true nature. *Yoga* literally means "union." Full enlightenment is a vow to save "all sentient beings."

This wholeness encompasses self, others, ideas.

Love is felt as a dynamic state of consciousness rather than as an emotion. Just as fear is constricted and chaotic, love is wide and coherent—a creative flow, harmony, acceptance of human frailty imbedded in deep self-knowledge. It is defenseless power, communication, vanished boundaries, closure.

You are joined to a great Self: *Tat tvam assi*, "Thou art That." And because that Self is inclusive, you are joined to all others. In the mystical vision of William Blake:

Awake! awake o sleeper of the land of shadows, wake! expand!
I am in you and you in me, mutual in love...
Fibers of love from man to man...
Lo! we are One.

Or, as a contemporary mystic expressed it on a personalized license plate, *IMU URI.*

This wholeness unites opposites. This Radical Center, this healing of the separation of human beings from each other and from nature is described in all mystical traditions. Nicholas da Cusa called it the *coincidentia oppositorium*, the union of opposites. In the Hasidic writings it is "the union of qualities, twos which oppose each other like two colors... but seen with the true inner eye form one simple unity." In Buddhism it is *madhya*, the transcendent middle way. The Kogi Indians of Colombia speak of the Way of the Souls leading at once upward and downward, the joining of polarities, the black sun.

In these spiritual traditions there is neither good nor evil. There is only light and the absence of light... wholeness and brokenness... flow and struggle.

A young therapist said:

An image occurs to me: the ocean shore. An outcropping of rock extending into the sea, strong and narrow. Which, when I restrict my field of vision sufficiently, appears to split the water into two distinct and separate bodies. The action of the waves lapping up on either side makes it seem as though these two are ever straining toward one another, striving with each surge to overcome this rock which prevents their joining... when, by simply stepping back and seeing more, by taking an all-encompassing perspective, expanding consciousness, I see that the separation is only an illusion—that both waves are and always were part of the one ocean, separated only by choice of my perception and my notion of striving to be one....

I see that I am already whole, that there is nothing to overcome. In those moments of emptiness, of letting be, of complete contact with another, I know that I am all I can be.

He is whole, "in place," awake to what Huxley called the "Allrightness" of the world, what Milton Mayerhoff described as knowing that "life is enough," the creative insight Rollo May called "this-is-the-way-things-are-meant-to-be." Home is not a place but an experience. The open secret of the spiritual disciplines is becoming whole, becoming oneself, going home. "The way home," said Colin Wilson in his study of mystics and artists, "is the way forward, more deeply into life." By definition, the Aquarian Conspiracy is in the world, like the "hidden yogis" of which Sri Ramakrishna spoke.

In this wholeness, oddly enough, virtues we might once have sought in vain through moral concepts now come spontaneously. It is easier to give, to be compassionate.

GOD WITHIN: THE OLDEST HERESY

In the emergent spiritual tradition God is not the personage of our Sunday-school mentality but more nearly the dimension described by William James:

> The further limits of our being plunge, it seems to me, into an altogether other dimension of existence from the sensible and merely "understandable" world. . . . We belong to it in a more intimate sense than that in which we belong to the visible world, for we belong in the most intimate sense wherever our ideals belong. . . .
>
> I will call this higher part of the universe by the name of God.

God is experienced as flow, wholeness, the infinite kaleidoscope of life and death, Ultimate Cause, the ground of being, what Alan Watts called "the silence out of which all sound comes." God is the consciousness that manifests as *lila*, the play of the universe. God is the organizing matrix we can experience but not tell, that which enlivens matter.

In J. D. Salinger's short story, "Teddy," a spiritually precocious youngster recalls his experience of immanent God while watching his little sister drink her milk. ". . . All of a sudden I saw that she was God and the *milk* was God. I mean, all she was doing was pouring God into God. . . ."

Once you have achieved the essence of religious experience, asked Meister Eckhart, what do you need with the form? "No one can know God who has not first known himself," he told his medieval followers. "Go to the depths of the soul, the secret place . . . to the roots, to the heights; for all that God can do is focused there."

British theologian John Robinson writes of a "shot-silk universe, spirit and matter, inside and outside, divine and human, shimmering like aspects of one reality which cannot be separated or divided." To Alfred North Whitehead, whose influence has risen like a flood tide in recent years, God is "the mirror image to structure in the [material] world. The world is incomplete; in its very nature it requires an entity at the base of all things, to complete it. This entity is God, primordial nature."

Buckminster Fuller tried to capture the sense of God as process:

For God, to me, it seems
is a verb
not a noun,
proper or improper;
is the articulation
not the art . . .
is loving,
not the abstraction of love . . .

Yes, God is a verb,
the most active, connoting the vast harmonic
reordering the universe
from unleashed chaos of energy.

We need not postulate a purpose for this Ultimate Cause nor wonder who or what caused whatever Big Bang launched the visible universe. There is only the experience. To Kazantzakis, God was the sum total of consciousness in the universe, expanding through human evolution. In the mystical experience there is the felt presence of an all-encompassing love, compassion, power. Individuals revived after clinical death sometimes describe passage down a dark tunnel to an unearthly light that seems to emit love and understanding. It is as if the light itself is a manifestation of universal mind.

Mystical experiences nearly always lead one to a belief that some aspect of consciousness is imperishable. In a Buddhist metaphor the consciousness of the individual is like a flame that burns through the night. It is not the same flame over time, yet neither is it another flame.

A number of those filling out the Aquarian Conspiracy questionnaire commented that their experiences had forced them to give up their previous assumption that bodily death ends consciousness. Despite their disaffiliation with formal religion, 53 percent expressed strong belief in such survival and another 23 percent said they were "moderately sure," a total of 75 percent. Only 5 percent were skeptical and 3 percent disbelieving.

The strongest believers were those who recounted brushes with death. Belief correlated strongly with the incidence of peak experiences and the pursuit of spiritual disciplines. A famous actress attributed her lifelong interest in the spiritual to a near-drowning when she was three: "Euphoria, music, and color surpassed anything known in the natural physical state."

Although he did not mention the incident in his 1927 account of his famous flight, Charles Lindbergh described in *The Spirit of St. Louis* (1953) an experience of disembodiment, the transcendence of space and time, loss of the fear of death, a sense of omniscience, remembrance of other lives, and a lasting shift in values.

Lindbergh wrote that in the eighteenth hour of his journey, he felt himself as "an awareness spreading through space, over the earth and into the heavens, unhampered by time or substance. . . ." The fuselage behind him filled with ghostly presences, "vaguely outlined forms, transparent, moving, riding weightless with me in the plane." He "saw" them behind him "as though my skull was one great eye." They conversed with him, advised him on problems of his navigation, "giving me messages of importance unattainable in ordinary life."

There was no weight to his body, no hardness to the stick. He felt more akin to the spirits, "on the borderline of life and a greater realm beyond, as though caught in the field of gravitation between two planets. . . ." He felt as if he were acted upon by forces too weak to be measured by normal means, "yet representing power incomparably stronger than I've ever known."

The presences seemed neither intruders nor strangers, more like a gathering of family and friends long separated, as though he had known them in some past incarnation.

"Death no longer seems the final end it used to be, but rather the entrance to a new and free existence," he wrote. The values of his twenty-five years — even the importance of the long-dreamed-of flight—altered sharply.

Fifty years later, when Lindbergh lay dying in his cottage in Hawaii, his wife asked him to share with her the experience of confronting the end. What was it like to face death? "There isn't anything to face," he said.

THE VISION: LIGHT AND THE COMING OF LIGHT

Contemporary mystical experiences from many individuals and many parts of the world have centered in recent years on a collective and intensifying vision, the sense of an impending transition in the human story: an evolution of consciousness as significant as any step in the long chain of our biological evolution. The consensual vision, whatever its variations, sees this transformation of consciousness as the moment anticipated by older prophecies in all the traditions of direct knowing—the death of one world and the birth of a new, an apocalypse, the "end of days" period in the Kabbalah, the awakening of increasing numbers of human beings to their godlike potential. "The seed of God is in us," Meister Eckhart said. "Pear seeds grow into pear trees, nut seeds into nut trees, and God seed into God."

The instruction booklet for Stargate, a contemporary symbolic game relating to consciousness, opens: "The turning-about is upon us, the turning of mind, the expansion of eyes . . . the light that shapes from within."

Always, the vision of evolution toward the light. Light is the oldest and most pervasive metaphor in spiritual experience. We speak of enlightenment, the city of light, the Light of the World, children of light, the "white-light experience."

"Light . . . light," wrote T. S. Eliot, "visible reminder of invisible light." To Honoré de Balzac, it seemed that humankind was on the eve of a great struggle; the forces are there, he insisted: "I feel in myself a life so luminous that it might enlighten a world, and yet I am shut up in a sort of mineral." In *The Reflexive Universe* Arthur Young, inventor of the Bell helicopter, offered in speculative scientific terms an idea as old as myth and Plato: We represent a "fall" into matter from light, and the lightward ascent has begun again.

Lawrence Ferlinghetti wrote a poem about "Olbers' paradox," the observation of a learned astronomer that there were relatively few stars nearby; the farther away he looked, the more there were.

> So that from this we can deduce
>   that in the infinite distances
>   there *must* be a place
>   there must be a place
>   where all is light

and that the light from that high place
where all is light
simply hasn't got here yet . . .

"Let the light penetrate the darkness until the darkness shines and there is no longer any division between the two," says a Hasidic passage. Before the soul enters the world, it is conducted through all the worlds and shown the first light so that it may forever yearn to attain it. The *sadik* in the Hasidic tradition, like the Bodhisattva of Buddhism, has allowed the light to enter him and shine out into the world again.

To the third-century mystic, Plotinus, it was "the clear light which is Itself." The Sufi dervish dancer does the "turn" with upraised right hand, symbolically bringing light onto the earth. The shaman achieves a state of perfect balance so that he might see a blinding light.

The dream of light and liberation is poetically expressed in an apocryphal contemporary *Aquarian Gospel of Jesus the Christ*. For too long, it says, our temples have been the tombs of the hidden things of time. Our temples, crypts, and caves are dark. We have been unable to see the patterns. "In light there are no secret things. . . . There is no lonely pilgrim on the way to light. Men only gain the heights by helping others gain the heights. . . .

"We know that the light is coming over the hills. God speed the light."

12

Human Connections: Relationships Changing

All real living is meeting.
—*MARTIN BUBER*

Each of us is responsible for everything to everyone else.
—*FYODOR DOSTOEVSKI*

The personal paradigm shift is like a sea-crossing to the New World. The immigrant, try as he might, cannot persuade all his friends and loved ones to make the journey. Those who stay behind cannot understand why the familiar did not hold the immigrant. Why did he abandon his accustomed homeland? Saddest of all, how could their affections not hold him?

And the immigrant learns that you cannot really restore the Old World on the new continent. New England is not England; Nova Scotia is not Scotland. Distance weakens the old reality, and communications become difficult, poignant. Letters to the Old World cannot evoke all the canyons and peaks that pulled the immigrant relentlessly across the unknown.

Ongoing personal transformation moves one away from the Old World—sometimes abruptly, more often over years. As we have seen in an earlier chapter, people change jobs, even voca-

tions, in the wake of shifting perceptions. If the powerful interest in the transformative process and the search for meaning
are not shared by one's marriage partner, the marriage is likely
to suffer. Over time, differences may seem more and more
pronounced, old schisms widen. Many old friendships and ac-
quaintances fall away; new friendships, even a whole new
support network, take their place. Based as they are on shared
values and a shared journey, these new relationships are
perhaps more intense.

Relatives, colleagues, friends, and marriage partners, understandably threatened by these changes, often exert pressure on
the individual to drop the practices or friendships involved in
the change. These pressures only widen the gap. You don't
stop an immigrant by trying to revive his hopes for the Old
World.

In this chapter we will look at changing personal relationships, the nature of transformative relationships, and the effect
of the transformative process on life transitions or "passages."

Relationships are the crucible of the transformative process.
They are bound to alter, given the individual's greater willingness to risk, trust in intuition, sense of wider connection with
others, recognition of cultural conditioning.

We are seeing the subtle power *custom* has wielded over our
lives. Cultural norms and mores are the great unexamined assumptions that run our lives. We become *accustomed* to roles;
they become *customary* and therefore unchallenged. Custom
is like a buildup of smog. We only notice it when it has
been swept away on a clear, clean day. We may fail to see the
outlines of a new cultural development until its effects are
pervasive.

Once-entrenched patterns of marriage, family, sexuality, and
social institutions are being shaken by radically new, or radically old, alternatives. There are no formulas and there are
many failures, but there are increasing numbers of individuals
trying to see more clearly, love more honestly, and do less
harm. Attitudes, not answers per se, are the key.

In early chapters we looked at the ways in which a new
consensus is emerging in such collective institutions as government, medicine, education, and business. But "the family,"
"marriage," and social relationships in general cannot be rethought by a committee or reformed by a program. These are
not true institutions but millions upon millions of relationships—connections—that can only be understood at the level

of the individual, and then only as a dynamic process. Social custom is perhaps the deepest of cultural trances.

TRANSCENDING CULTURAL ROLES

When one begins the transformative process, death and birth are imminent: the death of custom as authority, the birth of the self.

In a sense our simultaneous effort toward autonomy and connection, contradictory as it seems, is an attempt to be real. We are stripping away the trappings and constraints of our culture: false machismo, false eyelashes, barriers, limits.

Several men who filled out the Aquarian Conspiracy questionnaire noted that the women's movement was important in their own change—not only because it focused on the trampled potentials of half the human race but also because it questioned the supremacy of those masculine characteristics valued in the society: competition, manipulation, aggression, objectivity. One said, "Much of the transformation was catalyzed by relationships. Having loving women help me let go of sexist attitudes contributed greatly to the increased 'yin' nature I have acknowledged in myself, which has unified my life and work."

As women in transformation are discovering their sense of self and vocation, men are discovering the rewards of sensitive relationships. During these equalizing shifts, the basis for male-female interaction is being redefined. Men are becoming more feeling and intuitive; women, more autonomous and purposeful.

According to very old wisdom, self-discovery inevitably involves the awakening of the traits usually associated with the opposite sex. All of the gifts of the human mind are available to the conscious self: nurturance and independence, sensitivity and strength. If we complete such qualities within ourselves, we are not as dependent on others for them. Much of what has been labeled love in our culture is infatuation with, and the need for, our missing inner halves.

The transformed self breaks out of the compartments structured by cultural role assignments, not only by acknowledging aspects long suppressed but also by recognizing how the assigned traits can become distorted. Strength may become caricatured as machismo, aggression, taciturnity. Nurturance may be exaggerated into smothering. Whatever short-circuits our

spontaneity, be it denial or exaggeration, contributes to unconsciousness and unreality.

Conventional terms of relationship—husband, wife, father,
son, daughter, sister, in-law, lover, friend of the family—do
not identify us as persons and, in fact, may mask our authentic
selves if we keep trying to match our behavior and feelings to
the "job description."

THE THREAT TO OLD RELATIONSHIPS

Personal transformation has a greater impact on relationships
than on any other realm of life. It may be fairly said that the *first*
impact is on relationships; they improve or deteriorate but
rarely stay the same.

There are myriad changes: the ways we use power, openness
to experience, capacity for intimacy, new values, lowered competition, greater autonomy in the face of social pressures. A
formerly authoritarian person may no longer enjoy having
power over others, and a passive person may become assertive.

In some cases these changes are welcomed. More often they
are threatening. The game-playing inherent in most relationships cannot withstand the departure of one player. Just as the
larger cultural trance is shattered in transformation, so is the
trance of our miniculture, the relationship. We see that its
habits and fences may have kept us from richer, more creative
lives, from being ourselves. If one partner now feels that vocation and day-to-day living are more urgent than long-range
goals, the partner who still supports the old agenda may feel
angry and abandoned.

"Gus is gone, and he's not coming back," one woman said of
her husband's new world. Their inability to share the transformative journey had created an ever-widening chasm, and she
felt she could not find a bridge.

The most significant force in changing relationships is the
transformation of fear. Beneath the surface, most intimate relationships pivot on fear: fear of the unknown, fear of rejection,
fear of loss. In their most intimate bonds, many people seek not
just sanctuary but a fortress. If, through whatever medium—
meditation, a social movement, assertiveness training, quiet
reflection, est—one partner breaks free of fear and conditioning, the relationship becomes unfamiliar territory.

Reassurances help very little. The threatened partner may

show open disapproval, either through anger, mockery, or argument. People want us to change, but to meet their needs, not ours. And the partner who feels threatened cannot see why the other does not just change back ("If you loved me . . .")—or hopes that this is a passing phase, like adolescent rebellion or midlife crisis.

But you can't quit a new reality the way you might resign from a job, the Democratic party, or the Presbyterian church. This new perspective defuses your fears, electrifies your awareness, links you to the human company, enlivens your days.

If the fearful partner cannot adjust or join, there will eventually be a rift, either actual or psychological. Those who stay in a relationship hostile to their new world have two choices: to be open about their interests, which may fuel the misunderstanding . . . or to become clandestine. Either way, they can no longer explore, *within the relationship*, the most meaningful developments in their lives.

A New York artist whose husband belittles her spiritual search put it bluntly: "I lead a double life."

This anguish is the dearest price we pay for the New World, as we gradually concede that it cannot be explained, only seen. There is a deep sadness, not only for the loss of what might have been a shared journey but more intensely for what the companion seems to be rejecting: freedom, fulfillment, hope. Yet trying to argue someone into a paradigm shift, telling him to disregard old cynicism or limiting beliefs, is as futile as telling someone blinded by cataracts to open his eyes wider. Our fears, motives, and needs are idiosyncratic. We come to understandings in our own time and in our own ways. We remember that we ourselves initially rejected ideas that later became central to our lives—once we *experienced* them to be true.

Whatever the cost in personal relationships, we discover that our highest responsibility, finally, unavoidably is the stewardship of our potential—being all we can be. We betray this trust at the peril of mental and physical health. At bottom, Theodore Roszak observed, most of us are "sick with guilt at having lived below our authentic level."

If one partner develops a strong sense of vocation and the other has none, that commitment can become a source of jealousy and antagonism, creating, in effect, a triangle.

Relationships have a mathematics of their own, either enriching or destructive. As social critic Norbert Prefontaine described this phenomenon:

When one thing and one thing are added together, the result is two things, be those things oranges, pistons, or buildings. However, if one person is added to another person, the result is always more than two or less than two, but never merely two. That is, persons who genuinely meet and interact either strengthen each other so that they are stronger together than the sum of them separately or they damage each other so that they are weaker together than the sum of them together.[1]

Psychologist Dennis Jaffe pointed out that two people can be a source of growth, support, and health for each other or they can be what he calls "lethal dyads."

A closed relationship, like a closed system in nature, loses energy. A schoolteacher said, "The old conventional relationships, in their exclusivity and ego massage, isolated us even more than if we were alone. The only difference was now it was the *two* of us, an island."

The transformative process, while making ever more apparent the narrowing aspects of our relationships, also introduces us to new possibilities.

TRANSFORMATIVE RELATIONSHIPS

A transformative relationship is a whole that is more than the sum of its parts. It is synergistic, holistic. Like a dissipative structure, it is open to the world—a celebration and exploration, not a hiding place.

As we become more concerned with the essence of relationship and less with the form, the quality of human interaction changes. Experiences of unity, fullness, awakened senses, empathy and acceptance, flow—all of these open us to more possibilities for connection than we had before.

This is the union described by Martin Buber:

In a real conversation, a real lesson, a real embrace . . . in all these, what is essential takes place between them in a dimension which is accessible only to them both. . . . If I and

---

[1] A management consultant, Ben Young, had a slightly different qualitative metaphor: "In every relationship there are two ways of adding. One plus one equals two—two independent individuals. But they can also make a whole—one half plus one-half equals one. We all enjoy feeling part of a single whole, but we need to allow each other to be separate individuals, too. The problem is that most people try to take their 'half' out of the other person's 'one.'"

another "happen" to one another, the sum does not exactly divide. There is a remainder somewhere, where the souls end and the world has not yet begun.

This dimension, "the between," the I-Thou, Buber also called "the secrecy without a secret." It is a conspiracy of two, a momentarily polarized circuit of consciousness, an electrified linking of minds. It neither asks nor answers; it simply connects. As Buber said, it may only be a look exchanged on a subway. And at its most complex and dynamic, it is the planet's brain, the accelerating awareness of brotherhood anticipated by Teilhard, Buber, Maslow, and others.

It is strangely impartial, turning frogs into princes, beasts into beauties. As more individuals open up to each other, expressing warmth and encouragement, love is a more available source of approval and energy. This can be a confusing phenomenon if seen through the lenses of the old paradigm.

One who believes in us, who encourages our transformation, whose growth interacts with and enhances our own, is what Milton Mayerhoff called "the appropriate other." Such caring relationships help us to become "in-place." We cannot find our growth alone, Teilhard said. He himself had intense friendships, many of them with women despite church strictures against even platonic closeness between priests and women. "Isolation is a blind alley.... Nothing on the planet grows except by convergence."

In his Aquarian Conspiracy questionnaire, a politician wrote of "the transforming power of liberating love relationships— occasionally experiencing myself more openly, fully, deeply, innocently than I had heretofore any sense of."

A number of those who responded to the questionnaire commented on the importance of powerful friendships that guided them across new territory. One, herself a therapist, remarked on the importance of "always meeting an essential strong person in my life when I need them. Each takes me to a certain point, then there's a period of integration, and the next one appears. These meetings are always accompanied by a deep sense of recognition and intense 'soul' involvement."

The loving, transformative relationship is a compass to our potential. It frees, fulfills, awakens, empowers. You don't have to "work at it." With its curious blend of intensity, ease, and spiritual connection, the transformative relationship contrasts with all the less rewarding connections in our lives and becomes as vital as oxygen. Each such relationship is also a compass to another kind of society, a model of mutual enrichment that can be extended throughout the fabric of our lives. Yet it requires that we first redefine our terms.

"When you ask what love is," said Krishnamurti, "you may be too frightened to see the answer.... You may have to shatter the house you have built, you may never go back to the temple." Love is not fear, he said. It is not dependence, jealousy, possessiveness, domination, responsibility, duty, self-pity, or any of the other things that conventionally pass for love. "If you can eliminate all these, not by forcing them but by washing them away as the rain washes away the dust of many days from a leaf, then perhaps you will come upon this strange flower man hungers after."

The transformative relationship is more easily described in terms of what it does not include. Our cultural concept of love's possibilities has been so limited that we don't have the proper vocabulary for a holistic experience of love, one that encompasses feeling, knowing, sensing.

To have a transformative relationship you must be open and vulnerable. Most people meet only at their peripheries, Rajneesh, an Indian teacher, said. "To meet a person at his center is to pass through a revolution in yourself. If you want to meet someone at his center, you will have to allow him to reach your center also."

Transformative relationships are characterized by trust. The partners are defenseless, knowing that neither will take advantage or cause needless pain. Each can risk, explore, stumble. There is no pretense, no façade. All aspects of each partner are welcome, not just agreed-upon behaviors. "Love is more important than romance," a magazine editor asserted. "Acceptance is more important than approval."

Past the old conditioning of competition, the partners cooperate; they are more than two. They dare and challenge each other. They take pleasure in each other's capacity to surprise.

The transformative relationship is a shared journey toward meaning. The process itself is paramount and cannot be compromised. One is faithful to a vocation, not a person.[2]

[2]In a forthcoming book, *The Couple's Journey*, Susan Campbell reports on her study of one hundred fifty couples, ranging in age from the twenties to the seventies, "who were engaged in developing greater awareness in their relationships." She has identified several stages of growth through which a couple pass en route to a transformative "co-creative" relationship. The preceding stages are an illusory romance, a power struggle, stability, mutual commitment, and finally a commitment to help one another realize a creative vocation in the world.

"Genuine love," Simone de Beauvoir said, "ought to be founded on the mutual recognition of two liberties; the lovers would then experience themselves both as self and the other; neither would give up transcendence, neither would be mutilated. Together they would manifest values and aims in the world."

Because there is a continuous change in a transformative relationship, there can be no taking for granted. Each partner is awake to the other. The relationship is always new, an experiment, free to become whatever it will. It rests on the security that comes from giving up absolute certainty.

The transformative relationship defines itself; it does not try to conform to what society says it should be but serves only the needs of the participants. There may be guiding principles, even flexible agreements, but no rules.

Love is a context, not a behavior. It is not a commodity, "won," "lost," "earned," "stolen," "forfeited." The relationship is not diminished by either partner's caring for others. One can easily have more than one transformative relationship at a time.

Both partners feel bonded to the whole, the community. There are new capacities to give and receive love, joy and sympathy for many. This intense communion with the world cannot be pressed into a narrow channel. A physician said, "It's as if you've been withholding your empathy with the world, and suddenly you lose your virginity. You feel as if you want to make love to the cosmos. Now, how are you going to explain that to anybody?"

THE TRANSFORMATION OF ROMANCE

At first we may try to fit this new cosmic caring into conventional structures, the kind of romantic expressions conditioned by our culture. We soon learn that the old forms of relationship are inappropriate to the demands of the transformative journey. One woman said of a brief remarriage after the end of a long marriage, "In retrospect, I realize that I was trying one last fling with the Old World, I was running away from my own spiritual drive."

A businessman said that for a time he tried to be more creative in his work and sought out sexual relationships "all trying to fill up the empty hole in the middle—the spiritual hunger. But once you recognize what you're doing, you stop. You can't keep doing it."

As transformative relationships evolve in our lives, we may find in them qualities that evoke the *original* meaning of romance, as it emerged in the nineteenth century. Romance referred then to the infinite and unfathomable, those forces in nature which are ever forming. Although it preferred the natural to the mechanistic, the Romantic movement was by no means anti-intellectual or anti-rational. Ironically, in their eagerness to probe the mysteries of nature, the Romantics generated the scientific curiosity that finally led to the glorification of reason. Romance was then reduced to a cosmetic and trivial role, representing all that is unreal, the gilt that hides the tarnish of life.

In its heyday the Romantic movement celebrated family, friendship, nature, art, music, literature, drawing on what one historian called "the mystery of the spirit, the larger self, the sense of quest." In a very real sense romance was identical with what we now call the spiritual. It trusted direct experience; it sought meaning.

Our cultural romance, however, is external, the product of conditioning: movies, television, commerce, custom. No wonder we become apostates from conventional romance! It's like second-hand God. And there is the same sense of loss and disillusionment as when we rebel against organized religion. We abandon the adventure; we say it is a sham. Yet the hunger is still there, the haunting suspicion that we are missing something central to life.

In the transformative process, romance—that numinous, spiritual, *inward* quality—is embodied in an adventure that evokes its own symbols and language, that feels like "the real thing," a dream from which you don't awaken. De Beauvoir conceded that certain forms of the sexual adventure would be lost as we became more real, "but this does not mean that love, happiness, poetry, dream will be banished.... Our lack of imagination always depopulates the future."

A Taoist meditation says, "Seek no contract, and you shall find union." One of the transformative shifts is an ebbing away of what the Eastern philosophies call "attachment." Non-attachment is a compassion that does not cling, love that accepts reality and is not needy. Non-attachment is the opposite of wishful thinking.

The old familiar emotions like jealousy, fear, insecurity, and guilt are unlikely to evaporate. But the overall patterns are changing. For some this means confronting and transcending internal contradictions, like the desire for freedom for oneself and fidelity in a partner. Coming to terms with such deep conflict is difficult, painful, and, for many, rewarding.

One woman said in her Aquarian Conspiracy questionnaire, "I spent two years learning how to love without possessing. I decided that when I got married it would be that way for me, and it has been for thirteen years. I've learned that you can love more than one person, that you may be jealous, but you can never possess someone, only make desperate tries at it. *We possess nothing, least of all each other.*"

Writing in a Quaker newsletter, one woman envisioned a near future in which everyone is more able to relate to others—husbands and wives not possessing each other, nor parents their children, in the old constricting ways.

> We will recognize that each person needs to nourish and be nourished by many persons, and we will not seek to restrict them through fear. We will know that we can only keep that which we set free. . . . We recognize ourselves as members of the family of human beings. It is right, even necessary, to make yourselves available to one another in new loving, caring, and fulfilling ways—without the spectres of old guilts at loving widely.

In new-paradigm relationships, the emphasis is not so much on sexuality as intimacy. Intimacy is prized for its shared psychic intensity and transformative possibilities, of which sex is only a part—and often a latent part at that.

For many people, giving up the idea of exclusive relationships is the most difficult paradigm shift in their own transformation. Some choose to limit their sexual expression to a primary relationship. Others may give priority but not exclusivity to the primary relationship. The desirability of exclusive relationships is a deep cultural belief, despite contradictory evidence — and behavior.[3] For many people, giving up the old

---

[3]Many sociologists anticipate the "evolution" of monogamy. Marriage, they say, must be transformed as an institution if it is to survive at all. In an article titled "Is Monogamy Outdated?" Rustom and Della Roy said that "about half of all marriages now existing will, and probably should, be terminated." If monogamy is tied inextricably with the restriction of all sexual expression to the spouse, they said, it will ultimately be monogamy that suffers." Instead it should be tied to more basic concepts (fidelity, honesty, openness) which do not necessarily exclude deep relationships with others, possibly including various degrees of sexual intimacy."

In our highly eroticized environment, the Roys said, people are brought together in all kinds of relationship-producing situations. Traditional

need for exclusivity was the most difficult paradigm shift of all, yet necessary if they were to be true to their own mores.

Trying to analyze the sexual revolution, contemporary sociologists have commented that the difference is in attitudes, not behavior. Our culture's traditional sexual mores have been widely violated in this society since the twenties, if not before. John Cuber, a sociologist at Ohio State University, found that, compared to their counterparts in 1939, young people in 1969 did not accept the old sexual rules. Even if they did not wish to engage in the once "forbidden" behavior, they challenged the validity of the law. Cuber said:

> *There is a profound difference between someone who breaks the rules and someone who does not accept the rules.* One is a transgressor; the other is a revolutionary. No government trembles before the tax evader. But no government could brook a Boston Tea Party; that was revolution.
>
> . . . Will the revolutionaries ever return to the fold, mend their ways, recant? I think not. It is a comfortable cliché among the middle-aged that the restive young when faced with responsibilities will settle into traditional viewpoints. That is not so for this generation. . . . As long as the sinner acknowledges his guilt, there is a chance that he may reform and repent. But the key to this generation is precisely its freedom from guilt.

Others are challenging the very context of sexuality in our culture. We have been conditioned to approach all sexual relationships in terms of conquest, they say, and this precludes deep trust and intimacy. We are "turned on" to a surprising degree by that which our culture has programmed us to associate with sexuality. This programming also sets us up for rejection and frustration.

In workshops around the country Joel Kramer and Diana Alstad talk about a sexual paradigm shift—freeing sexuality from "the context of conquest." Conditioned desires and stereotypes have to change, they say, if we are to appreciate the

---

monogamy contravenes the growing sense "that the greatest good of human existence is deep interpersonal relationships, as many of these as is compatible with depth." They concede that most middle-class, educated Americans over thirty-five" are so schooled into both exclusivity and possessiveness that very few could accept any kind of structured non-exclusivity in marriage," but they note that younger people are trying to devise and invent a form of marriage appropriate to a new era.

integrated person—a strong woman, a sensitive man."Men are still sexually turned on to beauty and women to power in very deep ways. What is new is that people are no longer satisfied with this way of relating." The old paradigm automatically puts love and sexuality "out of kilter" with each other. People who are "good for you" are often not those who excite you sexually, they said.

> What we are talking about is another way of looking at relationships and sexuality, in which the major interest is in exploring and growing together. We all hunger for solutions, but rather than defining or laying out a new way to be, we must be pioneers if we're going to create a new way to live together.
>
> No real solution can come until both men and women truly see the nature of the problem, which lives in each of us.... Seeing the patterns changes you.
>
> As long as men and women are hooked into romance, they can never meet each other totally. If we are to open opportunities to meet human beings, we must leave the whole context of conquest. It takes equals to create the possibility of mature love.

THE TRANSFORMATIVE FAMILY

The novel *Anna Karenina* begins, "Happy families are all alike; every unhappy family is unhappy in its own way."

Suddenly we aspire to a society in which we may be happy in different ways. As the old social structures break, millions have been cast loose from the conventional support systems of the past. The Carnegie Council on Children estimated in 1978 that as many as four of every ten youngsters born in the 1970s will spend part of their childhood in a one-parent family. Three out of five women polled recently by the Roper organization preferred divorce to staying with an unsatisfactory marriage. One urban study showed that 40 percent of the city's adults were totally without family ties. Only one of four families fits our stereotype of the breadwinner husband and homemaker mother.

It's ten o'clock, says the public service radio announcement. *Do you know where your child is?* A better question: It's late in the twentieth century.... Amidst experimentation, changing social structures, broken relationships, new relationships, demands for freedom, demands for security—do we know where our connections are?

The family can nurture the child so effectively, with warmth and stimulation, that we call the result giftedness. But if the family fails to nurture, if the emotional bonds are weak, the child will not thrive. Studies of infants in institutions have shown that the development of normal intelligence requires human interaction. Without love, without input and response from the world, we can make no sense of the world. Retardation is the result for babies who are fed but not played with, safe but not spoken to.

An atmosphere of trust, love, and humor can nourish extraordinary human capacity. One key is authenticity: parents acting as people, not as roles. The poet Adrienne Rich recalled one summer in Vermont when she and her three young sons lived spontaneously, without schedules. Late one night, driving home from a movie, she felt wide awake and elated. "We had broken together all the rules of bedtime, the night rules, rules I myself thought I had to observe in the city or become a 'bad mother.' We were conspirators, outlaws from the institution of motherhood. I felt enormously in charge of my life." She did not want her sons to act for her in the world. "I wanted to act, live, in myself and to love them for their separate selves."

Parents often pretend to endorse rules, institutions, and behavior because they trust authorities more than their own experience and intuitions. This perpetuates hypocrisy and the power of the institutions from generation to generation. Children, teenagers especially, tend to assume that their own feelings are unacceptable, and so they withdraw from their parents.

"Many, perhaps a majority, of young people are looking for deep, intimate relationships," said Ted Clark and Dennis Jaffe of their experiences counseling youths. "They need a supportive, understanding, and tolerant person for a guide. Nothing has to be 'done.' They just want a place where they can be themselves."

Like the transformative adult relationship, the transformative family is an open system, rich in friends and resources, giving and hospitable. It is flexible, adaptive to the realities of a changing world. It gives its members freedom and autonomy as well as a sense of group unity.

Long before the educational system exacts its psychological

costs, the family has defined roles and expectations, teaching a benign, cooperative attitude toward the world or a competitve, paranoid one. The family rewards or punishes innovation. The family is a setting for self-disclosure, for intimacy—or for the repression of feelings, for hypocrisy. In its rigidity or flexibility, its exclusive or inclusive attitudes, the family patterns our later relationships.

The child develops self-esteem in an atmosphere of unconditional caring, mastery in an atmosphere of appropriate challenge.

Insecurity keeps many families from outside relationships that could change them. They are closed systems. Fearful families, said Hossain Danesh, a Canadian psychiatrist, "perceive the world in dichotomies: men and women, old and young, emotions and intellect, power and weakness, self and others." They discourage members from friendships with people different from themselves. The child gains approval only by conforming to the parent's wishes.

The power of parent-child relationships is tragically evident in a phenomenon called emotional dwarfism. A six year old with this syndrome may be the size of a three year old. Typically, when placed in a good foster home, such a child begins to grow normally but stops again if returned to the hostile biological family. Emotional dwarfism is relatively unusual, but a more common stunting of growth occurs in families all the time when children are thwarted in their unfolding as individuals.

Frederick Perls, the famous psychologist, once said that dissociation—the split between emotions and conscious thinking—begins with a parent's *conditional* love. Because many adults were betrayed as children—not rewarded for being themselves, always urged to "do better" however hard they tried—they find it difficult to trust that they are loved. The chain is perpetuated if they become parents because they may find it hard to accept their own children unconditionally. Not until we have discovered the extent of our own programmed fears can we forgive the imperfections and weaknesses of others. When we have touched the healthy center in ourselves, we know it exists in others, whatever their outward behavior. Consciousness enables us to care about them.

The transformative process is a second chance for many people to achieve the self-esteem they were denied as children. By reaching the center in themselves, the healthy self, they discover their own wholeness.

THE PLANETARY FAMILY

The wider paradigm of relationships and family transcends old group definitions. The discovery of our connection to all other men, women, and children joins us to another family. Indeed, seeing ourselves as a planetary family struggling to solve its problems, rather than as assorted people and nations assessing blame or exporting solutions, could be the ultimate shift in perspective.

If we consider that any child being abused is *our* child, the problem changes. When we see our culture, our social conditioning, or our class as an artifact rather than a universal yardstick, our kinship expands. We are no longer "ethnocentric," centered in our own culture.

A society in flux will have to create its families in new ways. The new family is emerging from networks and communities, experimental and intentional groups, friendships. The American Home Economics Association redefined the family in 1979 as "two or more persons who share resources, share responsibility for decisions, share values and goals, and have commitment to one another over time. The family is that climate that one 'comes home to,' and it is this network of sharing and commitments that most accurately describes the family unit, regardless of blood, legal ties, adoption, or marriage."

Human beings have a kind of optical illusion, Einstein once said. We think ourselves separate rather than part of the whole. This imprisons our affection to those few nearest us. "Our task must be to free ourselves from this prison by widening our circle to embrace all living creatures.... Nobody achieves this completely, but the striving itself is part of the liberation."

The "transcenders" Maslow studied, Einstein included, seemed sadder than the other healthy, self-actualizing persons; they saw more clearly the gap between potential and reality in human relationships. Any one of them could have written a workable recipe for social transformation in five minutes, Maslow said.

"I have seen the truth," Dostoevski said. "It is not as though I had invented it with my mind. I have seen it, *seen it*, and the living image of it has filled my soul forever.... In one day, one hour, everything could be arranged at once! *The chief thing is to love*." He said he realized that this truth had been told and retold a billion times, yet it had never transformed human life.

Love and fraternity, once part of an ideal, have become crucial to our survival. Jesus enjoined his followers to love one

another; Teilhard added, "or you perish." Without human affection, we become sick, frightened, hostile. Lovelessness is a
broken circuit, loss of order. The worldwide quest for community typified by the networks of the Aquarian Conspiracy is an
attempt to boost that attenuated power. To cohere. To kindle
wider consciousness. When man reclaims this energy source,
the sublimation of spiritual-sensual love, Teilhard once said,
"for the second time he will have discovered fire."

During the second New York City blackout, while some
people were looting, others were beaming their flashlights
from apartment-building windows to the sidewalks, "moving"
pedestrians from one building to the next, creating a path of
light and safety. In this time of uncertainty, when all our old
social forms are crumbling, when we cannot easily find our
way, we can be lights to each other.

CHAPTER *13*

The Whole-Earth Conspiracy

*When you come to be sensibly touched, the
scales will fall from your eyes; and by the penetrating eyes
of love you will discern that which your other
eyes will never see.*

—*FRANÇOIS FÉNELON, 1651–1715*

 Victor Hugo prophesied that in the twentieth century war would die, frontier boundaries would die, dogma would die—and man would live. "He will possess something higher than these—a great country, the whole earth . . . and a great hope, the whole heaven."

Today there are millions of residents of that "great country, the whole earth." In their hearts and minds, war and boundaries and dogma have indeed already died. And they possess that large hope of which Hugo wrote.

They know each other as countrymen.

The Whole Earth is a borderless country, a paradigm of humanity with room enough for outsiders and traditionalists, for all our ways of human knowing, for all mysteries and all cultures. A family therapist says she urges her clients to discover not who is right or wrong but *what they have as a family*. We are beginning to make such an inventory of the Whole Earth. Every time one culture finds and appreciates the discovery of another, every time an individual relishes the talents or unique insights of another, every time we welcome the unexpected knowledge emerging from inside the self, we add to that inventory.

Rich as we are—together—we can do anything. We have it within our power to make peace within our torn selves and with each other, to heal our homeland, the Whole Earth.

We look around at all the reasons for saying No: the failed social schemes, the broken treaties, the lost chances. And yet there is the Yes, the same stubborn questing that brought us from the cave to the moon in a flicker of cosmic time.

A fresh generation grows up into a larger paradigm; thus it has always been. In many science-fiction tales the adults are barred from the transformation experienced by a new generation. Their children grow irrevocably beyond them, into a larger reality.

Those of us born into the "broken-earth" paradigm have two choices: We can go to our graves with the old view, like the generations of die-hard scientists who insisted there were no such things as meteorites, or germs, or brainwaves, or vitamins — or, we can consign our old beliefs unsentimentally to the past and take up the truer, stronger perspective.

We can be our own children.

NEW MIND, NEW WORLD

Not even the Renaissance has promised such a radical renewal; as we have seen, we are linked by our travels and technology, increasingly aware of each other, open to each other. In growing numbers we are finding how people can enrich and empower one another, we are more sensitive to our place in nature, we are learning how the brain transforms pain and conflict, and we have more respect for the wholeness of the self as the matrix of health. From science and from the spiritual experience of millions, we are discovering our capacity for endless awakenings in a universe of endless surprises.

At first glance, it may seem hopelessly utopian to imagine that the world can resolve its desperate problems. Each year fifteen million die in starvation and many more live in unrelenting hunger; every ninety seconds the nations of the world spend one million dollars on armaments; every peace is an uneasy peace; the planet has been plundered of many of its nonrenewable resources. Yet there have been remarkable ad-

vances as well. Just since the end of World War II, thirty-two
countries with 40 percent of the world's population have overcome their problems of food scarcity; China is becoming essentially self-sufficient and has controlled its once-overwhelming
population growth; there is a net gain in world literacy and in
populist governments; concern for human rights has become a
stubborn international issue.

We have had a profound paradigm shift about the Whole
Earth. We know it now as a jewel in space, a fragile water
planet. And we have seen that it has no natural borders. It is
not the globe of our school days with its many-colored nations.

We have discovered our interdependence in other ways, too.
An insurrection or crop failure in a distant country can signal
change in our daily lives. The old ways are untenable. All countries are economically and ecologically involved with each
other, politically enmeshed. The old gods of isolationism and
nationalism are tumbling, artifacts like the stone deities of Eas-
ter Island.

We are learning to approach problems differently, knowing
that most of the world's crises grew out of the old paradigm—
the forms, structures, and beliefs of an obsolete understanding
of reality. Now we can seek answers outside the old
frameworks, ask new questions, synthesize, and imagine. Science has given us insights into wholes and systems, stress and
transformation. We are learning to read tendencies, to recognize the early signs of another, more promising, paradigm.

We create alternative scenarios of the future. We communicate about the failures of old systems, forcing new frameworks
for problem-solving in every area. Sensitive to our ecological
crisis, we are cooperating across oceans and borders. Awake
and alarmed, we are looking to each other for answers.

And this may be the most important paradigm shift of all.
*Individuals are learning to trust—and to communicate their change of
mind.* Our most viable hope for a new world lies in asking
whether a new world is possible. Our very question, our anxiety, says that we care. If we care, we can infer that others care,
too.

The greatest single obstacle to the resolution of great problems in the past was thinking they could not be solved—a
conviction based on mutual distrust. Psychologists and
sociologists have found that most of us are more highly motivated than we think each other to be! For instance, most
Americans polled favor gun control but believe themselves in
the minority. We are like David Riesman's college students,

who all said they did not believe advertising but thought everyone else did. Research has shown that most people believe themselves more high-minded than "most people." Others are presumed to be less open and concerned, less willing to sacrifice, more rigid. Here is the supreme irony: our misreading of each other. Poet William Stafford wrote:

If you don't know the kind of person I am
and I don't know the kind of person you are
a pattern that others made may prevail in the world,
and following the wrong god home, we may miss our star.

Following the wrong god home, we have seen all of those we did not understand as alien, the enemy. Failing to comprehend each other's politics, cultures, and subcultures, which often are based on a different worldview, we questioned each other's motives ... denied each other's humanity. We have failed to see the obvious: "Most people," whatever their philosophy about how to get there, want a warless society in which we are all fed, productive, fulfilled.

If we see each other as obstacles to progress, our assumption is the first and greatest obstacle. Mistrust is a self-fulfilling prophecy. Our old-paradigm consciousness has guaranteed its own dark expectations; it is our collective negative self-image.

Now, as we are learning to communicate, as ever-increasing numbers of people are transforming their fear and finding their bonds with the rest of humanity, sensing our common yearnings, many of the planet's oldest, deepest problems show promise of breaking and yielding. The shift for which we have waited, a revolution of appropriate trust, is beginning. Instead of enemies, we are looking for allies everywhere.

When an international conference, "The Future of the West," convened at the University of Southern California, the authorities agreed firmly on one point: The conference had been misnamed. The West, they said, can have no future apart from the East. This awareness may signal what Martin Heidegger called "the still unspoken gathering of the whole of Western fate ... the gathering from which alone the Occident can go forth to meet its coming decisions—to become, perhaps, and in a wholly other mode, a land of dawn, an Orient."

Beneath the trappings of culture, anthropologists have said, lies a whole other world. When we understand it, our view of human nature will change radically. Now we confront an array of possible ways to be. The global village is a reality. We are joined by satellite, supersonic travel, four thousand international meetings each year, tens of thousands of multinational companies, international organizations and newsletters and journals, even an emergent pan-culture of music, movies, art, humor. Lewis Thomas observed:

> Effortlessly, without giving it a moment's thought, we are capable of changing our language, music, manners, morals, entertainment, even the way we dress, all around the earth in a year's turning. We seem to do this by general agreement, without voting or even polling. We simply think our way along, pass information around, exchange codes disguised as art, change our minds, transform ourselves.
> ... Joined together, the great mass of human minds around the earth seems to behave like a coherent living system.

The proliferating small groups and networks arising all over the world operate much like the coalitional networks in the human brain. Just as a few cells can set up a resonant effect in the brain, ordering the activity of the whole, these cooperating individuals can help create the coherence and order to crystallize a wider transformation.

Movements, networks, and publications are gathering people around the world in common cause, trafficking in transformative ideas, spreading messages of hope without the sanction of any government. Transformation has no country.

These self-organizing groups are very little like old political structures; they overlap, form coalitions, and support each other without generating a conventional power structure. There are environmental groups like Les Vertes in France and the Green Alliance in Great Britain, women's groups, peace groups, human rights groups, groups battling world hunger; thousands of centers and networks supporting "new consciousness," like Nexus in Stockholm; publications like *Alterna* in Denmark, *New Humanities* and *New Life* in Great Britain, linking many groups; symposia on consciousness in Finland, Brazil, South Africa, Iceland, Chile, Mexico, Rumania, Italy, Japan, the USSR.

The Future in Our Hands, a movement launched in Norway in 1974 and inspired by a book of that title by Erik Damman, now numbers twenty thousand of that country's total population of four million. The rapidly growing movement promotes

"a new lifestyle and a fair distribution of the world's resources." It emphasizes the need for industrialized nations to
curb their consumption patterns and seeks ways to boost the
living standard of Third World countries. According to a national survey, 50 percent of the Norwegian population supports the goals of the movement, 75 percent believe that their
nation's standard of living is too high, and 80 percent fear that
continued economic growth will lead to an increasingly stressful, materialistic lifestyle.

The movement is fueled by grass-roots power. Small local
groups determine their own course in furthering the collective
goals. A related movement started in Sweden in 1978 and
another is now under way in Denmark.

These social movements transcend traditional national borders, with Germans joining French demonstrators to protest
nuclear power plants. Johann Quanier, British publisher of *The
New Humanity* journal, said, "The strands of free thinking
within Europe are now being drawn together; despite the conflicts, the tension, and the differences, that territory is preemi-
nently suitable for the emergence of the new political-spiritual
framework."

To Aurelio Peccei, founder of the Club of Rome, such groups
represent "the yeast of change... scattered, myriad spontaneous groupings of people springing up here and there like an-
tibodies in a sick organism." An organizer of a peace group
remarked on his discovery of these networks and their sense of
"imminent world transformation." Many brilliant, creative
thinkers have affiliated internationally to help synthesize the
intellectual support for an emergent vision for the planet. To
them it is more than a mere scenario, one of many possible
futures, but rather a responsibility; the alternatives seem to
them to be unimaginable.

The Threshold Foundation, based in Switzerland, stated its
intent to help ease the transition into a planetary culture, "foster a paradigm shift, a new model of the universe in which art,
religion, philosophy, and science converge," and promote a
wider understanding that "we exist in a cosmos whose many
levels of reality form a single sacred whole."

FROM POWER TO PEACE

We are changing because we must.

Historically, peace efforts have been aimed at ending or preventing wars. Just as we have defined health in negative terms, as the absence of disease, we have defined peace as non-conflict. But peace is more fundamental than that. Peace is a state of mind, not a state of the nation. Without personal transformation, the people of the world will be forever locked in conflict.

If we limit ourselves to the old-paradigm concept of averting war, we are trying to overpower darkness rather than switching on the light. If we reframe the problem — if we think of fostering community, health, innovation, self-discovery, purpose—we are already engaged in waging peace. In a rich, creative, meaningful environment there is no room for hostility.

War is unthinkable in a society of autonomous people who have discovered the connectedness of all humanity, who are unafraid of alien ideas and alien cultures, who know that all revolutions begin within and that you cannot impose your brand of enlightenment on anyone else.

The Vietnam War protests in the United States marked a critical turning point, a coming of age, as millions said, in effect, that you can't consign an autonomous people to a war they don't believe in. Other phenomena in recent years have been equally significant: fifteen thousand Germans marching in Cologne to oppose a new flicker of Nazism and to express their individual grief for the Holocaust . . . Catholics and Protestants risking their lives to embrace at a bridge in Northern Ireland, promising each other to work for peace . . . "Peace Now," the Israeli movement launched by combat soldiers asking, "Give peace a chance."

After a recent congress in Vienna on the role of women in world peace, Patricia Mische wrote of "the transformation already slowly in process among individuals and groups who, in a deep probing of their own humanness, are discovering the bonds they have with people everywhere."

Can the arms race be reversed? "A prior question," Mische said, "would be, '*Can people—and nations—change their hearts and minds?*'" The Vienna participants seemed living testimony that the answer is Yes. At the close of the congress one participant asked, to tumultous applause, that at future conferences speakers not be required to identify themselves by nationality. "I am here as a *planetary* citizen," she said, "and these problems belong to all of us."

In *The Whole Earth Papers*, a series of monographs, James Baines described a "power paradigm" and a "peace paradigm." For millennia, he said, we have lived under the power paradigm, a belief system based on independence and domination. Yet it has always existed alongside the components for a peace paradigm: a society based on creativity, freedom, democracy, spirituality. To foster a global shift, Baines said, we can now create "a web of reinforcement": leadership comfortable with uncertainty, heightened public awareness of the contradictions in the power paradigm, exciting models of new lifestyles, appropriate technology, techniques for expanded consciousness and spiritual awakening. Once these ideas coalesce into a coherent new paradigm grounded in transformation, we will see that humanity is both a part of creation and its steward as well, "a product of evolution and an *instrument* of evolution."

We need not wait for a leadership. We can begin to effect change at any point in a complex system: a human life, a family, a nation. One person can create a transformative environment for others through trust and friendship. A warm family or community can make a stranger feel at ease. A society can encourage growth and renewal in its members.

We can begin anywhere—everywhere. "Let there be peace," says a bumper sticker, "and let it begin with me." Let there be health, learning, relationship, right uses of power, meaningful work. . . . *Let there be transformation, and let it begin with me.*

All beginnings are invisible, an inward movement, a revolution in consciousness. Because human choice remains sacrosanct and mysterious, none of us can guarantee a transformation of society. Yet there is reason to trust the process. Transformation is powerful, rewarding, natural. It promises what most people want.

Perhaps that is why the transformed society exists already as a premonition in the minds of millions. It is the "someday" of our myths. The word "new" so freely used (new medicine, new politics, new spirituality) does not refer so much to something modern as to something imminent and long awaited.

The new world is the old—transformed.

ENDING HUNGER—CREATING A PARADIGM SHIFT

Historically, movements for social change have all operated in much the same way. A paternal leadership has convinced people of the need for change, then recruited them for specific tasks, telling them what to do and when to do it. The new social movements operate on a different assumption of human potential: the belief that individuals, once they are deeply convinced of a need for change, can generate solutions from their own commitment and creativity. The larger movement inspires them, it supports their efforts and gives them information, but its structure cannot direct or contain their efforts.

The power of individuals to generate broad social change is the basis for the Hunger Project, an international charitable organization launched by est founder Werner Erhard in 1977 and headquartered in San Francisco. The Hunger Project's goal is to speed up a solution to the world hunger problem by acting as a *catalyst*. It is an intense, sophisticated large-scale effort to hurry a paradigm shift—to "make an idea's time come," as the project's organizers put it. The successes of the project and the ways in which it has been misunderstood are instructive.

The Hunger Project assumes that solutions do not reside in new programs or more programs. According to the best-informed authorities and agencies, the expertise to end hunger within two decades *already exists*. Hunger persists because of the old-paradigm assumption that it is not possible to feed the world's population.

In less than two years, *seven hundred fifty thousand* individuals in dozens of countries have pledged their personal commitment to help end world hunger by 1997; enrollment in the Hunger Project is increasing at the rate of more than sixty thousand per month. Three million dollars has been raised explicitly to increase public awareness of the tragic proportions of the problem, the available solutions, and the ways in which individuals and groups can accelerate an end to hunger and starvation.[1]

The Hunger Project does not compete with older hunger organizations; rather, it publicizes their activities and urges enrollees to support them. The project draws all concerned parties into its efforts. Just prior to the launching of the foundation, a delegation that included world food distribution experts met with India's prime minister. Advisers to the project represent many nations and existing hunger organizations; Arturo Tanco, president of the World Food Council, is one. Government data, like the National Academy of Sciences report on the means to end hunger, are promulgated.

[1]In response to media critics who charged that none of the money was buying food, the project's administrators explained in a financial report, "If our one million dollars can make the five billion spent annually on the development [of food resources] just one percent more effective, we will have had a *five thousand percent return on our money.*"

To create a sense of urgency, the project draws on the power of the symbol and the metaphor, describing the toll of starvation as "a Hiroshima every three days." When a Hunger Project relay of more than one thousand runners carried a baton from Maine to the White House, they did not ask the government to solve the problem. Rather, their message spoke of their own commitment to help end hunger and starvation.

The project uses models from nature and scientific discoveries as metaphors; the hologram, for example, is "a whole within a whole." Everyone who enrolls is "the whole project." The project is "an alignment of wholes." Everyone who signs up is told to "create your own form of participation." Some fast and contribute to the project what they would have spent on food. Many businesses have donated a day's receipts. A team of forty runners generated pledges of six hundred twenty-five thousand dollars for running in the Boston Marathon in 1979, and twenty-three hundred spectators were enrolled along the way. Eighty-eight fifth graders in a California school sponsored a Skate-a-thon and raised six hundred dollars; when they designated their funds for "the boat people," the Hunger Project put them in touch with Food for the Hungry, an organization directly assisting the refugees.

Everyone who signs up is encouraged to enlist others. Enrollees are told how to capture the interest of clubs, school boards, lawmakers; how to direct letters; how to make public presentations. Each enrollee is asked to become a teacher. Seminars emphasize the power of a single committed person, like the man in New Rochelle, New York, who enrolled his mayor, school superintendent, city manager, governor, and lieutenant governor; and the Honolulu woman who signed up the entire congressional delegation, governor, and most of the state legislature. At her urging the governor proclaimed Hunger Week, and state legislators passed a resolution to encourage Hawaiian agricultural research to help alleviate world hunger. A Massachusetts couple enrolled *fifty thousand*.

Prisoners have been among the most dedicated supporters of the Hunger Project. A prisoner in the correctional facility at San Luis Obispo, California, enrolled fifteen hundred of the twenty-four hundred inmates. A Leavenworth prisoner not only became involved in the project; he and seven other inmates also pooled their money to sponsor two Vietnamese children through Save the Children. A long-term prisoner in a Virginia women's penitentiary said, "The women get bitter and critical in here, the walls close in. Each day grinds. Finally you give up and close in on yourself. . . . I realized the Hunger Project is a way out of the trap—by reaching out to help others."

So long as we thought we couldn't do anything about the world's starving millions, most of us tried not to think about them; yet that denial has had its price. The Hunger Project emphasizes a key principle of transformation—the need to confront painful knowledge:

> We have numbed ourselves so that we do not feel the pain. We have to be asleep in order to protect ourselves from the horror of knowing that twenty-eight people, most of them young children, are dying this very minute—twenty-eight people no different from you or me or our children, except that we have food and they do not.
>
> We have closed down our consciousness and aliveness to a level where it doesn't bother us. So if you wonder if it costs us anything to allow millions to starve, it does. *It costs us our aliveness*.

Within a year after the launching of the project, ninety committees had been organized in thirteen countries. Celebrities spoke out for the cause, sometimes without specific reference to the project, much as movie stars helped sell war bonds in the 1940s. Singer John Denver made a documentary film on world hunger. He told a newspaper interviewer, "We're at a point in this planet where we're going to have to make a specific shift in attitude, in how we lend ourselves to life. Up until now it's been, 'If this were the last cup of grain, my very survival depends on my keeping it for me and my own.' Now we're at a time when we will shift to 'My survival depends on my sharing this with you. If this isn't enough for me, my survival *still* depends on my sharing this with you.'"

Denver, now on the Presidential Commission on World Hunger, wrote "I Want to Live," the title song in a gold-record album, for the Hunger Project. Its theme: We are on the threshold of the end of war and starvation. "It is only an idea—but I know its time has come."

Comedian Dick Gregory gave the project one of its most dramatic images:

> When people ask me, "Well, what do you think is going to happen with hungry folks?" I give them the kind of answer the fire marshal gives to the TV reporter when a forest fire is burning out of control: "It's out of our hands

now. If we don't get a shift in the wind, we can't save it."

For a while it looked like we weren't going to make it unless we got a shift in the wind. But I left leeway for that which controls *all* winds to step in. . . . Our Hunger Project *is* that shift in the wind.

A key point is made to those who sign up: A world in which hunger has ended will be not merely different or better but *transformed*. And those who take part will be transformed by their own participation — by telling friends, family, and co-workers of their own commitment, even if they feel self-conscious, and by searching for answers.

RE-CHOOSING

The Aquarian Conspiracy is also working to ease hunger—for meaning, connection, completion. And each of us is "the whole project," the nucleus of a critical mass, a steward of the world's transformation.

In this century we have seen into the heart of the atom. We transformed it—and history—forever. But we have also seen into the heart of the heart. We know the necessary conditions for the changing of minds. Now that we see the deep pathology of our past, we can make new patterns, new paradigms. "The sum of all our days is just our beginning. . . ."

Transformation is no longer lightning but electricity. We have captured a force more powerful than the atom, a worthy keeper of all our other powers.

We find our individual freedom, by choosing not a destination but a direction. You do not choose the transformative journey because you know where it will take you but because it is the only journey that makes sense.

This is the homecoming so long envisioned. "Condemn *me* and not the path," Tolstoi said. "If I know the road home, and if I go along it drunk and staggering, does that prove that the road is not the right one? If I stagger and wander, come to my help. . . . You are also human beings, and you are also going home."

The nations of the world, Tocqueville once said, are like travelers in a forest. Although each is unaware of the destination of the others, their paths lead inevitably toward meeting in the center of the forest. In this century of wars and planetary crisis, we have been lost in the forest of our darkest alienation. One by one the accustomed strategies of nation-states—isolation, fortification, retreat, domination—have been cut off.

We are pressed ever more deeply into the forest, toward an escape more radical than any we had imagined: freedom with—not from—each other. After a history of separation and mistrust, we converge on the clearing.

Our metaphors of transcendence have spoken of us more truly than our wars: the clearing, the end of winter, the watering of deserts, the healing of wounds, light after darkness—not an end to troubles but an end to defeat.

Over the centuries those who envisioned a transformed society knew that relatively few shared their vision. Like Moses, they felt the breezes from a homeland they could see in the distance but not inhabit. Yet they urged others on to the possible future. Their dreams are our rich, unrealized history, the legacy that has always existed alongside our wars and folly.

In a wider state of consciousness one can sometimes vividly re-experience a past trauma and, in retrospect and with imagination, respond to it differently. By thus touching the source of old fears, we can exorcise them. We are not haunted so much by events as by our beliefs about them, the crippling self-image we take with us. We can transform the present and future by reawakening the powerful past, with its recurrent message of defeat. We can face the crossroads again. We can re-choose.

In a similar spirit, we can respond differently to the tragedies of modern history. Our past is not our potential. In any hour, with all the stubborn teachers and healers of history who called us to our best selves, we can liberate the future. One by one, we can re-choose—to awaken. To leave the prison of our conditioning, to love, to turn homeward. To conspire with and for each other.

Awakening brings its own assignments, unique to each of us, chosen by each of us. Whatever you may think about yourself and however long you may have thought it, you are not just you. You are a seed, a silent promise. You are the conspiracy.

Afterword

After reading galleys of *The Aquarian Conspiracy* on an airplane in late 1979, a fellow writer called to say, "This isn't your book—it's ours." He echoed my sense of joint authorship. Many times I had felt like a spider spinning a web from a community of ideas and people, and the diarist of a vast emigration.

Perhaps for that reason, *The Aquarian Conspiracy* has proven to be more a phenomenon than a book, a statement that helped catalyze support for the shifts it described. As the conspiracy was mapped and named, as the web became visible, it gathered strength. In that sense, I was not so much an author as a midwife.

Even before publication, the reaction to the manuscript was reassuring. Four or five xeroxed copies given to friends turned into twenty or thirty in the hands of strangers. Within weeks after publication, leaders of the Solidarity Movement in Poland had ordered ten copies. The book became a text in a variety of college courses. It was published in the United Kingdom, France, Germany, the Netherlands, Sweden, Japan, Portugal, and Spain. Discussion groups were started in prisons, churches, government agencies, and even in a South African village.

Beyond the conspiracy I had described, there was a community of respected leaders scanning the horizon for helpful new ideas. This community was a dynamic counterpart to the traditional power structure. I found myself talking to—and learning from—such diverse groups as health educators, nuclear physicists, school counselors, Canadian farm wives, members of Congress, data processing managers, hotel executives, state administrators, medical librarians, college presidents, and international gatherings of youth and business leaders.

There were thousands of letters whose common motif was relief: "Thank God, I'm not alone." People said they were strengthened by knowing that change is not only possible but under way. One woman wrote, "The voices are no longer crying in the wilderness."

More hearts harbored the dream of a better world than I had imagined in my wildest moments. The impact of the vision continues to surprise me.

Two years after publication of the book, the World Future Society polled a large panel on the likelihood of "a dramatic cultural shift, such as the Aquarian Conspiracy, by 2000 A.D." Fifty-eight percent said such a shift was probable.

A number of critics, of course, were skeptical of that possibility. They saw me as too optimistic and unaware of the horrendous problems. Some social activists feared that the book's hopeful tone would give false reassurance that transformation was all but accomplished; they were understandably concerned that people might relax their effort. I saw how easily the ideas in the book could be construed as dangerous or naive. Certainly there have been times when I felt that the skeptics and naysayers must be right—that neither individuals nor societies can truly change.

With the growth of the movement, there were also more teachers, trainers, and project organizers who seemed to be exploiting the emerging values, overpromising what they could deliver, and creating a dependency in avid seekers.

On the other hand, I had the encouraging experiences and news from my travels, seminars, lectures, and from the grapevine of *Brain/Mind Bulletin* (and *Leading Edge,* a social-change newsletter I published from 1980–1985). In this kaleidoscope of living history, something authentic seemed to be on the move. Everywhere, it seemed, there was evidence of the awakening of a more artful humanity.

What was real? Buffeted from time to time by headlines of disaster and setback, then cheered by first-hand experience and upbeat news, I was becoming "skeptimistic." Eventually I began to see the seesaw itself as a clue to the problem. And that is a major point of this afterword.

The human brain, it has been pointed out, learns by story; it remembers facts if they are made meaningful. But the truly significant stories of our time will never be reported on the six o'clock news. They are not events but *patterns* of events. Recognition of these deeper tendencies gives us clues to what today's stories mean for tomorrow.

These larger contexts offer hope, however tentative, of a cultural renaissance. Decades from now we might look back on them as clear turning points in our thinking and our agendas. Some have to do with new internal processes, others with external developments.

Here are examples of some of the "breaking stories" of the 1980s and 1990s:

Story #1. Learning that bad news can be good news.

By the time a problem is serious enough to compel the attention of the public, not just a few reformers, it may be on its way to being solved. At that point we are likelier to acknowledge the need for deep housecleaning.

The popular will is energized only when a threat appears grave and leaders offer no believable reassurance. The old saying, "If it works, don't fix it," is a clue to the reluctance to experiment and innovate. For example, malfeasance in government has been a norm. As it becomes a raging fever, the citizenry is forced to find remedies. (At the same time, such scandals seem to provoke more soul-searching than before, a collective sense of responsibility rather than righteousness.)

People are also beginning to learn the costs of our preoccupation with facade. "Bad news" that exposes deeper social problems can show us how they have been camouflaged.

Another example of bad news/good news: We seem to be in the midst of a new Great Depression, this one not economic but psychosocial. Depression—the "common cold of mental health"—is reportedly on the increase in preschoolers, teenagers, those eighteen to thirty-four, those forty-five to fifty-five, and elderly men. According to one estimate, four out of five sufferers go untreated. What does this apparent epidemic mean? And why is it happening now?

In fact, the wave of depression may be a sign of impending health. As the late psychiatrist Karl Menninger once pointed out, a darkness or disturbance in the mind often precedes the deep reorganization that leads to a higher norm. People become "weller than well."

Depression can be a signal to reexamine assumptions and change strategies—a slowing down to reorient. If we are to deal effectively with problems, we have to see them realistically. And we have to define our purpose. As private persons and as members of a society, a special task of renewal lies before us. The best antidepressants are expression and action—engagement in the struggle. That way, depression is not an end, but a meaningful beginning.

Story #2. The evolution of revolution.

The very shape of cultural turning points may be shifting a little from the old predictable sequence—sharp swings of the pendulum—to more thoughtful forms of social renewal.

Revolutionaries have typically called for quick and final solutions, premature answers that failed to include ideas from all factions. By failing to integrate the best of the old values with the new, for example, revolutions themselves have often been disappointing, their gains gradually reversed. With a greater awareness of systems thinking, we may not have to subject ourselves to the far swings of the pendulum. Faced with the appalling costs of our rifts, our too-often empty "victories," whether in personal encounters or high-level negotiation, we are learning to respect the art and science of mediation. Training programs, books, and articles show us how to attack problems and not opponents. Change agents are starting to match the sense of purpose to the reality of the whole. This reflects a growing awareness in Western thinking of the balance described in Oriental thought as *yang* (identified with action, the masculine) and *yin* (the matrix in which events unfold, the receptive and feminine).

Story #3. Bridging the confusion gap.

"Confusion gap" is the name given by a management consultant to the period of implementing change. During this time we are tempted to give up the new and run back to the devil we know. We are learning to recognize chaos as an inevitable part of change, to distinguish the transition period from the goal.

Story #4. The rise of the Pacific Culture.

This new economic center is geographically rimmed by active volcanoes ranging from Japan and the Philippines to the San

Andreas Fault of the Western United States. Economically it includes the trading countries of the Asian Pacific, the western United States and Canada, and Australia and New Zealand.

The visionaries of the Pacific Culture tend to emphasize the future, ecology, high technology, inner development, cultural diversity, coalition, the joining of disciplines, and parallel spiritual truths.

The wealth of the new center, these forecasters say, both rises from and influences its worldview. Its values will increasingly affect the rest of the world. It is global in its sense of space, long-range in its sense of time. Economist Richard Kjeldsen observed that the Pacific economies are not monolithic but diffuse and complex. The new culture seems to epitomize the uncertainties of the times. Boundaries, both physical and abstract, are shifting, blurring, even dissolving. Bioregions (naturally independent areas) are seen as units, irrespective of national borders.

The Pacific Culture has been called a way of thinking, an emerging social vision. It may foretell something unprecedented—not a world order, but a world civilization.

Story #5. The advent of citizen diplomats.

The new ''citizen diplomats'' offer imaginative approaches to international problems. Just as the economic interdependence of the Pacific nations gives greater importance to dealings outside government, individual Americans have cooperated with Soviets to organize tours, cultural exchange programs, concerts, sporting events, entrepreneurial deals, and joint professional meetings. They have created space bridges and closed-circuit television broadcasts. Ever more frequently, influential Americans are invited to meet with high-level Soviet officials, both here and in the Soviet Union.

Examples of citizen diplomacy include: the 1986 Goodwill Games, organized by broadcaster Ted Turner and the Soviet government; the Health Promotion Project, sponsor of joint research and conferences, a collaboration of the Esalen Soviet-American Institute and Soviet officials; and the Entertainment Summit, the highly publicized 1987 series of meetings in Los Angeles and New York of American and Soviet filmmakers.

Story #6. Increasing media coverage of metaphysical/spiritual news.

The chroniclers and even the advertisers have noticed a growing and apparently insatiable popular appetite for mystery and self-transcendence.* In early 1987 alone, an exponential growth has generated a fresh momentum, an acceleration in the rate of acceleration.

On September 29, 1986, the *New York Times*, the number-one arbiter of the national reality for many intellectuals, ran a front-page feature about the growing number of adherents to spiritual views. One interview warned that such people may represent a new coalition, "the most powerful social force in the country today."

Over the next few months other major features on the "New Age," some positive, appeared in publications like *Time*, *U.S. News and World Report*, *The Los Angeles Times*, and on television ("20–20," "Sixty Minutes," network morning shows). Soon virtually all the popular magazines, major newspapers, and television networks were providing ongoing coverage. Since then, the emerging views and values have become the topic of TV dramas, even situation comedies.

Focusing on the bizarre or glamorous, the media have often missed the deeper significance of the movement's values, like personal responsibility, self-help, and mutual help. Even so, it is clear that the larger story is now nearly mainstream.

Story #7. Taking responsibility for the present reality.

New psychotechnologies are showing that people can change. And popular expression has been emphasizing the role and potential of the individual in bringing about change. It is as if we are graduating from a narrow glorification of individual freedoms to a larger exploration of what those freedoms can effect.

Whether in the calls to action of public speakers and writers, the themes of entertainment, or overheard private conversations, we are admitting that we have to change ourselves. As the relentless limelight is exposing the wrongs in every corner of every society, we have run out of scapegoats, the vague "they" who once were responsible for everything that doesn't work. The outer world reflects our inner wars, paralyses, and

---

*The so-called transpersonal may soon be reckoned normal, judging from recent surveys. And the spiritual values associated with the so-called New Age seem to be on the upswing in American political life.

The National Opinion Research Center of the University of Chicago has found a steep increase in spiritual and psychic experiences. The center, which has polled Americans on their spiritual life since 1973, reports that 67 out of 100 American adults say they have experienced extrasensory perception, for example. (This compares to 58 percent in 1973.) Various Gallup polls in the

guilt. Mostly we have sinned by omission—not so much by cheating or unkindnesses, but by failing to act, by tolerating wrongs. And the quality of life that is diminished is our own.

As we begin to see ourselves as prospective actors on the world stage, we may overcome inertia and narrow interests, our habit of having habits. As we become more aware of our actions and reactions, we see how we shape and are shaped by the environment. New light begins to shine through chinks in the fortress of personality ("this is who I am") and the bastion of beliefs ("this is what I think"). We can learn to recreate ourselves in the wake of new information.

At the same time, our loss of faith in institutions, experts, and technology may mark a new maturity. A greater number of us acknowledge that our own efforts are needed. The growing skepticism about authority may, in fact, force us to become the informed and thoughtful people for whom democracies were designed.

Story #8. The rediscovery of bodymind.

Of all the examples of change discussed in *The Aquarian Conspiracy*, the paradigm change in health care was the most solidly under way. That shift continues, supported by widespread and well-reported research. Epidemiological studies have shown the startling connection between healthy minds and well-being, between emotional patterns and susceptibility to illness. Practitioners continue to offer innovations that tap self-healing mechanisms, that employ imagery and stress-reduction techniques. The importance of emotional support and a sense of purpose are recognized.

Since 1980 there has been perhaps a twentyfold increase in investigations of the interface of mind and body. Modern neuroscience and allied disciplines are illuminating the once-mysterious interface of the mental/emotional and the physical.

Psychoneuroimmunology, an exciting new field, explores the interaction of the emotional brain and the immune system. The

---

1980s found increased reporting of mystical experiences. Forty-three of those questioned said they had had an unusual spiritual experience.

"A New Age for Metaphysical Books," an article in *American Bookseller* (February 1987), concluded that "the human potential movement is finally coming of age." In early 1987 the B. Dalton chain newsletter reported that solid growth in the market for spiritual and esoteric topics was reaching boom proportions.

see Story #1 — section on Depression

complexity of this link is seen in multiple-personality syndrome, the effects of light and sound, lucid dreaming, the chemistry of emotions, and memory.

Medicine is being critiqued from within. Physicians are challenging their profession sincerely and even publicly, urging a return to the healing arts, a greater respect for the patient's own observations, and emotional sensitivity.

The growing evidence of a brain/body dynamic makes more sense of mind-oriented therapies and body therapies that can affect depression and other mental disorders. Medical journals are reporting on the surprising effects of alternative and folk techniques, ranging from herbal remedies to acupuncture to "healing trance" (hypnosis). Because of objective laboratory evidence that *something* is going on, American physicians have agreed to cooperate with an official Chinese investigation of *gi gong*, apparent energy effects at a distance. Homeopathy was found effective in a well-controlled study reported in the British medical journal *Lancet*. In a Brazilian study, patients helped by spiritist healers fared better than those who received conventional treatment. In an elegantly designed double-blind experiment, an American cardiologist reported that prayer by others significantly affected recovery.

The new paradigm of health implies greater creativity on the part of both healer and patient. It means a greater respect for natural healing responses, promising a continuing shift away from the impersonal medicine that has caused such widespread bitterness. It does not imply a rejection of technological breakthroughs like new drugs or surgical innovations. It uses whatever works.

The bodymind paradigm also introduces a higher standard—well-being rather than an absence of disease. And, in its multi-faceted view of health, it tends to diffuse professional competition. There is greater parity between physicians and others who serve health, including nurses, psychotherapists, chiropractors, healers, acupuncturists, herbalists, homeopaths, bodyworkers, nutritionists, and religious counselors. As we know more about our brains and bodies, we have a more sophisticated sense of how once-mysterious remedies may work.

Story #9. The cultivation of intelligence.
The finding that intelligence can be enhanced is a breakthrough comparable to the discovery of agriculture. We can 'grow' intelligence as our prehistoric ancestors grew food.

For example, children are being taught "critical thinking skills." People are being trained to achieve learning states. Even old age can be a season of growth rather than decline. New research shows that some people get better as they grow older; this alternative life-path is almost wholly associated with a positive mental attitude—especially with the sense of choice. Passive, negative people decline; active, interested people thrive.

Increasingly, the psychotechnologies described in this book are being used all over the world to enhance learning.

One example of the cultivation of intelligence is a Venezuelan movement inspired by modern brain research. In 1979, inspired by Luis Machado's *The Right to be Intelligent,* a new Ministry for the Development of Human Intelligence initiated an ongoing national program based on Machado's book, *The Right to be Intelligent.* The program has led to a host of conferences and the creation of a global network. It is being emulated in a dozen or more countries.

In the Venezuelan program, parents are encouraged to stimulate their babies. Schoolchildren are trained in thinking skills and imagination. Educational programs on prime-time television offer adults ongoing opportunities to learn.

The Japanese government has announced an ambitious plan to reform schools so that children learn to think for themselves, to understand and create as well as memorize. American efforts at reform in recent years have emphasized "more of the same"—longer hours and increased homework, rather than a better grasp of how teaching and learning occur. Brain research is still only rarely applied to curriculum design and classroom methodology. Meanwhile, other countries increase their lead over us in test performance, a gap which business leaders see as a major cause of the relative decline of American productivity. The burning question: Will we wake up in time to reverse the much-discussed mediocrity? Those responsible for action are, in fact, of the very system that needs radical restructuring.

But there is far more light shed on the problem than ever. Since the publication of *The Aquarian Conspiracy,* the educational crisis has become a compelling national topic. A variety of large networks of educators and concerned citizens have been organized. These networks are models of cooperation. The organizing teachers have shown themselves to be more effective and heroic than even they believed possible.

Story #10. New respect for whole-brain thinking.

A new appreciation of intuition and the creative process, for example, extends even to university classrooms and research laboratories. The analytical brain recognizes and respects the gifts of its counterpart, the brain of web and novelty.

Scientists have been holding major meetings to discuss "serendipity," the opportunities presented by happy accidents. Serendipity, they say, is the fountainhead of scientific breakthroughs.

In a survey, chief executive officers of the fastest growing companies agreed that their greatest regret was not paying enough attention to their intuitions. "Vision," a more inclusive term for intuition, has come into popular use in business, politics, the arts, even in consumer advertisements.* People are paying more attention—and respect—to their hunches.

A new breed of professional trainers and consultants is untangling the strategies of self-starters and successful innovators, methods for accessing superior states for learning, and the capacity to shift from unproductive moods.

Story #11. A search for methods to achieve positive mental states.

It becomes increasingly evident that a certain state of mind facilitates creativity, health, and good timing. This state is similar to the glow of success. Learning to achieve it voluntarily, we can avoid the anxiety that too often keeps us from being clearheaded enough to carry off difficult tasks.

Modern society has tended to confuse pessimism with realism and optimism with rose-colored glasses. Actually, optimist and optimism are derived from the Latin *optimus* (best) related to *ops* (power). Pessimism derives from *pessimus* (worst) from the Greek *pedon* (ground).

A high vantage point offers power—and a far better perspective than does the ground. Perhaps the reason optimists work hard is because success is visible on the horizon.

In fact, faith based on experience is a tool, a calm state of mind geared to optimal performance. The current interest in more constructive attitudes may be not so much an innovation as a corrective—the inward/outward turn that can grant us, at

---

*The "visionary factor," the constellation of traits of those best able to translate dreams into action, is the subject of a forthcoming book I have been writing with my husband and colleague, Ray Gottlieb.

one time, both homecoming and new adventure. It is becoming common sense, as well as good science, to acknowledge that high-ground thinking is more fruitful than cynicism.

Story #12. The arts and entertainment as sensors of broad cultural change.

The visual arts and music are often forerunners of feelings and perceptions too vague to articulate, priorities too new to defend.

A convergence of art and conscience can be seen in fiction, films, and in a few bold television efforts. Leading rock groups and soloists attract capacity crowds to hear their poignant social/spiritual messages, often the concert centerpieces. The Band Aid recording, the "USA for Africa" album, and the Live Aid concert proved the eagerness of entertainers and their fans to contribute in some way.

An ambitious and nationally acclaimed retrospective exhibit, "The Spiritual in Art: Abstract Art 1890–1985," drew large crowds to the Los Angeles County Museum of Art before moving on to Chicago and the Hague. Even the negative critics hedged their remarks, confessing fascination with the subject matter.

For those with ears to hear, a new voice is beginning to sound in the marketplace of culture. This voice isn't a supplicant pleading for attention, nor is it prophetic; it is more immediate and practical. It comes from many different quarters, as if a wiser human core, ancient and new, has begun to transmit a new range of frequencies. Successful projects offer prototypes for evolutionary change. (See "Guidelines for Successful Projects" for tips to successful innovation.)

Story #13. The rediscovery of myth and metaphor as reshaper of social purpose.

Archetypes, metaphors, and myth have long been used to sell products and ideologies. Myths of a new culture can give us an alternative vision to nuclear/ecological disaster or mere nervous survival. Metaphors for our condition are all around us. For example, looking at mountains, valleys, canyons, peaks, and plateaus can remind us of the terrain of life.

According to a legend from the ancient mystical Judaic strain known as kabala, migrant beings—souls from a higher order— are born into every generation.* They are "children from the

*As recounted in *Nine-and-a-half Mystics* by Herbert Weiner (Collier).

chamber of yearning," also known as *tohu,* the state of chaos. They are destined to be triggers of evolution. These rebellious spirits, restless and alienated, unhappy with "surface relationships and surface truths," offend the good manners of the day.

At an end-of-days period, when the world is to be remade, an even greater number of such chaotic spirits arrive to shake the status quo to its roots. But the kabala says we should not be afraid of such times, for these people are only freeing the energy from dying forms. A new breed will emerge—"the masters of construction," who will focus the fire of revolution into practical improvements.

Story #14. The wealth of solutions to our problems.

Contrary to general belief, answers exist for nearly all of our most compelling problems. The trick is to initiate them and to appreciate multiple options. Our answers don't have to compete. As the head of an international foundation observed, "Each of us has acted as if our answer is a gladiator that has to come out of the arena as the sole winner."

New problem-solving processes—methods to orchestrate the warring solutions—are being invented. Too often we have not even identified the problem. This has led to an interest in what someone called "the jugular questions." Through the art and science of mediation, people are also learning to be more straightforward and to discover that we can help each other more readily if our agendas are on the table.

Breakthroughs like the rapidly evolving superconductor technology hint at powerful new possibilities; perhaps this time, recalling past mistakes, we will act more wisely.

Certainly these headlong years have seen the erosion of tradition and an escalation of chaos and rebellion. Yet here and there, as promised, we can see a rising force of creative organizers, some even drawn from the ranks of ex-rebels. We are beginning to realize—or remember—that ours is a common fate. And that may be the biggest news.

We need not know the outcome of these stories to play a part in them. Because there are always forces and countervailing forces, each day we choose which wave to support. Will we contribute to the problem or the solution? Will we see possibilities or impossibilities? From the perspective of critics, we will focus on what can't be done. From the perspective of creators, we will know what must be done.

The time of spectators is fast coming to a close. Let us choose, sooner rather than later, to be masters of construction.

Guidelines for Successful Projects

After more than a decade of publishing *Brain/Mind Bulletin* and five years of publishing *Leading Edge* we reviewed the track record of hundreds of innovations, projects, and events.

Some had thrived and had even become international models. Others turned out to be little more than good intentions or aggressive public relations. The concepts that succeeded shared certain qualities. They also steered clear of the rocks on which others went aground. Here are some rules of thumb for successful projects:

Do the do-able. Many plans fail because they are too grandiose for the available skills and resources.

Learn from your mistakes. Successful projects are often a new, improved version of an earlier effort.

Understand the technology that could help your project. Develop a professional attitude toward word processing, graphics, printing, mailing services, postal laws, and volunteer management.

Look at the entire project, and look ahead. Consider the system. No action is isolated; everything is in motion.

Get cooperation from a variety of groups or "stakeholders." If you can't get support in advance, your idea may not have enough appeal to be worth doing.

Recruit respected spokespeople and endorsers. The genuine support of such people is better than gold. But don't exaggerate your support, especially in trying to get publicity.

430

Be truthful. Be clear about how far along your plans are—what is hoped for, what is tangible. "Hype" is part of the problem, not the solution.

Raise your standards. Excellence is all it's cracked up to be. The look of your materials (meeting announcements, brochures, and the like) tells prospective supporters a lot about your seriousness and sophistication. Try to recruit someone with graphic skills.

Build on the quality of people. Don't compromise your goals by trying to include inappropriate people, even if they are your best friends or sources of funding.

Find flexible forms. Structure should be versatile enough to meet the unexpected.

Find a critical consensus. Hidden disagreements can sabotage the project.

Think in terms of solutions, not problems. Confidence is likelier than a crisis mentality to produce answers.

Don't get righteous and rigid about your values. Values come from perspectives, which can change as circumstances change. Today's enlightenment may be tomorrow's cliche.

Exploit differences. Many projects fail because the participants are too much alike, preaching to the converted. They can't anticipate a broad range of public response.

Find the middle path. Successful projects manage to combine freedom and discipline, individual expression and cooperation, the new and the traditional.

Tell a better story. People are moved by metaphors, drama, and symbols.

Train your intuition. Investigate technologies that help you achieve a creative, receptive state. Look into apparent intuitions so that you can track their validity and learn better how to distinguish wishful thinking from wisdom.

Go to the roots of your problems. If you don't, you postpone the day of reckoning at your expense.

Be realistic about the inevitable miscommunication between and confusion among people. Processes and policies can help, but establishing trust is even better.

Don't rely on miracles for money. If your project depends on grants or contributions, you will probably become endlessly enmeshed in fundraising or borrowing. Think like an entrepreneur even if your project is nonprofit.

Respect details and logistics. "Perfection is made of ten thousand trifles," Michelangelo once said, "and perfection is no trifle."

Summary of Questionnaire Responses

Of the 185 respondents, 131 were male and 54 female. Approximately 46 percent lived in California, 29 percent in the East, 9 percent in the Midwest, 6 percent in the West (excluding California), 6 percent in the South, and 4 percent outside the United States.

At the time of the survey, 101 (54.5 percent) of the respondents were married. Nearly half had been the only child or firstborn in their family. As noted in the text, they represented a wide range of vocations, but most were professionals.

Many preferred not to designate their positions on the political spectrum, saying that the old labels were no longer relevant. Of those who answered, 40 percent characterized themselves as liberal, 12 percent radical, 20 percent centrist, 7 percent conservative, 21 percent apolitical. Party affiliation: Independent, 47 percent; Democrat, 34 percent; Republican, 3 percent; other, 16 percent. Most (72 percent) saw government as *less* essential to problem solving than they had five years earlier; 28 percent, *more* essential. Decentralized government was favored by 89 percent, strong central government by 11 percent.

Fifty-eight percent said they had numerous contacts with individuals who shared their values and their interest in human potential; 42 percent, only a few.

They designated the institutions in transition they considered the most dynamic: medicine, 21 percent; psychology, 17 percent; religion, 13 percent; the family, 12 percent; business, 10 percent; media, 9 percent; education, 8 percent; the arts, 6 percent; and politics, 4 percent.

The greatest threat to social transformation: popular fear of change, 44 percent; conservative backlash, 20 percent; divisiveness among advocates for change, 18 percent; excessive claims by advocates for change, 18 percent. Fifty percent characterized their beliefs about humankind's future as optimistic, 38 percent as cautiously optimistic, 8 percent as uncertain, and 4 percent as pessimistic.

They each chose four instruments of social change they considered most important in terms of their own experience: personal example was checked off by 79 percent; support networks, 45 percent; electronic media, 39 percent; winning over influential persons, 38 percent; books, 38 percent; public education, 37 percent; conferences and seminars, 32 percent; newsletters and journals, 22 percent; professional education, 20 percent; pilot projects, 15 percent; funding sophistication, 12 percent; government programs, 9 percent.

Spiritual disciplines and growth modalities the respondents considered important in their own change: Zen, 40 percent; yoga, 40 percent; Christian mysticism, 31 percent; journals and dream journals, 31 percent; psychosynthesis, 29 percent; Jungian therapy, 23 percent; Tibetan Buddhism, 23 percent; Transcendental Meditation, 21 percent; Sufism, 19 percent; Transactional Analysis, 11 percent; est, 11 percent; the Kabbalah, 10 percent. Earlier religious background of the respondents: Protestant, 55 percent; Judaic, 20 percent; Catholic, 18 percent; other, 2 percent; none, 5 percent. Eighty-one percent were no longer active in the religion of their childhood.

Body therapies experienced by the respondents: T'ai Chi Ch'uan, 32 percent; Rolfing, 31 percent; Feldenkrais, 31 percent; the Alexander technique, 24 percent; and Reichian methods, 14 percent.

Many respondents chose not to answer the questions relating to former or present use of major psychedelic drugs. Thirty-nine percent of all respondents acknowledged that psychedelic experiences had been important in their own transformative process; 28 percent said they still used psychedelics on occasion; 16 percent said psychedelic experiences continued to be important to them.

Many respondents were engaged in aspects of science; the survey showed a high level of interest in the arts as well: 46 percent played a musical instrument, 43 percent engaged in arts or crafts on a regular basis, and 63 percent regularly read fiction and poetry.

Most respondents accepted psychic phenomena and the transpersonal dimension as a reality. Choosing from a spectrum of belief — strongly sure, moderately sure, unsure, skeptical, and disbelieving —

they tended to believe (strongly or moderately sure) in telepathy (96 percent), psychic healing (94 percent), precognition (89 percent), clairvoyance (88 percent), synchronicity (84 percent), psychokinesis (82 percent), cosmic intelligence (86 percent), consciousness that survives bodily death (76 percent), and reincarnation (57 percent). A number protested the use of the word *belief*, saying that they had accepted these phenomena because of direct experiences.

Peak experiences were described as frequent by 48 percent of the respondents, occasional by 45 percent, rare by 5 percent, non-existent by 2 percent.

Major personal change was characterized by 35 percent as very stressful on occasion, by 22 percent as "really rough," by 21 percent as mildly stressful, and by 22 percent as relatively smooth.

Asked to designate which of a list of ideas had been important in their own thinking, they chose as follows: altered states of consciousness research, 74 percent; discoveries about the brain's specialized hemispheres, 57 percent; parapsychological research, 55 percent; Jung's archetypes, 53 percent; paradoxes in physics, 48 percent; holographic models of reality, 43 percent; Kuhn's paradigm-shift concept of scientific revolutions, 39 percent; Teilhard's concept of evolving consciousness, 35 percent; paradoxes in evolution, 25 percent; and paradoxes in mathematics, 14 percent.

When respondents were asked to name individuals whose ideas had influenced them, either through personal contact or through their writings, those most often named, in order of frequency, were Pierre Teilhard de Chardin, C. G. Jung, Abraham Maslow, Carl Rogers, Aldous Huxley, Roberto Assagioli, and J. Krishnamurti.

Others frequently mentioned: Paul Tillich, Hermann Hesse, Alfred North Whitehead, Martin Buber, Ruth Benedict, Margaret Mead, Gregory Bateson, Tarthang Tulku, Alan Watts, Sri Aurobindo, Swami Muktananda, D. T. Suzuki, Thomas Merton, Willis Harman, Kenneth Boulding, Elise Boulding, Erich Fromm, Marshall McLuhan, Buckminster Fuller, Frederic Spiegelberg, Alfred Korzybski, Heinz von Foerster, John Lilly, Werner Erhard, Oscar Ichazo, Maharishi Mahesh Yogi, Joseph Chilton Pearce, Karl Pribram, Gardner Murphy, and Albert Einstein.

B

Resources for Change

The networks, periodicals, and directories listed here are only a few of hundreds of publications and literally thousands of social-action and mutual-help networks and organizations with an essentially "new paradigm" orientation. Those included have a relatively broad focus and are open to anyone.

Readers may also be interested in the following materials:

Brain/Mind Bulletin, a four-page news bulletin, has been edited and published by Marilyn Ferguson since 1975. It covers developments in learning, creativity, health-care, and new scientific models for an inter-disciplinary readership. One year subscription, $35. (First class mail, $40; outside U.S., $45 U.S. funds.) Collected issues of prior volume year (17 issues), $20. First eleven years (222 back issues), $195.

Complete set of back issues of *Leading Edge*, a four-page bulletin on social change published from 1980–1985; 85 issues, $30. (Limited supply.) Collected articles from both bulletins are also available as "theme packs."

Aquarian Conspiracy Discussion Packet for groups exploring ideas encompassed by the book. Supplementary material, $7.50.

Transformation Curriculum Packet for educators, trainers, and group leaders. Assortment of course outlines, projects, and reading lists developed by university and college instructors, $10. All orders should be sent to Interface Press, P.O. Box 42211, Los Angeles, CA 90042. For telephone credit card orders, (800) 626-4557; in California, (800) 233-9228; other calls, (213) 223-2500.

For a sample issue of *Brain/Mind Bulletin* and information on articles collected by theme, send a self-addressed envelope with two stamps.

NETWORKS AND ORGANIZATIONS

Action Linkage
P.O. Box 2240
Wickenburg, AZ 85358
  Networks, task groups,
  international newsletter.

Ark Communications Institute
250 Lafayette Circle
Lafayette, CA 94549
(415) 283-7920
  Computer network of peace
  organizations, publishes
  newsletter, sponsors other
  activities.

Association for Humanistic
  Psychology
325 Ninth Street
San Francisco, CA 94103
(415) 626-2375
  Publishes journal and
  newsletter.

Association for the Study of
  Dreams
Jayne Gackenbach
Department of Psychology
University of Northern Iowa
Cedar Falls, IA 50614
(319) 273-2286

Association for Transpersonal
  Psychology
P.O. Box 3049
Stanford, CA 94305
(415) 327-2066
  Publishes journal and
  newsletter.

Better World Society
1140 Connecticut Avenue, N.W.,
#1006
Washington, D.C. 20036
(202) 331-3770
  Ted Turner's foundation to
  support socially significant
  television programming.

Beyond War Project
222 High Street
Palo Alto, CA 94301
(415) 328-7756

Brain Trainers Network/
  Brainware Development Group
Box 7117
Falls Church, VA 22046
  Sponsored by the American
  Society for Training and
  Development; applies brain
  research to training and
  organizational change.

Canadian Council on Social
  Development
55 Parkdale, P.O. Box 3505
Station C
Ottawa, Ontario K1Y 4G1
Canada
  Promotes volunteer activities.

Center For a Post-Modern World
2060 Alameda Padre Serra, #101
Santa Barbara, CA 93103
(805) 965-0366

Coalition of Holistic Health
  Organizations
1424 Sixteenth Street, N.W.
Suite 105
Washington, D.C. 20036
(202) 328-8600
  Operates Holnet, an
  alternative medicine computer
  network.

Creative Education Foundation
437 Franklin Street
Buffalo, NY 14202
  Publishes the *Journal of Creative
  Behavior.*

Econet
Farallones Institute
15290 Coleman Valley Road
Occidental, CA 95465
(707) 874-3060
  An environmental computer
  network.

Education 2000
Futures Foundation
Box 2451
Denver, CO 80201
(303) 778-1001
    National network of
    community leaders and
    educators.

The Elmwood Institute
P.O. Box 5805
Berkeley, CA 94705
(415) 848-1127
    Founded by Fritjof Capra,
    author of *The Tao of Physics* and
    The Turning Point. Aims to
    facilitate shift to a holistic and
    ecological world view.

Esalen Institute Soviet-American
    Exchange Program
Esalen Institute
Big Sur, CA 93920
(408) 667-2335
    Major organizer of
    conferences; facilitator of
    citizen diplomacy.

John E. Fetzer Foundation
9292 W. KL Avenue
Kalamazoo, MI 49009
(616) 375-2000
    Research and development in
    holistic medicine.

Global Education Associates
552 Park Avenue
East Orange, NJ 07017
(201) 675-1409
    Publishes newsletter and
    monographs.

The Grail Foundation
4717 N. Figueroa Street
Los Angeles, CA 90042
(213) 223-2500
    Marilyn Ferguson's foundation
    invites donations to efforts to
    disseminate new-paradigm
    information and research

findings to relevant networks
and leaders.

Holyearth Foundation
6330 Eagle Harbor Drive, N.E.
Bainbridge Island, WA 98110
(206) 842-7486
    Earthstewards Network,
    journal.

The Hunger Project
P.O. Box 789
San Francisco, CA 94101
(415) 928-8700

Ideas Festival
Telluride Institute
Box 1770
Telluride, CO 81435
    A yearly gathering of and for
    creative people, sponsored by
    Megatrends author John
    Naisbitt.

Institute for Security and
    Cooperation in Outer Space
8 Logan Circle, N.W.
Washington, D.C. 20005
(202) 462-8886
    Promotes peaceful
    development of space, with
    emphasis on ending arms race.
    Publishes newsletter.

Institute for the Advancement of
    Near-Death Studies
Department of Psychiatry
University of Connecticut
    Health Center
Farmington, CT 06032
    Publishes newsletter and
    journal.

Institute of Noetic Sciences
475 Gate Five Road, Suite 300
Sausalito, CA 94965
(415) 331-5650
    Publishes newsletter and
    journal. Supports research,
    conferences on the mind-body
    link.

Interfaith Center on Corporate
  Responsibility
475 Riverside Drive, Suite 566
New York, NY 10115
  Sponsors conferences,
  publishes newsletter.

Learning Resources Network
  (LERN)
P.O. Box 1448
Manhattan, KS 66502
(913) 539-5376
  National consulting center for
  noncredit adult learning.
  Publishes newsletter.

Meta Network
Metasystems Design Group, Inc.
2000 N. 15th Street, Suite 103
Arlington, VA 22201
(703) 243-6622
  International home computer
  network of those interested in
  human potential. Publishes
  newsletter and reports from
  conferences.

The Networking Institute
296 Newton Street, Suite 350
Waltham, MA 02154
(617) 891-4727
  Computer network, publishes
  quarterly *Networking Newsletter*
  and semiannual journal.
  Membership $75 per year.

New Dimensions Radio
  Network News
New Dimensions Foundation
P.O. Box 410510
San Francisco, CA 94141
(415) 563-8899
  Independent producer of radio
  programs on personal and
  social change aired on 100
  stations. Publishes newsletter.

New Horizons For Learning
Box 51140
Seattle, WA 98115

(206) 621-7609
Helps other networks get started.
International network, publishes
newsletter on educational
innovation.

Organization Transformation
Metasystems Design Group, Inc.
2000 N. 15th Street, Suite 103
Arlington, VA 22201
(703) 243-6622
  Professional network.

Peacenet
1918 Bonita
Berkeley, CA 94704
(415) 486-0264
  International personal
  computer-based network of
  peace movements throughout
  the world.

Planet Art Network
262 Spruce Street
Boulder, CO 80302
(303) 443-4328
  International artists network.

Public Interest Media Project
P.O. Box 14066
Philadelphia, PA 19123
(215) 992-0227
  Publishes newsletter.

Results
245 Second Street, N.E.
Washington, D.C. 20002
(202) 543-9340
  Anti-hunger lobbying
  network.

Search for Common Ground
1701 K Street, N.W., Suite 403
Washington, D.C. 20006
(202) 835-0777
  Approaches arms control
  issues by bringing together
  people of dissimilar views.

Spiritual Emergency Network
Institute of Transpersonal
    Psychology
250 Oak Grove Avenue
Menlo Park, CA 94025
(415) 327-2776
    Worldwide network for
    individuals experiencing
    "severe spiritual distress."

Wondertree Education Society
P.O. Box 35243, Station E
Vancouver, B.C. V6M 4G4
Canada
(604) 732-9902
    Publishes journal.

World Future Society
4916 St. Elmo Avenue
Bethesda, MD 20814
(301) 656-8274
    Publishes magazine, quarterly,
    and newsletter. Sponsors large
    annual conference.

World Research Foundation
15300 Ventura Boulevard
Suite 405
Sherman Oaks, CA 91403
(818) 907-5483
    Collects and disseminates
    information on
    complementary medicine
    worldwide; international
    personal computer network.

PERIODICALS
AND RESOURCE
DIRECTORIES

Advances
Institute for the
    Advancement of Health
16 E. 53rd Street
New York, NY 10022
(212) 832-8282
    Quarterly journal exploring
    connections between bodily
    health and the mind; $35 per
    year.

Brain/Mind Bulletin
P.O. Box 42211
Los Angeles, CA 90042
(213) 223-2500
    Six-page news bulletin
    published monthly by
    Marilyn Ferguson, $35
    per year.

Chop Wood, Carry Water
Rick Fields and editors of
    New Age Journal, 1984; $11.95.
Jeremy P. Tarcher/
St. Martin's Press
175 Fifth Avenue
New York, NY 10010
(800) 221-7945

The Essential Whole Earth Catalog
Point Foundation, 1986; $14.
27 Gate Five Road
Sausalito, CA 94965
(415) 331-6249

John Naisbitt's Trend Letter
Naisbitt Group
P.O. Box 25536
Washington, D.C. 20007
(202) 833-3822
    Biweekly, $87 per year.

The Kids' Whole Future Catalog
Paula Taylor, 1982; $8.99
  hardcover/$6.95 softcover.
Random House
201 E. 50th Street
New York, NY 10022
(800) 638-6460

The Networking Book:
People Connecting With People
Jessica Lipnack and Jeffrey
  Stamps, 1986; $12.95.
Routledge and Kegan Paul
The Networking Institute
296 Newton Street, Suite 350
Waltham, MA 02154
(617) 891-4727

New Age Journal
342 Western Avenue
Brighton, MA 02135-9907
(617) 787-2005
  Bimonthly, $24 per year.

New Options
New World Alliance
P.O. Box 19324
Washington, D.C. 20036
(202) 822-0929
  Monthly, politically oriented
  newsletter; $25 per year.

The Rapids of Change:
  Social Entrepreneurship
  in Turbulent Times
Robert Theobald and the Action
  Linkage Network, 1987; $16.95.
Knowledge Systems, Inc.
7777 W. Morris Street
Indianapolis, IN 46231
(317) 241-0749
  Includes resource list.

Revision: A Journal of Consciousness
  and Change
Rudi Foundation
P.O. Box 1973
Cambridge, MA 02238
(617) 354-5827
  Biyearly, featuring scholarly
  philosophical inquiries on
  holism; $16 per year.

The Self-Help Sourcebook
Edward Madara and Abigail
  Meese, 1986; $8.
St. Clares-Riverside Foundation
Self-Help Clearinghouse
(Attn: *Sourcebook*)
1 Indian Road
Denville, NJ 07834
(201) 625-7101

Utne Reader
2732 W. 43rd Street
Minneapolis, MN 55410
(612) 929-2670
  Bimonthly, $24 per year. "The
  best of the alternative press."

Whole Again Resource Guide
  (1986-87 ed.)
Tim Ryan and Patricia J. Case;
  $24.95.
SourceNet
P.O. Box 6767
Santa Barbara, CA 93160
(805) 964-6066
  Forty categories of personal
  and social interest, including
  local alternative directories.

Whole Earth Review
27 Gate Five Road
Sausalito, CA 94965
(415) 332-1716
  Quarterly, $18 per year. An
  offshoot of Stewart Brand's
  Whole Earth Catalog.

Windstar Journal
The Windstar Foundation
P.O. Box 286
Snowmass, CO 81654
(303) 927-4777
  Quarterly, $18 per year.
  Published by John Denver's
  center for ecological concerns.

Readings
and References

This bibliography was designed to provide access to further exploration rather than for scholarly documentation. Most books are listed without detailed publishing information because they can be readily found through libraries, bookstores, and *Books in Print.* Many books are available in a number of different editions. For references more difficult to obtain, more detailed information is given.

These lists are by no means inclusive, as there are many valuable books available on most subjects covered. For the most part, those mentioned are in print, communicate clearly, and will lead the reader to further resources. Note that Appendix B lists supplementary resources: networks and periodicals.

In addition to technical scientific references cited for chapters 3, 6, 8, and 9, a major source was the author's newsletter, *Brain/Mind Bulletin* (interviews, summaries of papers delivered at conferences and published in scientific journals); listing all of the original citations would make for a voluminous bibliography, since material was drawn from ninety-six issues — four years of reporting. Those wishing to pursue a specific topic via *Brain/Mind Bulletin* "theme packs" can find further information in Appendix B.

CHAPTER 1. The Conspiracy

Sources of quoted material, other than those cited in the chapter, include Beatrice Bruteau's essay in *Anima* Spring 1977, Ilya Prigogine's lectures at the University of Texas, April 1978, *The Phenomenon of Man* by Pierre Teilhard de Chardin, *Democracy in America* by Alexis de Tocqueville, *Understanding Media* by Marshall McLuhan, *The Transformations of Man* by Lewis Mumford, *An Experiment in Depth* by P.W. Martin, and *The Whole Earth Papers* (see periodicals list in Appendix B).

CHAPTER 2. Premonitions of Transformation and Conspiracy

In addition to the books named in the text, sources for quoted material include *Saviors of God* by Nikos Kazantzakis, *The Growth of Civilization* by Arnold Toynbee, *The Hunger of Eve* by Barbara Marx Hubbard, *The New American Ideology* by George Cabot Lodge, *The Transformative Vision* by Jose Arguelles, *Survival of the Wisest* by Jonas Salk, *Between Man and Man* by Martin Buber, *Sources*, edited by Theodore Roszak, a lecture by Roszak at the Claremont Colleges in 1976. Authors of *The Changing Image of Man* (Policy Research Report #4 of the Center for the Study of Public Policy, Stanford Research Institute, Menlo Park, California, prepared for the Charles F. Kettering Foundation) were Joseph Campbell, Duane Elgin, Willis Harman, Arthur Hastings, O. W. Markley, Floyd Matson, Brendan O'Regan, and Leslie Schneider.

CHAPTER 3. Transformation: Brains Changing, Minds Changing

Sources not identified in the text: *Flatland* by Edwin A. Abbott, *Choices* by Frederic Flach, *The Varieties of Religious Experience* by William James, *My Belief: Essays on Life and Art* by Hermann Hesse, *Focusing* by Eugene Gendlin, and various writings and lectures by Ernest Hilgard, including an article in *Pain* 1: 213–231. Meditation increasing blood flow to the brain was reported by Ron Jevning and co-workers at the University of California/Irvine to the American Physiological Society annual meeting in 1979; the functional split-brain of psychosomatic patients in *Psychoanalytic Quarterly* 46: 220–244; the psychedelic effect of paying attention to one's awareness was reported in *Archives of General Psychiatry* 33: 867–876; theta bursts in the EEGs of long-term meditators in *Electroencephalography and Clinical Neurophysiology* 42: 397–405. Data on meditation phenomena, shifts in states of consciousness, brain chemicals, and specialized functions of the left and right hemisphere were drawn from various issues of *Brain/Mind Bulletin*.

Books of related interest: *The Language of Change* by Paul Watzlawick, *The Brilliant Function of Pain* by Milton Ward, *The Experience of Insight: A Natural Unfolding* by Joseph Goldstein, *The Natural Mind* by Andrew Weil, *The Brain Revolution* by Marilyn Ferguson, *The Stream of Consciousness*, edited by Kenneth Pope and Jerome Singer, and *Conscious-*

ness: Brain, States of Awareness, and Mysticism, edited by Daniel Goleman and Richard Davidson.

CHAPTER 4. *Crossover: People Changing*

Edward Hall's discussion of time appears in *Beyond Culture* and in an interview in *Psychology Today*, July 1976; Jonas Salk's remarks were made at the theory conference of the Association for Humanistic Psychology in 1975. *On Waking Up* by Marian Coe Brezic is published by Valkyrie Press, 2135 1st Ave. S., St. Petersburg, Florida 33712. Gabriel Saul Heilig's statement is in his afterword to *Tenderness Is Strength*, by Harold Lyons, Jr. Aldous Huxley's discussion of psychedelic drugs originally appeared in the *Saturday Evening Post* and is included in *Collected Essays*.

Related reading: On the over-all subject of personal transformation, Viktor Frankl's *Man's Search for Meaning*, Roberto Assagioli's *Psychosynthesis*, Abraham Maslow's *Toward a Psychology of Being* and *The Farther Reaches of Human Nature*, and C. G. Jung's *Modern Man in Search of a Soul* and *The Development of Personality*.

A variety of approaches to the transformative process: *Halfway Through the Door* by Alan Arkin, *The Centered Skier* by Denise McCluggage, *The Ultimate Athlete* by George Leonard, *Open Secrets: A Western Guide to Tibetan Buddhism* by Walt Anderson, *The Gurdjieff Work* by Kathleen Speeth, *The Last Barrier* by Reshad Feild, *Mindways* by Louis Savary and Margaret Ehlen-Miller, *At a Journal Workshop* by Ira Progroff, *Awakening Intuition* by Frances Vaughan, *Meditation: Journey to the Self* by Ardis Whitman, *The Varieties of the Meditative Experience* by Daniel Goleman, *Journey of Awakening: A Meditator's Guidebook* by Ram Dass, *Freedom in Meditation* by Patricia Carrington, *The TM Technique* by Peter Russell, *Mind Therapies/Body Therapies* by George Feiss, *Giving in to Get Your Way* by Terry Dobson and Victor Miller, *Zen and the Art of Motorcycle Maintenance* by Robert Pirsig, *The Silva Mind Control Method* by Jose Silva and Philip Miele, *Getting There Without Drugs* by Buryl Payne, *Body Awareness in Action: A Study of the Alexander Technique* by Frank Pierce Jones, *The Roots of Consciousness* by Jeffrey Mishlove, *Books for Inner Development: The Yes! Guide*, edited by Cris Popenoe; *Mindstyles, Lifestyles* by Nathaniel Lande; *The Art of Seeing* and *The Doors of Perception* by Aldous Huxley; *Jacob Atabet* by Michael Murphy, *Drawing on the Right Side of the Brain* by Betty Edwards, *Est: 60 Hours That Transform Your Life* by Adelaide Bry, *Making Life Work* by Robert Hargrove, *Actualizations: Beyond Est* by James Martin, and various books of Carlos Castaneda (*The Teachings of Don Juan, Journey to Ixtlan, A Separate Reality, Tales of Power*). See also listings under Chapter 11.

CHAPTER 5. *The American Matrix for Transformation*

American Transcendentalism 1830–1860: An Intellectual Inquiry by Paul F. Boller, Jr.; *Revivals, Awakenings, and Reform* by William McLoughlin;

California: The Vanishing Dream by Michael Davy; *California: The New Society* by Remi Nadeau; *The California Revolution* by Carey McWilliams; *The Next Development in Man* by Lancelot Law Whyte. George Leonard described his encounter with Michael Murphy in his foreword to *Out in Inner Space* by Dr. Stephen A. Applebaum; James Alan McPherson's statement in *Atlantic*, December 1978. Anthony F. C. Wallace's classic essay on revitalization movements was first published in *American Anthropology* 58: 264–281.

CHAPTER 6. Liberating Knowledge: News from the Frontiers of Science

Alfred Korzybski's ideas, set forth in *Science and Sanity*, have been explained in simpler terms by a number of authors, including Stuart Chase in *Power of Words*. Barbara Brown's views on the implications of biofeedback have been expressed in interviews, lectures, and three books (*New Mind, New Body; Stress and the Art of Biofeedback*, and the forthcoming *Supermind.*) See also *Beyond Biofeedback* by Elmer and Alyce Green.

The punctuated equilibrium theory of evolution was discussed by Stephen Jay Gould in *Natural History*, May 1977 and by Niles Eldredge at "New Horizons in Science," a 1978 meeting sponsored by the Council for the Advancement of Science. Evidence for multiple hominid ancestors of human beings was reviewed by Gould in *Natural History*, April 1976, in an article on Richard Leakey in *Time*, November 7, 1977, and in Leakey's book, *People of the Lake*. Szent-Gyorgyi's remarks on chance mutation appeared in *The Journal of Individual Psychology* and in *Synthesis* Spring 1974. The report on intervening sequences in genetic material appeared in *New Scientist* May 1, 1978.

Ilya Prigogine's statements were taken from interviews, lectures, a special December 1977 edition of the *Texas Times* (published by the University of Texas system, Austin), an article on social dynamics in *Chemical and Engineering News*, April 16, 1979, and *Thermodynamic Theory of Structure, Stability, and Fluctuations* by P. Glandsdorff and Prigogine. Prigogine's somewhat technical book on the theory of dissipative structures, *From Being to Becoming*, will be published by W. H. Freeman Co. in 1980; his popular book, tentatively titled *A Dialogue with Nature*, will be published by Doubleday. The theory of dissipative structures is central to Erich Jantsch's *The Self-Organizing Universe: Scientific and Human Implications of the Emerging Paradigm of Evolution*. (To receive the special issues of *Brain/Mind Bulletin* on Prigogine's theory, send a stamped, self-addressed business-size envelope to Box 42211, Los Angeles 90042.) The relationship of dissipative structure to brain function is discussed in *Neurosciences Research Progress Bulletin, Volume 12*, MIT Press, by A. K. Katchalsky et al.

A long technical article in *Scientific American*, November 1979, examines the evidence for Bell's theorem. The excerpts quoted from Jeremy Bernstein and Robert Jastrow appeared in essays in the *Los*

Angeles Times. For current surveys and bibliographies of parapsychology: *Advances in Parapsychological Research, Volume 1, Psychokinesis*, and *Volume 2, Extrasensory Perception*, edited by Stanley Krippner (Plenum), and *Brain, Mind, and Parapsychology*, edited by Betty Shapin and Lisette Coly.

Karl Pribram's synthesis of his holographic brain model with David Bohm's view of the physical universe is in *Consciousness and the Brain*, edited by Gordon Globus et al. and *Perceiving, Acting, and Knowing*, edited by R. E. Shaw and J. Bransford. Pribram's remarks in the text were taken from lectures, conference proceedings, and interviews (*Human Behavior*, May 1978, and *Psychology Today*, February 1979). David Bohm's theory of the implicate universe is in *Quantum Theory and Beyond*, edited by Ted Bastin; *Foundations of Physics* 1 (4), 3 (2), and 5 (1); *Mind in Nature*, no named author, published by University Press of America, and a long interview in *Re-Visions* (Summer/Fall 1978).

Other books of interest: *Sensitive Chaos* by Theodor Schwenk, *Stalking the Wild Pendulum* by Itzhak Bentov, *Janus* by Arthur Koestler, *The Silent Pulse* by George Leonard, *On Aesthetics in Science*, edited by Judith Weschler, *The Reflexive Universe* and *The Bell Notes* by Arthur Young, *Grow or Die: The Unifying Principle of Transformation* by George T. L. Land, *The Intelligent Universe* by David Foster, and *Personal Knowledge* by Michael Polanyi.

CHAPTER 7. *Right Power*

In addition to books and authors identified in the chapter, *New American Ideology* by George Cabot Lodge, *Democracy in America* by Alexis de Tocqueville, John Stuart Mill's essay, "On Liberty" and Henry David Thoreau's essay, "Civil Disobedience"; *Gandhi's Truth* by Erik Erikson; *Gandhi the Man* by Eknath Easwaran is published by Nilgiri Press, Box 477, Petaluma, CA 94952; interviews with Jerry Rubin and his book, *Growing (Up) at 37*; article by Tom Hayden in the *Los Angeles Times*; John Platt's *Step to Man*; essay by Melvin Gurtov adapted from *Making Changes: Humanist Politics for the New Age*; *Man for Himself* and *The Sane Society* by Erich Fromm; *On Personal Power* by Carl Rogers; interview with James MacGregor Burns in *Psychology Today*, October 1978; *An Incomplete Guide to the Future* by Willis Harman; "The Pornography of Everyday Life," an essay by Warren Bennis in the *New York Times*; interview with John Vasconcellos in *New Age*, October 1978; Harold Baron's article in *Focus/Midwest*, Volume 11, No. 69; "Women and Power" monograph from *Whole Earth Papers* (see Appendix B, periodicals); *After Reason* by Arianna Stassinopoulos, scenarios of the future by Stahrl Edmunds in *The Futurist*, February 1979. *Revivals, Awakenings, and Reform* by William McLoughlin, *Beyond Culture* by Edward Hall and interview with Hall in *Psychology Today*, July 1976.

Virginia Hine's description of SPINS, "The Basic Paradigm of a Future Socio-Cultural System" first appeared originally in *World Issues*, April/May 1977, published by the Center for the Study of Democratic

Institutions. Hine and Luther Gerlach wrote *People, Power, Change: Movements of Social Transformation* and *Lifeway Leap: The Dynamics of Change in America*. See also Gerlach's article on movements of revolutionary change in *American Behavioral Scientist* 14 (6): 812–835.

Related books of interest include *A Liberating Vision* by John Vasconcellos, *New Age Politics* by Mark Satin, *Many-Dimensional Man* by James Ogilvy, and *The Making of a Counter Culture, Where the Wasteland Ends*, and *Person/Planet* by Theodore Roszak. *Resource Manual for a Living Revolution* by Virginia Coover et al. is available from Movement for a New Society (see Appendix B).

CHAPTER 8. *Healing Ourselves*

Richard Selzer's essay about Yeshi Donden, the Tibetan doctor, appeared in *Harper's*, January 1976 and *Reader's Digest*, August 1976. The U.S. Senate Subcommittee on Health report #94–887 on humanistic medicine was issued May 14, 1976. Edward Carpenter's view of health as a governing harmony appears in his book, *Civilization: Its Cause and Cure*. The experiments on the role of the physician's belief in placebo effect were described in *Persuasion and Healing* by Jerome Frank. Rick Ingrasci on the placebo: *New Age*, May 1979. Kenneth Pelletier on stress: *Medical Self-Care* 5. The effect of confronting or avoiding: *Psychophysiology* 14: 517–521.

The role of the brain in the immune response, *Science* 191: 435–440, and *Psychosomatic Medicine* 37: 333–340; the new model of the immune system as a cognitive process, proposed by Francisco Varela of the University of Colorado Medical Center, Denver, and a Brazilian allergist, Nelson Paz, *Medical Hypothesis* and *Brain/Mind Bulletin* February 6, 1978; the effect of bereavement on the immune system, *Lancet*, April 16, 1977; the link between heart and brain, *Journal of the American Medical Association*, 234: 9 and *Science* 199: 449–451; stress as a "co-carcinogen," *Clinical Psychiatry News* 5 (12): 40 and *Science News* 113 (3): 44–45. See also *The Broken Heart: The Medical Consequences of Loneliness* by James J. Lynch; *Getting Well Again: A Guide to Overcoming Cancer for Patients and Their Families* by Carl and Stephanie Simonton; *Imagery of Cancer* by Jeanne Achterberg and Frank Lawlis.

On the body as pattern and process: *Rolfing: The Integration of Human Structures* by Ida Rolf; Wallace Ellerbroek's article on disease as process first appeared in *Perspectives in Biology and Medicine*: 16 (2): 240–262.

Anatomy of an Illness, a book by Norman Cousins, describes his treatment and recovery, based on the much-reprinted article from the *New England Journal of Medicine*; see also *Saturday Review*, May 28, 1977; George Engel's essay appeared in *Science* 196: 129–136. The new test for entry into medical college: the author's article, "Once and Future Physician," in *Human Behavior* February 1977. Maggie Kuhn's comments were made during a lecture in Los Angeles in 1977.

For further reading: *Healing from Within* by Dennis Jaffe, *Bodymind* by Ken Dychtwald, *Free Yourself from Pain* by David Bresler, *The Mind/Body*

Effect by Herbert Benson, *Mind as Healer, Mind as Slayer* by Kenneth Pelletier; *Therapeutic Touch* by Delores Krieger; *Wellness*, edited by Cris Popenoe (compendium of 1,500 books with publishers' addresses); *Maggie Kuhn on Aging* by Dieter Hessel; *Your Second Life* by Gay Gaer Luce (based on the SAGE program); *Life's Second Half: The Dynamics of Aging* by Jerome Ellison; *Maternal-Infant Attachment* by Marshall Klaus; *The Competent Infant: Research and Commentary*, edited by Joseph Stone et al.; an article on hospices, *Science* 193: 389–391.

CHAPTER 9. *Flying and Seeing: New Ways to Learn*

Leslie Hart's article on "brain-antagonistic schools," *Phi Delta Kappan*, February 1978; Hermann Hesse's essay on school from *Beneath the Wheel*; John Gowan on creativity from *Journal of Creative Behavior*, 2 (2); Edward Hall on culture from *Psychology Today* interview, July 1976; Synectics and Title I students, *Psychiatric Annals* special issue on creativity 8 (3); Joseph Meeker on "ambidextrous education" in *North American Review*, Summer 1975; Eskimo children, volume 4 of *Children of Crisis* by Robert Coles; expectations, *Pygmalion in the Classroom* by Robert Rosenthal and Lenore Jacobson and *Experimenter Effects in Behavioral Research* by Rosenthal; "Miss A," *Harvard Educational Review* 48: 1–31; movement toward transpersonal education, *Phi Delta Kappan*, April 1977; over-obedience, *Obedience to Authority* by Stanley Milgram, *Science News*, August 20, 1977, and *Journal of Personality and Social Psychology*, July 1977; on "Why Johnny Can't Disobey" in *The Humanist*, September-October 1979. The Milwaukee Project has been described in a number of articles and book chapters; for a list of publications, send a stamped, self-addressed envelope to Rehabilitation Research, Waisman Center, University of Wisconsin, Madison, Wisconsin 53706. Material on brain-hemisphere specialization, nonverbal sensitivity, the facilitative behaviors movement, the value of reframing problems, and many other topics was drawn from *Brain/ Mind Bulletin*, October 1975–November 1979.

Related reading: *Education and the Brain*, edited by Jeanne Chall and Allan Mirsky; *Alternatives in Education: Schools and Programs* by Allan Glatthorn; *Beyond the Scientific*, edited by Arthur Foshay and Irving Morrissett (published by Social Science Education Consortium, 855 Broadway, Boulder, Colorado 80302); *Values in Education* by Max Lerner; *The Metaphoric Mind* by Bob Samples; *The Wholeschool Book* by Robert Samples, Cheryl Charles, Dick Barnhart; *Transpersonal Education: A Curriculum for Feeling and Being* by Gay Hendricks and James Fadiman; *The Centering Book* by Hendricks and Russell Wills; *The Second Centering Book* by Hendricks and Thomas B. Roberts; *Meditating with Children* by Deborah Rozman; *The New Games Book*, by Andrew Fleugelman; *The Brain Revolution* by Marilyn Ferguson; *The Brain Book* by Peter Russell; *Suggestology* by Georgyi Lozanov; *Superlearning*, by Sheila Ostrander and Lynn Schroeder; *The Relevance of Education* by Jerome S. Bruner; *The Success Fearing Personality* by Donnah

Canavan-Gumpert et al.; *Four Psychologies Applied to Education*, edited by Thomas B. Roberts; *Reversals* (an account of dyslexia) by Eileen Simpson; *Self-Fulfilling Prophecies* by Russell A. Jones.

CHAPTER 10. *The Transformation of Values and Vocation*

In addition to books and other sources mentioned in the text: Willis Harman on values, *Fields Within Fields* 5 (1); Lawrence Peter on voluntary simplicity, *Human Behavior*, August 1978; L. R. Mobley's "Values Option Process," a paper delivered at the 1978 conference of the General Systems Research Association; *On Caring* by Milton Mayerhoff; study of high-achieving managers summarized in *Training*, February 1979; problems of productivity, *Training*, January 1979; information on voluntary simplicity report and VALS reports Center for the Study of Social Policy, Stanford Research Institute, Menlo Park, California. Right- and left-brain strategies of managers and planners, *Psychophysiology* 14: 385–392; McGill study, *Brain/Mind Bulletin*, August 2, 1976; intuition and inference in executive decision-making: *Fortune*, April 23, 1979; readiness of workers to learn intuitive methods: *Planning Review*, September 1978; interview with Sim Van der Ryn, *New Age*, March 1979; quote on "high intention" from *Werner Erhard* by William W. Bartley III; creative imagination as wealth from *Humanomics* by Eugen Loebl; danger of technology as master, *Computer Power and Human Reason* by Joseph Weizenbaum. A book by Bob Schwartz on the new entrepreneur will be published in 1980 by Simon and Schuster.

CHAPTER 11. *Spiritual Adventure: Connection to the Source*

Zbigniew Brzezinski's comments appeared in a James Reston interview for the *New York Times* syndicate, December 31, 1978; Sy Safransky's essay in *The Sun*, published in Durham, North Carolina; Robert Ellwood's historic view, *Alternative Altars: Unconventional and Eastern Spirituality in America*. Herbert Koplowitz's monograph on Unitary Operational Thinking was summarized in *Brain/Mind Bulletin*, October 2, 1978. Ron Browning's statement on transcending the system is from his 1978 dissertation, "Psychotherapeutic Change East and West: Buddhist Psychological Paradigm of Change with Reference to Psychoanalysis." Jung's comment on the transpersonal perspective is taken from his foreword and commentary in *The Secret of the Golden Flower* by Richard Wilhelm; Karl Pribram's speculation on mystical access to the implicate order, *Psychology Today* interview February 1979; Capra's "seeing" of cascades of energy, *The Tao of Physics*; psychedelics facilitating access to the holographic domain, Stanislav Grof's article in *Re-Visions*, Winter-Spring 1979 and his book, *LSD Psychotherapy*; the image of the ocean and outcropping of rock in Karl Sperber's article in *Journal of Humanistic Psychology* 19 (1); William James's definition of God from *The Varieties of Religious Experience*.

Related reading: *Forgotten Truths* by Huston Smith; *A Sense of the*

Cosmos: The Encounter of Modern Science and Ancient Truth by Jacob Needleman; *The Road Less Traveled* by M. Scott Peck; *Life After Life* and *Reflections on Life After Life*, by Raymond Moody, Jr.; *Meister Eckhart*, translated by Raymond Blakney; *The Way of a Pilgrim* and *The Cloud of Unknowing*, authors unknown; *Coming Home* by Lex Hixon; *Shamanic Voices* by Joan Halifax; *Ten Rungs* by Martin Buber; *Tales of the Dervish* by Idries Shah; *Reflections of Mind* by Tarthang Tulku; *Meditation in Action* by Chogyam Trungpa; *What Is Zen?* and *An Introduction to Zen Buddhism* by D. T. Suzuki; *The Master Game* by Robert S. de Ropp; *Transpersonal Psychologies*, edited by Charles Tart; *The Rediscovery of Meaning* by Owen Barfield; *The Book (on the Taboo Against Knowing Who You Are)*, *The Wisdom of Insecurity*, *The Joyous Cosmology* and *The Essence of Alan Watts* (a posthumous anthology) by Alan Watts; *Process Theology: An Introductory Exposition* by John B. Cobb, Jr. and David Griffin; *Toward Final Personality Integration* by A. Reza Aresteh. See also listings under Chapter 4.

A scholarly selected bibliography, "Science and Parascience," relating to the integration of scientific and mystical views, has been compiled under the auspices of the Program for the Study of New Religious Movements in America ($2 from the Graduate Theological Union Library, 2451 Ridge Road, Berkeley, California 94709).

CHAPTER 12. *Human Connections: Relationships Changing*

Martin Buber's "secrecy without a secret" passage is in *Between Man and Man*; Krishnamurti on love from *Freedom from the Known*; John Cuber on the changing attitude toward "rules" and the views of Rustum and Della Roy on monogamy are in *Intimate Life Styles: Marriage and Its Alternatives*, edited by Jack and Joann DeLora; Joel Kramer and Diana Alstad on transforming sexuality, from *New Age* August 1978; Adrienne Rich account from *Of Woman Born*; Ted Clark and Dennis Jaffe in *Grassroots*, July 1973; Hossain Danesh's article on the authoritarian family and its adolescents, *Canadian Psychiatric Association Journal* 23: 479–485. See also *Androgyny* by June Singer.

CHAPTER 13. *The Whole-Earth Conspiracy*

Aurelio Peccei's reference to the groups that are the "yeast of change" appeared in *The Futurist*, December 1978; The Future in Our Hands movement, in *New Age*, October 1979; the efforts of Les Vertes in *Co-Evolution Quarterly*, Winter 1977-1978; Patricia Mische on women and power, *Whole Earth Papers* 1 (8) and James Baines on the peace paradigm, *Whole Earth Papers* 1 (1); some of the material about the Hunger Project was taken from various issues of the project's newspaper, *A Shift in the Wind*. The Tolstoi passage was published in *The New Spirit*, edited by Havelock Ellis.

Name Index*

See Also Subject Index

Adams, John, 121
African Genesis, 161
Airliehouse, 261
Alcott, Bronson, 47
Alighieri, Dante (*see* Dante), 150
Alliance for Survival, 200
Alstad, Diana, 398–399
Alternative Birth Centers, 270–271
American Association for the
  Advancement of Science, 147
American Association of Medical
  Colleges, 267
American Council of Life
  Insurance, 351
American Holistic Medical
  Association, 265
American Home Economics
  Association, 402
American Medical Association,
  269n, 270
American Medical Students
  Association, 264
American Productivity Center, 350
American Psychological Asso-
  ciation, 221
American Society for Psychical
  Research, 175n
Amnesty International, 240
Anna Karenina, 399
Another Place, 336
Appollinaire, Guillaume, 293
Arcosanti, 336
Ardrey, Robert, 161
Arguelles, Jose, 62, 214, 319–320
Arnheim, Rudolf, 160n
Ashen, Ruth Ananda, 55
Assagioli, Roberto, 220, 365, 420
Association for Holistic Health, 262
Association for Humanistic Psychol-
  ogy, 39, 141n, 220, 236, 313
Aurobindo Ashram, 138
Aurobindo, Sri, 420
Auroville, 336
Avery, Oswald, 177

Bach, Richard, 115
Baines, James, 411–412
Baker, Russell, 33
Balzac, Honoré de, 385

Barker, Eric, 117
Baron, Harold, 208
Bartley, William, 90n
Bates, William, 100
Bateson, Gregory, 59, 420
Bay Area Association for Alternatives
  in Psychiatry, 274
de Beauvoir, Simone, 395–396
Belas, Ula, 179n
Bell, J. S., 171
Bellow, Saul, 107, 110, 366
Benedict, Ruth, 420
Bennis, Warren, 194
Benson, Herbert, 237
Bentov, Itzhak, 179n
Bergier, Jacques, 53–54, 152
Bergson, Henri, 167, 184
Berkeley Christian Coalition, 369–370
Bernstein, Jeremy, 170
Berry, Wendell, 336
Berryman, John, 99
Bhagavad Gita, 47
Birth Without Violence, 234
Blake, William, 46–47, 119, 379, 381
Bohm, David, 46, 180–181, 186, 321
Bohr, Niels, 151, 173
Book of Mirdad, 176
Boorstin, Daniel, 124
Borghese, G. A., 65
Borman, Leonard, 218
Boulding, Elise, 420
Boulding, Kenneth, 55n, 222, 305, 420
Boyle, Kay, 85
Bradbury, Ray, 92
Brave New World, 54
Brezic, Marian Coe, 114–115
Briarpatch, 220, 353–354
British Broadcasting Corporation, 218
Broder, David, 133
Brooke, Rupert, 361
Brown, Barbara, 153
Brown, Charlie (*Peanuts*), 310
Brown, Jerry, 216, 231, 235
Brown, Norman O., 137
Brown, Sam, 207
Browning, Ron, 372
Bruner, Jerome, 298, 310
Brunner, John, 88, 99
Bruteau, Beatrice, 26
Brzezinski, Zbigniew, 363–364
Buber, Martin, 52, 80, 191, 244, 387,
  392–393, 394, 420

*Many of the names and titles that appear in References and Readings are not included in this index. See also alphabetical lists of networks and periodicals in Appendix B.

Bucke, Richard, 48
Burbank, Luther, 175n
Burns, James MacGregor, 121, 201–202, 208, 227, 231, 266
Business Exchange, 333
Butler, Samuel, 73

California Commission on Crime Control and Violence Prevention, 235
California: The Great Exception, 133
Callenbach, Ernest, 358
Campbell, Joseph, 58
Campbell, Susan, 394n
Cappa, Laurel, 265
Capra, Fritjof, 145, 149–150, 152, 172, 261n, 374
Carlson, Rick, 261, 261n
Carlyle, Thomas, 47
Carnegie Council on Children, 399
Carnegie Foundation for the Advancement of Teaching, 305–306
Carpenter, Edward, 30–31, 48, 63, 69, 101, 105, 214, 248, 310
Carrel, Alexis, 175n
Carter, Jimmy, 231
Castaneda, Carlos, 59, 95, 97, 130, 137, 184, 291–292, 321
Catherine of Siena, Saint, 102
Cavafy, C. P., 102, 189
Center for the Advanced Study in the Behavioral Sciences, 137, 178
Center for Attitudinal Healing, 272
Center for Integral Medicine, The, 262
Center for the Study of Democratic Institutions, 137
Central Intelligence Agency, 126n
Challenge of California, 133
Changing Image of Man, The, 61, 342
Channon, Jim, 347
Chapin, Harry, 346, 347
Charge-a-Trade, 333
Chew, Geoffrey, 172
Childhood's End, 62, 157–158, 294
Clark, Barbara, 309
Clark, Ted, 400
Clarke, Arthur, 62, 157–158, 294
Cobbs, Price, 139
Coleridge, Samuel, 47
Commager, Henry Steele, 230
Committee for the Future, 57
Commonweal, 39
Communications Workers of America, 351
Continental Drift, 133
Cooperative College Community, 335–336

Copernicus, 27
Cori, Carl, 311
Corrigan, Mairead, 240
Cosmic Consciousness, 48
Couple's Journey, The, 394n
Cousins, Norman, 264
Crossing Point, The, 60
Cuber, John, 398
cummings, e. e., 68
da Cusa, Nicholas, 381

Damman, Erik, 409
Dancing Wu Li Masters, The, 172
Danesh, Hossain, 401
Dante Alighieri, 150
Darwin, Charles, 53, 158
Daumal, René, 82
Davy, Michael, 134, 135
Death at an Early Age, 284
Demian, 49, 82
Democracy in America, 37–38
Denver Free University, 319
Denver, John, 113, 415
Dewey, John, 47
Dial, The, 123
Dickinson, Emily, 47
Dirac, Paul, 173
Divine Comedy, The, 150
Dolgoff, Eugene, 179n
Donne, John, 256
Doors of Perception, The, 105–106
Dorothy (*Wizard of Oz*), 85
Dostoevski, Fyodor, 387, 402
Dubos, René, 55n
Durrell, Lawrence, 187

East/West Journal, 130
Easwaran, Eknath, 238–239, 335
Eccles, John, 152
Economics As If People Mattered, 356
Ecotopia, 358
Eddington, Arthur, 182
Edge of History, The, 317
Edison, Thomas, 175n
Edmunds, Stahrl, 238
Einstein, Albert, 27, 149, 150, 175n, 402, 420
Eldredge, Niles, 158
Eliade, Mircea, 55n
Eliot, T. S., 117, 184, 363, 385
Ellerbroek, Wallace, 257
Ellis, Havelock, 227–228
Ellis, John Tracy, 368–369
Ellison, Jerome, 273
Ellwood, Robert, 367
Emerson, Ralph Waldo, 47, 122, 123, 135, 184, 367

Engel, George, 266
Erhard, Werner, 113, 261n, 351–352, 413, 420
Erikson, Erik, 200
Esalen Institute, 87, 98, 137–140
d'Espagnet, Bernard, 172
Eupsychean Network, 56
Executive Trade Club, 333

Family Hospital of Milwaukee, New Life Center, 270–271
Fantini, Mario, 281
Fegley, Robert, 340
Fehmi, Lester, 295
Feild, Reshad, 376
Feldenkrais, Moshe, 87, 255, 261n
Fénelon, François, 405
Ferguson, Charles, 121n
Ferguson, Tom, 268
Ferlinghetti, Lawrence, 385–386
Fields, Rick, 367
Findhorn, 336
Flach, Frederich, 73–74, 109–110
Flatland, 65–66, 69, 362
Flaubert, Gustave, 135–136
Fletcher, Jerry, 319
Floyd, Keith, 183
Foerster, Heinz von, 420
Forum for Correspondence and Contact, 220
Foster, David, 182
Francis of Assisi, Saint, 180
Frank, Jerome, 299, 259, 275
Frankl, Viktor, 69, 87, 115, 220
Franklin, Benjamin, 121n
Free for All, 333
Free Speech Movement, 58, 111, 138
French Academy, 151, 249
Freud, Sigmund, 53, 229
Fromm, Erich, 55n, 57, 62, 113, 225, 420
Frost, Robert, 135, 241
Fuller, Buckminster, 108, 259, 284, 307, 383, 420
Fuller, Margaret, 47, 123
Fuller, Robert, 113
Future in Our Hands, 409–410
Future Shock, 302

Gabor, Dennis, 178, 179n
Galbraith, John Kenneth, 197
Galilei, Galileo, 27, 187, 292
Galyean, Beverly, 303–314
Gamesman, The, 342
Gandhi, Mohandas, 47, 199–201, 214, 216, 224, 228, 239
Gandhi the Man, 239
Garcia Lorca, Federico, 102

Gendlin, Eugene, 79–80, 92, 169, 297
Geranium on the Window Sill Just Died, but Teacher You Went Right On, The, 311
Gerlach, Luther, 216, 217
Gift of Unknown Things, 321
Gilbert, Walter, 160
Glass Bead Game, The, 82
Goldenseal, 264–265
Goldstein, Joseph, 103
Gordon, William J.J., 304–305
Gottleib, Ray, 302
Gough, Harrison, 266–267
Gould, Steven Jay, 158, 159–160
Gowan, John, 302–303, 320
Grayson, C. Jackson, 350
Green Alliance, 409
Green, Edith, 286n
Greening of America, The, 60
Gregg, Richard, 338
Gregory, Dick, 415–416
Grof, Stanislav, 375–376
Gross, Ronald, 317–318
Growing Up Gifted, 309
Guide for the Perplexed, 357
Guillemin, Roger, 155
Gunther, Richard, 354
Gurdjieff, G. I., 86
Gurtov, Melvin, 190, 191, 224

Haldane, J. B. S., 148
Hall, Edward, 104, 229, 303
Hammarskjöld, Dag, 109
Haney, Craig, 301
Harman, Willis, 61, 226, 230–231, 339–340, 420
Harris, Evan, 179n
Harris, Lou, 227
Hart, Leslie, 296
Hawking, Stephen, 174
Hawthorne, Nathaniel, 47
Hayakawa, S. I., 139
Hayden, Tom, 208–210
Healy, Dorothy, 207
Heard, Gerald, 137
Heidegger, Martin, 408
Heilig, Gabriel Saul, 115
Heisenberg, Werner, 55n, 134–135, 151
Herbert, Nick, 172
Hesse, Hermann, 49, 76, 82, 116, 130, 301, 368, 420
Hiatt, Howard, 267, 268–269
Hilgard, Ernest, 75
Hine, Virginia, 216, 217
Hofmann-LaRoche, 340n
Holism and Evolution, 48, 156
Holt, John, 58

Houston, James, 133
Houston, Jean, 152
Hubbard, Barbara Marx, 57, 113
Hugo, Victor, 405
Human Systems Management, 62
Hunger Project, 413–416
Hutschnecker, Arnold, 266
Huxley, Aldous, 50n, 52, 54–55, 82,
    105–106, 130, 136, 138, 190, 223,
    271, 310, 327, 374–375, 381, 420
Huxley, Laura, 271
Huxley, T. H., 158

Ichazo, Oscar, 420
Illich, Ivan, 55n
Illusions of Urban Man, 193
Ingrasci, Rick, 249–250
Inkeles, Alex, 124
Institute of Humanistic
    Medicine, The, 262
International Trade Exchange, 333
Island, 54–55

Jacob Atabet, 45, 113
Jacobson, Lenore, 309
Jaffe, Dennis, 392, 400
James, Henry, 300
James, William, 48, 71, 87–88, 175n,
    189, 347, 365, 371, 382
Jampolsky, Gerald, 272
Janet, Pierre, 175n
Jastrow, Robert, 173
Jeans, James, 182
Jeffers, Robinson, 135
Jefferson, Thomas, 120
Johnson, Lyndon, 138
Jonas, Hans, 272
Journey to Ixtlan, 97n
Jung, Carl, 49, 50n, 96, 99, 109, 130,
    175n, 365, 372, 420
Justine, 187

Katchalsky, Aharon, 167–168
Katz, Alfred, 215–216
Kazantzakis, Nikos, 49, 81n, 102,
    106, 383
Keller, Helen, 124
Kelly, Walt, 59
Kettering Foundation, 61
King, Martin Luther, 47, 138
Koestler, Arthur, 185, 220
Kohlberg, Lawrence, 310
Koplowitz, Herbert, 371–372
Korzybski, Alfred, 51, 149, 420
Kostelanetz, Andre, 105
Kozol, Jonathan, 284
Kramer, Joel, 398–399
Krieger, Dolores, 275–276

Krippner, Stanley, 306
Krishnamurti, J., 130, 395, 420
Krupnick, Lou, 207
Kuhn, Maggie, 273
Kuhn, Thomas, 26, 27, 28, 151, 178n,
    197, 320
Kumarappa, J. C., 323

Lafayette, Marquis de, 121n
Laing, R. D., 274
Languages of the Brain, 178n
Lao-tse, 202, 357
Lashley, Karl, 177
Laurel's Cookbook, 335
Leadership and Management
    Training, 237
Leakey, Louis, 161–162
Leboyer, Frederick, 234, 271
Leibniz, Gottfried W., 183
Leonard, George, 59, 136–140, passim,
    370
Lerner, Max, 129–130, 286–287
Lerner, Michael, 39
Levin, Bernard, 39–40
Levy, Peter, 132
Lewis, C. S., 53
Lifeline, 313
Lilly, John, 420
Lindbergh, Charles, 81n, 124, 384
Lindner, Robert, 53
The Linkage, 218–219
Literature and Western Man, 54
Litwak, Leo, 139–140
Lives of a Cell, The, 62, 253
Locke, John, 326
Lockheed Corporation, 141n
Lodge, George Cabot, 61–62, 196
Loebl, Eugen, 360
Lonely Crowd, The, 52, 279
Longfellow, Layne, 353
Lord of the Rings, 366
Lucas Aerospace, 350
Lyell, Charles, 158

McCarthy, Sarah, 317
Maccoby, Michael, 342
McCready, William, 364
McGill University, 349
McInnis, Noel, 208, 284
McKenna, Dennis, 179n
McKenna, Terence, 179n
McLoughlin, William, 127, 128,
    231–232, 369
McLuhan, Marshall, 35, 55, 78, 129,
    189, 262n, 307, 420
McMaster University, 267
McPherson, James Alan, 142
McRae, Norman, 355

453

McWilliams, Carey, 133
Magical Child, 321
Maharishi Mahesh Yogi, 420
Man Who Gave Thunder to the Earth, The, 184–185
Mar'n, Peter, 90
Martin, P. W., 31–32
Maslow, Abraham, 50*n*, 56, 91, 130, 137, 146, 220, 309, 365, 393, 402, 420
Master Hakuin, 362
Matteson, Jay, 237–238
May, Rollo, 137, 227, 381–382
May, Scott, 268
Mayerhoff, Milton, 55*n*, 342, 381, 393
Mead, Margaret, 284, 420
Medved, Ron, 349–350
Meeker, Joseph, 305
Meister Eckhart, 46, 184, 382, 385
Melville, Herman, 47, 123
Memoirs of Hadrian, The, 145
Mendel, Gregor, 177
Mendell, Jay, 353
Menninger Foundation, 152, 350
Menninger, Karl, 274
Menninger, Roy, 260
Mental Radio, 175*n*
Merton, Thomas, 57, 420
Mesmer, Anton, 27, 299
Meyer, C. E., Jr., 340–341
Mid-Peninsula Conversion Project, 221
Milgram, Stanley, 316–317
Mill, John Stuart, 197–198, 330
Miller, Henry, 51–52, 117
Milwaukee Project, 284*n*
Mind Parasites, The, 193
Mische, Patricia, 226, 411
Mr. Sammler's Planet, 107
Mitchell, Edgar, 108–109
Mobley, Louis, 327
Morning of the Magicians, The, 53–54, 152
Mott, Benjamin, 135
Mount Analog, 82
Movement for a New Society, 335
Muir, John, 135
Mumford, Lewis, 42, 55*n*, 57
Murphy, Gardner, 53, 55*n*, 420
Murphy, Michael, 45, 94, 113, 137–140, *passim*
Murray, W. H., 108
Murry, John Middleton, 81
Must We Conform? 53
Myrdal, Gunnar, 220

Nadeau, Remi, 132–133
NAPSAC (National Association of

Parents and Professionals for Safe Alternatives in Childbirth), 271
Narcissus and Goldmund, 82
Nasafi, Aziz, 172–173
Nash, Paul, 321
National Academy of Sciences, 135
National Association for Humanistic Gerontology, 273
National Commission on Drug and Marijuana Abuse, 126*n*
National Endowment for the Humanities, 306
National Humanities Center, 306
National Institute of Mental Health, 263
National Opinion Research, 365
National Training Laboratories, 87
Nazarea, Apolinario, 186*n*
Needleman, Carla, 346
Needleman, Jacob, 60–61, 140, 364, 367–368
Nelson, Ruben, 191, 193
New Dimensions Foundation, 130–131
New Earth Expo, 339
New Religions, The, 140
Newton, Isaac, 26, 149, 198
Nexus, 409
1984, 193
"Notes on the Tao of the Body Politic," 207

Office of Technology Assessment, 191
Ogilvy, Jay, 224
On Waking Up, 114
O'Neill, Eugene, 117–118
Open Conspiracy: Blueprints for a World Revolution, 49
Open Network News, 220
Oregon Urban-Rural Credit Union, 333
Origin of the Species, The, 158
Orwell, George, 193
Our Ultimate Investment, 271
Outcalt, Douglas, 265
Outsider, The, 56

Pacific Institute, The, 349
Padovano, Anthony, 368
Paine, Thomas, 119, 122
Paracelsus, 277
Pasteur, Louis, 27, 253
Pauli, Wolfgang, 175*n*
Pauling, Linus, 137
Pauwels, Louis, 53–54, 152
Peace People, 240

Pearce, Joseph Chilton, 321, 420
Peccei, Aurelio, 410
Pelletier, Kenneth, 251, 257
People Index, 221
Perls, Frederick, 139, 293, 401
Peter, Laurence, 338–339
Peter Principle, The, 338–339
Phenomenon of Man, The, 50–51
Piaget, Jean, 371
Pico della Mirandola, Giovanni, 46, 70
Pietsch, Paul, 179
Pirsig, Robert, 106–107, 356
Planck, Max, 175n, 327n
Plato, 239
Platt, John, 56–57, 162, 215, 222, 240
Polanyi, Michael, 107, 177
Postman, Neil, 282–283
Prefontaine, Norbert, 391–392
Pribram, Karl, 152, 177–187, *passim*, 320–321, 373–374, 420
Price, Richard, 137
Priestley, J. B., 54
Prigogine, Ilya, 25, 163–169, *passim*, 173–174, 186, 327
Process and Reality, 49–50
Project Change, 313
Proust, Marcel, 117
Provender, 334
PUSH Program, 318

Quanier, Johann, 410

Radio and Television Belgium, 141
Ram Dass, 364–365
Ramagiri, 335
Raymond, Dick, 354
Razor's Edge, The, 138
Reflexive Universe, The, 385
Reich, Charles, 60
Renascence Project, 220, 355
Revel, Jean-François, 58, 125, 131
Revere, Paul, 121n
Revolution of Hope, 57
Rich, Adrienne, 227, 400
Richards, M. C., 60, 108
Richet, Charles, 151n, 175n
Riesman, David, 52–53, 279, 407–408
Rig Veda, 380
Rinzai, 377
Roberts, Tom, 308
Robertson, Laurel, 206
Robinson, John, 383
Rogers, Carl, 35, 57, 62, 130, 137, 233, 420
Rolf, Ida, 87, 255
Rolling Thunder, 276

Rosenthal, Robert, 309, 311
Rossman, Michael, 58, 59, 111–112, 207
Roszak, Theodore, 33–34, 36, 62, 99, 114, 130, 190, 213, 391
Rothman, Esther, 312
Rowland, Vernon, 168
Roy, Della, 397n–398n
Roy, Rustom, 397n–398n
Rubenstein, Arthur, 366
Rubin, Jerry, 206
Ruck, Frank, 350
Rumi, 88, 184
Rush, Benjamin, 121

Safransky, Sy, 366
de Saint-Exupéry, Antoine, 108
St. Christopher's Hospice, London, 272
Salinger, J. D., 382
Salk, Jonas, 55n, 57, 109, 370
Satir, Virginia, 197
Saxon, David, 235
Schrödinger, Erwin, 151, 173, 175n
Schumacher, E. F., 220, 325–326, 339, 356–357
Schutz, Will, 139
Schwartz, Bob, 354–355
Schwarz, Jack, 259, 276
Seeing Yourself See, 68
Self Determination, 62, 232
Seven Arrows, 308
Shanti Project, Berkeley, 272
Sherrington, Charles, 175n
Shimotsu, John, 321
Shockwave Rider, 88, 99, 113
Siddhartha, 82
Siegel, Mo, 355
Simon, Herbert, 327
Sinclair, Upton, 175n
Skinner, B. F., 139, 229, 280
Sloan-Kettering Institute, 62
Small Is Beautiful, 356
Smith, Page, 136
Smuts, Jan Christian, 48–49, 156
Snow, C. P., 134, 147
Snyder, Gary, 135
Society for Physical Research, 175n
Soleri, Paolo, 220, 347
Solomon, Paul, 276
Solomon, Robert, 36
Solzhenitsyn, Alexander, 363
Spiegelberg, Frederic, 420
Spiritual Counterfeits Project, 369–370
Sri Ramakrishna, 382
Stafford, William, 408

Stanford Research Institute, 61, 137, 338
Stapleton, Ruth Carter, 370
Stapp, Henry, 171
Stassinopoulos, Arianna, 39
Steiger, William, 243–244
Stein, Gertrude, 129
Stent, Gunther, 177
Step to Man, 222, 240
Steppenwolf, 82
Sternlight, David, 325
Stevens, Wallace, 23
Stokowski, Leopold, 105
Storm, Hyemoyohsts, 308
Stratton, George, 228
Structure of Scientific Revolutions, The, 26, 178n
Strutt, J. W., 175n
Stulman, Julius, 326
Suzuki, D. T., 420
Swami Muktananda, 420
Swami Rama, 152
Swank, Calvin, 347
Swearingen, Robert, 276–277
Swedenborg, Emanuel, 46, 47
Szent-Gyorgyi, Albert, 161, 305

Tanco, Arturo, 413
Tao of Physics, The, 172
Taylor, Matt, 222
Teaching as a Subversive Activity, 282–283
Teachings of Don Juan, The, 291–292
Teilhard de Chardin, Pierre, 25, 43, 50–51, 68, 101, 113, 130, 184, 225, 243, 289, 294, 393, 402–403, 420
Theobald, Robert, 59, 191, 205, 218–220, 224, 353
Thomas, Irving, 58
Thomas, Lewis, 62, 253, 407
Thompson, Francis, 279
Thompson, J. J., 175n
Thompson, William Irwin, 135, 317
Thoreau, Henry, 47, 136, 198–199, 201, 206, 208, 339, 367
Threshold Foundation, 410
Thurber, James, 106
Tiller, William, 62, 179n
Tillich, Paul, 137, 420
Tilopa, 379
de Tocqueville, Alexis C., 34, 37, 38, 190, 194–195, 225, 348, 360, 363, 416
Todd, Malcolm, 260–261
Toffler, Alvin, 302
Tolkien, J. R. R., 321, 366
Tolstoi, Leo, 416
Toynbee, Arnold, 51, 131, 137, 330

Trade-Americard, 333
Transformation, The, 59
Troubled Teachers, 312
Tulku, Tarthang, 241, 420

de Unamuno, Miguel, 142
Understanding Media, 55
Union of Experimenting Colleges and Universities, 319
United Nations, 217, 369n
United States Department of Transportation, 163
University Without Walls, 319
Unsettling of America, The, 336
Upanishads, 103

Van der Ryn, Sim, 358–359
Vasconcellos, John, 233–235, 259
Les Vertes, 409
Von Bertalanffy, Ludwig, 52, 157, 220

Wadsworth, William, 98
Wallace, Anthony C. W., 127
Washington, George, 121n
Watson, Diane, 312
Watson, Lyall, 156, 178–179, 321
Watts, Alan, 137, 382, 420
Way of All Flesh, The, 73
Weiner, Norbert, 255
Weingartner, Charles, 282–283
Wells, H. G., 49, 213, 222
Wheeler, John, 173
Whitehead, Alfred North, 49–50, 167, 184, 383, 420
Whitman, Walt, 47, 117, 123, 132, 367–368
Whole Earth Catalog, 339
Whole Earth Papers, 39, 411
Whorf, Benjamin, 149
Whyte, Lancelot Law, 55n, 58
Wigner, Eugene, 152, 174
Will to Live, The, 266
Williams, Roger, 134
Williamson, John, 281
Wilson, Colin, 56, 162, 193, 382
Wilson, James Q., 133, 333n
Wisdom of the Heart, The, 51–52
Without Marx or Jesus, 58, 125
Wolf, Alvin, 217n
Wolfe, Tom, 90
Women and Power, 226
Wood, Grant, 254
Wood, Nancy, 184–185
Woodward, C. Vann, 131
Wordsworth, William, 98
World Future Society, 221
Worrall, Olga, 276

Young, Arthur, 385
Young, Ben, 392n
Yourcenar, Marguerite, 145

Zen and the Art of Motorcycle Maintenance, 106–107, 356
Zimbardo, Philip, 301
Zukav, Gary, 172
Zumwalt, Elmo, 237

Subject Index
See Also Name Index

aging, 272–273
American dream, 119–225; and fourth "great awakening," 127; and imagination, 142; *see also* United States
American Transcendentalists, 120–123, 367
appropriate technology, *see* technology
Aquarian Conspiracy, 19–21, 23–43, 202 205, 220–221, 228, 238, 320, 346, 383–384, 377; and California, 136–141; and government, 235; and medicine, 259–269; as network of networks, 216–217; and paradigm shifts, 151; *see also* Aquarian Conspiracy questionnaire, networks
Aquarian Conspiracy questionnaire, 20, 85–87, 115, 118, 141, 175, 230, 265, 280–281, 343, 367, 374, 383–384, 418–420
attention, 68, 77–79, 87, 250–252, 295, 361
autarchy, 102; *see also* autonomy, freedom
autonomy, 99, 120, 205, 225; in education, 292; in medicine, 241; and others, 198; and personal relationships, 351; in workers, 348
awakening, capacity for, 406; as discovery of transformation, 97–98

barter, 333
Bell's theorem, 171–172, 275
bioenergetics, 102, 256
biofeedback, 86, 153–154, 206, 250, 258–259, 277
birth and bonding, 269–270
body, as pattern and process, 255–257
bodymind connection, 102, 142–143; and health, 252–256; *see also* health
brain research, 77–81, 167–169, 179–186, 295–300, 317
Buddha, eightfold path of, 190

business, transformation of, 340–342; *see also* vocation

California, 132–141; center of spiritual unrest, 60–61; conspiracy and cultural change in, 136–141; and democratic experiment, 133; laboratory of change, 132–136; politics of, 232–235
cancer, *see* immune system
center, transcendent, 32, 81–83; *see also* Radical Center
change, 70–76, 112; avoidance of, 74–76; types of, 71–72
Cheyenne Medicine Wheel, 306–308
collective unconscious, 49, 96, 146
communication, 34–36, 408; and new consciousness, 34; as social nervous system, 128–132
communities, 334–337; *see also* relationships, support systems
complementary, theory of, 173
connectedness, discovery of, 99–101
consciousness, 55, 58, 65 71, 75 83, 112, 153–156, 362, 375
conservation, 357–360
context, 297, 303–306; *see also* connection
cooperation, 187, 215; *see also* barter, New Games, support networks, synergy
cooperatives, 334–337
counterculture, 58–59, 126–128, 208
culture, 37–45; limits of, 104; transcendence of, 389, 390; and values, 389–390; *see also* counterculture, cultural trance
cultural trance, freedom from, 103; and social customs, 389; and transformation, 390
curriculum, new, 314–317

decentralization, power of, 223; in education, 317–320; *see also* paradigms: assumptions of old and new
déjà vu, 185
democracy, 194 196, 198; hidden powers of, 226; and spirituality, 207
despair, 21, 36–37, 142
direct knowing, 371–376; stages of, 371–372; tradition of, 378
dissipative structures, 162–170, 223, 327; and learning, 291; and relationships, 392; and societies, 205, 327
dying, 272, 383–384
dyslexia, 299

ecology, *see* conservation

economics, 323–327; assumptions of old and new paradigms, 328–330; *see also* values

education, 279–282; and appropriate stress, 291–292; beyond schools, 317–320; for context, 303–306; and new society, 280; and "pedogenic illness," 282–285; transpersonal, 287–288; *see also* learning, teaching

endorphins, 154–156; *see also* placebo

entrepreneurship, 353–356

euphenics, 307

evolution, 157–167; conscious, 69–71; and dissipative structures, 25, 162–167; and genes, DNA, 160–161; individual and collective, 70, 183, 385; of new species, 157; and transformation, 161

failure, 118, 346

family, 399–403; planetary, 402–403

fear, of creative behavior, 274; of heresy, 198; of higher potential, 91; of knowing, 91, 146; and learning, 291–295; of mystical states, 274; transformation of, 115–116

fear-of-success syndrome, 294

freedom, discovery of, 103; evolution of, 142; *see also* autonomy

General Systems Theory, 52, 156–157

God, 370, 382–385

government, conspiracy in, 235–240; and health, 259–260; as paternal power, 193–196; *see also* politics, power

healing, 275–277; and altered awareness, 250; and caring, 259; and electrical stimulation, 256; folk systems of, 274–275; and imagination, 277; models, 275; power, 275; and spiritual networks, 259; and will, 277; *see also* health, psi

health, 241–277, 294–296; assumptions of old and new paradigm, 246–248; attention, 250–252; and belief systems, 248–250; and body-mind, 252–255; and health, 282–284; and networks, 262; and transformation, 257–259; and wholeness, 242; *see also* healing, medicine

Hidden Observer, 75–76

high expectations, 308–310

"high intention," 351–352

holism, 49, 156–157

holographic theory, 177–187; and brain, 179–182; and Eastern philosophy, 373; and Hunger Project analogy, 414; and medical model, 275

holomovement, 180–181

hope, 21, 36–37, 142

Hunger Project, 412–416

iatrogenic illness, 245

immune system, 253–254

Indian Medicine Wheel, *see* Cheyenne Medicine Wheel

integrity, 199–200

interdependence, 407

intuition, 267, 295–297, 353; collective, 225; discovery of and trust in, 107

I-Thou, 243–244

language, limits of, 66–67, 149

leadership, 205–210; transforming, 266

learning, 279–321; assumptions of old and new paradigm, 286–291; and brain specialization, 295–300, 305, 315, 317; and connection, 303–306; and health, 282–284; and intuition, 296; role of metaphorical thinking, 305; and transformation, 291–295; *see also* education, teaching

light, in spiritual experience, 385–386

logic, limitations of, 106; *see also* intuition

love, 392–395, 402–403; discovery of, 100; power of, 240; as state of consciousness, 380; and universal synthesis, 243

meaning, search for, 363–367; *see also* transformation, discoveries of

media, 55; *see also* communication

meditation, 82, 86, 250, 258–259, 274; *see also* spiritual disciplines

mind, 65–83; the body's, 252–255; and disease, 260; healing power of, 54–249; new, new world, 406–410; and reality, 175; *see also* consciousness

monads, 183

mystical experience, 65–67; 362–366; defined, 371; flow and wholeness, 379–382; *see also* direct knowing, spiritual disciplines

nature, 145–146, 161, 171; *see also* science

Navy training program, 237

networks, 25, 39, 48, 62-63, 86, 421–427; SPINs, 216-217; support, discovery of, 112-115; tools for social transformation, 213-221
New Age Caucus, 240
non-attachment, 104–105, 228, 396

Omega Point, 50
oxherding pictures, 378

paidea, 307, 317
pain, 74–76, 78; and learning, 291–295, 308; in relationships, 387–392; *see also* dissipative structures, placebo stress
paradigms and paradigm shifts, 26–30, 196–201, 286–291, 326–330; assumptions of old and new paradigm of economics/values, 328–330; assumptions of old and new paradigm of education/learning, 289–291; assumptions of old and new paradigm of medicine/health, 246–248; peace, power paradigms, 410–412; assumptions of old and new paradigm of politics/power, 210–212; "whole-earth paradigm," 405
parapsychology, *see* psi
physics, 170–176; *see also* under Name Index: Bohm, Bohr, Capra, Einstein, Heisenberg, Newton, Schrödinger
placebo effect, 249–250; *see also* endorphins
politics, 189–241; *see also* power
power, discovery of, 100; other sources of, 221–226; of Radical Center, 192, 228–232; "right power," 190; *see also* autonomy, freedom, politics, responsibility
pravritti, 185
process, discovery of, 101–102; and transformed life, 116–118; *see also* learning, vocation, health, relationships
psi, 170–176, 275–276, 420
psychedelics, 89–90, 94–95, 106, 110–111, 126, 374–376
psychiatry, new approaches, 274–275
psychology, *see* consciousness, mind, psychotechnologies, transpersonal psychology
psychotechnologies, 31, 97, 105; Actualizations, 37; Applied Kinesiology, 87, 255; Arica, 86; autogenic training, 86; body disciplines, 87;

and brain synchrony, 79; Course in Miracles, 87; dervish dancing, 87; dream journal, 86; est, 87; Feldenkrais, 87, 255; Fischer-Hoffman process, 87; focusing, 79, 169; Gestalt therapy, 87; guided imagery, 87; Gurdjieff work, 86; and healing, 259; hypnosis, 75–76, 86; improvisational theater, 86; and learning, 315; Lifespring, 86; Logotherapy, 87; music, 86; and nervous system, 88; Neurokinesthetics, 102, 255; Primal Therapy, 87; psychotherapies, 87; psychosynthesis, 86; Reichian therapy, 102; resistance to, 88; Rolfing, 102, 253; Science of Mind, 87; self-help, mutual-help networks, 86; sensory isolation, 86; Silva Mind Control, 86; sports, 87; structural integration, 255; Sufi stories, 86; Theosophy, 86; ultimate placebo, 277; *see also* bioenergetics, biofeedback, meditation, spiritual disciplines
punctuationalism or punctuated equilibrium theory, 158–159

questions, new, 29, 76, 107, 116, 292, 376

Radical Center, 228–232, 287, 317, 381–382; *see also* center
re-choosing, 416–417
relationships, 387–403; changing paradigm of, 397; transformative, 392–395; working, 348–351
religion, 361–385; *see also* spirituality
responsibility, discovery of, 110–112, 194; *see also* autonomy, freedom, power
revolution, inwardness of, 206; "second American," 125–128; as a way of life, 24
romance, defined, 396; transformation of, 395–399

Satyagraha, 199–201, 228, 273; *see also* under Name Index: Gandhi
science, 145–187; model for social change, 152; of transformation, 162–167; *see also* brain research, dissipative structures, evolution, holographic theory, nature, psi, physics
self, 99–101; *see also* autonomy
self-actualizers, as transcenders, 56, 402; and "new cops," 347; values

of, 285; *see also* under Name Index: Maslow
self-fulfilling prophecy, 232, 272, 309
sex differences in perception, 229
sexuality, 397–399
social movements, 62, 126
society, *see* culture
spiritual experience and spirituality, 361–385; teachers, disciplines, 376–379
stewardship, 225
stress, and health, 250–252; and learning, 291–295; and revolution, 126–128; *see also* dissipative structures, punctuationalism
success, 118, 346
Suggestology, 315
synchronicity, 108, 114, 174, 182
Synectics, 304–305
synergy, 156; and cooperation, 215; as new wealth, 332 – 337; value of, 332–337
synthesis, defined, 156; and nature, 156
syntropy, 156, 161, 214

teaching, 292–295; *see also* education, learning, spiritual experience
technology, 222, 356–359
time, 104, 115
transformation of brain and mind, 32, 65–67; and business and work, 340–342, 346–351; and critical mass, 62; defined, 68; discoveries of, 97–116; fear of, avoidance of, 33, 74–76; and medicine, 264–266; men and women in, 389; and myths, 308; personal, 24, 65–118; and political crisis, 191; premonitions of, 43, 45–63; of quantity to quality, 176–177; and relationships, 388–395; science of, 162–167; stages of,

89–97; role of stress, crisis, paradox, 39, 73; and trust, 33; and values, 24, 323–324
transformative process, 65–118, 207; and business, 353–354; and death-birth, 389; and "the great learning," 317–319; and relationships, 392–395; *see also* psychotechnologies, transformation
transformed life, qualities of, 116–118; is the message, 118; and nature, 166; and social action, 192
transpersonal education, 287–288; *see also* curriculum, education
transpersonal psychology, 372–373

uncertainty, discovery of, 105, 221, 248, 327, 375, 412
United States, 119–143, 367–368; *see also* American dream, American Transcendentalists
universe, 156, 182, 410

values, 323–360; of conservation, 357–360; "etherealization" of, 331–332; of knowing what you want, 337–348; and paradigm shift, 197; of personal development, 351–353; transformation of, 24; *see also* economics
vocation, 342–348; discovery of, 108–110; as vehicle for transformation, 342
voluntary simplicity, 80, 338–339

walkabout, 307
wealth, sources of, 332–337, 360; *see also* values
women, and power, 226–228

Zhabotinskii reaction, 165